Get the ebook FREE!

To get a free PDF copy of this book
(sold separately for $34.99) purchase the print
book and register it at the Manning website
following the instructions inside this insert.

That's it!

Thanks from Manning!

Continuous Integration in .NET

Continuous Integration in .NET

MARCIN KAWALEROWICZ
CRAIG BERNTSON

MANNING

Greenwich
(74° w. long.)

For online information and ordering of this and other Manning books, please visit
www.manning.com. The publisher offers discounts on this book when ordered in quantity.
For more information, please contact

    Special Sales Department
    Manning Publications Co.
    180 Broad St.
    Suite 1323
    Stamford, CT 06901
    Email: orders@manning.com

Manning Publications Co.   Development editor: Emily Macel
180 Broad St.   Copyeditor: Tiffany Taylor
Suite 1323   Typesetter: Dennis Dalinnik
Stamford, CT 06901   Cover designer: Marija Tudor

ISBN: 9781935182559
Printed in the United States of America
1 2 3 4 5 6 7 8 9 10 – MAL – 17 16 15 14 13 12 11

brief contents

contents

ix

12 Extending continuous integration 276

After completing my master's degree, I moved from Poland to Germany and began working as a .NET developer for a company full of experts in … Clarion. The Clarion folks were developing the company's flagship—very successful leasing software—and I was left to do "the rest": a bit of interfacing with web services (no way to do it from Clarion at that time), a rewrite of a Pocket PC leasing calculator, a piece of a website for a customer in Switzerland, and so on.

Over time, I was given more and more small software gems to manage. "How about introducing a source-control system?" I thought. I was uneasy about the "zip and store on a share" method my old friends were using. Fortunately, my bosses were open-minded, and I was given a free hand. I could do whatever I wanted to make my work life easier. And believe me, there was a lot to change! I started with Visual SourceSafe and a plug-in for Visual Studio. This made a difference, but I didn't stop searching.

It was a time of Agile hype. The popularity of test-driven development was increasing, and my adventure with unit testing began. We moved from Visual SourceSafe to Subversion, and about that time I saw some information about CruiseControl.NET. It was a *build server*. I thought that was cool: all I had to do was write a build script and check the source into the version-control system, and CruiseControl.NET would detect my changes, pull the source, and perform the build; it would include the tests automatically, deploy the created bits to the test server, and tell me right away if something was wrong. I knew this continuous integration (CI) process would change the way software was developed on my team. All the pains of late consolidation were alleviated: we had a fairly ready, tested piece of software every time we checked in to the source-control system.

I had to learn MSBuild to write my build scripts. The learning curve wasn't too steep; soon, I had a custom-built script for every project we worked on. I was lucky to have virtually no hardware limits from my bosses. I got a fairly old server and created my first build machine. Boy, was it cool to see all the "yet another successful build" messages from the Windows tray-notification tool.

From day one, I was a fan of and a believer in the CI concept. I'm strongly convinced that it was the sole attraction that kept me in the Chaos Developer Club in those days. Now I'm running my own company, and one of the most important tools in my repertoire is the CI server.

Back in 2007, I wrote an article about CI for a Polish computer magazine. It resonated in the community and was generally well received. Sometime after that, a friend suggested that the topic was worth more exploration—perhaps in a book. I couldn't have agreed more. I ran the idea by a few Polish publishers, but they all said the topic was too specific for the Polish market. "Well," I thought, "if the Polish market is too narrow, how about the global market?" It was the first time I'd considered writing the book in English. I was concerned because English isn't my mother tongue. I knew the language well enough to read just about anything written in English, but would I be able to write in it? With the support of Manning, and Craig as coauthor, I decided to give it a try. You are holding the result!

MARCIN KAWALEROWICZ

acknowledgments

Writing a book is a long and arduous process. Many people were involved and we're sure to forget someone here. Our sincere thanks to all of you.

We must acknowledge the entire staff at Manning, especially Emily Macel who guided us through most of the writing process, and Michael Stephens for his support and patience when things got tough. There were others, including Maureen Spencer, Karen Tegtmeyer, Christina Rudloff, Tiffany Taylor, Katie Tennant, Mary Piergies, and Dennis Dalinnik, who helped along the way, and of course, publisher Marjan Bace who green-lighted the project.

Thanks to all the technical reviewers listed here and to Margriet Bruggeman and Nikander Bruggeman who did a final technical proofread of the manuscript shortly before it went to press. Your valuable feedback made this book better: Erik D. Lane, Craig Smith, Rob Reynolds, Aleksey Nudelman, Darren Neimke, Dave Corun, Jonas Bandi, Derik Whittaker, Sebastien Vaucouleur, Amos Bannister, Philippe Vialatte, Eric C. A. Swanson, Marc Gravell, Anil Radhakrishna, and Lester Lobo.

Finally, we would like to thank all of the readers of Manning's Early Access Program (MEAP) who added comments and corrections to our manuscript via the Author Online forum.

Marcin Kawalerowicz

I would like to thank the people who made me the developer I am today: Paweł Jackowski (without you, I wouldn't have become a software developer and this book wouldn't have been written), Jacek Jarczak (my long-time friend and business associate), Bernhard Korn (a man I've learned a lot from), and Harald Cich (my first boss at C.I.C. Software GmbH; his brilliant mind was always open to innovation). Thanks also to Michal Sodomka, Błażej Choroś, Mateusz Łoskot, Aleksej Kirschner, Łukasz Stilger, Tomasz Rospond, and my fellows at CODEFUSION.

Thanks to the people who made me the person I am today: my parents, Barbara and Krzysztof; my lovely wife, Sylwia; and my daughter (born between chapters 8 and 9), Zosia.

Craig Berntson

First and foremost, I need to thank my coauthor. Marcin made the initial contact with Manning and got the project started. Being almost half a world apart didn't help, but we were able to meet briefly in Germany. It's mostly through his work that we finally got to the end of this journey.

I had other help with my research and with answers to many questions about different tools and how things work. David Starr and Richard Hundhausen were great sounding boards.

Thanks to all the people on the C# and VB.NET Insiders lists for answering my simplest of questions about the CI process in their environments. Also, thanks to the people at Microsoft, JetBrains, and ThoughtWorks for making great products.

Finally, a personal thank you to the people close to me: my coworkers and managers for putting up with hearing me talk about this project; and most of all to Jason, Johnathan, and especially Laurie for supporting me in this effort.

about this book

Continuous integration is what it is, regardless of whether it's done in .NET or some other technology. It's a set of best practices aimed at easing the integration pains that arise during the course of a software project. .NET has its own set of tools to make CI happen, but the basic rules stay the same: use a source-control system, build by issuing one command, test, analyze, and deploy. Be ready.

Who should read this book?

This book is for developers who want to dive into state-of-the-art CI techniques. It provides simple guidance on how to create a full CI process with minimal effort and cost. The book wasn't written for experienced build masters and old-time CI practitioners, but we hope they will find some gems of knowledge as well.

Roadmap

The book is divided into three parts:

- Part 1 "Make it happen" includes chapters 1-6
- Part 2 "Extend it" consists of chapters 7-8
- Part 3 "Smooth and polish it" covers chapters 9-12

Marcin wrote chapters 2 through 10. Craig contributed chapters 1, 11, and 12.

Chapter 1 lays the foundation. It describes the CI process and gives you advice about how to introduce it to your company. We'll show a simple way to set up a CI process using a CMD file.

Chapter 2 describes the *sine qua non* for CI: a source-control system. You'll learn what the code repository is and how to use it. We'll help you choose the right tool for your needs. We'll describe Subversion and TFS source control as examples of source-control systems that are ready to be used in CI.

Chapter 3 goes deep into build automation. We'll describe how to set up a system that lets you build an entire project using one command. We'll present MSBuild as our tool of choice.

In chapter 4, we'll help you choose a CI server. We'll describe how to install and set up CruiseControl.NET, TFS in its basic configuration, and JetBrains TeamCity.

In chapter 5, we'll examine the responsiveness of CI servers. We'll look at the feedback mechanisms available in these systems, including web-based reports, system tray notifications, email, and SMS notifications. At the end, you'll use a USB LED toy to get immediate feedback from your system.

Chapter 6 describes unit testing and how it's a characteristic of the CI process. You'll use NUnit and MSTest to build a simple test suite, and you'll integrate the test results with the CI server. We'll examine test coverage and sending reports as feedback to developers. You'll learn how to mock some of the tests and how doing so affects the CI process.

In chapter 7, we'll extend your test repertoire with integration, system, functional, and acceptance tests. You'll use various frameworks to test various technologies: White to test Windows Forms and Silverlight, Selenium to test Web Forms, and FitNesse to establish user-acceptance testing. You'll learn if and when it's OK to introduce these kinds of tests to the CI process.

Chapter 8 describes how to perform static code analysis. You'll analyze precompiled .NET intermediate language using FxCop. We'll show how to use StyleCop to analyze C# code even before it's precompiled. And we'll explain how to use NDepend to do additional analysis. We'll provide information about how to extend and integrate this analysis with CI.

Chapter 9 describes XML comment notation and how to generate MSDN-style documentation from it. We'll show you how to generate documentation continuously.

Chapter 10 deals with deployment and delivery, including using Visual Studio to create setup files, and using WiX and MS Deploy. We'll show you how to use these techniques on the CI server.

Chapter 11 deals with continuous database integration. We'll show you how to maintain a database using Visual Studio and how to perform tests at the database level.

Chapter 12 is about extending CI. We'll explain how to deal with slow builds, how to scale the CI process, and how to check the maturity of the CI process you're using.

Code conventions and downloads

All source code in listings or in text is in a `fixed-width font like this` to separate it from ordinary text. Code annotations accompany many of the listings, highlighting important concepts. In some cases, numbered bullets link to explanations that follow the listing.

This book includes a fair amount of source code that is available for download. The source code illustrates the techniques described in the book. It is *not* production code. We provide many configuration files, especially for CruiseControl.NET. You can access the source code from the publisher's website at www.manning.com/ContinuousIntegrationin.NET.

Author Online

Purchase of *Continuous Integration in .NET* includes free access to a private web forum run by Manning Publications where you can make comments about the book, ask technical questions, and receive help from the authors and from other users. To access the forum and subscribe to it, point your web browser to www.manning.com/ContinuousIntegrationin.NET. This page provides information on how to get on the forum once you are registered, what kind of help is available, and the rules of conduct on the forum.

Manning's commitment to our readers is to provide a venue where a meaningful dialog between individual readers and between readers and the authors can take place. It is not a commitment to any specific amount of participation on the part of the authors, whose contribution to the book's forum remains voluntary (and unpaid). We suggest you try asking them some challenging questions lest their interest stray!

The Author Online forum and the archives of previous discussions will be accessible from the publisher's website as long as the book is in print.

about the authors

MARCIN KAWALEROWICZ has a master's degree in computer science from the Technical University of Opole, Poland, and more than eight years of experience in software development. He started programming in PHP and Java during his studies. After graduation, he lived and worked in Munich, Germany, where he learned the basics of .NET development. He's back in Poland now, writing software and running his own company, CODEFUSION. Through his German contractors, he worked for the financial branch of a large car manufacturer based in Munich and an even bigger credit bank based in Zurich, Switzerland. He writes about the stuff that matters on his blog, www.iprogrammable.com, and contributes articles to Polish computer magazines. Marcin lives in Silesia, Poland, with his wife and daughter.

CRAIG BERNTSON has been writing software for over 25 years. He's worked in several different fields and felt the same pain in his processes that you have. He has been named a Microsoft Most Valuable Professional (MVP) every year since 1996 and is currently an MVP for Visual C#. He speaks at developer events across the US, Canada, and Europe and has written articles for several magazines. This is his second book; he forgot everything he said about never doing it again after the first one. Craig is active in his local developer community, helps organize Utah Code Camp, and speaks at and attends several area .NET and software craftsmanship groups. Craig lives in Salt Lake City, Utah, where he works for a Fortune 100 company developing database software in C# and C++ for use in hospitals worldwide. He blogs at www.craigberntson.com/blog.

about the cover illustration

The figure on the cover of *Continuous Integration in .NET* is captioned "Bride from Sinj in Dalmatia, Croatia." The illustration is taken from a reproduction of an album of Croatian traditional costumes from the mid-nineteenth century by Nikola Arsenovic, published by the Ethnographic Museum in Split, Croatia, in 2003. The illustrations were obtained from a helpful librarian at the Ethnographic Museum in Split, itself situated in the Roman core of the medieval center of the town: the ruins of Emperor Diocletian's retirement palace from around AD 304. The book includes finely colored illustrations of figures from different regions of Croatia, accompanied by descriptions of the costumes and of everyday life.

Sinj is a small town in the center of an area in Dalmatia known as *Cetinska krajina*, a group of settlements situated on a fertile plain through which the river Cetnia passes. Sinj lies between four mountains which give the area its specific sub-Mediterranean climate. The town grew around an ancient fortress (held by the Ottomans from the sixteenth century until the end of seventeenth century) and a Franciscan monastery with the church of Our Lady of Sinj, a place of pilgrimage.

The bride on the cover wears a red cap over which she ties a blue scarf, and a white dress embroidered with red wool that she wears over a white shirt. She has tied a red linen apron around her waist and added a long, dark blue vest decorated with red wool. A small bouquet of flowers completes the bridal costume.

Dress codes and lifestyles have changed over the last 200 years, and the diversity by region, so rich at the time, has faded away. It is now hard to tell apart the inhabitants of different continents, let alone of different hamlets or towns separated by only a few miles. Perhaps we have traded cultural diversity for a more varied personal life—certainly for a more varied and fast-paced technological life.

Manning celebrates the inventiveness and initiative of the computer business with book covers based on the rich diversity of regional life of two centuries ago, brought back to life by illustrations from old books and collections like this one.

Part 1

Make it happen

A technically savvy programmer and project manager once asked how we'd describe continuous integration (CI) to someone who had never heard of it. We said there are two types of answers, and which one to give depends on how much time the listener has. The longer answer starts with part 1 of the book. The shorter one is not really an answer—it's another question that can give you an idea about what CI is. Do you remember the last time you released software? That's the time in the project when you gather all the bits and pieces required to deliver the software to the customer. Was it painful? Yes? Well, that's where CI can come to the rescue.

In the first part of this book (chapters 1 through 6), we'll lay the groundwork for a well-designed CI process in .NET. You'll learn the basics required for any CI system. We'll start by looking at CI in general. We'll define the term and talk a little about how to do CI in .NET. After that, we'll introduce the source control system as part of the CI tool chain that can't be omitted. We'll help you choose the right one and introduce it into your day-to-day work.

As a second ingredient that's required for CI, we'll describe build automation. We'll show why you need a single command-build process and how modern XML-based build systems are perfect for the .NET CI process. You'll also find out how to choose the right CI server to bind all the ingredients into one.

We'll then look at unit testing—what it is and how to use it in CI. You'll learn to write unit tests and automate their execution. We'll discuss CI servers and their ability to give immediate feedback about the state of the build process. It's a core concept of the CI process that every degradation in code quality should be immediately visible, so the team can react as swiftly as possible to make obstacles disappear. This is the purpose of controlling and reporting mechanisms in modern CI servers. We'll look at how you can extend these reporting capabilities with your software.

After reading this part of the book, you'll be able to set up your own CI process using free or inexpensive software. You'll understand what the CI process is and how to use it to your team's benefit. And you'll be ready to extend CI to better suit your needs.

Understanding
continuous integration

As developers, we're interested in creating the best possible applications for our customers with the least amount of work. But with applications becoming more complex and having more moving parts, creating great applications is getting harder, even with advances in tools such as Visual Studio and the .NET Framework.

One of the keys to improving applications and productivity is to automate some of the work. Continuous integration (CI) is one of the best ways to do this.

Have you ever written code that did its small task perfectly, but then discovered unexpected side effects when you integrated that piece of code with the rest of the application? Do you always have success integrating your code with code from other developers? Have you ever shipped an application, only to find that it didn't work for the customer but you couldn't duplicate the error? Can you always predictably measure the state of the code for your current project? CI helps alleviate these problems and more.

In this chapter, you'll learn what CI is all about, why should you use it, and how to overcome objections to its adoption from your team. We'll briefly introduce you to several free or low-cost tools such as CruiseControl.NET, Subversion, MSBuild, Team Foundation Server, and TeamCity that are part of a complete CI process. Throughout the rest of the book, we'll explain in detail how to use these tools.

This chapter also demonstrates a simple CI process through an example using batch files. We'll also get started on a more complex Visual Studio Solution that we'll use to demonstrate various CI tools and techniques. But before we do any of that, you need to understand exactly what CI is.

1.1   What does it mean to integrate continuously?

When you adopt CI, it's likely that you'll make major changes in your development processes because you'll move from a manual system to an almost completely automated system. Along the way, you may meet resistance from your team members. This section provides you with reasons to use CI and how to overcome objections. But before we take you there, we need to define CI.

1.1.1   Defining continuous integration

One of the best definitions of continuous integration comes from Martin Fowler (www.martinfowler.com/articles/continuousIntegration.html):

> *Continuous Integration is a software development practice where members of a team integrate their work frequently, usually each person integrates at least daily—leading to multiple integrations per day. Each integration is verified by an automated build (including test) to detect integration errors as quickly as possible. Many teams find that this approach leads to significantly reduced integration problems and allows a team to develop cohesive software more rapidly.*

This definition contains an important phrase: "multiple integrations per day." This means that several times each day, the CI system should build and test the application. But multiple integrations per day isn't where you begin your journey into CI; we recommend against this because many shops not using CI will meet enough resistance just automating the build, let alone doing multiple builds per day. (We'll talk more about overcoming team resistance later in this chapter.) Ideally, you should set up your CI process just as you create software: by taking small steps, one at a time.

Here is another definition:

> *CI is the embodiment of tactics that gives us, as software developers, the ability to make changes in our code, knowing that if we break software, we'll receive immediate feedback … [It is] the centerpiece of software development, as it ensures the health of software through running a build with every change.*
>
> —Paul Duval, *Continuous Integration*
> (Addison-Wesley, 2007)

The key phrase here is "the centerpiece of software development." This means whatever development process and methodology you use, CI is a key part of it.

Our definition is similar to those we've mentioned. Here's how we define continuous integration:

An automated process that builds, tests, analyzes, and deploys an application to help ensure that it functions correctly, follows best practices, and is deployable. This process runs with each source-code change and provides immediate feedback to the development team.

As we were discussing this definition, we wondered what a *build* is. Is it the same as clicking Build on the Visual Studio menu, or something more? We finally decided that the definition varies depending on what you're doing. Early in the development process, a build can be as simple as compiling and unit testing the code. As you get closer to release, a build includes additional and more complete testing and running code metrics and analysis. You can also go as far as combining all the different files into an install set and making sure it works correctly.

Finally, don't get caught up with the meaning of *continuous*. CI isn't truly continuous, because integration occurs only at specific intervals or when triggered by a specific event. Integration is continuous in that it happens regularly and automatically.

Now that you know what CI is, let's see how it changes your development process.

1.1.2 *CI and your development process*

Is your development process agile? Do you use extreme programming (XP), scrum, or something else? Is your company deeply rooted in waterfall methodologies? Does your process fall somewhere between agile and waterfall?

It really doesn't matter which methodology you use, because you probably follow pretty much the same process when it comes to writing code:

1 Check out the needed source files from your source code repository.
2 Make changes to the code.
3 Click Build on the Visual Studio menu, and hope everything compiles.
4 Go back to step 2. You did get compile errors, didn't you?
5 Run unit tests, and hope everything is green. We hope you're running unit tests.
6 Go back to step 2. Unit tests do fail. In this case, you'll see red. Perhaps in more ways than one.
7 Refactor the code to make it more understandable, and then go back to step 5.
8 Check the updated code into the source code repository.

When you start using CI, you'll follow the same process. But after you check in the source code, you'll take additional steps (see figure 1.1).

9 An automated system watches the source control system. When it finds changes, it gets the latest version of the code.
10 The automated system builds the code.
11 The automated system runs unit tests.
12 The automated system sends build and test results to a feedback system so that team members can know the current status of the build.

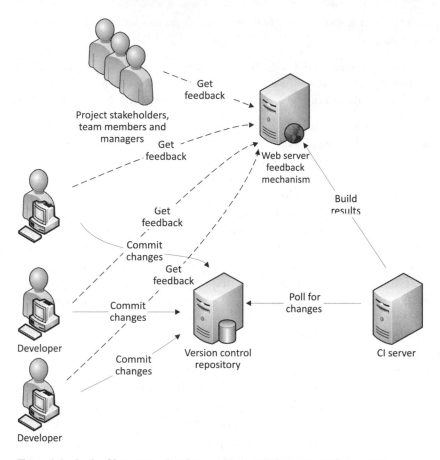

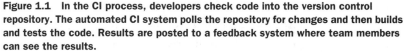

Figure 1.1   In the CI process, developers check code into the version control repository. The automated CI system polls the repository for changes and then builds and tests the code. Results are posted to a feedback system where team members can see the results.

At this point, you may be asking yourself several questions, such as, "Why do tests need to be run multiple times?" or "Why can't I just click Build in Visual Studio?" The answer to these questions is the same: automating the building, testing, and running of other processes through CI ensures that the code from multiple people integrates, compiles, and functions correctly, and that it can be reproduced the same way every time on a different machine than your workstation. Also, consider that you may have an application with many assemblies. When you click Build, you may only build the assemblies you're responsible for. Even if you're a one-person shop, adopting CI will improve the quality of your software.

Automating the build and the unit tests are steps in the right direction, but a good CI process can do more—and eventually you'll want it to, so you can maximize its usefulness. Things like running code-analysis tools, running tests in addition to unit testing, building an install package, and simulating an install on the customer's PC are all possible through a CI process. But you won't do all these things with every change.

1.1.3 Do I need to build with every change?

The CI steps we've outlined make it sound like every time a developer checks in code, a build is triggered. This is the ultimate goal and the reason it's called *continuous integration*. Reread the quote from Paul Duval: he says you should build "with every change." Martin Fowler says, "multiple integrations per day." That's pretty close to continuous. But, remember, continuous is the eventual goal. You don't want to start there.

One way to begin to set up your CI system is to start by getting the latest changes from source code and building the application. Then add unit tests. And only do this daily at first. You can call this a *daily build*; but as you'll see in a moment, a daily build includes other things that don't run when you do the incremental build.

When you have this build running every day, add two or three builds per day that only build and test. It won't take long, and you'll be building continuously and adding different builds to do different things. The exact types of builds you need depend on your environment and applications. Some of the more common builds are listed in table 1.1.

Table 1.1 Some of the different types of builds you can do with CI

Build type	How it's used
Continuous/Incremental	Runs when code is checked in. Does a quick compile and unit test.
Daily/Nightly	Does a compile and full suite of unit tests and possibly additional testing such as FitNesse.
Weekly	Does a compile, full unit testing, and additional testing such as FitNesse.
Release	Creates an install set and then runs and tests the inst all process.
QA	Creates a build just for the QA team.
Staging	Builds and copies assemblies to a staging server.

The most important build, and the one you want to get to, is the *continuous* or *incremental* build. This build is automatically triggered whenever source code is checked in to the repository. Because this build can potentially run several times per day, and one build may run immediately upon completion of another, you want the continuous build to run quickly—preferably in under 5 minutes. This build should get the updated code, rebuild the assembly it's in, and then run some preliminary unit tests. Reports are sent to the feedback mechanism.

Next is the *daily build*, often called the *nightly build*. Rather than running whenever the code changes, the daily build is scheduled to run once per day, usually in the middle of the night. Because you don't need to worry about the next build starting immediately, the daily build typically runs a complete suite of unit tests against all the code. Depending on your environment, you may want to add additional automated tests or code analysis.

Another build type is the *weekly build*, which runs automatically and usually on the weekend. Once a week, you should run a code analysis and additional tests with tools like Selenium, FitNesse, and NUnitForms. You may also want to create documentation with Sandcastle or do continuous database integration. As you get closer to your release date, you may want to run the weekly test build more often. You'll also want to run a *release build*.

The purpose of the release build is to create and test an install set. The release build is typically manually triggered. But after the build is started, all the other steps are handled automatically. In a release build, you'll build all the source code, increment the version number, and run a full suite of tests. You'll then create the install set and simulate the install. Good CI server software will have a way to check if the install was successful and then roll back the changes, so that the test system is ready for the next round of install testing.

Your environment may require other types of builds. For example, you may have a build that copies assemblies to a QA environment after the build. Or you can copy files to a staging or production server. The bottom line is that many different types of builds are needed for different purposes. But because steps are automated, you can be sure that things are done the same way every time.

As you introduce CI and different types of builds, some team members may resist the changes. It's important to overcome these objections so your CI process is successful.

1.1.4   Overcoming team objections

With all these builds going on and developers having to change their routine and check in code more often, you may get objections from team members. Some common objections are as follows:

- *CI means increased maintenance.*
  Someone will have to maintain the CI system. This will take them away from programming duties. At first, there will be extra overhead to set up the system; but when a project is fully integrated, your team will save time because it will be faster and easier to test the application and detect and fix bugs. Many teams report that after the CI process is running, maintenance takes less than an hour per week.

- *This is too much change, too fast.*
  It's difficult to adapt to the new way of doing things. Don't implement everything at once. Start out with a simple build once per day, and then add unit testing. After the team is comfortable with this, you can add one or two additional

builds per day or start doing code analysis. By taking the process in baby steps, you'll get more buy-in into the process.

- *CI means additional hardware and software costs.*

  Start out small with an old PC as your CI server if you need to. Eventually, you'll want better hardware so that you can run builds quickly (remember, the integration build should run in under 5 minutes); but for a build two or three times a day, older hardware will work. If you use the tools we discuss here, your software costs will be minimal.

- *Developers should be compiling and testing.*

  We're not taking those responsibilities away from developers. We're moving much of the grunt work to an automated system. This allows programmers to use their brains to solve the business problems of the application. This makes the developers more productive where it counts: writing and debugging code.

- *The project is too far along to add CI.*

  Although it's better and easier to place a new project under a CI process, the truth is, most of the work we do is maintenance on existing projects. An existing project may not have unit tests, but you'll still use source control and need to do builds. You can benefit from CI no matter how far along your project is.

One of the authors once worked in an environment where each developer was responsible for a different executable in a 15-year-old C++ application. Each executable was built locally and then copied to a shared folder on the network where QA picked it up and tested it. Problems arose because each developer used a different version of third-party components, and each developer used different compiler switches. This meant that if one developer was on vacation, and a bug in their code needed to be fixed, it was difficult to reproduce their development environment on another developer's workstation. It was so troublesome that management finally decided that unless the customer was down due to the bug, the fix would wait for the responsible programmer to get back to the office. If CI had been in place, many of the issues with the software wouldn't have happened.

Here are several reasons to use CI in your development process:

- *Reduced risks*—By implementing good CI processes, you'll create better software, because you'll have done testing and integration earlier in the process, thus increasing the chances of catching bugs earlier. We'll talk more about reducing risks in the next section.

- *Deployable software*—If you automate the installation process, you'll know that the software installs as it should.

- *Increased project visibility*—The feedback mechanism allows project members to know the results of the build and where the problems are. Bugs can be fixed sooner rather than later, reducing costs and the time spent fixing bugs.

- *Fast incremental builds*—In October 2009, ZeroTurnaround released results of a survey of more than 500 Java developers. In the survey, 44% said their incremental builds took less than 30 seconds, and another 40% said build times were between 1 and 3 minutes. The overall average build time was 1.9 minutes.[1] Although the survey was for Java apps, there's no reason not to believe your .NET projects will have fast incremental build times. Fast incremental build times means you get build and test results sooner, helping you to fix bugs earlier in the development process.

Don't let team objections get you down. The initial resistance will eventually give way to acceptance as the team works with the CI system. Virginia Satir, a family therapist, developed the Satir Change Model, which shows how families deal with change. Steven Smith wrote that the same model can be used to show how new technology is adopted (http://stevenmsmith.com/ar-satir-change-model/). The change process involves five steps:

1 *Late status quo*—Everyone is working in the current process and knows how it works.
2 *Resistance*—A new element is introduced. People are hesitant to change how they're working. The late status quo works fine. Why change it?
3 *Chaos*—The new element is adopted. There is no longer a normal way of doing things. Daily routines are disrupted.
4 *Integration*—People slowly become adjusted to the new way of doing things. It gets easier to do their jobs with the new methodology.
5 *New status quo*—The new element becomes fully integrated into the system. People now look at it as normal.

Almost every team has adopted new methodologies at one time or another. This process should sound familiar to you.

As you meet resistance from the team, be persistent in implementing the changes. Team members will eventually accept them. Some team members will adopt CI more quickly than others, who may need more convincing. Perhaps you should show them how CI reduces risk in the development process.

1.1.5   *It's all about reducing risk*

Your customer doesn't like risk. Your manager doesn't like risk. Your project manager should have plans in place to mitigate risk. In the end, you shouldn't like risk either. CI is all about reducing risk.

Perhaps the biggest risk in software development is schedule slippage—in other words, the project being delivered late. Because of the feedback mechanism in the CI

---

[1] Alex Handy, "Survey finds that incremental Java builds are speeding up," *Software Development Times*, Oct. 29, 2009, www.sdtimes.com/link/33867.

process, team members always know the status of the current build, which helps you know whether the project is getting behind schedule. Feedback mechanisms will be presented in chapter 5.

The next biggest risk is bugs. It's been shown that the later in the process you find a bug, the more costly it is to fix. Some estimates suggest that it costs as much as $4,000 to fix a single bug in internal, home-grown corporate web applications. In 2005, a well-known antivirus company had a bug in an update. That single bug caused customers to lose confidence in the antivirus software and forced the company to lower its quarterly income and revenue forecasts by $8 million. Do you want your company to experience similar costs? One of the caveats of CI is that bugs are fixed as soon as they're reported. By integrating and testing the software with each build, you can identify and fix bugs earlier in the process. We'll discuss unit testing in chapter 6 and application testing in chapter 7.

Have you considered how many different code paths exist in your application? Have you tested each `if/else` combination? How about every case of a `switch` statement? In his book *Testing Computer Software* (John Wiley & Sons, 1999), Cem Kaner mentions a 20-line program written by G. J. Meyers that has 100 trillion paths. *Code coverage* is a methodology that checks which paths are tested and which aren't. A great thing about code coverage is that you can automate it in your CI process. It's impossible to test every combination; but the more you test, the fewer issues will be uncovered by your customers. Code coverage will also be presented in chapter 6.

Another risk is database updates. It's never easy to add columns to a table or new tables to a database. With continuous database integration, you'll know that database changes work properly and without data loss. We'll discuss continuous database integration in more detail in chapter 11.

Developers often hate coding and architectural standards, but they have a useful purpose: they ensure that the application follows best practices, which in turn makes the application perform better and makes it easier to maintain. Code reviews catch some of these issues; but because code reviews are a manual process, things are missed. Why not automate standards compliance as part of your CI process? We'll cover code analysis in chapter 8.

Comments are rarely put in code, and documentation is generated even less often. Many people say that if you're agile, you don't have documentation, but this isn't true. Agile says that you value working software over documentation. But some documentation is still needed, especially if you're creating assemblies for use by other developers. Here's another opportunity for automation in your CI process, and one that'll be covered in chapter 9.

How do you know that your installation process works correctly? There are few things that frustrate users more than when they can't install an application. Create and test the entire installation process in your CI system. We'll cover deployment and delivery in chapter 10.

Finally, CI also increases visibility. It's easier to see problems hiding in the project that without CI wouldn't be found until much later in the development process, when they would be harder and much more costly to fix.

Now that you know what continuous integration is and how it can improve your development process, let's see CI in action.

1.2 A simple Hello World–type CI example

It seems that just about every computer book starts with a Hello World application. To help you understand the CI process, we've developed a simple C# application and simulated a CI server using a Windows script. Make sure you have .NET Framework 4.0 Extended installed. Throughout the book, we'll use Visual Studio 2010. If you have it installed, you're good to go.

To install the demo, create a miniCI folder, and then copy the demo files into it. To run the demo, open a command window, change the directory to the miniCI folder, and type `Build`. The results are shown in figure 1.2.

The build script is an old command-line batch file. We used this tool to show you how easy it is to create something that resembles the CI process. We aren't the only ones to try something like this: there are PowerShell scripts made to do the CI server's job (see http://ayende.com/Blog/archive/2009/10/06/texo-ndash-my-power-shell-continuous-integration-server.aspx). The CI script, shown next, verifies that the input and output folders exist, compiles the Equals.cs file into an .exe, and then runs it to

```
C:\Windows\system32\cmd.exe

Compiling
        1 file(s) copied.
Microsoft (R) Visual C# 2008 Compiler version 3.5.30729.4926
for Microsoft (R) .NET Framework version 3.5
Copyright (C) Microsoft Corporation. All rights reserved.

Testing
        1 file(s) copied.
Test passed. Application deployed.
Checking for changes in files
Checking for changes in files
Checking for changes in files
Checking for changes in files
Checking for changes in files
Checking for changes in files
Checking for changes in files
Checking for changes in files
Checking for changes in files
```

Figure 1.2   The miniCI application builds updated files, tests and deploys them, and then keeps checking for changes in the source code files.

verify that it works. The application takes two parameters and returns `true` if they're equal or `false` if they aren't.

Listing 1.1   Script for the miniCI demo system

```
@echo off
cls
echo Setting up environment
if not exist work md work
if not exist deploy md deploy
if not exist equals.cs echo Dummy >> work\equals.cs
:Start
echo Checking for changes in files
fc equals.cs work\equals.cs /b > nul
if not errorlevel 1 goto :End
echo Compiling
copy equals.cs work\equals.cs
C:\Windows\Microsoft.NET\Framework\v3.5\Csc.exe work\equals.cs
echo Testing
equals.exe test test
if errorlevel 0 goto :TestPassed
echo Test failed. Application not deployed
goto :End
:TestPassed
copy equals.exe deploy\equals.exe
echo Test passed. Application deployed.
:End
ping 1.1.1.1 -n 1 -w 5000 > nul
goto :Start
```

❶ Verifies build environment

❷ Builds source file

In the CI script, you verify that the work area on the build server is set up correctly ❶. The original source file is compared to the file in the work area. If it's different, it's copied to the work area. To detect the differences, you can use the fc.exe tool that comes with Windows, which compares two text files, prints the differences on screen, and redirects the output of the command to the null device to hide it from the user. The new work-area source file is then compiled into an .exe and tested ❷. To test the application, the script uses a little fake: it outputs 0 if the strings are identical. This is because you have to check the error level in the batch file. If the program returns something bigger than 0, you'll assume it's an error. If the test is successful, the .exe is copied to the deploy folder. The feedback mechanism is also updated with the result.

Now that you've seen a simple example of how CI works, it's time for us to introduce you to the tools that do the real work in continuous integration.

1.3   CI tools

A complete CI process consists of several tools. You can buy expensive CI systems that are feature rich and often easy to set up and maintain; or you can use tools that aren't as feature rich and often require some work to set up but are either free or low cost. Either way, no one tool does everything you need in a complete CI system. In this book, we'll work with free or low-cost tools and show you how they work and how to integrate them into a fully functional CI process. In this section, we'll give a brief introduction to several tools, starting with those that you must have.

1.3.1 Essential tools

Five tools are required to get started with CI. At a minimum, you should have these tools as part of your initial CI setup.

SOURCE CODE CONTROL

The first essential tool is source control. Source control systems are most often used to store each revision of the source code so that you can go back to any previous version at any time. But you should also use the source control system to store customer notes, development documentation, developer and customer help files, test scripts, unit tests, install scripts, build scripts, and so on. In fact, every file used to develop, test, and deploy an application should be saved into source control. There's a debate in the developer community about whether this should include binaries that you can build; that decision is up to you and should be based on the needs of your team.

You have many source control options, ranging from high-end enterprise tools from IBM Telelogic that integrate with requirements and bug-reporting systems, to Visual SourceSafe (VSS) from Microsoft, which has been around for years. You can spend thousands of dollars on these tools or find ones like Subversion and Git that are open source and free. Even if you don't use CI, you should have source control, no matter the size of your team.

> **NOTE** Microsoft discontinued the aging and not well-respected VSS in early 2010 and replaced it with Team Foundation Server Basic. But many teams continue to use VSS and have no plans to change in the near future.

This book looks at mostly free tools from the Subversion family and mostly paid tools related to Microsoft Team Foundation Server (TFS). If you choose Subversion, make sure you also install another tool such as AnkhSVN (http://ankhsvn.open.collab.net/), VisualSVN (www.visualsvn.com/visualsvn/), or TortoiseSVN (http://tortoisesvn.tigris. org/) that integrates into Windows Explorer or Visual Studio and makes it easy to work with Subversion. TortoiseSVN (see figure 1.3) seems to be the most popular (according to StackOverflow[2] and SuperUser[3]), so that's what we'll use for our examples. If you're using TFS and have Visual Studio 2010 installed, you're ready to go.

---

[2] http://stackoverflow.com/questions/108/best-subversion-clients-for-windows-vista-64bit
[3] http://superuser.com/questions/33513/which-subversion-client-should-i-use

CONTINUOUS INTEGRATION SERVER

The second and most important tool you need is one to drive your CI process. This sits on the CI server, watches for changes in the source code repository, and coordinates the other steps in the CI process. It also allows on-demand builds to be made. Essentially, this application is the traffic cop of any CI system. The CI server software typically has its own feedback mechanism that's used to aggregate feedback from the other tools and provide it to the feedback mechanism.

The most common CI tools for .NET development are Team Foundation Server from Microsoft and open source tools such as CruiseControl.NET and Hudson. TeamCity is another application that sits between these two options, because it's free for small teams but requires licensing fees as the size of the team or number of projects increase. We'll discuss CI servers in more detail in chapter 4. Most CI tools are driven by a configuration file (see figure 1.4) that specifies when a build should take place and what specific steps are taken during the build or integration process.

FEEDBACK MECHANISM

The feedback mechanism is another essential part of the CI process. Your team needs to know the status of any build at any time, especially when the build fails. There are many ways to provide feedback to the team, and we'll discuss them in chapter 5. But the most common method is through a website.

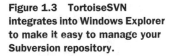

Figure 1.3 TortoiseSVN integrates into Windows Explorer to make it easy to manage your Subversion repository.

BUILD MANAGER

Next, you need something to do the actual build. The two most common options are MSBuild and NAnt. MSBuild is part of the .NET Framework, so it's free and most closely matches what happens when you click Build from the Visual Studio menu. NAnt is designed after the Java tool Ant. It's an open source solution, but it has received few updates in the past couple of years. Both applications are controlled by XML configuration files, but you can find GUI tools such as MSBuild Sidekick (see figure 1.5) to make the configuration files easier to maintain.

The build-manager application takes a Visual Studio solution or individual project files and calls the correct compiler, generally C# or VB.NET. The compilers come free as part of the .NET Framework. Some shops use MSBuild for the actual compilation of the source and then use NAnt for the remaining steps, such as running unit tests.

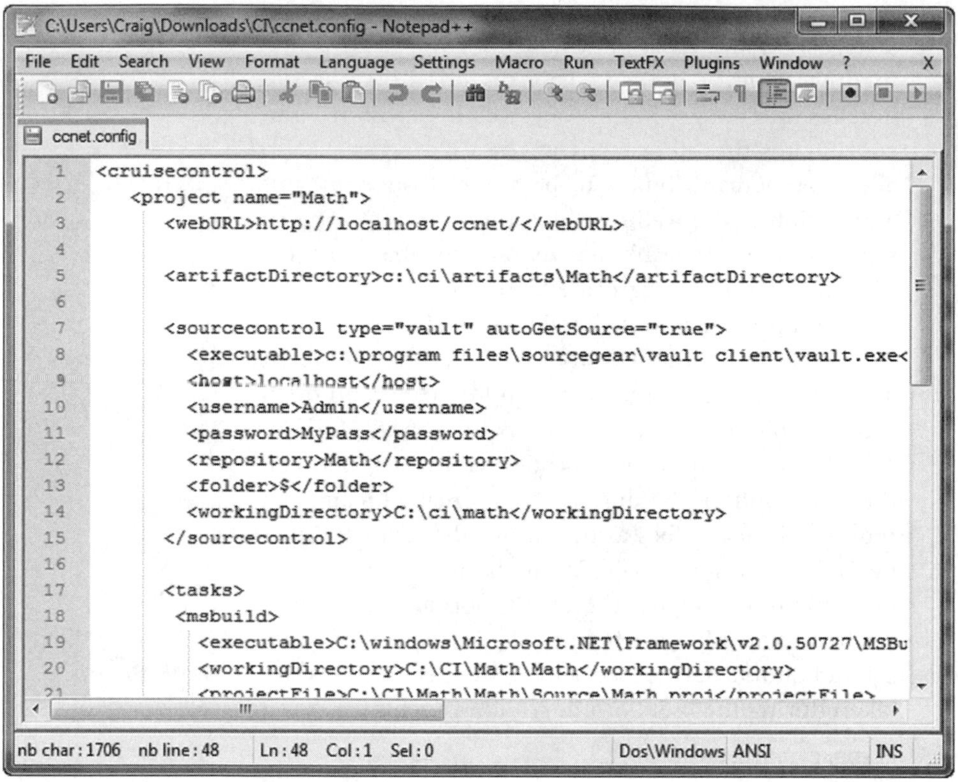

Figure 1.4   Part of the XML configuration file for CruiseControl.NET

UNIT TEST FRAMEWORK

The last essential tool you need is a unit testing tool. The two most common options are MSTest and NUnit (see figure 1.6), but there are others such as MbUnit and xUnit.net. These tools run the unit tests that you write for your application and then generate the results into a text file. The text file can be picked up by your CI server software; a red/green condition for fail/succeed is reported to the team through the feedback mechanism.

Although NUnit has a GUI tool, it can also be run as a console application as part of your CI process. Many of the tools we'll discuss in this book have both a GUI and a command-line version. The command-line tools provide results as text or XML files that can be processed by your CI server software; the results are displayed using the feedback mechanism.

Now that you know the required tools, let's turn our attention to other tools that will help you write better code: code-analysis tools.

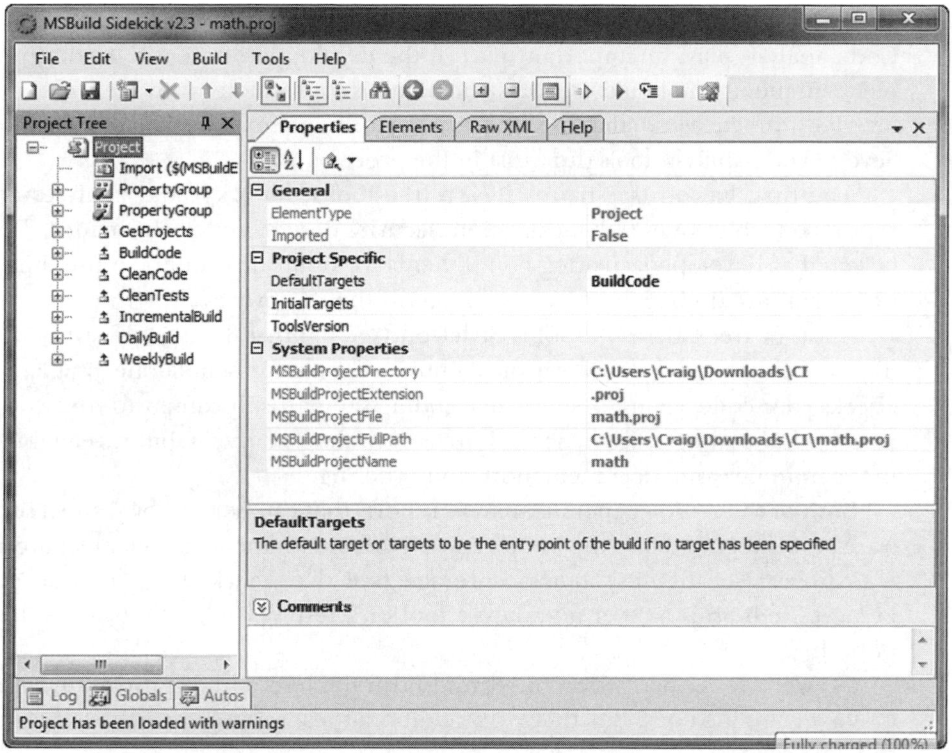

Figure 1.5 MSBuild Sidekick from Attrice makes it easy to develop and maintain MSBuild scripts.

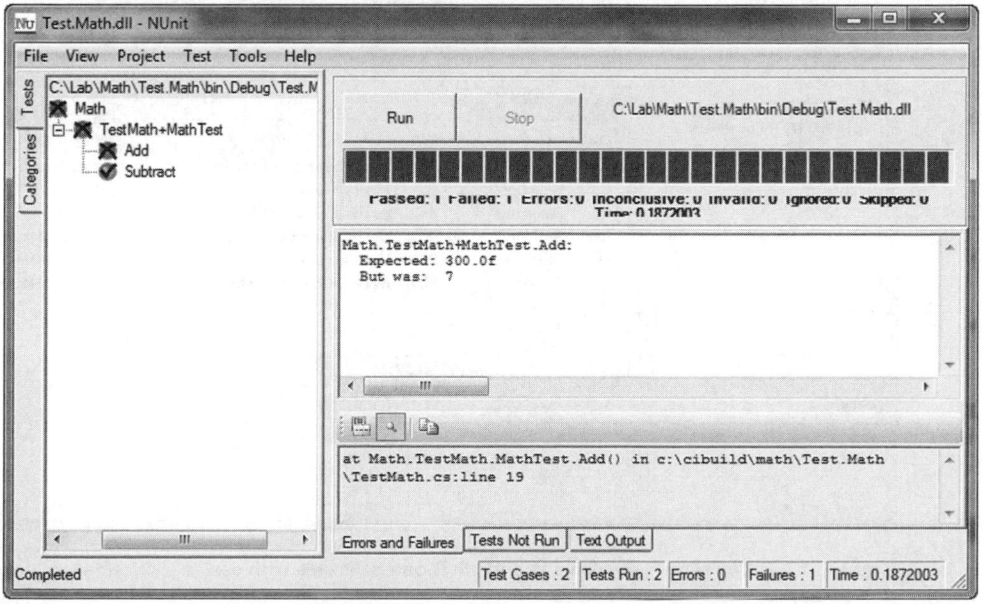

Figure 1.6 NUnit runs unit tests on your code and reports the results as red/green for failure or success.

1.3.2   *Code-analysis tools*

Code analysis plays an important part in the development process. Code from multiple team members should use the same naming conventions. And the code should follow best practices so that it's robust, performant, extensible, and maintainable. Several code-analysis tools can assist in the process.

The first, FxCop (see figure 1.7), a free tool from Microsoft, analyzes code and reports possible issues with localization, security, design, and performance. The tool is targeted at developers creating components for other developers to use, but application teams are finding FxCop a useful part of their CI process.

Another free Microsoft tool is StyleCop (see figure 1.8). It comes with Visual Studio and is delivered with a set of MSBuild plug-ins for standalone usage. This tool checks your code against best-practice coding standards. It compares your code to recommended coding styles in several areas including maintainability, readability, spacing, naming, layout, documentation, and ordering.

Both of these tools generate analysis reports that can be used by your CI server software and integrated into the build report available via the feedback mechanism.

NCover (see figure 1.9) is a coverage tool that checks that all code paths are being tested. So is NCover an analysis tool or a testing tool? The truth is, it's a little of both.

NCover uses either MSTest or NUnit to run the tests and can integrate with several CI server applications. But there are additional test tools, and they're the subject of the next section.

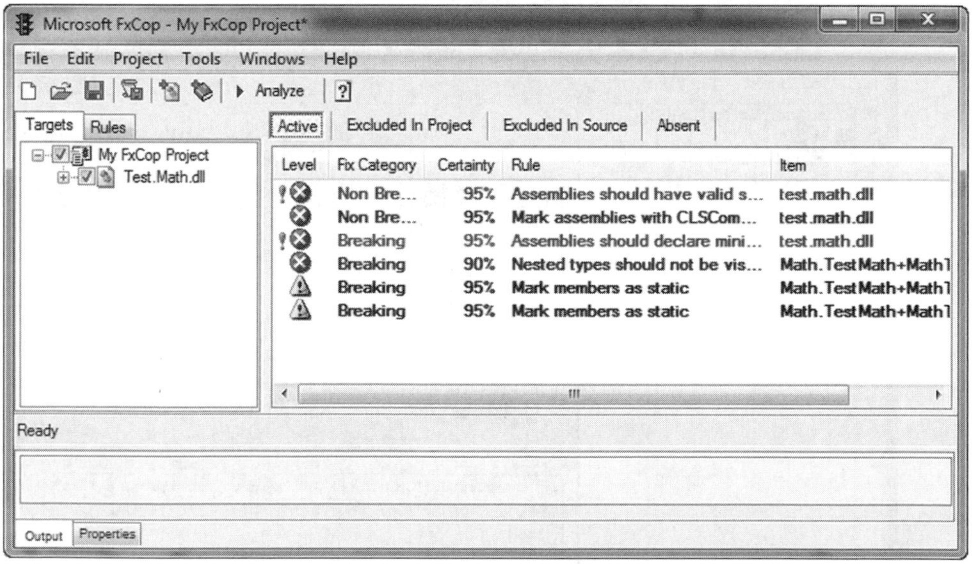

Figure 1.7   FxCop reports problems in code that can be issues with design, performance, security, or localization.

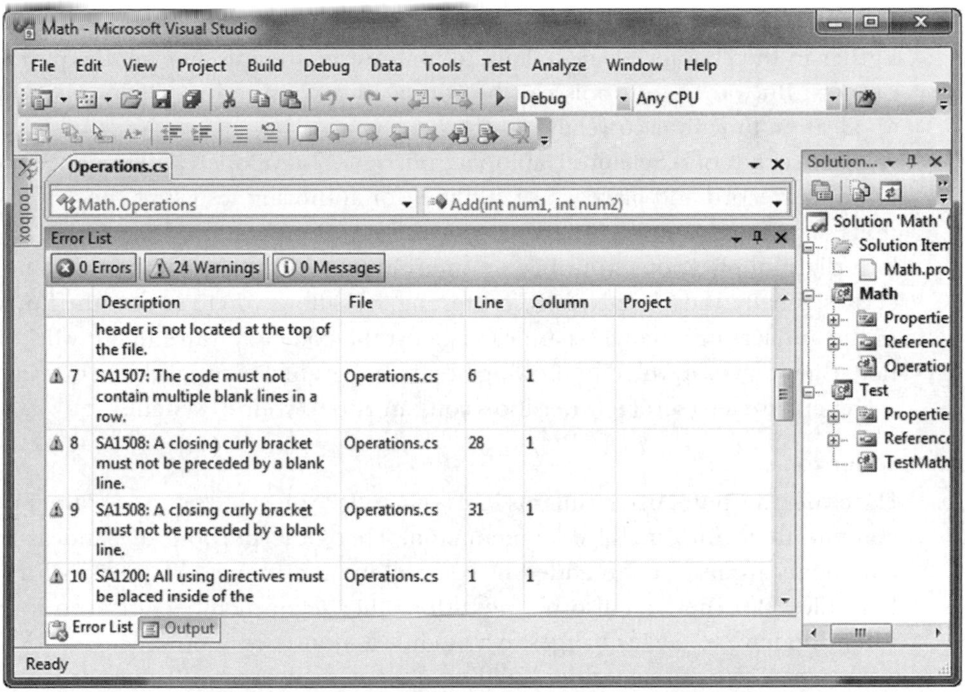

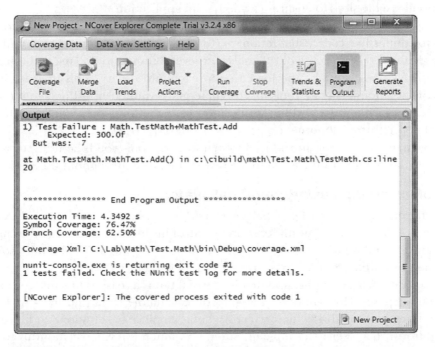

Figure 1.8 The StyleCop GUI integrates with Visual Studio and reports issues with coding style.

Figure 1.9 NCover reports the results of testing code paths through the application.

1.3.3   *Testing tools*

Earlier in the chapter, we talked about unit testing tools as an essential part of the CI process. But other test tools can be run against your code to help ensure that the application functions correctly.

One such tool is Selenium, an open source tool developed by ThoughtWorks. Selenium has record and playback capabilities for authoring tests that check web applications. If you're creating WinForms, Windows Presentation Foundation (WPF) or Silverlight applications, you may be interested in White: it allows testing of your UI classes. Finally, there's FitNesse. This testing tool allows you to specify the functionality of the application; then tests are run against the code to ensure that it works as specified. Chapter 6 is devoted to showing how to integrate these tools with your CI process.

There are also several other tools you can add to your CI system.

1.3.4   *Other tools*

Have you ever put XML comments into your code? You can, and then extract them and compile them into useful documentation. That's the purpose of Sandcastle. These comments are most often added by component and framework vendors for building help files. But they can also be useful for other team members or even for yourself when you have to make changes to a module a month from now.

You can also automate the building of your deployment. It doesn't matter if you use ClickOnce, Visual Studio Installer, WiX, Inno Setup, or something else. Having your CI process automatically build the application, create the install set, and then test the install are big steps to ensuring a good, solid application.

The tools presented here are by no means an exhaustive list. You can find many tools for things like code visualization, performance testing, static analysis, and more through a web search. Some of the tools cost several thousand dollars, and others are free. In this book, we take the low-cost approach and discuss tools that are free or available at a minimal cost. Tools like this emerge continuously in the community. To keep track of what's new and hot, you can check community sites like StackOverflow and ALT.NET (http://altdotnet.org/).

Now that you've been introduced to many of the tools you'll be using in your CI process, it's time to introduce you to the project we'll use throughout the book.

1.4   *A project for CI: leasing/credit calculator*

To better understand the CI process, you should have a simple but real-world example of software that you can put under source control in the next chapter and eventually integrate continuously. At this early point, you'll only create a Visual Studio solution and the project files. You'll add the code in later chapters.

You want a sample application that isn't trivial but is as easy as possible for demonstration purposes. How about a leasing/credit calculator? It may not be a tool that'll prevent the next worldwide financial crisis, but it's a piece of software that'll provide a straightforward answer to a simple question: how much will you pay monthly for your dream car or house?

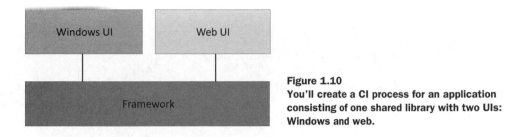

Figure 1.10
You'll create a CI process for an application consisting of one shared library with two UIs: Windows and web.

The architecture will be sophisticated, as you can see in figure 1.10.

The application will consist of one shared library with two clients. One client will be made using WPF and the other with Web Forms. You'll create a full CI process for this tool throughout this book. But remember, the project is only a pretext to show you how to set up a CI process and not a goal in itself.

You'll use Visual Studio 2010 to develop the application. In this chapter, we'll present two examples using ASP.NET and WPF, but the techniques described are suitable for other kinds of .NET applications like Windows Forms, ASP.NET MVC, Silverlight, and mobile apps. The details may differ, but the easiest way to set the CI process correctly is to think about it from the beginning. It never hurts to first think about what you want to accomplish and then do it afterward—not the other way around. The first part of the example we'll look at is the core of the application: a shared library used with the finance mathematical part of the software.

1.4.1 Calculation core

The financial library project will contain all the necessary code to perform the financial calculation. You'll start small with one class to perform a leasing/credit installment calculation.

DIRECTORY STRUCTURE

Pick a directory to work with. By default, Visual Studio stores projects somewhere deep in the user folder structure, which makes all the paths long and error prone. It's better to make the path shorter—anything on the first level in the directory structure will do, such as C:\Project, C:\Development, or C:\Work. For this example, let's use C:\Dev.

Consider organizing your project directory a little better than the Visual Studio defaults. If you create a project, you'll get a solution file named after the project. Visual Studio will also create a directory under the solution file, again named after the project, and place the project file inside. That may be all right for a quick shot, but you should consider taking this structure under your control.

First, if you plan to have more than one project in a solution, consider naming the solution differently than any of the projects. Second, remember the golden rule of CI: keep everything you need to integrate inside the repository. To meet this rule, you'll need a directory to keep all your stuff in. You can name it lib or tools. And you can go even further, as you can see in figure 1.11.

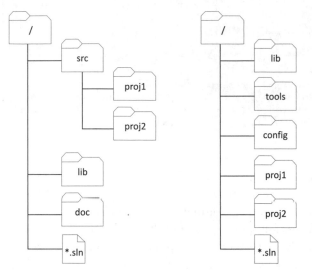

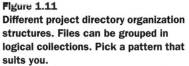

Figure 1.11
Different project directory organization structures. Files can be grouped in logical collections. Pick a pattern that suits you.

Organizing your files in logical groups makes the solution directory tidy. For example, source files go in a directory called src, and documentation-related stuff goes in the doc directory. Of course, this isn't divine knowledge, and you may have a good reason to do it differently. You may want to put the documentation in another repository or to not have a separate source directory. It's up to you, but you should at least think about it.

ORGANIZING THE PROJECT STRUCTURE
Here are the steps to organize the project:

1   Launch Visual Studio, and create a new solution. Select File > New > Project from the Visual Studio menu. The New Project dialog box opens (see figure 1.12).

2   In the Installed Templates list, select Other Project Types > Visual Studio Solutions, and then choose Blank Solution.

3   Enter Framework for the solution name and C:\Dev\ for the location, and click OK.

4   To add the financial-calculation library to the newly created solution, first choose File > Add > New Project. Then choose Visual C# > Windows, select Class Library, and name the library CalcCore. (In a real solution, you may have other libraries parallel to the core—for example, a project containing database-access classes or controls ready for reuse in various projects.) Your Solution Explorer should look similar to figure 1.13.

5   You need to change some Visual Studio defaults to give better results when you build the project and put it under the CI process. From the Solution Explorer, right-click the CalcCore project, and select Properties.

6   Switch to the Build tab. Under Errors and Warnings, check if the warning level is set to 4 (see figure 1.14).

7   Under Treat Warnings as Errors, select All.

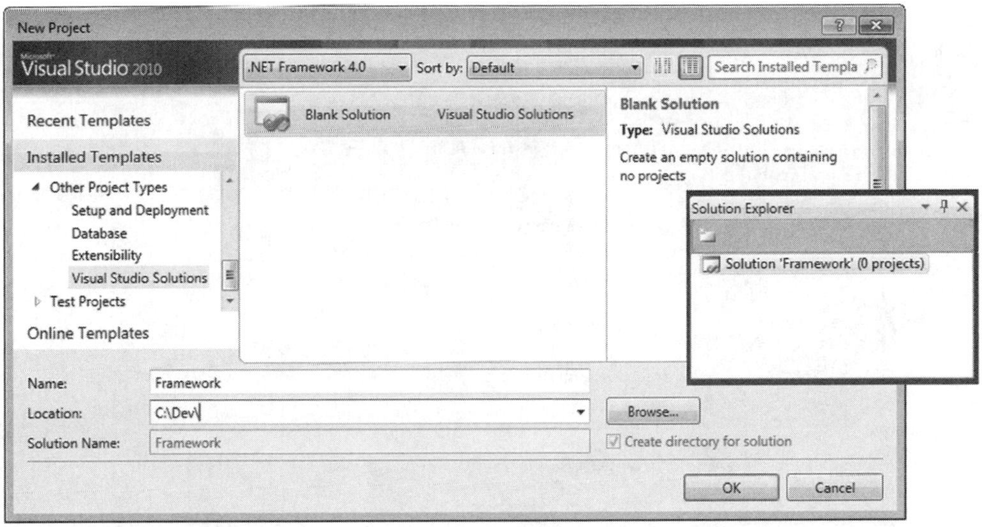

Figure 1.12 **You should start with a blank solution. Doing so will give you the ability to name it differently than the project inside and to place the projects where you want them. Don't take a shortcut by creating a project first and letting Visual Studio create the solution file for you. You'll end up with the Solution Explorer window shown.**

These settings will cause the compiler to throw an error every time your code contains the slightest warning (including the least severe and even informational warnings). It's because the number of warnings have the tendency to grow and in end effect can be completely ignored. If you're conscious that there's no way around the warning you can always suppress it by typing its number into the "Suppress warnings" text box. You do this to eliminate unnecessary noise. If you're like many developers, you have a tendency to stop reacting to too-frequent stimulation. Soon enough, you'll have dozens of warnings and miss an important one that may lead to a problem. And you don't need any problems, do you?

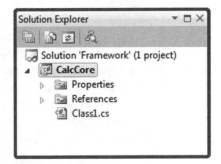

Figure 1.13 **The initial project structure in the Visual Studio Solution Explorer. Remember, it's not necessary to correspond to the folder structure on the hard drive.**

NOTE Pay close attention to the platform shown in figure 1.15. In Visual Studio 2010, it defaults to x86 by executable .NET applications and to Any CPU for class libraries. This is different than in Visual Studio 2008, which defaults to Any CPU. If your assembly doesn't use native Windows functionality, it's safer to set it to Any CPU. It'll run properly on either a 32- or 64-bit processor.

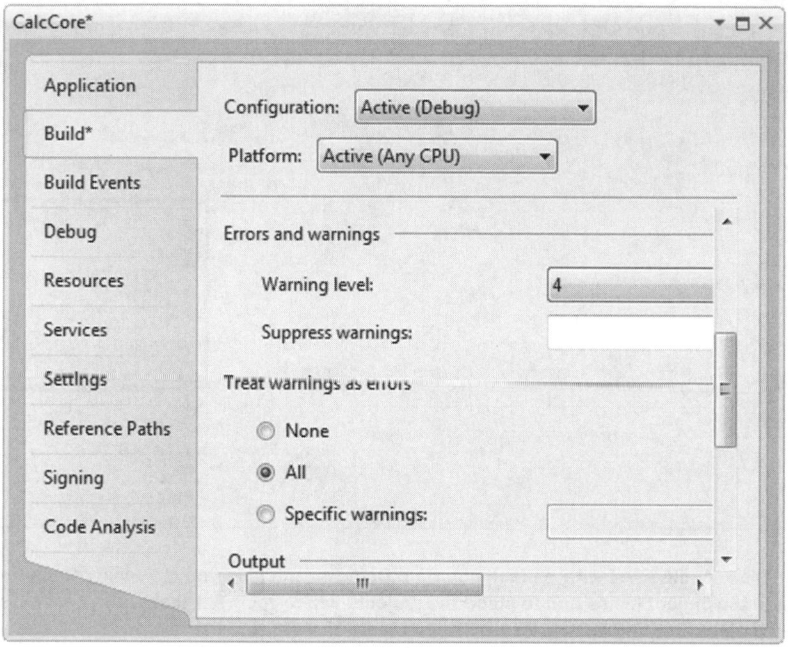

Figure 1.14 Build properties set the right way. All warnings are treated as errors and given the maximum warning level. This setup is used for every configuration defined.

8 Signing the assembly with a strong key gives your assembly a globally unique name. It makes identification and administration easier. It makes it possible to create a reference to an explicit version of software, and it prevents others from spoofing your libraries. Without a strong name, you won't be able to add a library to the Global Assembly Cache (GAC), which may be a good idea for the financial-calculation library. But keep in mind that signing the library will make the versioning more complex. You can't call a nonsigned library from a signed one. The general rule of thumb is to sign the libraries and leave the executables alone; you'll have to decide for yourself what to do.

To sign the assembly, switch to the Signing tab (see figure 1.15), and select the Sign the Assembly check box.

9 From the Choose a Strong Name Key File drop-down list, select New. The Create Strong Name Key dialog box opens.

10 Enter CalcCore for the Key File Name, and deselect Protect My Key File with a Password. Press Enter in the resulting dialog box (shown in figure 1.15).

11 Delete the default Class1.cs file. You need to add a new program file that'll eventually contain the code.

12 Delete all unused references. Everything that's mentioned in the references is loaded into memory at runtime. If it isn't needed in your program, it will have nothing to do in memory.

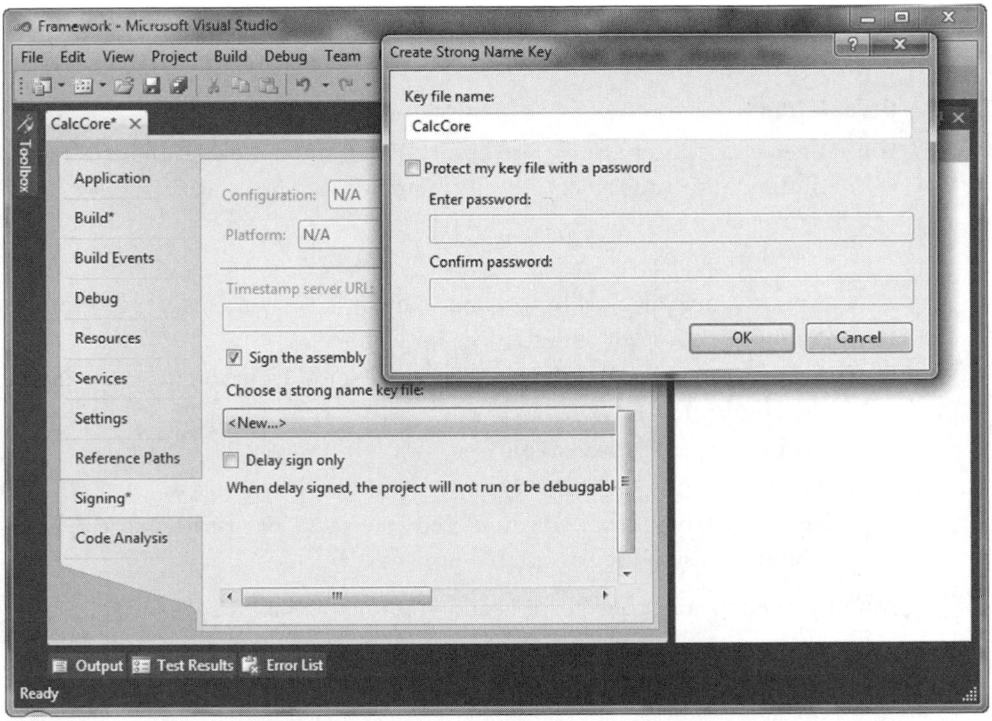

Figure 1.15 It's worth signing your reusable assemblies. Doing so makes it possible to reference them using strong assembly names.

13 Right-click the `CalcCore` project, and select Add > New Folder from the context menu. Name the folder Math.

14 Create a class called `Finance` inside the folder. Did you notice that the namespace in the new program file contains the path to the file? It's generally a good idea to have the path and namespace match. Using folders, you won't clutter your solution with files, and it'll be easier to manage a lot of files in the Solution Explorer window. Your Solution Explorer should look like figure 1.16.

Figure 1.16 Model solution with no unnecessary references. The project is signed and uses folders (that match the namespaces).

The `Finance` class will contain simple financial mathematical operations. The implementation details are irrelevant now; we'll pay closer attention to the financial library in chapter 6, where you'll write unit tests for the library.

Now, let's create two additional projects that you'll put together with the core library in the source control repository.

1.4.2 Calculators

You'll need a user interface for the library. Using the same technique as for the framework solution and core project, you'll create two user interfaces: one for Windows and one for the web.

Follow these steps:

1 Create a new blank solution and name it `WindowsCalculator`. From the Visual Studio menu, select File > Add > Project...
2 Select Visual C# > Windows > WPF Application from the list of project templates (see figure 1.17).
3 Name the project `WinCalc`.
4 Set the location to `C:\Dev\`.
5 Set the warning level as you did for the CalcCore project in the previous section. Don't sign the executable project.

You now need to create a web application for the web-base UI for the calculator project:

1 Create a new blank solution and name it `WebCalculator`. From the Visual Studio menu, select File > Add > Project.

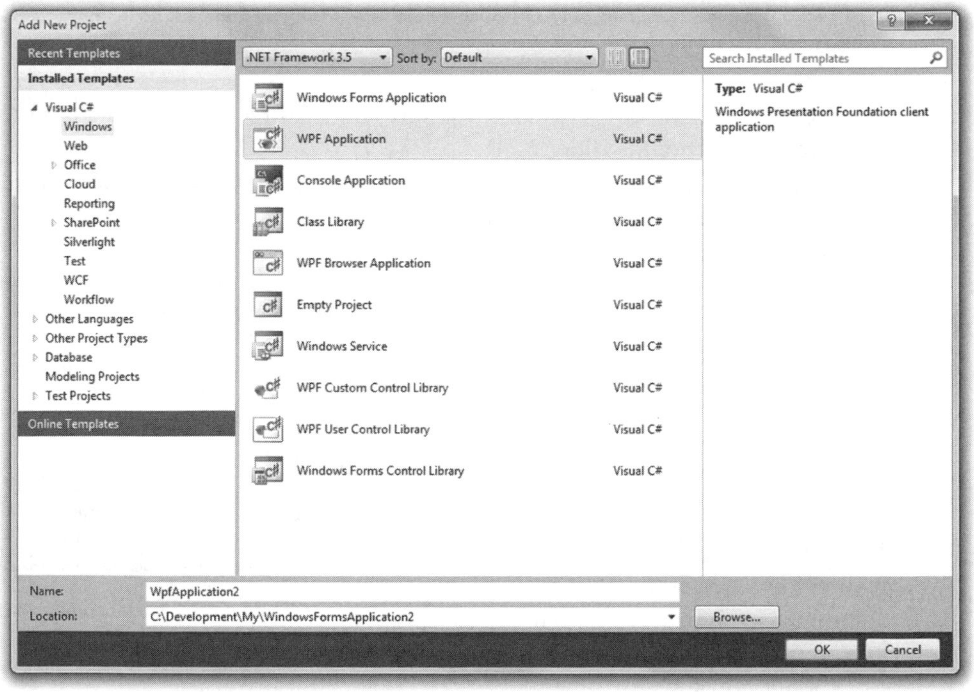

Figure 1.17   Create a Windows Forms application for the finance calculator project.

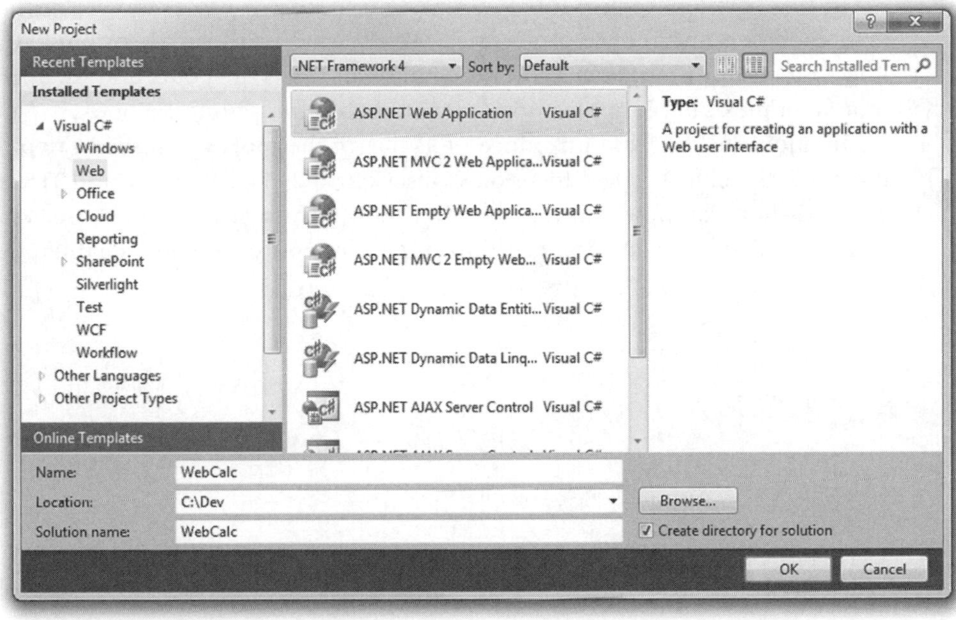

Figure 1.18 shows the New Project dialog in Visual Studio 2010.

Figure 1.18 Creating the web calculator solution in Visual Studio 2010 is straightforward and should be familiar to users of earlier versions.

2 Select Visual C# > Web > ASP.NET Web Application from the list of project templates (see figure 1.18).

3 Name the project `WebCalc`.

4 Set the location to `C:\Dev\`.

5 Set the warning level as you did for the CalcCore project in the previous section. Don't sign the executable project.

The solutions and projects for the loan calculator are now finished. Your folder structure should look like figure 1.19.

You've built the initial construction site. It contains three solutions, each with one project. In the next chapter, you'll place the application under source control.

1.5 Summary

You should now understand what continuous integration can do for you and your team. It may seem confusing to set up and maintain CI with all the essential tools; but as you'll learn throughout this book, it's simple if you take things a step at a time.

Figure 1.19 If you've followed the steps in this chapter, you should end up with a directory structure similar to this.

In this chapter, we presented information to help you overcome objections from team members and reduce project risk. We also gave you a simple example that shows how CI looks for file changes and then builds and tests the code; and we introduced a more complex sample application that you'll use throughout the book.

In addition, you were introduced to some of the tools you'll see in depth later in the book. Specifically, we'll focus on CruiseControl.NET, TeamCity, and TFS as CI servers, and show you how to integrate other tools with them. One of those, source control, is the first tool you need to set up and is the topic of the next chapter.

Setting up a source control system

Continuous integration (CI) isn't possible without a source control system. As a matter of fact, it's difficult to set up any reasonable software manufacturing process without one, regardless of whether you're using CI. As soon as you progress beyond being a lonely developer spitting out code in a dark corner of a dorm room, you'll have to think about setting up a proper place for your code to reside. You need a place you can send the fruits of your work and from where you can receive the work of your colleagues.

In the dawn of time, there was a harsh division of functionality, and every developer had their own EXE or DLL to work on. Everyone worked on a separate part of the code and submitted their work to someone whose sole task was to integrate the code from various developers into one codebase. Those times are long gone. We now have automated systems that do the trick. They reside somewhere in the net (intra or inter doesn't matter). Every developer works closely with the system. They

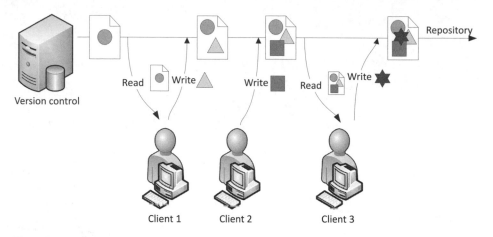

Figure 2.1   Most common source control systems involve a centralized server and a bunch of clients reading from and writing to the source control repository.

push their work onto it and regularly pull the work of others out to a local construction site.

Source control systems, also called *version* or *revision control systems,* are programs that let you manage changes in files. More important, source control systems hold the files containing the source code for your software. But generally, it doesn't matter what kind of files are managed: documents or binary files are also welcome. As shown in figure 2.1, source control clients are able to read from and write to a revision control repository.

In this chapter, you'll learn why a source control system is essential not only for the CI process, but also in the day-to-day life of the developer. You'll choose a suitable tool for your needs, taking into consideration a number of attributes. Subversion (SVN) and Team Foundation Server (TFS) source control will prove to be the source control systems to choose from. We'll look at the VisualSVN Server as a suitable Subversion package for the Windows platform. You'll learn how to use TortoiseSVN, a great SVN Windows client. And last but not least, you'll prepare and dispatch to source control the sample project introduced in chapter 1. After that, you'll learn how to do the same with TFS source control. But first, why do you need a source control system in your CI environment?

2.1   *Choosing the right source control system for you*

Let's imagine a CI process without a source control system. It could be a one-person shop where everything happens on a single machine. That's fine, but as soon as you start to work on a team, you'll run into problems.

There must be one single place where developers commit their work and the CI process pulls it to integrate. It may be a single folder on network share where developers manually copy their new features; the CI process periodically checks the folder for changes and integrates the code when something new is detected. That approach will probably work too. But why do it the hard way? Why not make a full-blown system to do the job?

Many great source control systems are available. Many of them are free—and free in this field doesn't mean an inferior product. They're feature rich and well-established. Installation is easy, and the list of benefits is huge. Let's examine them quickly before you decide what source control system to use.

2.1.1 Benefits of source control systems

With a source control system, you have a full development history of everything you've committed—always. Have you ever wished you had the version from last Friday where everything worked correctly, and not the mess you created on Monday when you were tired after a long and eventful weekend? Of course, you didn't think about making a secure copy on Friday. And now you have to look for a nasty bug, and you don't have working code to compare. With a source control system, that's not a problem. You always have a full history of everything you've done. You can pull the version from Friday (assuming, of course, that you didn't forget to commit!). You can pull and check every version from the time you set up your source control system.

If you can pull every historical version that exists in your repository, nothing prevents you from reverting the changes you made to the current version. For example, the bad code you wrote after an eventful weekend can be replaced with a working copy in a minute.

Most source control systems let you lock a file one way or another. Think about a situation in which you want to have a file just for you. You don't want anyone changing something while you work on this particular-new-very-important feature. With some source control systems, you can explicitly lock the file you're working on: no one can edit the file, but everyone can still pull it and compile with it. Some systems only let you mark the file as locked: others aren't prevented from editing other files, but no one can check out a file someone else locked. Either way, you can have the file available to only you.

Source control systems let you label revisions if you want. Assume you're releasing a new version. The revision number is 4711. Do you have to remember it, in case you have to fix a bug in this particular version when it's in production with a customer? No: you can label this revision by giving it a meaningful name and marking it so it will be easy to find and work with. If needed, you can take the labeled version, fork it, and set a separate CI process for it.

Let's say you've found a bug in a labeled production version. You've fixed the bug in this version, but it also resides in the main version. That means you'll have to implement the fix there, too. But you don't have to do this manually. In most cases, you can merge the changes you've made in the labeled version with the main version using only source control system features.

Or, suppose you're working on a new feature. You aren't sure the technique you've chosen is the right one. No problem: you set a labeled version and don't mess with the main version. But in the end, you realize that your technique was correct (of course!). What do you do? You merge.

One more thing is especially important if you're considering setting up a CI process. The golden rule of CI says to keep all the files you need to fully integrate your software in the project directory. You should keep not only your source but also all the tests and third-party tools and libraries you use—literally everything you need for full integration, including executables for documentation generation, installation, and deployment. Now, think about this project directory residing in your source control system. You can point new developers to one place and have everything ready for them to pull and start to work. They don't need to install anything extra to start compiling, testing, and working. The same setup applies to the CI process. You can point it to the same place every developer uses, and it can do the work it's designed for, wherever it's installed. Not bad, eh?

Now that you know the most important source control system benefits, let's look for the right one for you.

2.1.2 *Source control aspects to consider*

The benefits we've discussed are mostly universal among modern version control systems. If you find one that doesn't perform all the functions described earlier, you should forget it. The important aspects to consider are the following:

- Centralized vs. distributed
- Transactional vs. nontransactional
- File blocking vs. non–file blocking
- Free vs. paid

Table 2.1 lists several popular source control systems; you can use it as a reference for your decision making.

Table 2.1 Important source control aspects of several different tools

	Subversion	TFS Version Control	Visual SourceSafe	Git	Vault
Free vs. paid	Free	$	$	Free	$
Centralized vs. distributed	Centralized	Centralized	Centralized	Distributed	Centralized
Transactional vs. nontransactional	Transactional	Transactional	Nontransactional	Transactional	Transactional
File blocking vs. non–file blocking	Non–file blocking	Both	File blocking	Non–file blocking	Both

FREE VS. PAID

The first thing you should consider is the cost-benefit factor. Commercial version control systems like that included in Microsoft TFS tend to do a lot more than you'd expect. For a lot of money, you get a lot of functionality. (Beginning with Visual Studio 2010, anyone with an MSDN Professional subscription or above gets a license for TFS. This significantly drives down the cost of implementing TFS.) The revision control system is a small part of the TFS infrastructure; we'll look at TFS features in the next chapter.

Other commercial tools are available, such as Vault. It was designed to replace the old Microsoft Visual SourceSafe (VSS).[1] If you're familiar with VSS, and you're afraid of the learning curve with something else, consider using Vault (it has the coolness factor of being written in .NET, too).

> **NOTE** Microsoft discontinued Visual SourceSafe with the release of Visual Studio 2010. It was replaced with Team Foundation Server Basic.

On the other hand, you have free systems like SVN and Git. Most of them are even open source. They control your source—period. For everything else, you have to use other tools.

CENTRALIZED VS. DISTRIBUTED

Another important aspect is the choice between centralized and distributed source control systems. You can see the concept behind distributed version control systems in figure 2.2.

Maybe because Linus Torvalds, the creator of Linux, started to work on Git, distributed source control systems are gaining popularity. The idea is to have a full repository containing all the revision history locally on the developer's machine. There is no single central server to administer the source—instead, there are many "central repositories." You initially commit locally; what to merge globally is up to a superuser. Distributed source control is a fairly new concept, but it's used to develop the Linux kernel and many other open source applications.

On the opposite end of the spectrum are centralized systems, with one server somewhere that manages the source. This group includes Subversion, TFS, VSS, and Vault.

Both distributed and centralized systems have their advantages and disadvantages. From the CI point of view, the centralized approach can be considered better. With a single repository and full control over history, centralized systems are easier to incorporate for a wider audience, and they demand less knowledge about source control system infrastructure.

---

[1] To use Visual SourceSafe with Visual Studio 2010 you will need to install additional package from here: http://code.msdn.microsoft.com/KB976375.

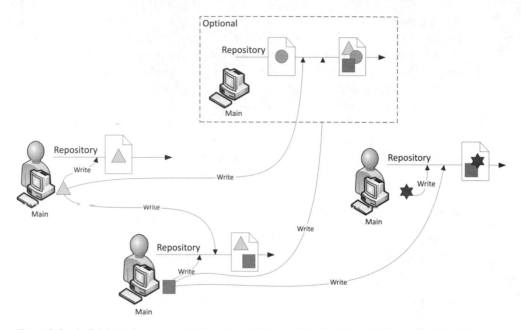

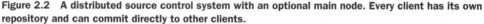

Figure 2.2   A distributed source control system with an optional main node. Every client has its own repository and can commit directly to other clients.

TRANSACTIONAL VS. NONTRANSACTIONAL

Although it almost isn't an issue with modern source control systems, this aspect is something you should keep in mind. It wasn't so long ago that repository operations within the source control system weren't atomic. If the operation to pass new files to the repository failed due to a network error or some other problem, some of the files were checked in to the repository and some weren't. This situation could easily render the repository unstable, in an unknown state and prone to further errors. For example, the VSS was nontransactional. Almost all of the modern source control systems are transactional. You should definitely go this way, too.

FILE BLOCKING VS. NON–FILE BLOCKING

Another aspect you may consider while choosing a source control system is the ability to explicitly check out files from the repository, preventing others from modifying them. Essentially, a file-blocking system is able to prevent you from editing a file someone else has blocked. A non–file blocking system lets you edit everything every time, which may eventually lead to a conflict.

Think about a situation where two developers have made changes to the same file. The first developer checks his changes into the repository, and the second developer is blocked from check-in because her version of the file conflicts with the one already in the source control system. This aspect often isn't addressed directly, but it may be essential if your build depends on files that can't be automatically merged. Two developers working on such a file could be a disaster. It's a question of work culture, too: a sick developer with an explicitly checked-out file is a real problem. You often end up with a lot of partial classes in separate files that have been created by various developers to bypass another user's blocks.

TFS can work in both modes. Subversion can only lock files, preventing parties from checking in rather than stopping them from editing. VSS works only in explicit checkout mode. From our experience working with text-only .NET source files, you don't need an explicit checkout mode; work goes smoothly if you don't block anything. Conflicts are an exception rather a day-to-day problem.

MAKING A CHOICE

We don't know if you're lucky if you're in a situation where you can choose among the various source control systems. If you're a startup, you can take your choice. If you're offered a job at a company that develops without one, consider running away unless they give you permission to set one up before you write the first line of code. If you have a system that works fine, and everybody is happy with it, you should stick to it. Just make sure the source control system you choose will work with your CI server.

If you're in the luxury position where you can choose, and you want to do it cheaply but professionally, pick Subversion. We're totally convinced that you won't be disappointed. Working with SVN is where we're heading in the next section.

2.2 Setting up a Subversion source control server

Subversion is a good, established, free, and open source version control system. It's widely adopted in open source projects and in corporations. It has a neat feature to make all the operations on the repository atomic. That means all you do is check-in, checkout, merge, whatever, all enclosed in a transaction. Either all the files go through or none at all. And there is no way someone else checks in the same time you do.

> **TIP** A great source of information about SVN is a free book called *Version Control with Subversion* by Ben Collins-Sussman, Brian W. Fitzpatrick, and C. Michael Pilato, available online at http://svnbook.red-bean.com/.

In this book, you'll use SVN as the tool of choice for setting up a source control process. Installation is straightforward. Let's set it up.

2.2.1 Installing VisualSVN Server

VisualSVN Server is a great choice if you want to quickly set up the SVN server on a Windows machine. It contains all you need to set up a Subversion server. It has a user interface to create repositories and users. It cuts out all the friction you'd have with setting up an Apache server on a Windows machine, configuring SSL to work on it, creating users, and setting repositories manually. It comes in a free version that has some limitations.

One of the limitations of a free VisualSVN Server version is the lack of remote control. You'll have to install both the Server and the Management Console together on one machine. If you want to manage your server remotely, you must buy the Enterprise version.

You can get the latest version from www.visualsvn.com/server/. If you have a dedicated machine to host your source control server, you obviously should install VisualSVN Server on this machine. This book's example uses a standalone Windows 2008 server to host the Subversion server.

Figure 2.3 shows the most important step in the installation process. You need to decide where to install the server software and where to place the repositories. Please consider a good location for the repositories. They should reside on a reasonably fast hard disk. You should activate SSL to encrypt communication; it will be difficult to read the content of the files you host on the source control server if you aren't authorized to do this. If you don't plan to make your repositories available from the internet, you don't have to activate a secure connection. Although it isn't considered a good idea, your server will react faster if you don't use SSL, because SSL connection negotiation is a fairly expensive process. The port use must be free in order for VisualSVN Server to use it. You can select Subversion authentication or choose to integrate user management with Windows authentication for additional security. If you're running Active Directory in your organization, you should obviously go with it and use Windows authentication (keep in mind that the version of VisualSVN that integrates with Active Directory isn't free). You'll avoid managing your users separately and in

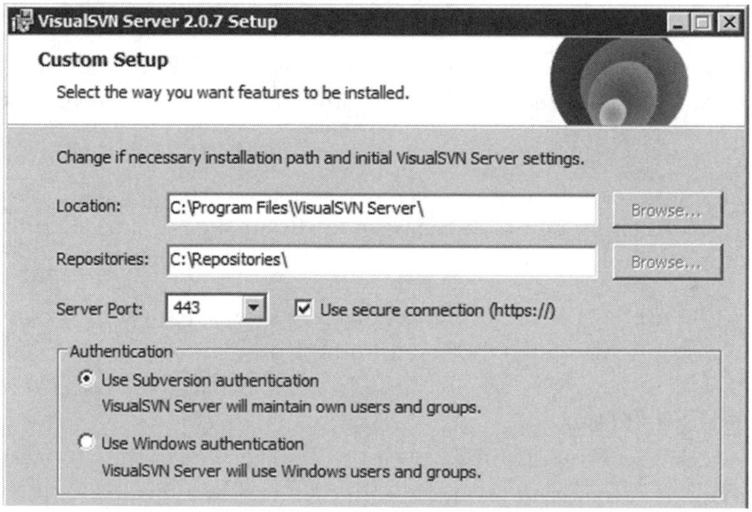

Figure 2.3   Where to store your repositories, whether to encrypt communication, and what user management to use are some of the important decisions you need to make when you install VisualSVN Server.

effect doubling your administrative effort. If you don't have Active Directory, it'll be easier to go with the built-in Subversion authentication (accounts are kept in text files with passwords hashed).

When all the necessary processes are installed, your source control server is ready to be used. You can administer VisualSVN Server using the VisualSVN Server Management Console (or VisualSVN Server Manager, as it's called in the Start menu). You'll find it in Windows by choosing Start > All Programs > VisualSVN.

2.2.2 Creating users and groups

VisualSVN Server comes with a handy Management Console. Using this tool, you can easily organize your source control system, manage your repositories and users, organize them into groups, and issue rights to the repositories.

If you associated your Windows authentication with SVN authentication in the Setup dialog box in figure 2.3, you can use your Windows user credentials to log in. If not, and you decided to let the VisualSVN Server manage your users, you'll have to create accounts for every member of your team, as shown in figure 2.4.

You can put users together in groups, as shown in figure 2.5.

After you create the users and groups, you can start creating repositories.

2.2.3 Creating the repository

You'll store your source code on the server in a structure called the *repository*. Keeping a healthy source code repository is important, even if you don't use CI. But in this scenario, it's somewhere near vital. You want to have the repository organized the right way. You don't want it to be cluttered with unnecessary files. You need a clean division for your customer between work in progress and work being used. You also want to easily manage the content of the repository and probably cross-reference repositories between each other.

Creating a repository in VisualSVN Server is as straightforward as creating a user. As you can see in figure 2.6, you have to assign a repository name, and you can decide to create the default structure right away. You'll learn why this is a good idea later in the chapter.

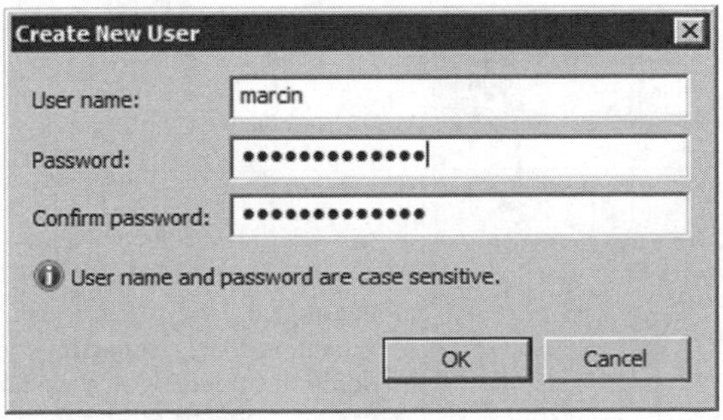

**Figure 2.4
Creating users managed by VisualSVN Server is straightforward: just assign a username and password. But you should consider associating SVN with Windows authentication so you won't double the administration effort.**

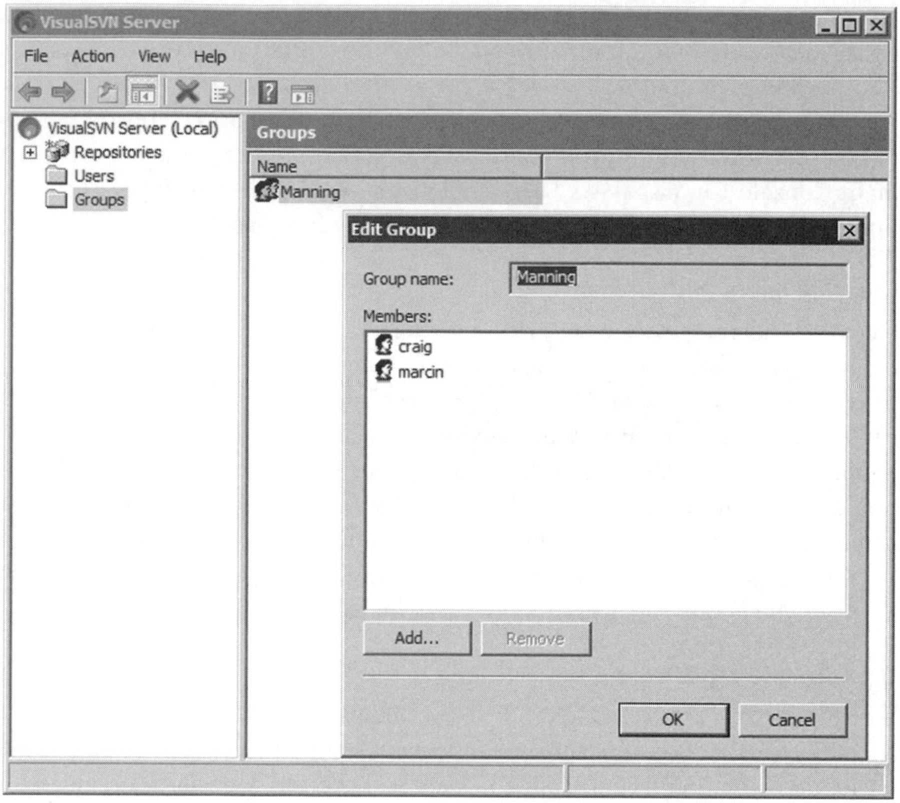

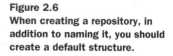

Figure 2.5   Creating groups using the native user management in VisualSVN. This step isn't necessary if you use Windows authentication. The way you set the rights to the repository stay the same: use the repository context menu.

To connect to the repository, you must provide an address to your files, in the form of a URL (see figure 2.7). The VisualSVN Server Management Console is kind enough to show you that address. If the address looks familiar, you're right: VisualSVN Server is nothing more than Subversion bound to a web server (Apache, in this case).

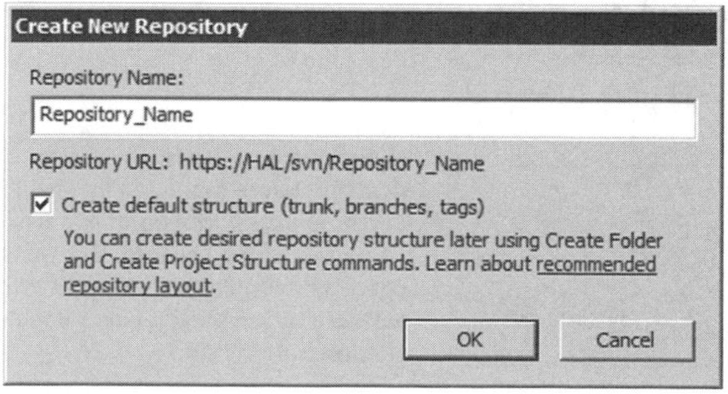

Figure 2.6
When creating a repository, in addition to naming it, you should create a default structure.

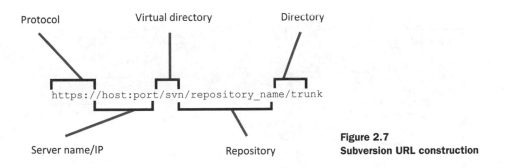

Figure 2.7
Subversion URL construction

The URL contains the protocol or file-access method name. You'll connect to the server using HTTP if you're using non-encrypted communication or HTTPS if you turned on SSL. It's also possible to use SVN with local folders or to use other protocols. We won't cover these in this book.

You connect VisualSVN Server using the server name or IP address and a port number. If you have firewalls on the way from the client to the server, remember to open this port. VisualSVN Server creates a kind of virtual directory named svn. The rest is the path to the files. The path always starts with a repository name and can be supplemented with directories in the repository.

2.2.4 *Keeping a healthy repository*

It's sometimes considered good practice to have one repository throughout a whole company or department; this means you store all your projects in one repository, using directories to logically divide it. Others prefer to have one repository per project.

The first approach makes a lot of things easier, such as source control server administration. After assigning users to the single repository and giving them enough rights, you can virtually forget about administration. Adding a new project is a matter of adding a new directory to the existing repository—no other administration is needed. Daily work with the repository is also easier. Copying, merging, and peeking for the differences (diff) is easier when you do it on a path basis rather than cross-repository. And you don't lose any historical data while moving, copying, and merging files.

You can set up something similar to the structure shown in figure 2.8. This is a single repository, called Projects, with a directory structure underneath.

A single repository isn't a good idea if you have a lot of users with different permissions to the code base. For example, it's difficult to assign one user only the read permission to one project and read/write to another. You should consider using multiple repositories if you plan to store different file types or when the revision number plays a special role in your development process. Another possible layout is shown in figure 2.9: Framework, WebCalculator, and WinCalculator are all separate repositories.

Look closely at the URLs shown in figures 2.8 and 2.9. Do you see the difference? The first figure shows http://HYMIE:81/svn/Projects/Framework, where Projects is a

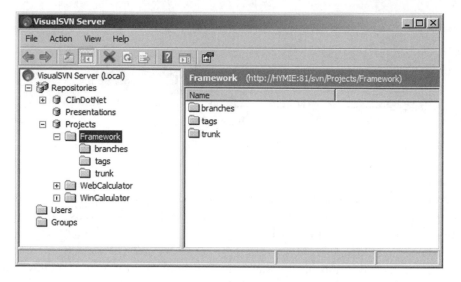

Figure 2.8   One repository throughout a company or department makes it easier to maintain the structure. You don't have to set up every repository separately.

repository and Framework is a directory within this repository. The second, http://HYMIE:81/svn/Framework, has Framework as the repository. From the client point of view, it doesn't matter. With SVN, you can pull a given directory. You don't have to work at the repository level.

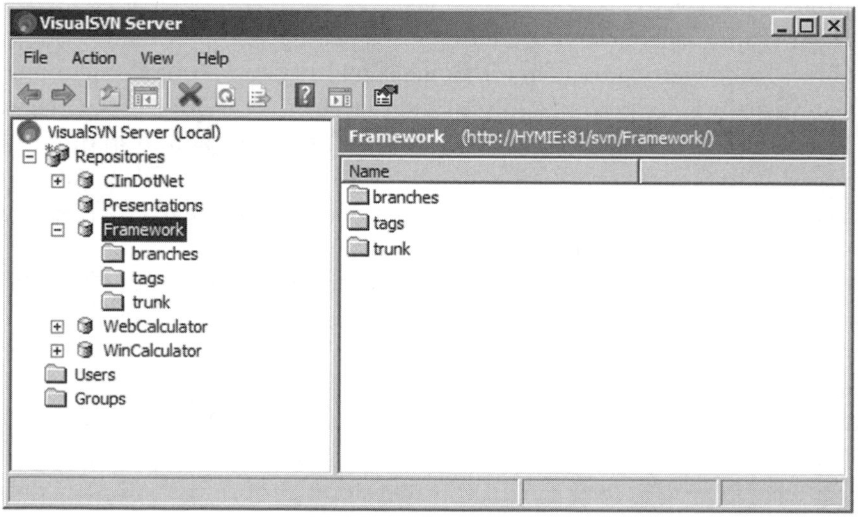

Figure 2.9   One repository for (roughly) every solution makes it possible to vary the user rights to the repositories. Generally, this approach is used to store various types of files— separating documentation and source code.

BRANCHES, TAGS, AND TRUNK

One other thing you have to consider when setting up your repository is the division of the branches, tags, and trunk. Creating these directories in your repository isn't mandatory, but it helps to maintain the project. The *trunk* is the main development line. Think of it like a tree trunk. It's the place where you spend the most time and where new features are implemented. The trunk drives new development. It's the obvious place to hook up to the CI process.

A *branch* is a separate line of development. It shares the same history but lives independently from the trunk and other lines of development. It's used mostly for release stabilization (long-lived branch), a place where you can work on a feature without considering influence from others (medium-lived branch), or as a try-out field for experimental development (short-lived branch). Generally, it's a good idea to have a branch for every software version used by a customer. This makes it easier to find and fix bugs in a particular version.

Some branches can be considered good material for the CI process. For example, release-stabilization branches should be continuously integrated, experimental ones shouldn't, and feature branches may be.

A *tag* is a snapshot of your repository taken at a given time and given a meaningful name. It's used every time something important happens, such as when you make a release or implement an important feature. We consider tags irrelevant for the CI process.

CREATING THE DIRECTORY STRUCTURE

You should go with the repository layout that works best for you. In this case, you'll use a repository per project, with the default directory structure shown in figure 2.9. Follow these steps:

1. From your source control server, launch the VisualSVN Server Management Console.
2. Right-click the Repositories node in the tree view in the left panel, and select Create New Repository. The Create New Repository dialog box opens (see figure 2.10).

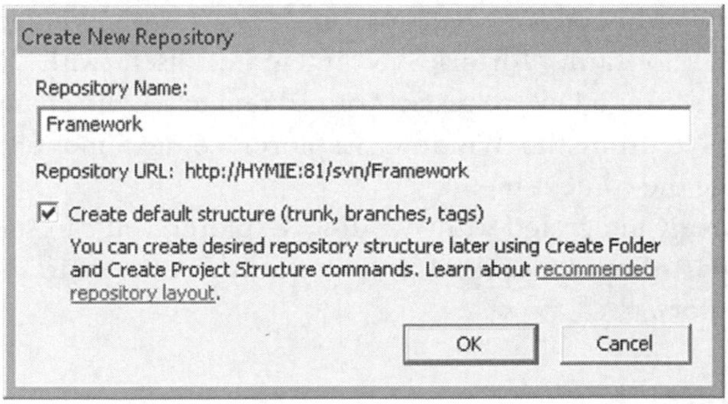

Figure 2.10
When creating a new SVN repository, you can optionally create a structure for the trunk, branches, and tags.

3 In the Repository Name text box, enter Framework.

4 Select the Create Default Structure (Trunk, Branches, Tags) check box, and then click OK to create the repository.

5 Use the same steps to create two more repositories: one named WebCalculator and the other named WinCalculator.

Notice how the repository names match the Visual Studio solutions you created in chapter 1. It's a good idea to keep these names the same to make source code management easier. With a repository structure in place, you can feed it some data. To do this, you need an SVN client.

2.3   *TortoiseSVN and working with the repository*

Thus far, we've shown you the SVN server. To work with it, you can use command-line utilities supplied with SVN, but it's much easier to work with the repository with an SVN client. A client allows you to send files to and receive them from the repository, by supporting one or many of the Subversion protocols (http://, https://, svn://, svn+ssh://, file:///, and svn+XXX://). Many clients are available with various interfaces, from a command-line interface to standalone programs to tools that integrate with Windows Explorer or Visual Studio.

The command-line tools are great for automation. You'll use them a lot in your CI process. They let you script things so the process can perform unmanaged, but they aren't so good for day-to-day work. And there is a learning curve for all the commands, switches, and parameters.

If you feel geeky enough to use the command-line interface feel free to do so. If not, think about using something with an easier user interface. You can use a standalone SVN client such as SmartSVN. You may also choose a plug-in for Visual Studio. The creators of VisualSVN Server have one called VisualSVN, but it isn't free. There's also a free plug-in for Visual Studio called AnkhSVN. But in this case we'll go with TortoiseSVN, which is one of the most popular SVN clients for Windows. It integrates with Windows Explorer and is easy to use.

2.3.1   *Subversion client: TortoiseSVN*

You can download the last version of TortoiseSVN from http://tortoisesvn.tigris.org/. The installation is straightforward. TortoiseSVN integrates itself with Windows Explorer (see figure 2.11), so you'll have to restart your system to see the changes. You can then access TortoiseSVN from the Windows Explorer context menu: select a folder and right-click to see the context menu.

With TortoiseSVN properly integrated with Windows Explorer, you can start using your repository. Let's import the solution and project files you created in chapter 1 into the SVN source repository.

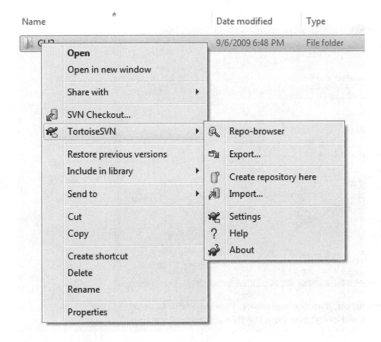

Figure 2.11 TortoiseSVN integrates itself with Windows Explorer by adding a context menu you can use to manage your source.

2.3.2 *Creating a working copy*

If you followed along in section 2.2.4, you should have a repository layout similar to the one shown in figure 2.9. The repositories are empty except the initial trunk, branches, and tags structure. Before you can start normal work with the repository, you have to populate it with some real data.

There are lots of ways to do that. You can import data into the repository and pull it out again and do additional maintenance, but probably the easiest way is to check the empty trunk into the folder with your project. Doing so creates a working or local copy of your repository.

In addition to your files, the working copy contains SVN artifacts (in the svn directory). This svn directory is vital for the SVN client to work. You should never mess with it or try to manage it manually—let the client do this work for you.

Follow these steps to create a working copy in the Framework directory:

1 Using Windows Explorer, navigate to the Framework directory, right-click, and choose SVN Checkout. The Checkout dialog box opens (see figure 2.12).

2 You can read the repository URL in the VisualSVN Server Management Console (shown earlier in figure 2.9). After you enter the server URL, and click OK, TortoiseSVN informs you that the folder you're trying to check out to isn't empty (see figure 2.13).

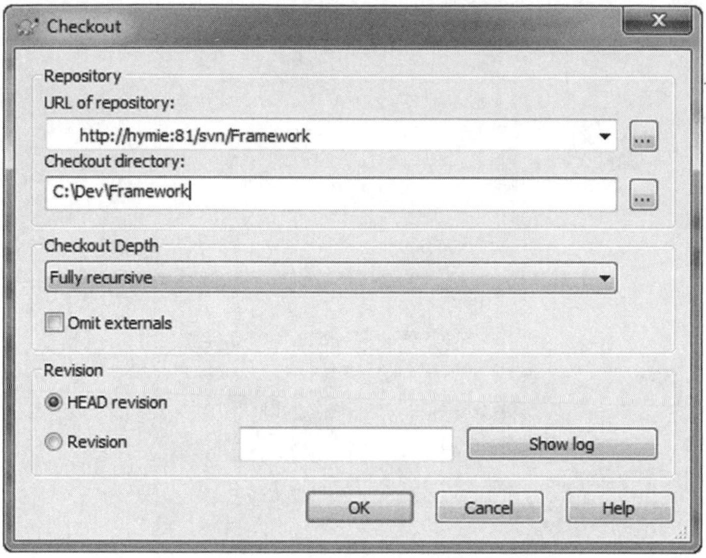

Figure 2.12   Checking out from the repository. Provide a URL to your repository, and check out everything from the HEAD (newest) revision.

3   It's all right, because you created your Visual Studio project in this folder and you do want the local copy to exist in this folder. Click Yes.

4   If you set up the SVN server to use SSL, you have to accept the SSL certificate issued by VisualSVN Server (if you're using SSL).

5   If prompted, enter your repository credentials.

   TortoiseSVN pulls the empty repository to the folder with your project, as shown in figure 2.14.

6   Follow the same steps to create a local repository for WebCalculator and WinCalculator.

Notice the new icons associated with the development folders on your local drive. The integration of TortoiseSVN with Windows Explorer tells you either that the files are checked in (a green checkmark) or that the state of the file is unknown (a blue question mark). As you work with the files and folders, you'll see other icons, most of which are self-explanatory.

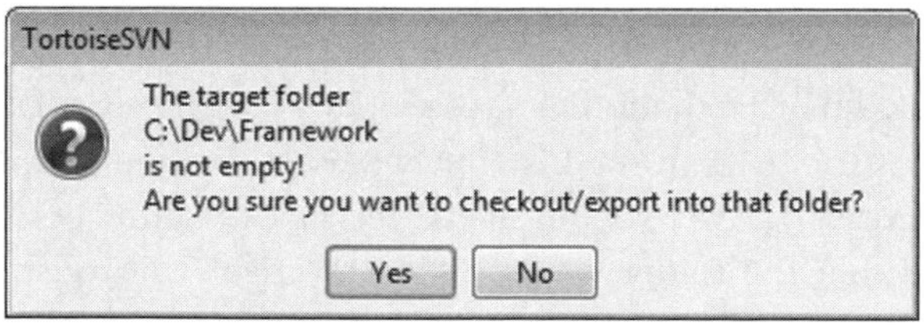

**Figure 2.13
TortoiseSVN displays a warning if you initially check out into a populated directory.**

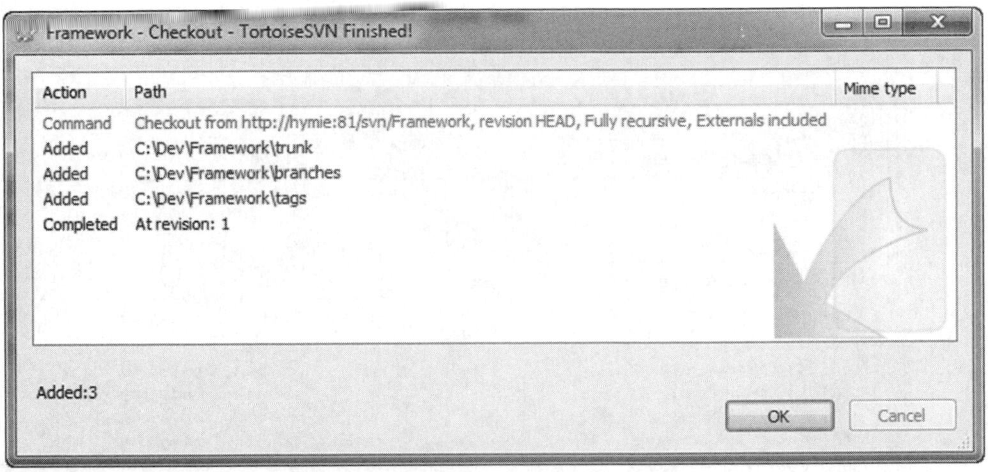

Figure 2.14 The initial checkout into the project folder. TortoiseSVN creates a working copy.

You now have a local copy of the repositories, but none of the source code has been stored on the server. Committing the changes to the repository is the next step.

2.3.3 Committing changes

You now have to send files to the repository and fill it with your project:

1 Right-click the Framework folder in Windows Explorer, and select SVN Commit from the context menu. TortoiseSVN searches in the folder for everything different than the checked-out version and presents you with a Commit dialog box (see figure 2.15).

2 Enter some text in the Message box. You should make it a habit to provide a message for everything. The message should clearly explain what changes were made in this revision. This way, you'll always have historical information that you may need in the future. Because the messages are searchable in Tortoise-SVN, it's easy to find a particular revision where you fixed a specific issue or bug if you use, for example, the reference number assigned to the bug. Some tools can resolve the issue based on the commit message.

3 Working with your project re-creates Visual Studio artifacts that aren't welcome in the repository: temporary data, compiled output, and user-specific files. Currently you have the normal results of the Visual Studio build: the bin and obj folders (containing compilation artifacts) and all the *.suo files (personalized additions to solution file) and *.user files (additions to project files). You shouldn't include these files in the repository. Select everything, and then deselect the files and directories you don't want to have in the repository.

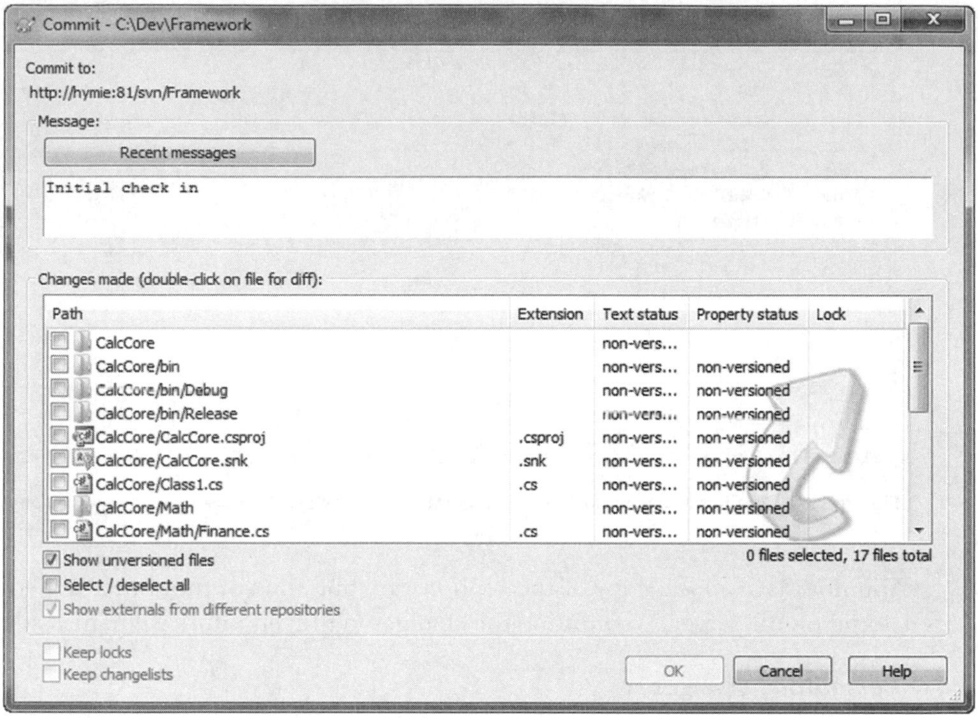

Figure 2.15   Initial commit. TortoiseSVN finds everything that's different from the checkout.

4   Click OK to begin checking in the project files. The progress dialog box is displayed (see figure 2.16). If all goes well, the Framework source files will be stored in the repository.

5   Repeat the commit process for the Windows and web calculator projects.

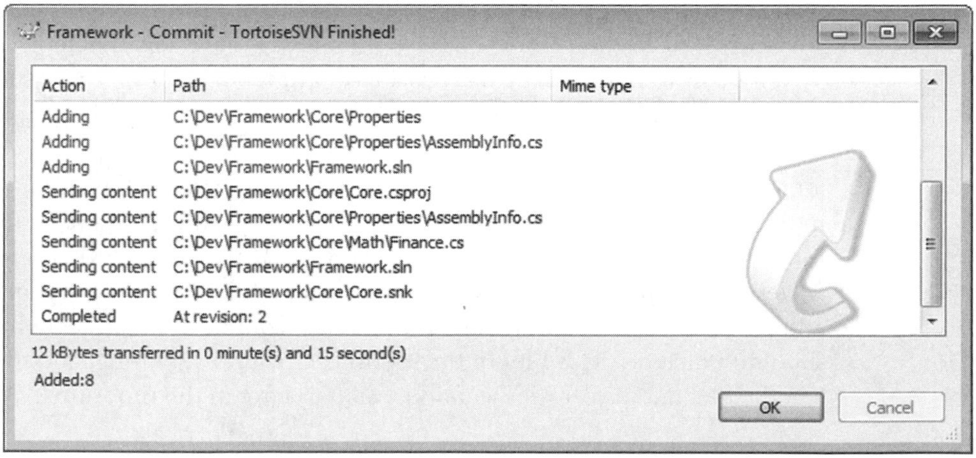

Figure 2.16   TortoiseSVN displays a progress dialog box as it sends files into the repository.

As you work with the project further, you'll end up with more and more artifacts that shouldn't be included in the repository. Your build process is likely to produce many artifacts that you don't want to host in the repository, including reports, deployment files, and so on. All these files can be ignored. You can ignore entire directories, separate files, and files with wildcards. You can clear the check boxes to do this, but it's inconvenient to browse the file list every time you want to commit something. To help, you can permanently ignore some files (see figure 2.17). TortoiseSVN will never try to commit the ignored files.

> **NOTE**   Using TortoiseSVN, you can right-click an artifact and tell Subversion to ignore it. After you mark a file or directory to be ignored, you have to commit it to the repository. If you want to include something you've ignored earlier, choose Add from the TortoiseSVN context menu.

As usual, that's only one way of preparing your construction site. You could create the project in Visual Studio after making the initial checkout or import everything into the repository and then make it clean. The thing is, you want to make the repository clean at the beginning and quickly get to your day-to-day tasks: working with files, updating, and committing.

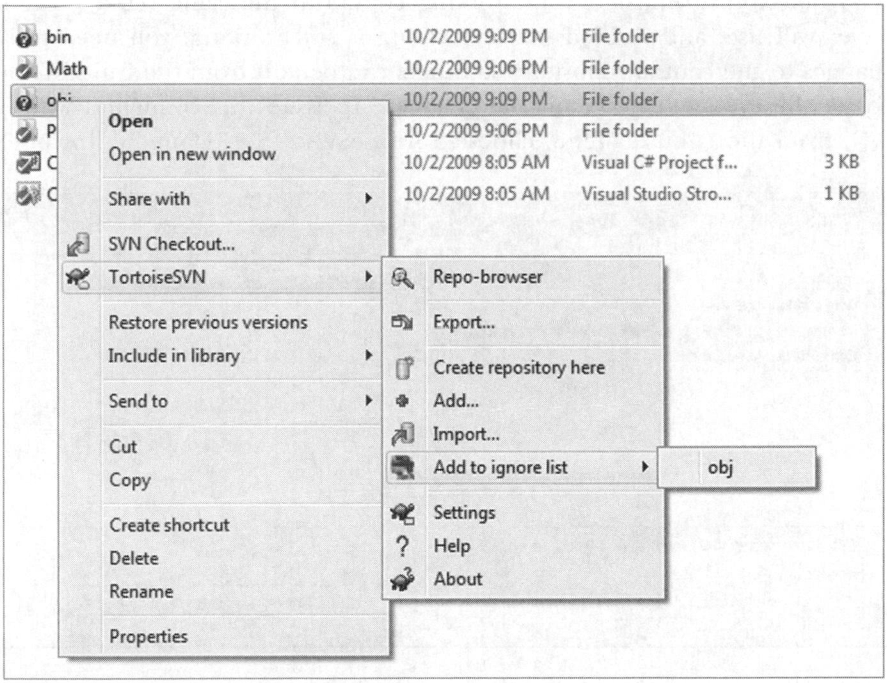

Figure 2.17   Making your repository tidy requires you to ignore files that you don't want in your repository.

2.3.4 *Updating and committing files*

Day-to-day work with the source control system consists mostly of updating and committing to and from the repository. As we said in chapter 1, when you have a real CI process, the developers on the team commit their work at least once a day. Generally, the more commits the better.

Pull the changes before you commit, and check if everything is still working fine. It's possible that someone committed something while you were working, and your copy of the file is out of date. It's even possible that someone worked in the same file you did. The Update function pulls all the changes from the central repository to your working copy. If necessary, SVN merges the changes others made into files you've worked with (see figure 2.18).

If TortoiseSVN isn't able to merge the files properly, you may get a conflict that you have to resolve. You can do so using the context menu for the conflicted item in the Update window, as shown in figure 2.19.

Conflicts occur rather infrequently on a well-organized team. But when they do occur, you must resolve them manually. A clean code base is important for a frictionless CI process. TortoiseSVN les you easily resolve conflicts using the Merge dialog box (see figure 2.20).

When you've updated your working copy, run the same build process the CI server will use, and verified that everything is still working, you need to send the changes to the central repository so others can benefit from the fruits of your work. To do this, you must commit the changes. To issue this command with TortoiseSVN, from the context menu, choose TortoiseSVN > SVN Commit. TortoiseSVN will

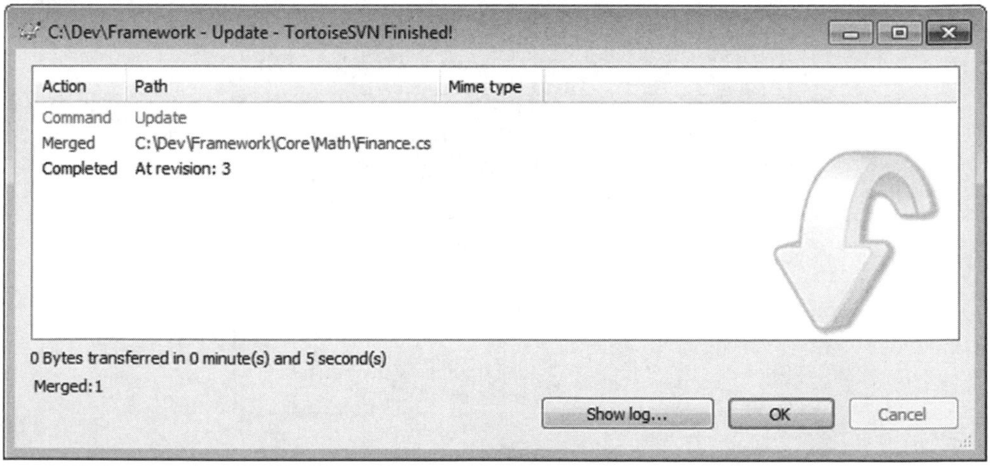

Figure 2.18 Always pull the changes before you commit. There may be changes already in the central repository. Check if everything still works after update. Commit only if you're sure you won't break the CI build.

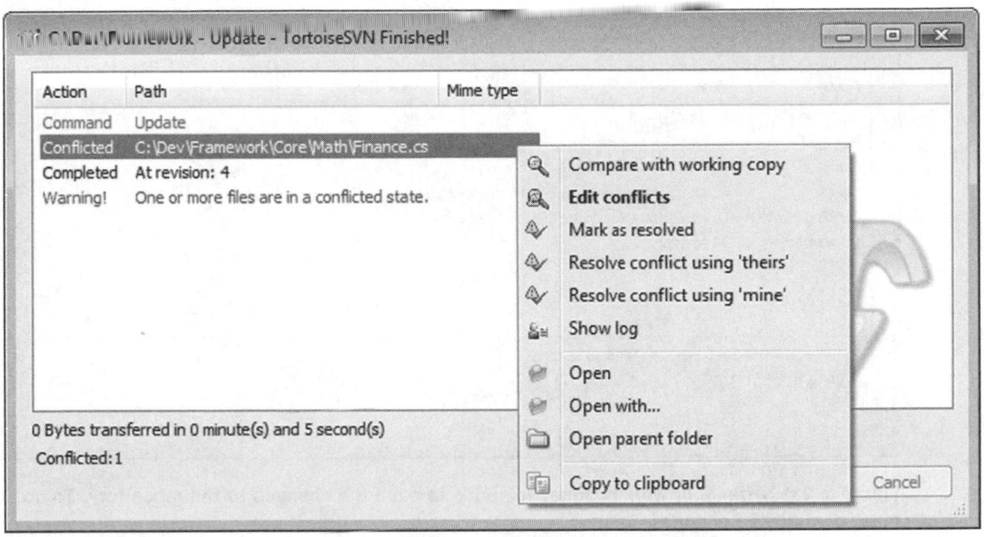

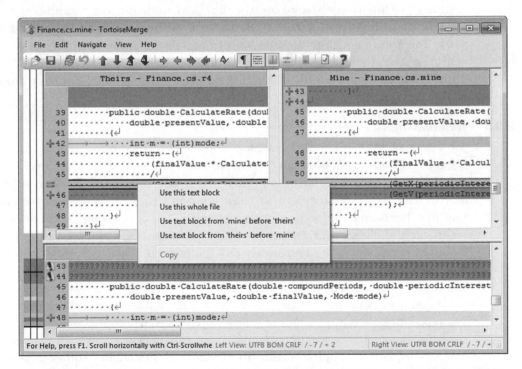

Figure 2.19 Changes in the repository and in your local copy overlap and are too big for TortoiseSVN to resolve. You have to step in and resolve the conflict.

Figure 2.20 Resolving the infrequent case of a conflict with TortoiseSVN. You must do this if you update changes that someone made to the same files as you and SVN can't automatically merge the files.

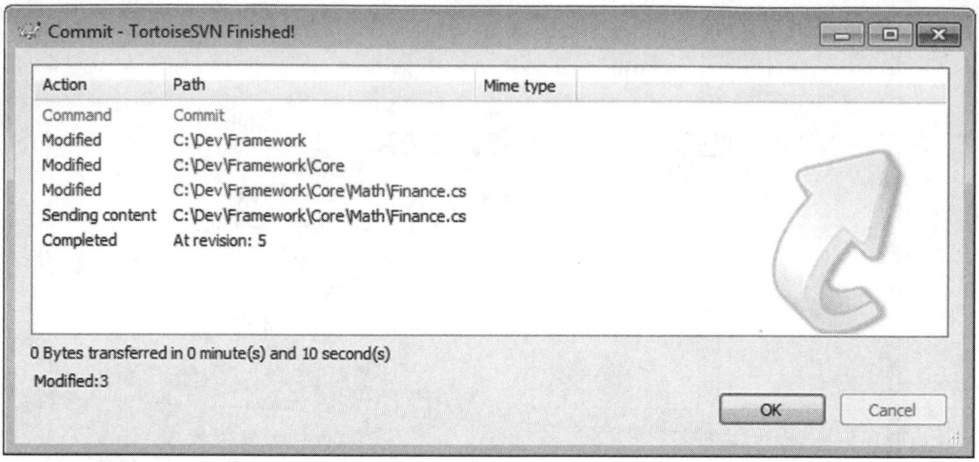

Figure 2.21   After your work is done, you have to send the changes to the repository. To do so, you must commit the changes.

push the changes into the repository and display the progress dialog box (see figure 2.21).

There's a lot more to source control management than updating and committing. By now, you should have a pretty good idea how the Subversion server and client work. You know enough to use it in your CI process. If you want to master your SVN skills, see the Subversion book at http://svnbook.red-bean.com/. Try reverting changes, copying within the repository, and branching the trunk. We'll now pay close attention to referencing.

2.3.5   *Referencing*

Let's go back to the example calculator project. It's divided into a shared calculation library CalcCore (from the Framework solution) and two clients, WinCalc (from the WindowsCalculator solution) and WebCalc (from the WebCalculator solution). You've built your repository structure, as shown in figure 2.9. But the shared library and the clients aren't referenced with each other. You could compile the library and reference the clients with a DLL, but you'll probably want to work in the projects simultaneously. You want to separately pull the projects from its repositories and create one solution that references them. One of the solutions to this problem is provided with Subversion external definitions.

When you set up an external reference, you tell Subversion to check out a different repository when you pull something else. This way, you can automatically have an external directory or repository present in your working copy. You'll set Framework as an external definition in the Windows and web calculator clients. Follow these steps:

1   In Windows Explorer, go to the WindowsCalculator folder, and bring up the context menu. Select TortoiseSVN > Properties. The Properties dialog box opens (see figure 2.22).

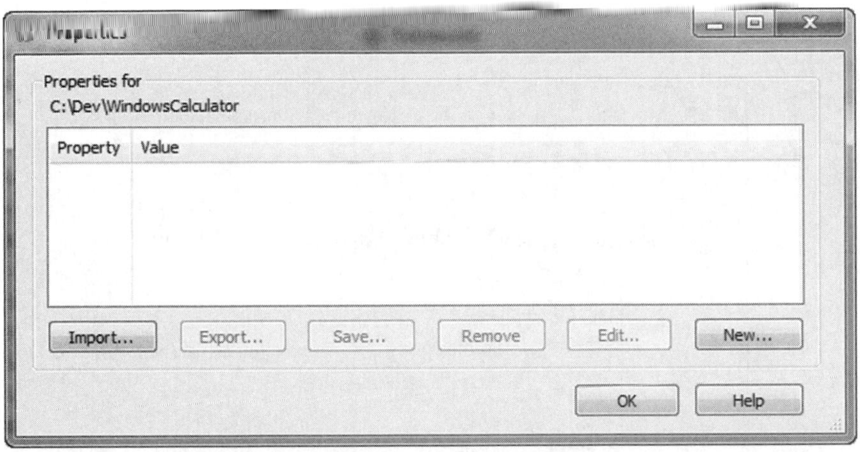

Figure 2.22   The TortoiseSVN Properties dialog box is used to manage properties for a particular item.

2 Click New. The Add Properties dialog box opens (see figure 2.23).

3 In the Property Name drop-down menu, select svn:externals.

4 In the Property Value field, enter the word Framework, press the spacebar, and then enter the URL to the Framework repository. The easiest way to get the URL is to right-click the Framework folder in Windows Explorer, select TortoiseSVN > Relocate, and copy the URL from the Relocate dialog box.

5 Click OK in the Add Properties dialog box, and then click OK to close the Properties dialog box.

6 Right-click the WindowsCalculator folder, and select SVN Update. Doing so pulls the Framework folder into the WindowsCalculator folder. To inform the repository about the external reference, you'll have to do the commit.

7 Repeat these steps for the WebCalculator folder.

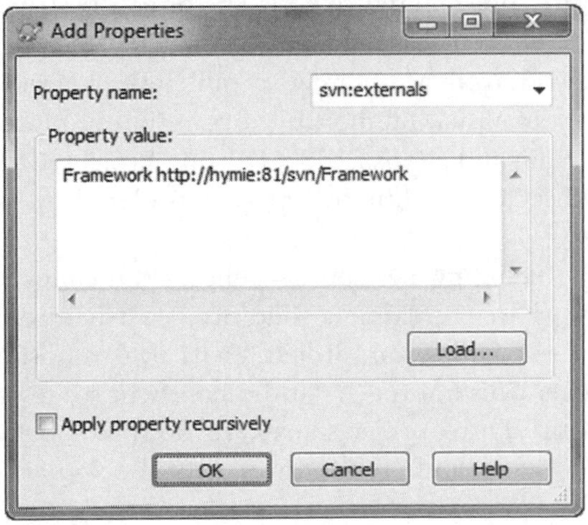

Figure 2.23
You can add many different properties using the Add Properties dialog, including references to external repositories.

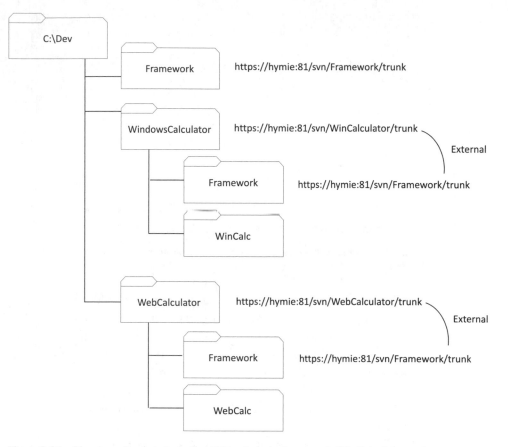

Figure 2.24   Directory structure including SVN external references to WinCalculator and WebCalculator, which contain the folder Framework that points to another repository or directory

You now have the directory structure shown in figure 2.24. The directory structure has changed, whereas the repository layout remains the same.

Now you can reference Framework from a subdirectory pulled by SVN within your Windows and web clients. Go back to Visual Studio. In the Solution Explorer, right-click the Windows Calculator solution, and choose Add > Existing Project. Choose the CalcCore project from the subdirectory within the project folder. Your solution should look like figure 2.25.

The library project is shared (including the source) among the client projects. Doing it this way requires more work than creating a solid project structure up front and checking it in. But this way, you have every project in its own repository, and you can reference them as you like. This approach can be handy in some scenarios such as simultaneous development of two projects that are destined to live separately in the future and are placed in separate repositories. In some scenarios (such as after release), it isn't advisable to use externals. Let's say you're ready to deliver the software to the end user. You must tag both the client project and the referenced project. The same thing applies to branching: if you branch one project, the external reference stays unchanged, and you must branch and re-reference it manually.

After the project is released, you may want to switch to referencing compiled libraries. It will be much easier to manage the files in a lib directory than to use external references.

The external definitions are also read by the CI servers. If you use them, you can be sure that the CI server will be able to read and resolve the externals without any problem.

Figure 2.25   Visual Studio solution layout with a reference to a library project from the client project. This way, you can work simultaneously with two separate repositories.

2.4   Setting up Team Foundation Server

Team Foundation Server 2010 brings a big change to the TFS licensing model. It's much more affordable than the earlier versions. Whereas an average setup of TFS 2008 with server, user licenses, and Visual Studio Team System (VSTS) cost around $10,000, the new TFS 2010 for five users is about $500. It works with all editions of Visual Studio except the Express Editions. And even better, if you have a Visual Studio Professional with MSDN subscription or higher, TFS is included. The cost factor is no longer a big deal.

One thing that drove this change was Microsoft's desire to encourage VSS users to move to TFS Version Control, which is a part of the TFS family of tools. The old VSS is infamous (for good reasons or not) for its instability. A corrupted repository is the last thing you want to experience after a hard day of work. And the sad truth about VSS is that corruption happens way too often. TFS Version Control can't be compared to VSS: it uses a completely different file-access mode (changes are transactional), and it uses SQL Server as its repository. You can also use SQL Server Express. TFS scales safely to a large number of users. Now that it isn't so expensive, you definitely should give it a try.

2.4.1   Installing TFS 2010

The TFS installation process has been completely reworked in TFS 2010. In earlier versions, you had to walk through a pre-install checklist and make sure all the prerequisites were in place before you could continue. The new process installs many of the prerequisites for you.

There's also a new TFS Basic, designed for VSS users, that installs a subset of TFS. If you select the Basic configuration during installation, you don't get the full TFS experience, but you get source code control, work items, and CI automation. It lacks the SharePoint portal and Reporting Services integration, but it can be a good first step for getting source code control and a CI system set up and running.

You can install the Basic configuration on a local workstation. It can also use SQL Server Express for its data store. We elected to go with the TFS Standard Single Server configuration for this book. The only prerequisite is that SQL Server needs to be installed on the server, including Reporting Services, Analysis Services, and Full-Text Search.

Follow these steps:

1 Launch the TFS Setup program.

2 Select Team Foundation Components and Team Foundation Server (see figure 2.26).

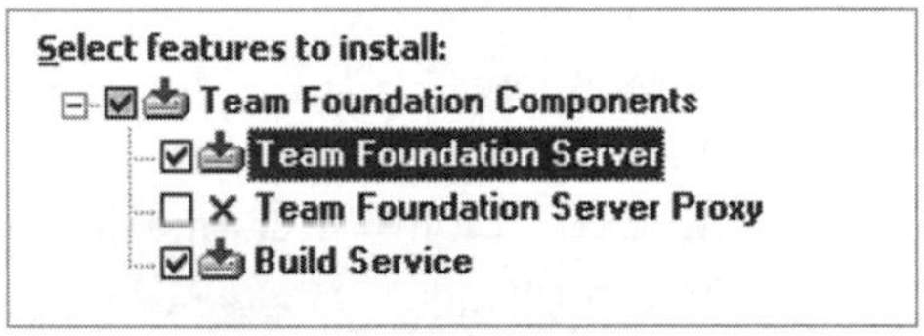

3 Make sure Team Foundation Server Proxy is unchecked.

Figure 2.26 Installing the core TFS features with the build service

The TFS Proxy is nothing more than a caching mechanism for distributed teams. Typically, it's installed in a local area network to provide a transparent service for a local team and connection to a real TFS server over a slower connection. We'll deal with it a little more in chapter 12, where you'll scale CI. If you don't need proxy/cache functionality, leave this feature unchecked.

4 Make sure Team Foundation Build Service is checked.

You'll definitely need it in chapter 4, where we'll deal with the CI server, so you want to install it here. It will be the workhorse for your CI setup. Although it's typically installed on a separate machine from source code control, for better performance you'll leave it selected. You can always install another build service on other machine later.

5 Click Install to begin the base install process. When it's completed, click Finish.

6 Make sure Standard Single Server is selected, as shown in figure 2.27, and click Start Wizard.

7 What happens next depends on how your server is already set up. For example, if Internet Information Services (IIS) is installed, the TFS Configuration wizard won't install it. Go ahead and work through the wizard, answering prompts as needed. Installation may take a while.

TFS 2010 installation has been greatly streamlined from earlier versions and is now a straightforward task. When installation completes, the TFS Administration Console is launched. Now you can begin organizing your Team Projects layout—and that's the topic of the next section.

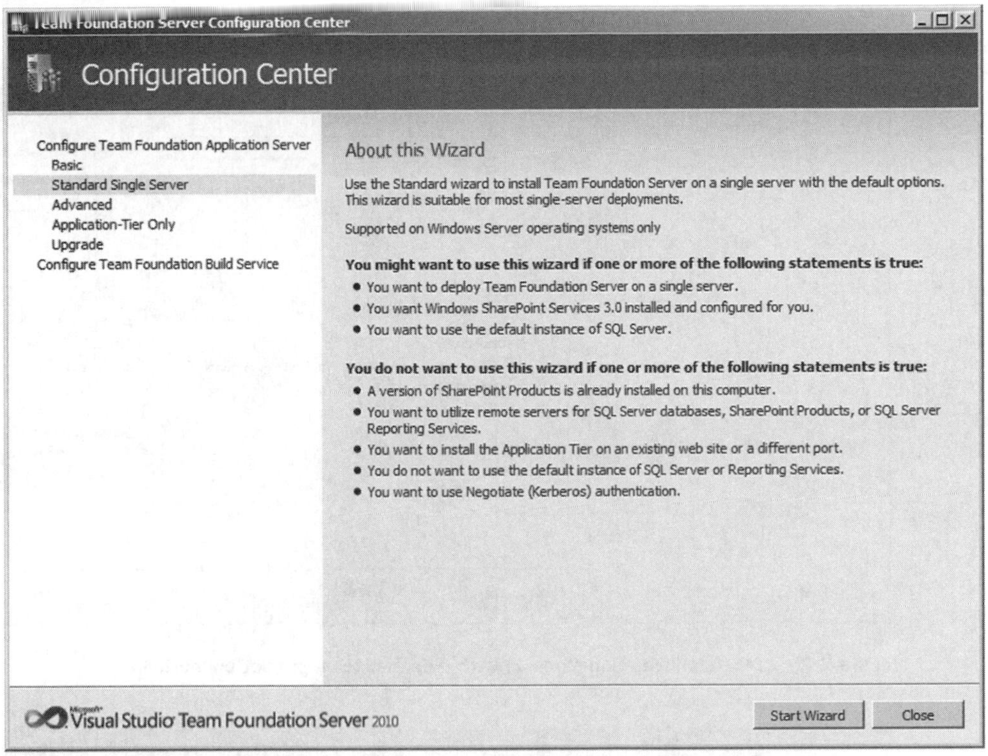

Figure 2.27 Choose the Standard Single Server configuration in the Team Foundation Server Configuration tool to set up one server with full TFS functionality.

2.4.2 *TFS collections*

The main organizational unit in TFS is a *team project*. To understand what a team project is, you have to remove yourself from the source control perspective: think about TFS as a general team-collaboration tool, with revision control as only a part of it. A team project is a set of work items, code repositories, build definitions, and so on. It's a central place that connects a software application with the team developing it.

Team projects are organized in *collections*. The team projects grouped in a collection can share the same resources and are stored in the same database. From the code point of view, a team project collection can share the same code base, and that makes possible branching, merging, and other common source control activities. Let's create a collection for the loan calculator application:

1 If it isn't running, launch the TFS Administration Console.
2 In the left panel, select Application Tier and then Team Project Collections (see figure 2.28).

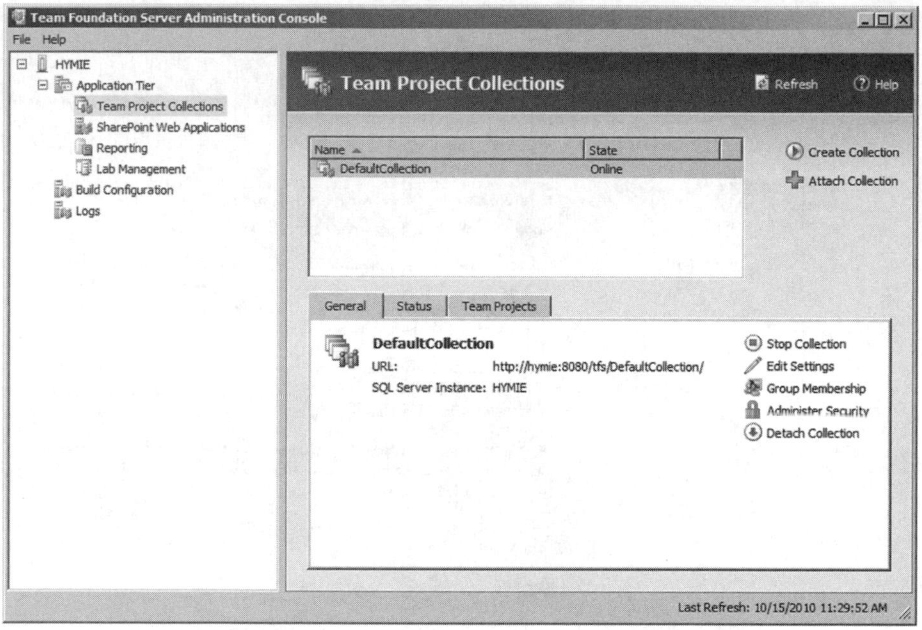

Figure 2.28   TFS Administration Console with a default team project collection

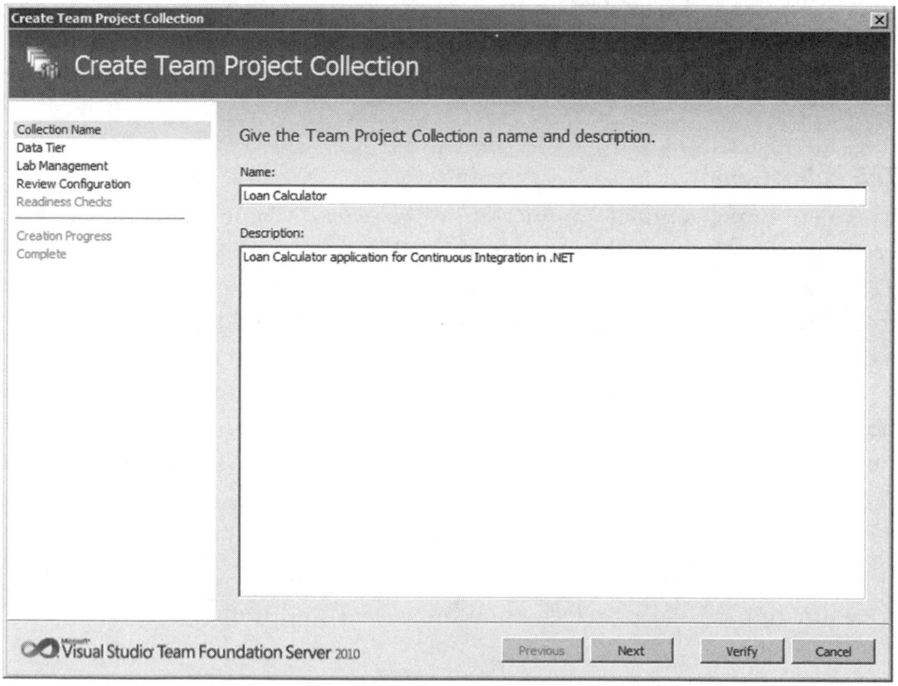

Figure 2.29   When you create a new team project collection, you give it a name and an optional description.

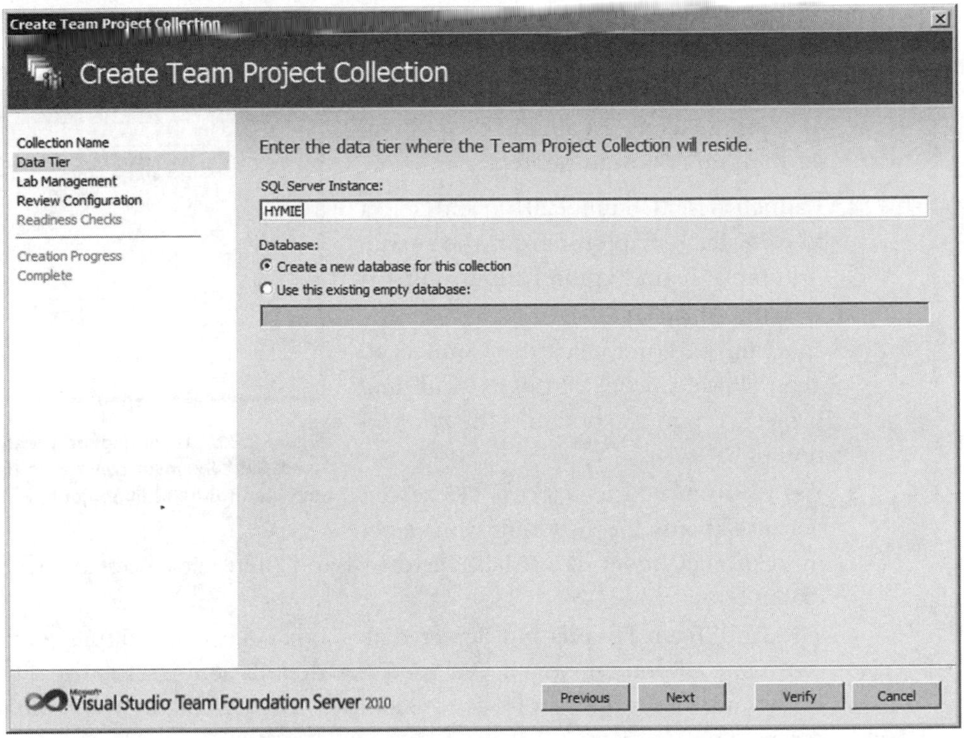

Figure 2.30 In the second step of creating a new team project collection, you specify the database settings for your source files.

3 Click the Create Team Project Collection link. The Create Team Project Collection wizard opens (see figure 2.29).

4 Enter `Loan Calculator` for the name, and an optional description; then click Next.

5 Select the SQL Server instance and database (see figure 2.30) to use to store the source files. In this case, keep the default settings. Click Next.

6 The remainder of the settings—SharePoint, Reports, and Lab Management—are beyond the scope of this book. Click Verify to have the wizard check whether everything is prepared for these settings. Then click Create.

7 It will take a few minutes for the wizard to complete. When it's finished, click Complete and then Close.

The newly created team project collection is ready. You can now populate it with some team projects. You won't do this from the TFS Administration Console. From now on, you'll work on your development machine with Visual Studio. Let's switch to it and populate the collection.

2.4.3 *Using Visual Studio Team Explorer*

All you need to manage your code with TFS 2010 is a copy of Visual Studio 2010. The available versions (except Express) have Team Explorer built in. Follow these steps:

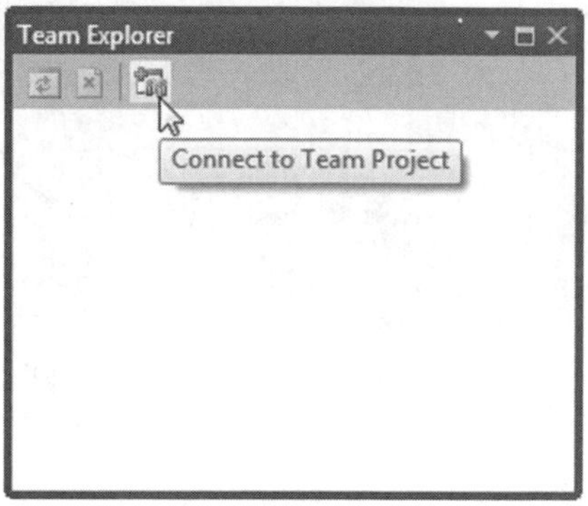

1 Launch Visual Studio 2010, and select View > Team Explorer from the menu. An empty Team Explorer window opens (see figure 2.31).

2 In Team Explorer, click the Connect to Team Project icon. If this is your first project, you must configure the connection to TFS.

3 You're prompted to select a TFS server, because this is the first time you've set up a project under TFS. Click Servers…, and then click Add in the resulting dialog box.

Figure 2.31   Team Explorer, ready to be used. First you must connect to the server and then to the team project.

4 The Add Team Foundation Server dialog box opens (see figure 2.32). Enter the name of your server. If you used the default settings for the TFS server, everything else is filled in for you. Click OK to finish making the connection to the server.

5 If you're prompted to log in, do so with proper credentials. The wizard should choose the newly created server connection for you, and you have to pick the collection. Choose the one you recently created, Loan Calculator, and click Connect. You'll land back in Visual Studio and see something like figure 2.33 in your Team Explorer.

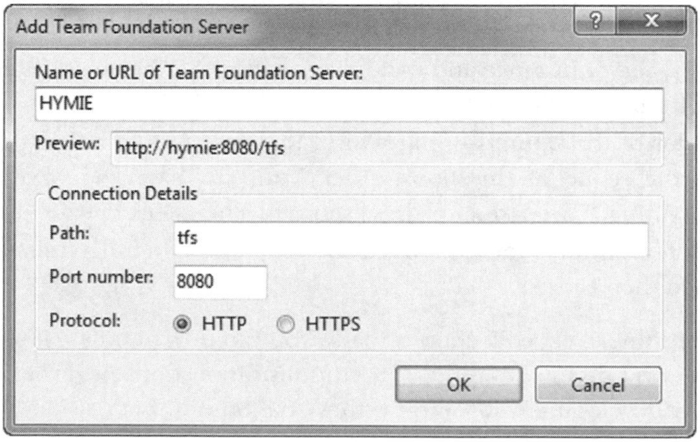

Figure 2.32   You need to tell Team Explorer which server has the TFS installation you're using.

6 Team Explorer now points to an empty project collection. You need to add a project to it. To do so, right-click the collection in Team Explorer, and choose New Team Project. The New Team Project wizard is launched (see figure 2.34).
7 Enter the name (for example, CIinDotNet Calculator Sample Application), and click Next.
8 You need to select the process template to use (see figure 2.35). In this case, choose the MSF for Agile Software Development template to work with, and then click Next.

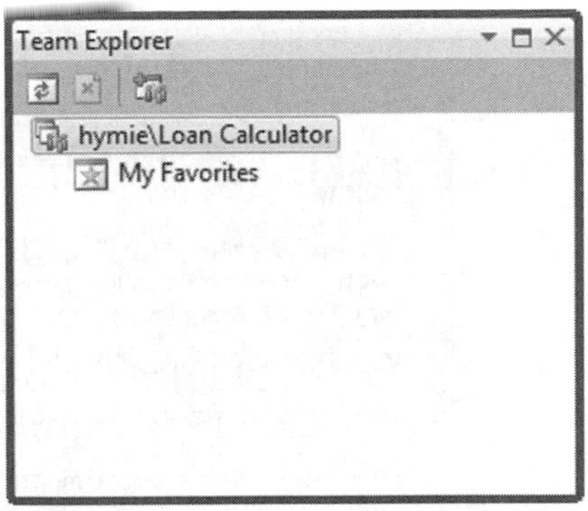
Team Explorer
hymie\Loan Calculator
My Favorites

Figure 2.33 Team Explorer now shows the Loan Calculator project collection.

TFS doesn't limit the methodology you use to develop your software. It comes with two process templates: Microsoft Solution Framework (MSF) for

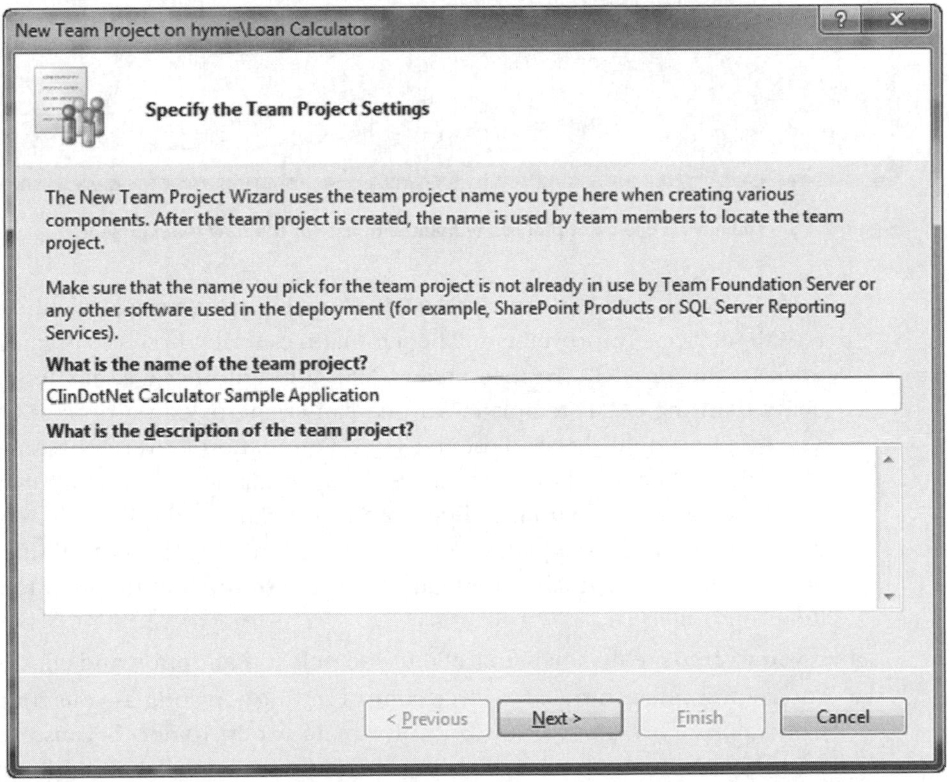
New Team Project on hymie\Loan Calculator
Specify the Team Project Settings
The New Team Project Wizard uses the team project name you type here when creating various components. After the team project is created, the name is used by team members to locate the team project.
Make sure that the name you pick for the team project is not already in use by Team Foundation Server or any other software used in the deployment (for example, SharePoint Products or SQL Server Reporting Services).
What is the name of the team project?
CIinDotNet Calculator Sample Application
What is the description of the team project?
< Previous
Next >
Finish
Cancel

Figure 2.34 When adding a team project to the collection, you need to specify a name and optional description.

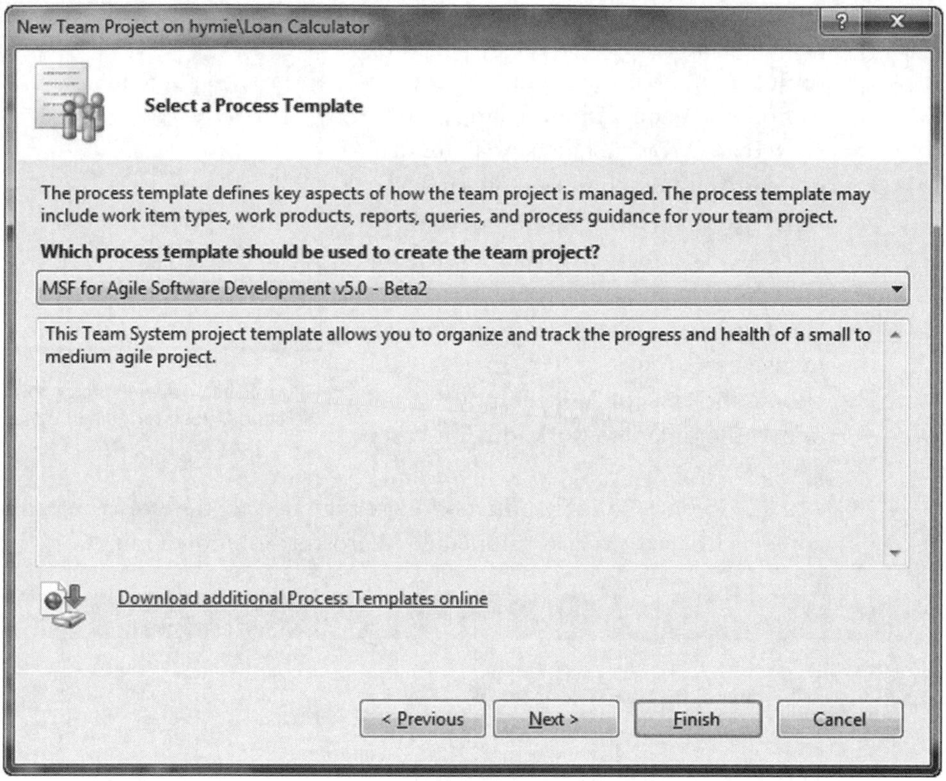

Figure 2.35   You have a choice of process templates to use for the new team project.

Agile Software Development and MSF for Capability Maturity Model Integration (CMMI) Process Improvement. The templates describe how TFS organizes your work in the project. We recommend MSF for Agile because it's less process-heavy than the CMMI template. Anyone can create or edit a process template. The best way to do this is to use the Team Foundation Power Tools and its Process Editor. The TFS Power Tools are freely available over the MSDN website. Additionally, at the bottom of figure 2.35, you can see the link where you can download prebuilt templates. An interesting one is Microsoft Visual Studio Scrum 1.0, which is suitable for teams using the scrum methodology to manage the project lifecycle.

9 If you wish to create a new SharePoint site, select that option and click Next.

10 You're prompted to specify source control settings. As long as your source control repository is empty, you can only create a new folder. Because you have nothing to branch yet, click Finish to complete the wizard. You'll be connected to the new team project (see figure 2.36).

You're now ready to manage your source code inside the team project.

2.4.4 Managing TFS source control

Unlike the example you saw earlier with Subversion, you don't need any external tools to manage code with TFS if you're using Visual Studio. As we said earlier, TFS is a lot more than source control. The source control tooling is tightly integrated with Visual Studio. From this perspective, it can be easier to use TFS than to gather all the SVN tooling, because everything is done from inside the development environment. It's possible to use command-line commands to manage TFS source control. In this case, you'll go the Visual studio way.

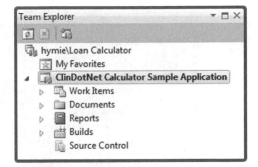

Figure 2.36   Team Explorer in Visual Studio 2010 connected to a server named hymie and Loan Calculator collection with one project inside.

Let's get the application source code checked in to TFS:

1 If you followed along earlier in this chapter and set up the loan calculator under Subversion, you need a fresh directory and project that aren't currently under source control. When that's done, continue to step 2.

2 Open the Framework solution in Visual Studio. Right-click the solution, and choose Add Solution to Source Control. The Add Solution to Source Control dialog box opens (see figure 2.37).

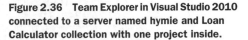

Figure 2.37
Adding the solution to
source control

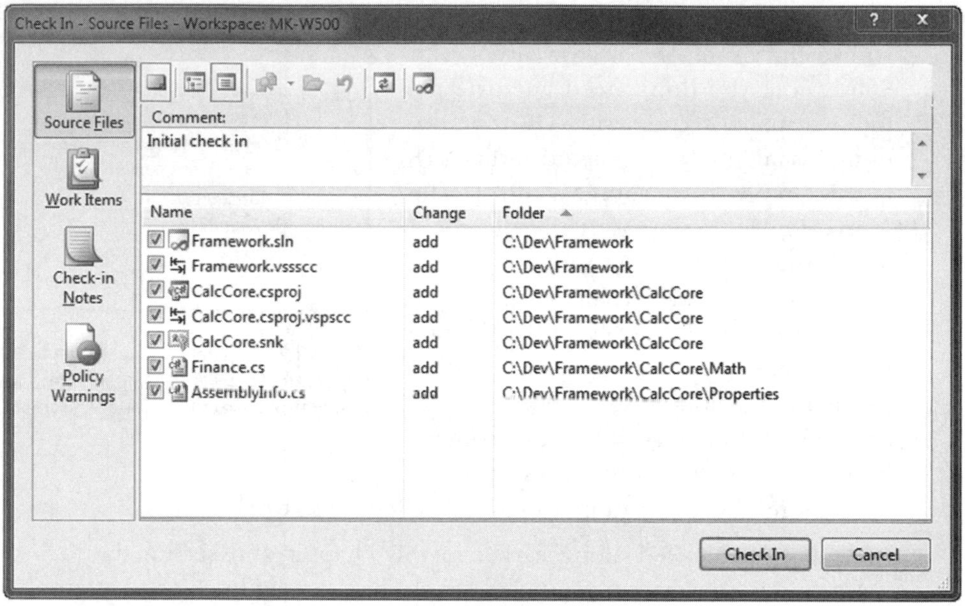

Figure 2.38   When you add files to TFS source code control, any files that are new or changed are flagged as pending changes.

3 Click OK to accept the default settings. The Pending Changes dialog box opens (see figure 2.38).

4 Because you want all the files to be saved, click Check In. If you're prompted to check in all items, select Yes.

5 Repeat these steps for the WebCalculator and WindowsCalculator solutions.

When all the files are checked in, notice the change in Solution Explorer. Each file now has a small lock icon displayed next to it (see figure 2.39) to indicate that the file is checked in. Other icons are used to indicate different source code control statuses. Consult the Visual Studio documentation for help understanding the different icons.

From now on, you can manage your code from the context menu in the Solution Explorer. The management concepts are the same for TFS as for SVN. You check in, check out, branch, merge, and so on. This time, you can perform all the operations from within Visual Studio. To check in files, right-click the solution, and issue the Check In command.

In a way similar to other revision-control software, you can add a message to every operation. TFS makes it possible to associate a work item with a given source control operation. We won't deal with work-item management and tracing in this book, but we strongly recommend that you look into it. You should start at http://msdn.micro-soft.com/en-us/vstudio, where you can find a lot of information about Visual Studio itself and TFS 2010 in particular. It helps the development process to know exactly why you're checking something in, what user checked in a file, and what work item was associated with it.

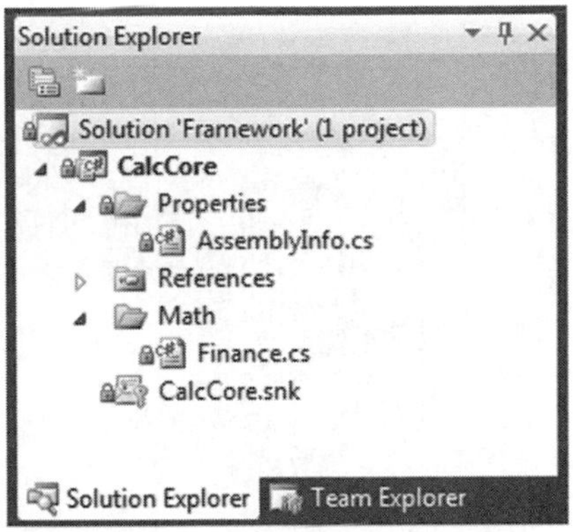

2.4.5 *Locking and shelving*

TFS source control, unlike SVN, lets you permanently lock the files you're working with. The difference lies in the fact that you can choose to prevent the files from being checked out by other users. This not only can prevent checking in changes to a locked file but also can prevent the file from being checked out.

To lock a file or directory, right-click in the Solution Explorer, and choose Check Out for Edit. The Lock dialog box opens, as shown in figure 2.40. Then choose a lock mode and click

Figure 2.39 A newly added solution source control. All the files are indicated as being ready for the first check-in.

Lock. Note that if you choose Check Out, other users will have to wait until you commit your changes to the repository before they can begin to work with the file.

Another useful feature of TFS source control is the ability to *shelve* changes. This lets you stack the changes you want to keep safe under source control but don't want to check in yet. Imagine that you've worked all day Friday on a new feature. You aren't

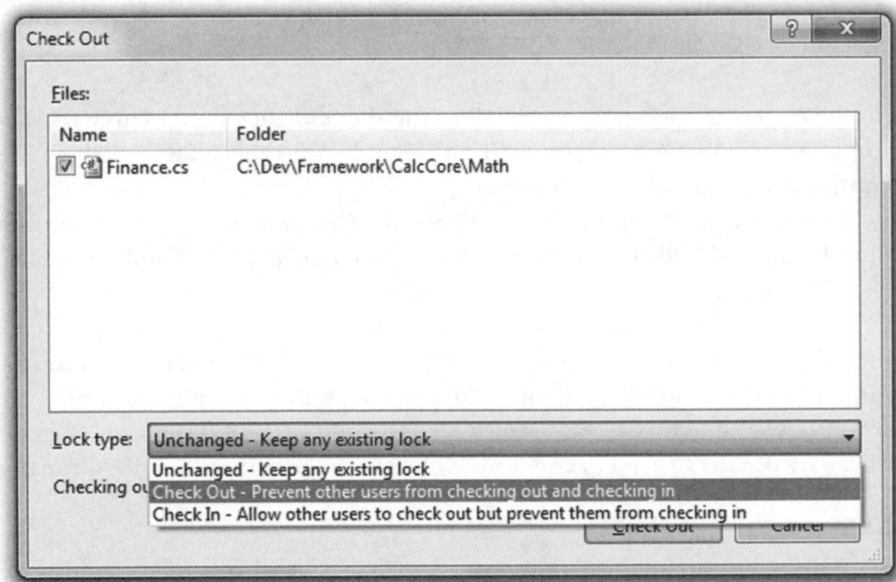

Figure 2.40 Locking a file in TFS source control prevents other users from checking in (just as with SVN) or prevents check in and check out.

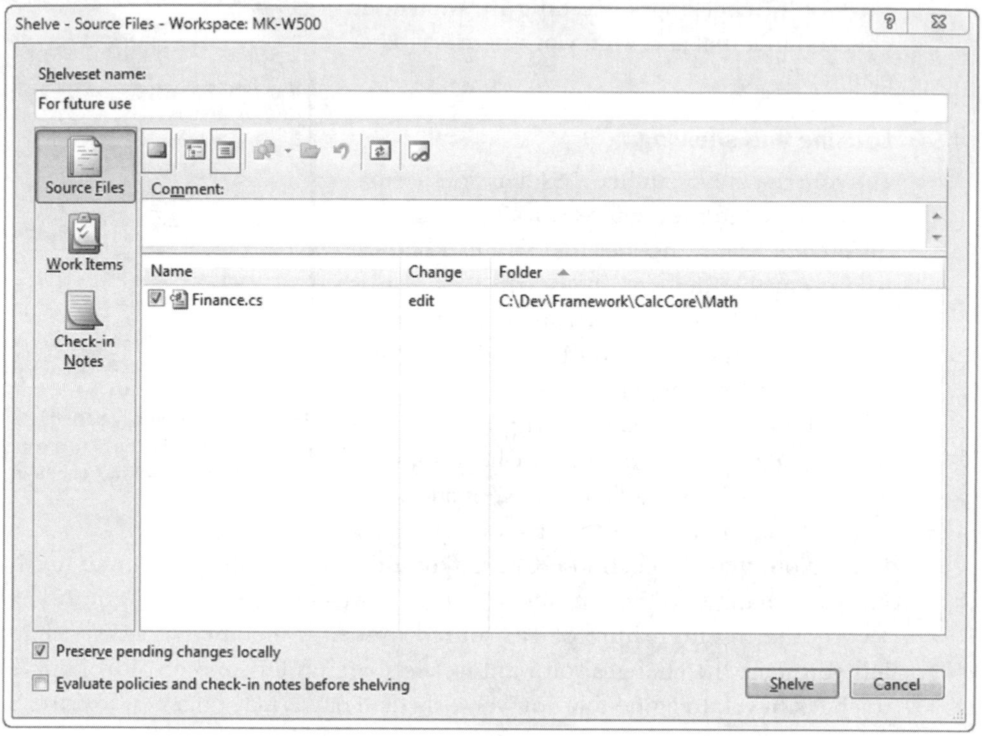

Figure 2.41   Shelving pending changes in TFS source control is nothing more than making a secure copy of work in progress under version control.

finished, so you don't want to check in the file; but the changes are too valuable for you to keep on your laptop over the weekend. You can create a shelf in TFS source control and send your changes there.

To create a shelf, right-click the file in Solution Explorer, and choose Shelve Pending Changes. The Shelve dialog box opens (see figure 2.41). Name the shelveset, and click Shelve.

TFS 2010 source control, unlike Visual SourceSafe, is a product worth recommending. If you're planning to base your CI process on TFS, make sure you're using its internal source control capabilities. Mixing SVN and TFS is possible but troublesome. If you have the luxury of choosing a source code control system, refer to chapter 4, where we discuss CI servers and how to choose the program that's best for you.

2.5   *Summary*

Setting up a clean and well-thought-out source control system is vital for the CI process. Without one, you won't be able to integrate your work continuously. There won't be a single repository containing all you need to build your software. It'll be difficult to know when something changed. It'll be impossible to trigger a CI build.

A well designed repository structure should play along with the project layout. Depending on your needs, you'll use single or multiple repositories to host your projects. You'll have to decide whether you need external references. The keys to the right solution are circumstances and experience. We're convinced that the solutions provided in this chapter play well while building a CI process.

If you're one of the rare software houses that hasn't been using source control systems until now, incorporating CI may be a great opportunity to introduce Subversion—a terrific, free revision control system. As you've seen, setting up a VisualSVN Server is simple, and administration with the VisualSVN Management Console is more than easy. If you choose to use the TortoiseSVN client, you'll be able to do anything you need to keep a consistent and clean code base.

If you're planning to use Microsoft Team Foundation Server, for which the 2010 version is a big milestone, especially for smaller teams, you should seriously consider using TFS source control to host the changes in your source code. TFS 2010 is affordable and is keeping up in the way of features with the best open source revision control systems.

The financial calculator you pushed to your source control system in this chapter will help provide a full-blown CI process later in the book. The next step will be to create a fully automated build process for this project. This build will be used within the CI process to check whether integration is going well, along with team commits. In the next chapter, you'll create a build process.

Automating the build process

3

This chapter covers

- Choosing a build-automation tool for the CI process
- Using MSBuild
- Extending MSBuild

Having a single repository that contains everything you need for building your software is the first step on the path to a good CI process. The second, which is also important, is to have the software build. To do this, you need a kind of metaphorical lever that will help you jack up your source code from transcription of ideas into working software. You'll use this lever in your day-to-day work as well as in the CI process you're building. Your build lever must be designed in a way that'll let you build your application in one step.

The first thing that may come to mind as a lever in the .NET Framework world is Visual Studio. It seems to have everything that makes for a good lever. When you press the F6 button, you start a build process that leads to working software. But is it enough? Does it make a good lever? We're afraid not. It's able to compile and start a program, but nothing else. We need more to incorporate CI: something that'll let you test everything, analyze the code, generate documentation, deploy, and create installation routines. We're looking for something powerful, customizable, and extensible. Visual Studio is a great development environment, but a poor software-automation tool—and we want to automate the entire software build process.

If your build process doesn't take care of everything in addition to compiling, those elements will most likely be neglected. You don't click one button to compile, another to test, and another to deploy. The key is automation—and that means you have to get rid of the human factor.

We want to create a build process that can work autonomously, without supervision. The way to achieve this goal is through an automation platform.

In this chapter, we'll browse through various build-management systems and determine which ones are suitable for the .NET integration process. We'll look at NAnt, but in the end we'll choose MSBuild as the best build tool. You'll use built-in and community-owned MSBuild features to create a build-and-deploy process. Finally, you'll extend MSBuild with your own functionality.

3.1 Build automation

In the CI context, an *automation platform* is a tool or a set of tools that helps automate the entire software build process, including doing the following:

- Compiling the source code
- Preparing the database
- Performing tests
- Analyzing the code
- Creating installation routines and deploying
- Creating documentation

What we're looking for should be easily maintainable. And it should be stored in the source control system like everything else that takes part in the CI process.

The obvious way to automate the build process is to script it using human-readable text. You should avoid everything that doesn't use text as a description of a build process. Compile managers are bad, bad things. You should ban from your mind any automation tool that keeps the build description in binary format and requires you to manually click to make it run. Text form is easier to create, read, edit, and keep track of (using version control) than binary form.

In chapter 1, you saw a simple example of automation using ordinary command-line commands organized in a batch file; software automation was done this way at the dawn of time. It makes the process faster in comparison to manually issuing commands, it reduces redundant tasks because you don't have to be involved in every build, and it lets others maintain the build. Now, let's walk through some *real* automation tools and search for the best one.

3.1.1 Make and its children

Software-automation platforms are older than most active software developers. The great-grandfather of almost all current tools is the UNIX make utility, which was created at the end of the 1970s and has been used mostly in the *ix world. It has a Windows version called *nmake* and a fairly good clone called *Opus Make*. All the make systems use a text file called a *make file* to describe the software build process.

Later-generation tools like Jam and Cook changed this. They used more sophisticated statements to hide some of the lower-level aspects of software automation. With time, the automation platforms became bigger and more complex and began to be called *automation systems*. One of them is GNU Automake with the GNU Build System (GBS—a set of small tools that comes in handy when you're building software on *ix systems).

Finally, we have automation tools that use a specific programming language to describe the build process. For example, SCons uses Python, and rake uses Ruby.

All the tools we've mentioned can be used to set up a CI process. But we'll look at the vanguard of build automation: the XML-based build systems Ant (NAnt) and MSBuild. The XML-based systems are a step away from tools that use fairly complicated commands or a programming language to describe the build process. Using them, you can declare the steps in an XML build script, and the steps are easy to extend and adapt.

NAnt and MSBuild are two of the tools you should choose from if you're creating a build process in a .NET environment. Both do the same job using similar techniques. NAnt is an open source tool maintained by the community, and MSBuild comes from Microsoft. Table 3.1 shows the most significant differences between them.

Table 3.1 NAnt vs. MSBuild: significant differences

Feature	NAnt	MSBuild
Actively developed	no	yes
Built-in features	yes	some
Open source	yes	no
Cross-platform (Linux, Mono)	yes	no
Good if you already know Ant	yes	no
Built in to .NET Framework	yes	yes
Integrated with Visual Studio	no	yes

Let's take a quick look at NAnt and see why we'll go with MSBuild instead.

3.1.2 *It's not an Ant*

Once upon a time, there was Ant. It was a good, established tool used to build applications in Java shops. It was ported to work in the .NET world and called NAnt (Not an Ant). From its Java ancestor, it inherited the XML declarative automation description language.

Let's try to use NAnt with this full-blown, single-line C# program:

```
class c{static void Main(){System.Console.Write("Hello NAnt");}}
```

Place this program in a file called HelloNAnt.cs. Now write the following NAnt script to build an application. Call it HelloNAnt.build.

Listing 3.1 NAnt build script to clean and compile a Windows application

```xml
<?xml version="1.0"?>
<project name="Hello NAnt" default="build" basedir=".">
    <property name="debug" value="true" overwrite="false" />
    <target name="clean">
      <delete file="HelloNAnt.exe" failonerror="false" />
      <delete file="HelloNAnt.pdb" failonerror="false" />
    </target>
    <target name="build" depends="clean">
       <csc target="exe"
       output="HelloNAnt.exe"
       debug="${debug}">
          <sources>
             <include name="HelloNAnt.cs" />
          </sources>
       </csc>
    </target>
</project>
```

An NAnt script is an ordinary XML document. First you declare the project, specifying the name (Hello NAnt), the default target (Build), and the working directory (dot [.] for the current directory). Next, NAnt gives you the ability to define properties. A *property* is a kind of named variable to which you can assign a value. The overwrite attribute lets you set the variable from the command line. The debug variable is used by the C# compiler task in a moment. The Clean target uses two delete tasks to erase unnecessary files. Setting the failonerror attribute tells NAnt to ignore possible errors—for example, if there's nothing to delete. The second target, Build, first runs the Clean target because of the depends attribute, and then runs the csc target to compile the source file.

One of the rules of CI that we keep mentioning is placing everything you need to fully build a project inside the project directory/repository. To use the script you just wrote, you need NAnt executables (available from http://nant.sourceforge.net). Place the NAnt executables in the tools/nant folder. NAnt is now ready to use.

Open a command window, navigate to the project folder, and type tools/nant/bin/nant.exe to launch NAnt (see figure 3.1). Run the script, and build your one-line program. Now that the script is working, you can extend it, declare more steps, and integrate more actions.

At the time we started writing this book, the open source NAnt project seemed to be dead. But in mid-2010, just as we were finishing writing, a new version of NAnt emerged. We felt that delaying publication didn't merit reworking examples and text to include NAnt. From a technical point of view, it isn't a big deal. NAnt is a good

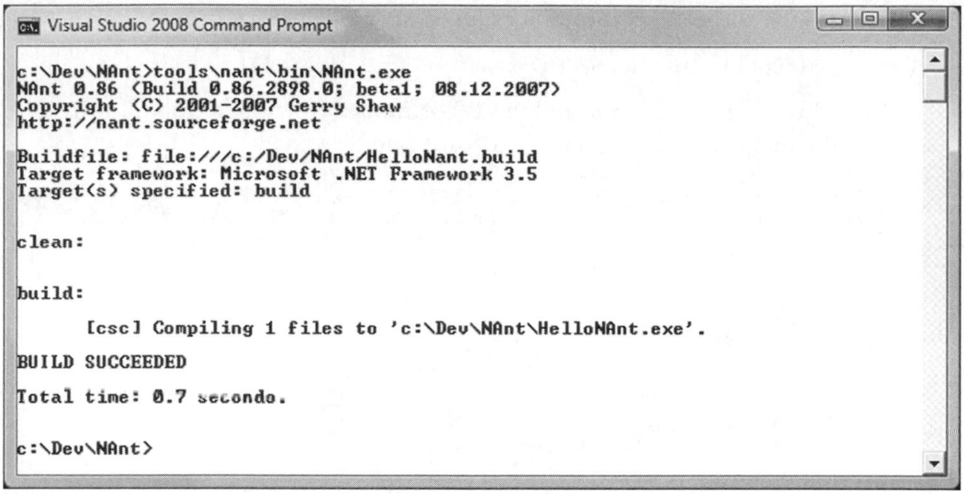

Figure 3.1   Starting a Hello World–style NAnt script. The build performs a `clean` followed by a `build` task. As an artifact, you get a compiled executable.

alternative for software developers with a Java background who are familiar with its ancestor, Ant. Many developers use MSBuild only to compile the source code and use NAnt to integrate all other tools into the CI process.

3.2   *The Microsoft worker: MSBuild*

Microsoft first shipped its own build tool for the .NET platform with the second version of the .NET Framework. Updated versions were shipped with .NET Frameworks 3.0, 3.5, and 4.0. If you check C:\Windows\Microsoft.NET\Framework\, you'll see that the subfolders for v2.0, v3.5, and v4.0 contain MSBuild.exe.

Using MSBuild means less work. You don't need to worry about third-party tools and how to integrate them with your environment. You don't have to worry about whether your favorite build tool is installed on the integration machine, because if you have .NET Framework installed, the tool will be there. Pragmatic people will find MSBuild appealing. Who knows how your business will grow? You may hit the scaling wall with the free software and have to think about something bigger. The entire Microsoft Team Foundation Server Build (more about it in chapter 4) is set on top of MSBuild. Keep this in mind, and you'll feel prepared.

MSBuild is freely distributed with the .NET platform. It has Microsoft's machinery behind it, so you don't need to worry about wide adoption and popularity. It won't die suddenly, leaving you without support. MSBuild is extensible and well-documented. It uses XML syntax similar to NAnt to perform build tasks. And it's closely integrated with Visual Studio: it understands Visual Studio solution files and makes it possible to compile Visual Studio solutions and projects without Visual Studio. It seems to be *the* build tool for .NET developers who want to set up a CI assembly line. But let's start small with a simple script that compiles a simple Hello World application.

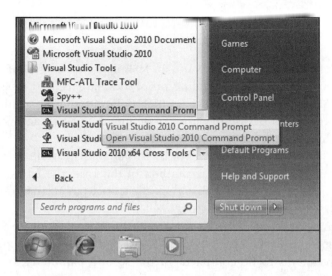

Figure 3.2
The Visual Studio Command Prompt knows the paths to various handy .NET tools. One of them is MSBuild.

3.2.1 First encounters with MSBuild

To use MSBuild from the command line, you have to write the full path for the executable or add it to your System Paths variable. But if you have Visual Studio installed, you can use the Visual Studio Command Prompt, which knows the path to MSBuild. You launch the Visual Studio Command Prompt from the Windows Start menu (see figure 3.2).

As a small workout in MSBuild, you'll perform the same tasks as you did previously with NAnt. Write another captivating one-liner:

```
class c{static void Main(){System.Console.Write("Hello MSBuild");}}
```

Compile it using the MSBuild script build.proj, shown next. The .proj file should go in the same folder as the source file for the program.

Listing 3.2 Simple MSBuild script

```
<?xml version="1.0" encoding="utf-8"?>
<Project DefaultTargets="Build"
 xmlns="http://schemas.microsoft.com/developer/msbuild/2003">
  <PropertyGroup>
    <Debug Condition="'$(Delete)'==''">true</Debug>
</PropertyGroup>
  <ItemGroup>
    <CompileFiles Include="HelloMSBuild.cs" />
    <DeleteFiles Include="HelloMSBuild.exe;HelloMSBuild.pdb" />
</ItemGroup>
<Target Name="Clean">
    <Delete Files="@(DeleteFiles)" />
</Target>
<Target Name="Build" DependsOnTargets="Clean">
    <Csc Sources="@(CompileFiles)"
        OutputAssembly="HelloMSBuild.exe"
```

```
                    EmitDebugInformation="$(Debug)" />
</Target>
</Project>
```

This script should look familiar. Just as with NAnt, an MSBuild script is an XML document, and it uses a similar set of ideas including properties, targets, and tasks. The main element of an MSBuild script is a `Project`, which defines the entire build process. It must be equipped with an `xmlns` attribute that defines the namespace. Optionally, you can define default targets. In this case, you use the `Build` target.

A `Target` is a logical part that declares a set of tasks. The target can be organized hierarchically, so that one target depends on another. In this case, the `Build` target depends on the `Clean` target, so MSBuild first runs the `Clean` target and then the `Build` target.

The `Build` target has only one task: `Csc`. This task calls the C# compiler with parameters. In the first parameter, specified by the `Sources` attribute, you provide an item containing a list of documents to be compiled. In the second parameter, `Output-Assembly`, you provide a name for the output file. In the last parameter, `EmitDebug-Information`, you specify whether you're interested in debug information for your program. The value for it is defined in the `Debug` property.

An `ItemGroup` contains a list of items. In the example, items contain one or more references to a file. You have two of them: the first defines the files to be compiled (in this case, one file, HelloMSBuild.cs) and the second contains the list of files that the `Clean` target should delete.

MSBuild properties are containers for values. Every property has a name and is defined in a `PropertyGroup`. You define only one property here: `Debug`. It contains a Boolean value and is used in the `Csc` target to determine whether the compiler should create a .pdb debug symbols file.

If the path to MSBuild exists in system variables or you're using the Visual Studio Command Prompt, the only thing you have to do is start MSBuild from the command line. Type `msbuild` to launch and run the build process (see figure 3.3).

Now that you've written your first MSBuild script, let's extend it a little.

Passing parameters to MSBuild scripts

Another neat thing you'll use often when creating a CI process using MSBuild is the ability to pass parameters from the command line to the script. Your `Debug` property has one attribute, `Condition`, which you can set from the command line like this: `msbuild /property:Debug=false`. This attribute helps set the default value if you call the script without setting the value explicitly.

After you do this, the condition `'$(Delete)'==''` isn't fulfilled. That is, the value is false and not empty. MSBuild uses what's defined at the command line. In the end, you get the compilation without the debug files.

```
Visual Studio 2010 Command Prompt                                    ☐ ◻ ✕

C:\Dev\MSBuild>msbuild
Microsoft (R) Build Engine Version 4.0.20506.1
[Microsoft .NET Framework, Version 4.0.20506.1]
Copyright (C) Microsoft Corporation 2007. All rights reserved.

Build started 10/4/2009 11:25:39 AM.
Project "C:\Dev\MSBuild\build.proj" on node 1 (default targets).
  Deleting file "HelloMSBuild.exe".
  Deleting file "HelloMSBuild.pdb".
Done Building Project "C:\Dev\MSBuild\build.proj" (default targets).


Build succeeded.
    0 Warning(s)
    0 Error(s)

Time Elapsed 00:00:07.83

C:\Dev\MSBuild>
```

Figure 3.3   MSBuild is less verbose than NAnt. If you have only one file with the *.proj extension in the directory where you start MSBuild, it's automatically executed.

3.2.2   *Using predefined tasks to extend an MSBuild script*

MSBuild comes with a set of predefined tasks. You've already used two of them: the C# compiler task `Csc` and the `Delete` task. Other useful MSBuild tasks include the following:

- `Copy` copies a file.
- `MakeDir` creates a folder.
- `RemoveDir` removes a folder.
- `Message` prints a message on the screen.
- `Exec` runs any program.

You'll use these tasks to extend your MSBuild script. Using the code from listing 3.3, you can create something like a mini-CI iteration step (without the loop). Using MSBuild, you clean up the building site, compile and archive the software, and then copy the output to a folder and start the program to test whether it works.

Listing 3.3   Extending the build script

```xml
<?xml version="1.0" encoding="utf-8"?>
<Project DefaultTargets="Build;Deploy;Execute"              ◁── ❶ Defines
  xmlns="http://schemas.microsoft.com/developer/msbuild/2003">        default
  <PropertyGroup>                                                     targets
    <Debug Condition="'$(Delete)'==''">false</Debug>
    <OutputFile>HelloMSBuild.exe</OutputFile>
    <OutputDirectory>Output</OutputDirectory>
  </PropertyGroup>
  <ItemGroup>
    <CompileFiles Include="HelloMSBuild.cs" />
    <DeleteFiles Include="HelloMSBuild.exe;HelloMSBuild.pdb" />
  </ItemGroup>
```

```
<Target Name="Clean">
  <Delete Files="@(DeleteFiles)" />
  <Delete Files="$(OutputDirectory)\**\*" />
  <RemoveDir Directories="$(OutputDirectory)" />
</Target>
<Target Name="Build" DependsOnTargets="Clean">
  <Csc Sources="@(CompileFiles)"
       OutputAssembly="$(OutputFile)"
       EmitDebugInformation="$(Debug)" />
</Target>
<Target Name="Deploy">
  <MakeDir Directories="Output" />
  <Copy SourceFiles="$(OutputFile)"
        DestinationFolder="$(OutputDirectory)" />
</Target>
<Target Name="Execute">
  <Message Text="Starting: $(MSBuildProjectDirectory)
    ➥\$(OutputDirectory)\$(OutputFile)"
           Importance="low" />
  <Exec WorkingDirectory="$(OutputDirectory)"
  ➥Command="$(OutputFile)"></Exec>
</Target>
</Project>
```

The first thing that catches your eye is probably the extended `DefaultTargets` list ❶. You define three new tasks, divide by semicolons. They're executed in the same order that they appear in the list. Note that the `Build` task still depends on `Clean`.

The `Build` target is the same as in the previous example. The `Deploy` target creates the output folder (`MakeDir` task) and copies the executable file (`Copy` task) to the folder defined in the property `$(OutputFile)`.

The `Execute` target first uses the `Message` task to write text to the screen. The message contains information about what will be executed and where. The message uses one of many predefined properties, `$(MSBuildProjectDirectory)`, which contains the path to the MSBuild project. The `Message` task has one more parameter, `Importance`, which defines the verbosity of the MSBuild execution. In a minute, you'll learn what this means and how to start MSBuild with different verbosity settings.

After the `Message` task, you use the `Exec` task to start the program. The `Exec` task uses two parameters: `Command` to define the program that needs to be started and `WorkingDirectory` to define where it needs to be started.

The `Clean` target is then extended with additional functionality to remove old folders (`RemoveDir`) and files (`Delete`).

Let's start the automated build process. For the sake of cleanliness, delete all the artifacts that remained in the project directory. You don't have to do this manually! You have all you need in your MSBuild script. You can start it with the `/target` command-line parameter. Using this parameter, you can start any target defined in your MSBuild project, disregarding the `DefaultTargets` project attribute.

Go to the command prompt, and type `msbuild /target:Clean`. You should see something similar to figure 3.4.

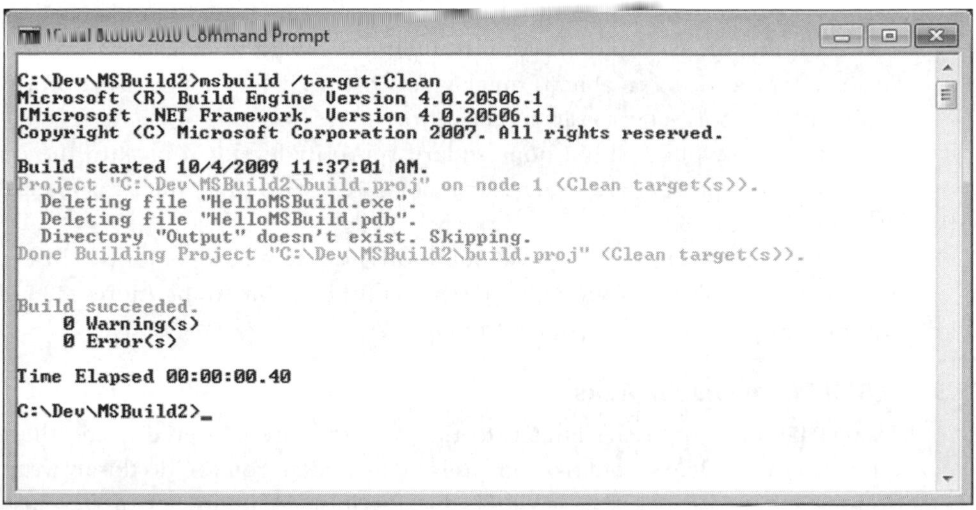

Figure 3.4 You can pass MSBuild a specific target—for example, one to clean folders and files—on the command line.

You've cleaned everything, and you're ready to start the actual build. Enter `msbuild` in the command window to build and run the program (see figure 3.5).

But what happened to the `Message` task in the `Execute` target? It's nowhere to be seen in the output. It was omitted because of MSBuild's default verbosity level. The *verbosity* level defines how much information the MSBuild process writes on the screen. The higher the level, the more information you see on screen. To see the messages with `Importance` set to `Low`, you must start MSBuild with high verbosity. It may sound trivial, but it's an art to set the correct verbosity level in the CI process. You have to set

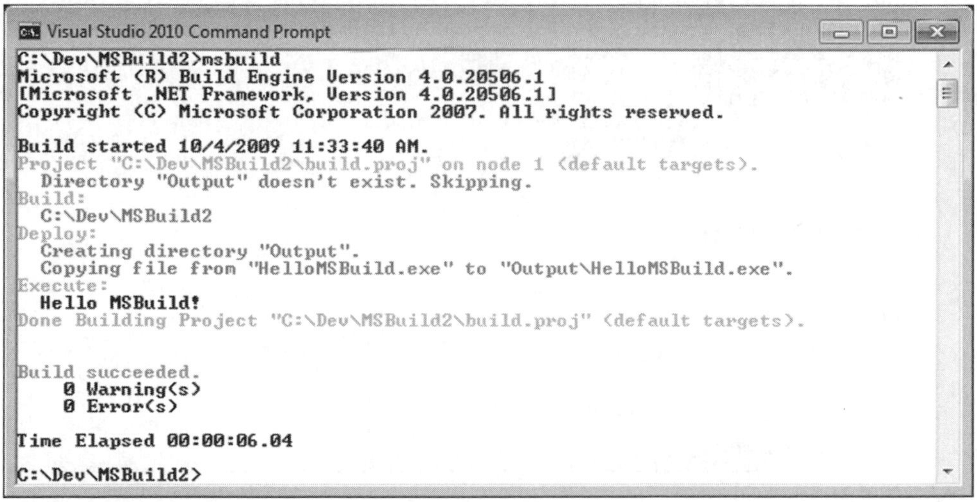

Figure 3.5 MSBuild can build and run a program.

verbosity this way to be able to quickly browse through and know what's going on. You'll do this often. You don't want to be flooded with information you don't need; instead, you want to be able to quickly and precisely locate the cause of a problem. Only with the correct verbosity level can you do this.

Let's run MSBuild with a nonstandard verbosity level. Go back to the command window, and type `msbuild /verbosity:detailed`. This time, the `Message` task is executed (see figure 3.6).

We've shown you how to use MSBuild with an essential set of tasks. These tasks are built in to MSBuild. But sooner or later, you'll need something more. MSBuild Community Tasks are a great set of additional tasks.

3.2.3   *MSBuild Community Tasks*

Using MSBuild, you aren't limited to the tasks that are delivered inside the program from Microsoft. The set of tasks can easily be extended. You can do this by writing a task yourself, or you can use tasks others have written. A useful set of free tasks called MSBuild Community Tasks is distributed as open source and contains a lot of ready-to-use functionality, such as using FTP servers, sending email, manipulating XML, managing SVN, getting the date and time, and much more. For the complete list, refer to http://msbuildtasks.tigris.org/.

The easiest way to start using the MSBuild Community Tasks is to download the MSI package and install it on the system. But this isn't the best way if you intend to set up a CI process. By installing the package, you get all the system variables set, and the Community Tasks are instantly ready to use. But if you do this, you must install the software on the build server as well. You'll encounter a similar problem if you want to use it on various machines for your team. Think about what it means to install the new version

```
Visual Studio 2010 Command Prompt                              [_][□][x]
Done executing task "Copy".
Done building target "Deploy" in project "build.proj".
Target "Execute" in file "C:\Dev\MSBuild2\build.proj" from project "C:\Dev\MSBu
ild2\build.proj":
Task "Message"
  Starting: C:\Dev\MSBuild2\Output\HelloMSBuild.exe
Done executing task "Message".
Using "Exec" task from assembly "Microsoft.Build.Tasks, Version=2.0.0.0, Cultur
e=neutral, PublicKeyToken=b03f5f7f11d50a3a".
Task "Exec"
  Command:
  HelloMSBuild.exe
  Hello MSBuild!
Done executing task "Exec".
Done building target "Execute" in project "build.proj".
Done Building Project "C:\Dev\MSBuild2\build.proj" (default targets).


Build succeeded.
    0 Warning(s)
    0 Error(s)

Time Elapsed 00:00:08.89

C:\Dev\MSBuild2>_
```

Figure 3.6   MSBuild is more verbose if you start it with a `/verbosity:detailed` switch.

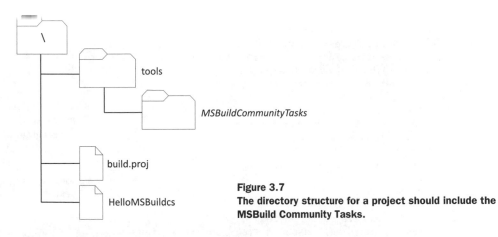

Figure 3.7
The directory structure for a project should include the MSBuild Community Tasks.

on every machine—that's one of the reasons to keep everything you need in the project directory.

Create the folder tools/MSBuildCommunityTasks under your project directory. Download the Community Tasks zip archive, decompress it, and copy the content of the bin directory into your tools directory (see figure 3.7). This way, everyone can use the Community Tasks after they get the latest version of the project from your source control system.

Now, let's put the Community Tasks to work. Listing 3.4 uses three of the many tasks that are available. These tasks let you archive your software, give the archive a unique name, and send it using email. To keep the script brief, it omits some parts that are duplicates from listing 3.3.

Listing 3.4   Build script using MSBuild Community Tasks

```xml
<?xml version="1.0" encoding="utf-8"?>                    Imports Community Tasks  ❶
<Project DefaultTargets="Build;Deploy;Execute"
        xmlns="http://schemas.microsoft.com/developer/msbuild/2003">
  <UsingTask
AssemblyFile="tools\MSBuildCommunityTasks\MSBuild.Community.Tasks.dll"
  TaskName="MSBuild.Community.Tasks.Zip" />
  <UsingTask
AssemblyFile="tools\MSBuildCommunityTasks\MSBuild.Community.Tasks.dll"
  TaskName="MSBuild.Community.Tasks.Mail" />
  <UsingTask
AssemblyFile="tools\MSBuildCommunityTasks\MSBuild.Community.Tasks.dll"
  TaskName="MSBuild.Community.Tasks.Time" />
  <PropertyGroup>
  </PropertyGroup>
  <ItemGroup>
    <DeleteFiles Include="*.zip" />
  </ItemGroup>
  <Target Name="Clean">
  </Target>
  <Target Name="Build" DependsOnTargets="Clean">
  </Target>
```

Insert code from listing 3.3

```
<Target Name="Deploy">
  <MakeDir Directories="Output" />
  <Copy SourceFiles="$(OutputFile)"
  ➥DestinationFolder="$(OutputDirectory)" />
  <Time Format="yyyyMMddHHmmss">
    <Output TaskParameter="FormattedTime"
            PropertyName="BuildDate" />
  </Time>
  <Zip Files="$(OutputFile)"
     ZipFileName="HelloMSBuild.$(BuildDate).zip" />
  <Mail
    SmtpServer="adres"
    To="email"
    From="email"
    Subject="New build!"
    Body="This is an automated message."
    Attachments="HelloMSBuild.$(BuildDate).zip"/>
</Target>
<Target Name="Execute">
</Target>
</Project>
```

2 Gets current time

3 Archives program

4 Sends email

Insert code from listing 3.3

First, you must inform MSBuild that you're about to use an additional task ❶. You do this in the UsingTask tag, giving it an attribute with the path to the MSBuild Community Tasks library and specifying what task you'll be using. Here, you use the Zip, Mail, and Time tasks in the Deploy target.

You use the Time task ❷ to set a new property with the current date and time. This property is named $(BuildDate) and is used in the next task, Zip ❸. This task creates an archive with the name defined in the attribute ZipFileName, which contains the files defined in the Files attribute. The last step is to send the archived file to a given email address using the Mail task ❹. The Mail task needs to be configured: you must provide the SMTP server name, the username and password if necessary, and the mail recipient. In a development environment, you might think about using a fake SMTP server to test the functionality. We like Antix SMTP Imposter (www.antix.co.uk/Projects/SMTPImpostor)—it has everything a normal SMTP server has, but it keeps the messages unsent and ready for review.

Run MSBuild as before, and you'll see that the MSBuild Community Tasks are run just like the native MSBuild tasks (see figure 3.8).

Additional Community Tasks are handy when you write your own build script. Another important feature of MSBuild is its integration with Visual Studio.

3.3 *The happy couple: Visual Studio and MSBuild*

MSBuild is used mostly in conjunction with Visual Studio, because they understand each other so well. MSBuild has tasks that can read and compile entire Visual Studio projects or solutions. And project files since Visual Studio version 2005 are nothing other than MSBuild scripts, which means you can extend your project file directly. IntelliSense and validation for MSBuild scripts are present in Visual Studio.

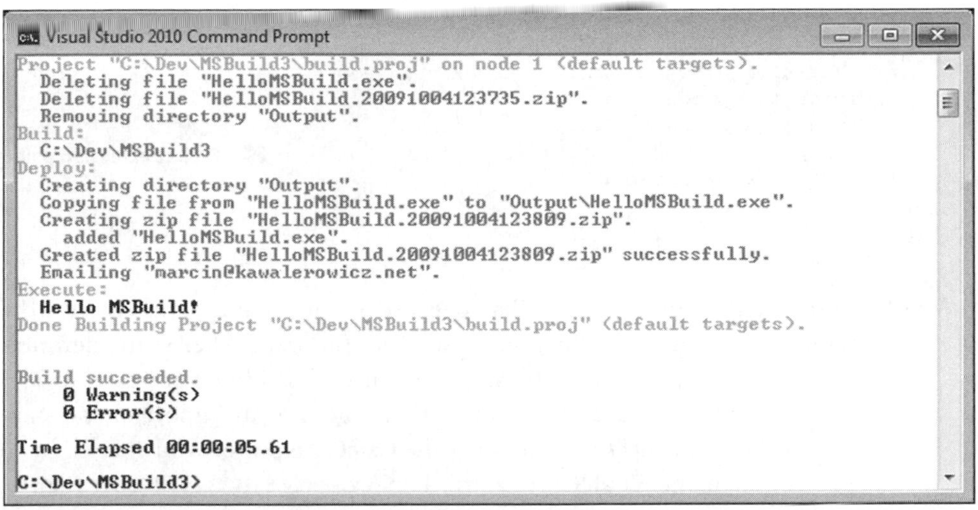

Figure 3.8   The extended MSBuild script in action. Using MSBuild Community Tasks, you can archive the output and send it as an email attachment.

3.3.1   Examining a project file

In chapter 1, you created some Visual Studio projects. This set contains one shared mathematical library and two clients for a leasing calculator. Open one of the project files: for C# projects, the name is *.csproj; and for VB, it's *.vbproj.

To open the project file in text form in Visual Studio 2010, unload the project (by choosing Unload Project from the project context menu in Solution Explorer) and edit it (also using the context menu). Don't forget to reload the project afterward. You can do the same thing using the PowerCommands plug-in (available from http://visualstudiogallery.msdn.microsoft.com). It'll let you open the project file by right-clicking in the Solution Explorer and choosing Edit Project File from the context menu.

The following listing shows part of a project file. To save space, we cut out the `PropertyGroups` responsible for project configuration and the `ItemGroups` that define references, includes, and files.

Listing 3.5   Visual Studio project file, which is an MSBuild script

```
<?xml version="1.0" encoding="utf-8"?>
<Project ToolsVersion="4.0" DefaultTargets="Build"
  xmlns="http://schemas.microsoft.com/developer/msbuild/2003">
  <PropertyGroup>
    <Configuration Condition="
      '$(Configuration)' == '' ">Debug</Configuration>
  </PropertyGroup>
  <ItemGroup>
    <Reference Include="System" />
  </ItemGroup>
  <Import Project=
    "$(MSBuildToolsPath)\Microsoft.CSharp.targets" />
```

Omitted project configuration

Omitted references, imports, compile items, embeds

❶ Does magic

```
<!-- To modify your build process, add your task
➥inside one of the targets below and uncomment it.
➥Other similar extension points exist, see
➥Microsoft.Common.targets.
  <Target Name="BeforeBuild">
  </Target>                                            ◄─┐
  <Target Name="AfterBuild">      ❷ Project extension points
  </Target>                                            ◄─┘
  -->
</Project>
```

This project file should look familiar, because it's an MSBuild script. It has a default target named `Build`, a `PropertyGroup`, and so on. But wait! Where's the definition of the `Build` target? It's nowhere to be seen. To solve this riddle, you have to look in the imported `Microsoft.CSharp.targets` project ❶. It's an import of the standard C# targets file. You can check it by opening the CalcCore project you created in chapter 1; the project file name is CalcCore.csproj. The property `$(MSBuildToolsPath)` points to the default MSBuild installation folder. Effectively, you're inserting the contents of the file C:\Windows\Microsoft.NET\Framework\[version number]\Microsoft.CSharp.targets into your project file. This file defines the standard targets in the compilation processes of C# projects. A similar file for Visual Basic resides in the same directory. Both of them import `Microsoft.Common.targets` that defines the common tasks for various project types.

The project files are ordinary MSBuild scripts, and it's possible to override and redefine the targets. You have to remember one rule: the target definition that's closer to your MSBuild script counts. So if you override the `BeforeBuild` or `After-Build` target in your file, MSBuild will take this definition and not the definition with the same name from an imported target file. `BeforeBuild` and `AfterBuild` are visible in every project file ❷. They're commented out, and all you have to do is to uncomment and define them to extend your build process.

Let's implement one of them to start the executable after the build. You can easily do so like this:

```
<Target Name="AfterBuild">
  <Exec Command="bin\$(Configuration)\WinCalc.exe"></Exec>
</Target>
```

Similar functionality is offered with the pre-build and post-build events. These are legacy events from pre–Visual Studio times. They're simple command-line commands that are executed line by line. You can use *macros* with them; these so-called macros are nothing more than MSBuild properties translated to strings by execution. These events are available in project properties in Visual Studio and are saved in the project file as `PreBuildEvent` and `PostBuildEvent` targets. To see the windows shown in figure 3.9, right-click the project file in Solution Explorer, choose Project Properties, click the Build Events tab, click the Pre- or Post-Build button, and click the Macros.

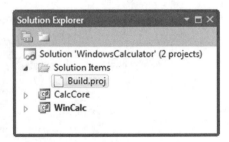

Figure 3.9   Using pre- and post-build events, you can add simple command-line commands enriched with MSBuild variables.

MSBuild integrates with Visual Studio solution files, but the integration looks different than it does with project files. MSBuild knows how to execute the solution files, as you'll see next.

3.3.2   *Examining the solution file*

Unfortunately, Visual Studio solution files (*.sln) aren't MSBuild projects. But MSBuild knows how to talk to them. Using a task called `MSBuild`, you can execute an MSBuild project from another MSBuild script. The `MSBuild` task has one neat feature: it can execute the Visual Studio solution file, which is the same thing Visual Studio does. Let's try it.

You can use the leasing calculator from chapter 1 as a test field. Your goal is to compile the solution without using Visual Studio. To do that, you'll need an MSBuild script. The easiest approach is to place it in the same folder as the solution file and make it a solution item (see figure 3.10). The Solution Items folder in Solution Explorer is created if you add any file directly to the solution. Create a text file, and name it build.proj. It helps to name the build scripts the same way in every solution (you'll learn why in the next section).

Figure 3.10   Custom build script as a solution item in Solution Explorer

To perform clean and rebuild operations on the solution, you must provide the `Targets` attribute to the `MSBuild` task. The targets are analogous to the action that Visual Studio performs when you choose Clean Solution and Rebuild Solution from the solution's context menu in Solution Explorer. The other attribute is the name of the solution file on which the MSBuild project file is to perform the targets. Here's the code:

```
<Project DefaultTargets="Build"
➥xmlns="http://schemas.microsoft.com/developer/msbuild/2003">
  <Target Name="Build">
    <MSBuild Targets="Clean;Rebuild" Projects="WindowsCalculator.sln" />
  </Target>
</Project>
```

Save this file and reopen it to make Visual Studio realize that it's an MSBuild script and turn on IntelliSense and code coloring.

3.3.3   *Starting an MSBuild script with Visual Studio*

During the course of setting up a CI process, you'll work extensively with MSBuild. So it's a good idea to integrate it more closely with Visual Studio. It would be handy to be able to execute the script directly from Visual Studio. To do so, you can set MSBuild as an external tool. In Visual Studio, choose Tools > External Tools, click Add, and name the tool MSBuild. Complete the definition as shown in figure 3.11 and outlined in table 3.2.

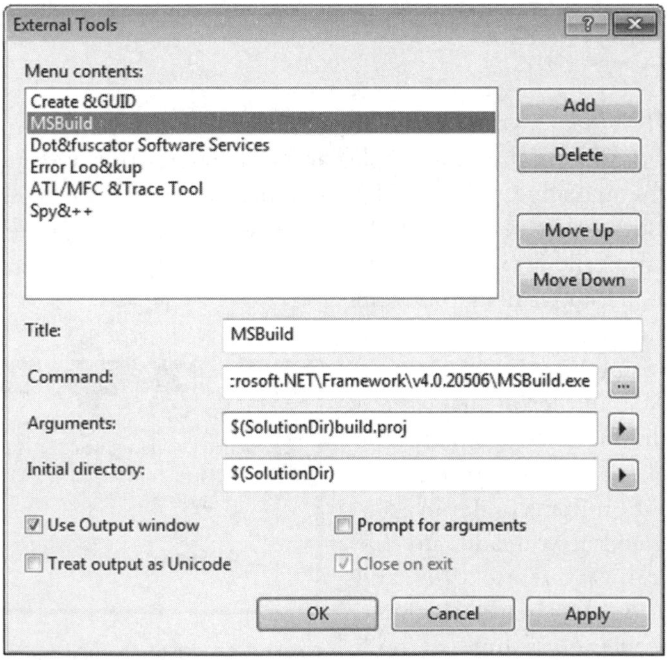

**Figure 3.11
Setting a new external tool in Visual Studio. The name will appear in the Tools menu. The command will be executed using the arguments provided in the Initial Directory field, and the output will be sent to the Output window.**

Table 3.0   MSBuild external tool definition in Visual Studio

Setting name (as in figure 3.11)	Value
Title	MSBuild
Command	C:\Windows\Microsoft.NET\Framework\[version number]\ MSBuild.exe
Arguments	$(SolutionDir)build.proj
Initial directory	$(SolutionDir)
Use Output window	Checked
Treat output as Unicode	Unchecked
Prompt for arguments	Unchecked

After you define the new external tool, an MSBuild item appears on the Tools menu. Click it, and look at the Output window. The script build.proj is executed. As you can see, the convention of always naming build projects the same way is necessary here: otherwise, you have to define the external tool for every project file name. The output of the MSBuild script is visible in Visual Studio, as shown in figure 3.12.

Visual Studio and MSBuild integration are a great productivity boost. A similar situation exists with MSBuild extensibility; it's easy to write your own custom tasks.

3.4   *Extending MSBuild by writing and using custom tasks*

Extending MSBuild is easy. To write your own tasks, you need to implement the Microsoft.Build.Framework.ITask interface or inherit from Microsoft.Build.Utilities.Task. The second solution is easier: all you have to do is override the Execute method. Let's use it to do something useful.

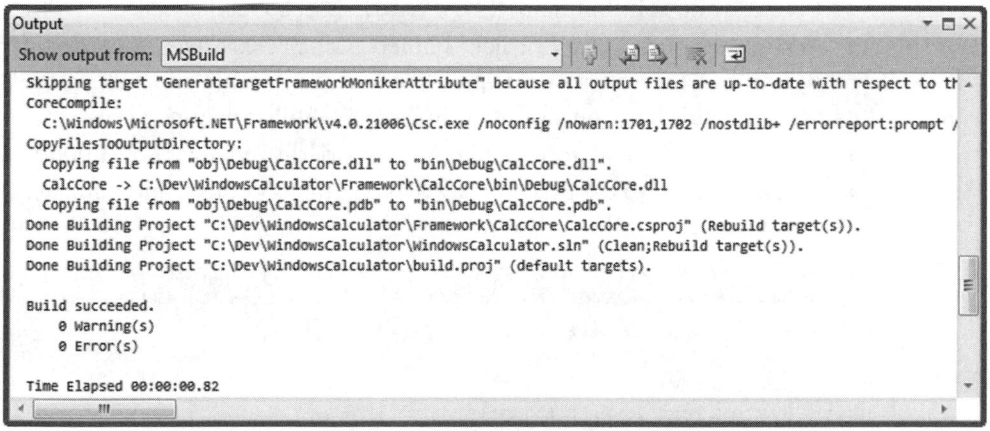

Figure 3.12   Custom build script output in the Output window in Visual studio

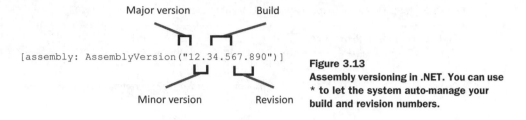

Figure 3.13
Assembly versioning in .NET. You can use
* to let the system auto-manage your
build and revision numbers.

Let's assume you want to associate the assembly version number with the Subversion (SVN) revision number. For some compelling reason, you decide that the revision part of the assembly version should be the current SVN revision number. For example, you want your CI process to update the version number every time it builds.

The assembly version is kept in the `assembly.AssemblyVersion` attribute in AssemblyInfo.cs. This file resides in the Properties folder in every project. Figure 3.13 shows how .NET Framework versioning works.

The revision number is easily readable with `SvnInfo`, a new MSBuild Community Task. It uses the SVN command-line client to read information about a given SVN path. So in addition to the MSBuild Community Tasks in your tools folder, you need the SVN client executable (available from http://subversion.tigris.org/).

Another MSBuild Community Task can help you easily update the AssemblyInfo.cs file with the new version number, including the revision number. Keep in mind that the version numbers have a maximum value of 65535.

One additional thing you want to do is archive the output in a zip file named after the version number. You can write your own MSBuild task to read this number directly from AssemblyInfo.cs.

3.4.1 *Implementing a custom task*

It's time to implement your custom task. Follow these steps:

1 Create a new solution named `CustomBuildExtensions`.
2 Add a new class library project named `BuildTasks.MSBuildTasks`. If you can go without the newest C# features, it's best to create the task in .NET Framework 2.0; this way, you can use it in every MSBuild version.
3 Add references to Microsoft.Build.Framework.dll and Microsoft.Build.Utilities.dll.
4 Add a new class to the `BuildTasks.MSBuildTasks` project, and name it `Assembly-InfoReader.cs`. Here's the code.

Listing 3.6 MSBuild task to read the assembly version from AssemblyInfo file

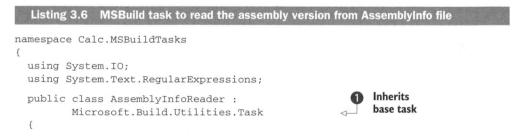

```
    private string path;
    private string property;
    private string value;

    [Microsoft.Build.Framework.Required]
    public string Path
    {
      get { return path; }
      set { path = value; }
    }

    [Microsoft.Build.Framework.Required]
    public string Property
    {
      get { return property; }
        set { property = value; }
    }

[Microsoft.Build.Framework.Output]
public string Value
{
  get { return this.value; }
  set { this.value = value; }
}

public override bool Execute()
{
  Regex regex = new
      Regex(@"^\[assembly:.+?" + Property + ".+?$",
          RegexOptions.Multiline);
  value = string.Empty;

  try
  {
    Match match = regex.Match(File.ReadAllText(path));
    if (match.Success)
    {
      value = match.Value.Substring(
            match.Value.IndexOf("\"") + 1,
            match.Value.LastIndexOf("\"") -
            match.Value.IndexOf("\"") - 1);
      return true;
    }
  }
  catch
  {
    // Ignore
  }

  return false;
}
    }
  }
```

❷ Contains path to AssemblyInfo file

❸ Contains property to be read

❹ Output property

❺ Does actual work

To implement your own functionality and be able to use it in an MSBuild script, you must inherit the `Microsoft.Build.Utilities.Task` class ❶. It has everything you need. The only thing you have to do is to override the `Execute()` method ❺. This method does the actual job and returns `true` if it succeeds or `false` if it fails. It uses custom properties that you can define, for example, to pass data in to the task. In the required property `Path` ❷, you must set the path to the AssemblyInfo file. The other required property is `Property` ❸, which contains the attribute to be read. The output is set in the `Value` ❹ property. The reading in the `Execute()` method is done with a mix of regular expressions and hack-and-slash string manipulation.

Another thing you can do here is synchronize the version number among all the assemblies in the project. Doing so may be a good idea if you always release the files simultaneously and you want to have the version synced over the release. You do this by creating a common assembly info file and adding it as a link in each project of the solution. The assembly info file must still be updated, but you can add that as a task in the build script. We leave the implementation of this as an exercise for you to complete.

Now, let's use your new task to do something useful.

3.4.2 *Putting it all together*

Your custom task is ready, so let's implement versioning using MSBuild and Subversion. To use your task, you have to put the compiled version in the tools directory of your framework. This is the project you intend to share with other projects. This way, the new `MSBuild` task is available in all the projects that are using it.

Do the same with the SVN client you downloaded. You should end up with the directory structure shown in figure 3.14.

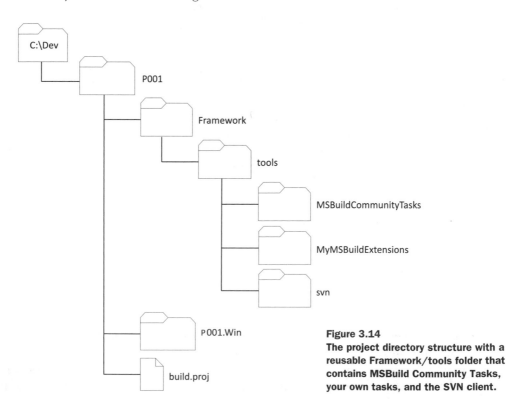

Figure 3.14
The project directory structure with a reusable Framework/tools folder that contains MSBuild Community Tasks, your own tasks, and the SVN client.

You'll version your leasing calculator. Go to the build.proj script you created in section 3.3.2, and extend it as follows.

Listing 3.7 Project versioning with Subversion and a custom `MSBuild` task

```
<Project DefaultTargets="Build;Deploy;"
    xmlns="http://schemas.microsoft.com/developer/msbuild/2003">
  <PropertyGroup>
    <MSBuildCommunityTaskPath>
      $(MSBuildProjectDirectory)\Framework\tools\MSBuildCommunityTasks
    </MSBuildCommunityTasksPath>
    <RevisionNumber Condition=" '$(RevisionNumber)' == '' ">
      x
    </RevisionNumber>
    <Configuration Condition=" '$(Configuration)' == '' ">
      Debug
    </Configuration>
  </PropertyGroup>
  <Import Project="Framework\tools\MSBuildCommunityTasks
➥\MSBuild.Community.Tasks.Targets"/>
  <UsingTask AssemblyFile="Framework\tools\MyMSBuildExtensions
➥\BuildTasks.MSBuildTasks.dll"
    TaskName="BuildTasks.MSBuildTasks.AssemblyInfoReader">        Maps task to
  </UsingTask>                                                    implementing
  <SetupSourceFiles Include="WinCalc\bin\                      ❶ assembly
➥$(Configuration)\WinCalc.exe" />
  </ItemGroup>

  <Target Name="Build">
    <SvnInfo RepositoryPath=
            "https://HYMIE/svn/WindowsCalculator/trunk"
            Username="[user]" Password="[password]"
                ToolPath="Framework\tools\svn">               ❷ Reads SVN
      <Output TaskParameter="Revision"                           revision number
                PropertyName="RevisionNumber" />
    </SvnInfo>
    <FileUpdate Files=" WinCalc\Properties\AssemblyInfo.cs"    ❸ Uses regex to
➥Regex="(\d+)\.(\d+)\.(\d+)\.(\d+)"                              update
➥ReplacementText="$1.$2.$3.$(RevisionNumber)" />                assembly info

    <MSBuild Targets="Clean;Rebuild" Projects="WindowsCalculator.sln" />
  </Target>

  <Target Name="Deploy">
    <AssemblyInfoReader
        Path=" WinCalc\Properties\AssemblyInfo.cs"            ❹ Custom task
        Property="AssemblyVersion">                              reads assembly
      <Output TaskParameter="Value" ItemName="Version" />       version
    </AssemblyInfoReader>

    <Zip Files="@(SetupSourceFiles)"
        ZipFileName="WindowsCalculator.%(Version.Identity).zip"
        Flatten="true" ContinueOnError="false" />

    <Copy SourceFiles="WindowsCalculator.%(Version.Identity).zip"
        DestinationFolder="c:\Dev\Release" />
```

```
    <Delete Files="WindowsCalculator.%(Version.Identity).zip"/>
  </Target>
</Project>
```

You extend the default build for the Windows calculator project and add the deploy target. You import the MSBuild Community Tasks using the predefined targets file. And you tell MSBuild that the task `AssemblyInfoReference` defined in `TaskName` that you intend to use is implemented in the assembly defined in the `AssemblyFile` attribute ❶. Then you extend the build target. You read the SVN revision number ❷ first, using the `SvnInfo` Community Task. The revision number is saved in the `$(Revision-Number)` property. Next, you use the `FileUpdate` Community Task ❸ to update AssemblyInfo.cs with the new version number. After that, you perform the build on the solution. When the build target is ready, MSBuild fires the `Deploy` target. Using your custom task, you read the version number into the `$(Version)` property ❹. Using the property metadata `%(Version.Identity)`, you create a zip file. The archive is copied into the release directory and deleted.

You've put everything together. The script you wrote is ready to be used as a part of a CI process.

3.5   *Summary*

Build automation is an essential part of the CI process, because CI occurs behind the scenes. You need an automated process that will perform the entire build every time it's needed.

Ideally, the automation process is scriptable. Changes can be made manually, or automatically with a tool like Visual Studio. You should be able to define various execution paths. Using conditions and parameterization, you should be able to perform various types of builds according to the situation. And your build process should be easily extensible.

Many tools deal with the build automation. Right now, MSBuild seems to be the best choice for .NET developers using Windows and Visual Studio; it's integrated with .NET Framework and used in the UI. But there are alternatives, such as NAnt. The choice is yours.

In the next chapter, we'll look at ways to bend the build process a little. You'll connect the end with the beginning and add some continuity to this process. To do so, you need a CI server.

Choosing the right CI server

This chapter covers

- CI server basics
- Choosing the right CI server
- Setting up CruiseControl.NET, TeamCity, and TFS Team Build
- Discussing build triggers
- Checking some extended capabilities of CI servers

In chapters 2 and 3, you gathered everything you need to perform full integration in a single repository. You now know how to build everything automatically. You're fully prepared for continuous integration (CI). You have all the bits and pieces to set up a fully automated process that eventually will build, test, deploy, and analyze an application to help ensure it functions correctly, follows best practices, and is deployable by the customer. It'll be a process that runs with each source code change and provides immediate feedback to the development team. To accomplish this, you need a CI server.

In this chapter, we'll give you an overview of what's on the market today. We'll look at the Microsoft flagship in this area: Team Foundation Server (TFS) 2010.

We'll also pay close attention to two leaders in the alternative .NET tooling list: Cruise-Control.NET and JetBrains TeamCity. But first, let's consider how far we are from a full-blown CI process.

4.1   A quick review of the CI process

Thus far, we've presented a sample application—a financial calculator—that you'll put under CI. It's been stored in the source code repository. You can get everything you need to build your software from the repository and then, with a single command, build it. Both actions are on a one-off basis. But you have to add continuity to the process and make the actions occur in a constant loop. They need to run continuously, preferably after every commit to the source control repository.

Right now, your process is a little flat. When something new happens, you start your build, it does all the things it was designed to do, and then it stops. The status quo is back in force until a software developer makes the next move (see figure 4.1).

The goal of this chapter is to introduce another player: a production-ready CI server that will work for you. The software developer works as shown in figure 4.1, but the new player gets more responsibility. Even if the software developer forgets to pull the "lever" to make a build and to check if everything is correct, the CI server never forgets, as shown in figure 4.2.

There are various ways to accomplish this manual build. First, you can try to build the system manually: *you* act as a CI server; you are the build master. You can perform a build once a day or after every check-in (for example, by using a physical item/token to show who has control, as we'll discuss later in the chapter). Think of hand-crafting a shell script similar to the example provided in chapter 1. You can try to write

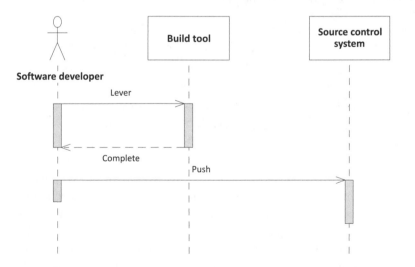

Figure 4.1   Until now, you've been able to push the lever and get the build done. If the application builds correctly, you can push your code into the source control system on a one-off basis. You get to do it all over again when you implement the next feature.

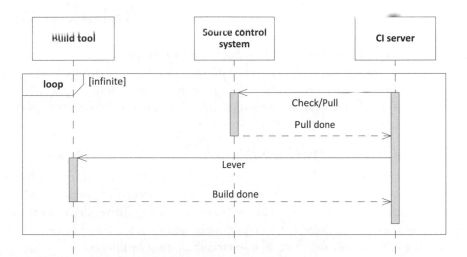

Figure 4.2 The CI server in action. It checks whether anything new is on the source control server. If so, it pulls the code and uses the lever to start the build. The whole process is enclosed in an infinite loop. Whenever the software developer pushes anything into the source control repository, sooner or later it's integrated.

your own task-loop software to mimic the CI server and extend it to a full-blown tool. Or you can use one of the ready-to-use tools on the market. In this chapter, we'll try to find the best way.

Choosing the right CI server isn't an easy task. You have to deal with both the hardware and software aspects. On the hardware side, you have to determine whether you have a separate physical machine on which to build your CI server. Is it a full-blown server with 99.9% uptime or only an old machine standing in the corner of your developers' room? If you don't have a physical machine, can you get a virtualized server running somewhere that every team member can access? If you're setting up a nonproductive CI process, just to check things out, it's all right to install it on your development machine, but that most likely isn't a production setup.

It's strongly suggested that you dedicate a separate machine to act as the CI server. Why? Because a correctly created CI process should have as few dependencies as possible. This means your machine should be as vanilla as possible. For a .NET setup, it's best to have only the operating system, the .NET framework, and probably the source control client. Some CI servers also need IIS or SharePoint Services to extend their functionality. We recommend that you not install any additional applications on the build server unless they're taking part in the build process.

Another reason to use a dedicated continuous build machine is that you can keep it clear of any configuration changes you normally do on a development machine or on a machine that's used for something else. This way, you're free from any assumptions about the installed software or machine configuration. You can be sure your vanilla machine stays vanilla—no toppings, no icing, nothing spoiling the vanilla taste. In other words, a machine brought to a known state every time the builds occur.

As for hardware, as usual, more is better. Your build should be as fast as possible. Every team member, after putting a new feature in the source control system, should wait for the CI build to finish and check it to be sure everything worked as expected. You don't want to keep developers from their work for too long. In the long run, a fast CPU and a fast hard drive are cheaper than your developers' time.

When you have a dedicated integration machine ready to host your CI server, you can figure out which server is right for you.

4.2 *Examining the CI server possibilities*

Before CI, a build master or release engineer had a build machine and integrated your software there. They received the code from the team and created working software, ready for shipment. They did the same set of repetitive steps over and over again. The work was boring, it was error prone, and it took a lot of time. The release build was made infrequently. Often, it led to integration problems.

Then someone came up with the idea of a manual integration build. With a build script in place, you can require developers to personally integrate new features or user stories into working software.

But someone else thought about changing the adjective to create automated integration builds. One thought led to another, and the CI server emerged. Let's try to walk this path—maybe it'll lead to the correct decision about how to establish your own CI server.

4.2.1 *Manual integration build or your own CI server?*

How about your own build server? Look at figure 4.3, which shows an ordinary build run as a simple directed graph.

Think about what it takes for the build process to run continuously. Perhaps you can squeeze or bend it a little, connecting the end with the beginning as shown in figure 4.4. With our warm apologies to all the math purists out there, you get a task loop.

The main reason to apply manual integration to builds is to prevent broken builds. The manual build technique is losing importance with the newest CI servers. All developers have to manually run the build and integrate the software before they check the software in to the repository. This task should be done in an environment as close to the customer's as possible. Running a manual integration build often involves using a physical marker (often a toy) to mark the developer who is currently holding up the

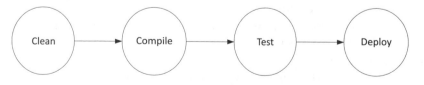

Figure 4.3   An ordinary build run. You clean the construction site, compile, test, and deploy. What can make this graph bend and become a task loop?

build or the person who checked in code that doesn't compile or fails tests, thus creating a broken build. Basically, it relies on starting the same build script in the integration environment that the software developers start on their machines to check if everything is still working.

If you apply this process, you can be sure that no code that can break the build gets into the repository. This technique can complement a normal CI server. Some modern CI servers can perform this kind of task out of the box. For example, TeamCity lets no code touch the source control repository without a prior integration build. But if you choose a server that doesn't have this fea-

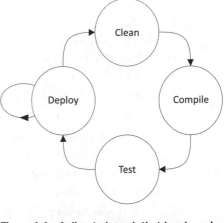

Figure 4.4 A directed graph that bends and closes in a task loop. It's almost a homemade CI server diagram.

ture, a manual integration build must be made by humans. And humans tend to neglect, forget, and make mistakes.

This approach has one fault: if nothing changes, you're building the same software over and over again. It's a pure waste of energy. How about adding one substantial element, something that'll periodically poll the changes from the repository? If nothing interesting has changed, the process waits. If not, it performs the build (see figure 4.5).

Scripting this scenario or writing a small program to do it shouldn't be too hard. You did it in chapter 1 using a command-line script. But the question is, do you have the time to do it? You won't do that in this book; but if you want to play, go ahead and write your own CI server. It'll take you a long time to get to the stage where the production-ready CI servers are right now. They've evolved over the years into feature-rich applications.

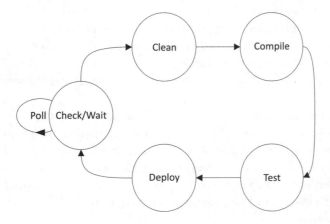

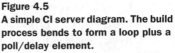

Figure 4.5
A simple CI server diagram. The build process bends to form a loop plus a poll/delay element.

4.2.2 *CI servers for .NET*

If you decided not to write your own CI server, you made the right decision. But now you have to decide which server to use. You have a lot of options to choose from. Several CI servers are on the market, and if you want to choose wisely, you must consider many aspects, such as the following:

- How much money do you have to spend?
- Do you want to pay the angle-bracket tax (write a lot of XML)?
- Does it support the other tools you need?
- How good are the documentation and support?
- Does it do what you want it to do?
- Does it do more than you need, not just now but into the future?
- Is it easy to use?
- Is it cool and hip?

Before we go into details, let's take a broader look at the tools available.

Programs and scripts that performed a task similar to a CI server existed for a long time. For example, they were used in the Linux community for kernel development (see http://test.kernel.org/tko/). But the era of CI servers started with CruiseControl in 2000 or 2001. It's a tool from ThoughtWorks, and it emerged about the same time as the first article about CI from Martin Fowler, who works at ThoughtWorks. Cruise-Control is a Java-based tool for performing continuous builds. It's widely adopted mainly in the Java community. It has a pluggable architecture and supports a wide range of source control systems. The build for CruiseControl is usually made using Ant as the build tool.

The first CI server aimed at the .NET community was CruiseControl.NET (CCNet). It's a form of the old CruiseControl made by ThoughtWorks, and it's been on the market since 2003. It has everything the older brother has, and it's written in .NET. It works as a Windows service and has a web dashboard to present the current state. It can remotely manage the process using a system tray program called *CCTray*. Just like CruiseControl, CCNet is open source.

CCNet was for years the automated integration server of choice for .NET teams that didn't have enough resources for commercial products, especially for Microsoft Team Foundation Server (TFS). As we mentioned in chapter 2, TFS is a suite of tools that supports collaborative software development. One of its features is the ability to perform CI builds.

Somewhere in between the totally free model of CCNet and the rather expensive model of TFS is another important player in the .NET CI server market: TeamCity from JetBrains, which was first released in 2006. The licensing scenario for TeamCity is a hybrid between free and propriety. You can start small without paying a penny for the Professional Edition license; but if you grow, and your needs expand, then you'll have to pay for the license. It's written in Java, is easy to set up, and has a few features that make it interesting to look at.

These three tools aren't all the CI servers you can use in .NET. You can also consider adopting Hudson, Bamboo, Electric Cloud, Anthill, or one of many others. A detailed CI feature matrix is available at ThoughtWorks' wiki page (http://confluence. public.thoughtworks.org/display/CC/CI+Feature+Matrix). We'll look at these three players from our point of view.

Earlier in this section, we listed some aspects to consider when choosing a CI server. Table 4.1 compares our three server choices on those aspects.

Table 4.1 CI server matrix that compares the features of three CI servers

Aspect	CruiseControl.NET	TFS 2010	TeamCity
Cost	yes	somewhat	somewhat
XML	no	yes	yes
Tools support	yes	somewhat	yes
Documentation	yes	yes	yes
CI functionality	yes	yes	yes
Additional features	no	yes	yes
Easy to use	no	somewhat	yes
Cool (subjective)	somewhat	somewhat	yes

When we were planning this book, we initially discussed going with CCNet. Our original goal was to provide you with all the information you needed to get up and running with no or little cost. We soon found that TeamCity was gaining a lot of interest from .NET developers, so we added it, knowing there would eventually be some cost to you. At that time, TFS was costly, so we ruled it out. But when Microsoft announced that TFS 2010 would be available at no extra cost to everyone with an MSDN Professional subscription or above, we knew it had to be included. We could have discussed other CI servers, but at some point, it would have been too many, and the book would have lost focus. We feel that with the CI servers we've selected, we meet our goal of no or little cost.

Now, let's start digging in to each server, beginning with CCNet.

4.3   *Continuous integration with CruiseControl.NET*

CruiseControl.NET is a CI server that is established in the .NET community. On the one hand, it's widely adopted and used with success in the production environment; but you have to pay a so called *angle-bracket tax* for using it. This is a loose term for the additional costs that are generated if you have to fight your way manually through the configuration, which is held in XML format (hence an angle-bracket tax).

With CCNet, you get the software for free, but you must deal with the configuration yourself. But on the other hand, if you're doing the configuration, nothing is hidden from you behind a wizard or UI.

You need a thorough understanding of what you're doing in order to do the configuration correctly. Let's set up a CCNet server to continuously integrate your project.

4.3.1 Starting with CCNet

You can get the last version of CCNet from the ThoughtWorks website (http://ccnet. thoughtworks.com). Get the setup installation file, and start it on your CI machine. The installation is easy. As shown in figure 4.6, you have to decide what components you want to install.

If you have Internet Information Server (IIS) installed on the same machine as CCNet, you can install Web Dashboard on the same machine. It can be also installed somewhere else. We strongly advise you to have an instance of the Web Dashboard running somewhere. If you don't have IIS installed on your server, we strongly recommend that you install it now. Depending on the operating system your server is running, you'll have to add the Web Server (IIS) role in Server Management in Windows Server 2008 or use the Programs and Features console to turn on IIS. If you get a message while installing Web Dashboard to choose an ASP.NET version, choose at least 2.0, and everything will work fine.

CI is all about the feedback. You should always know what's going on. Did the build fail? Why did it fail? You can obtain that information using the Web Dashboard, and CCNet would be handicapped without it.

During the installation, you're asked whether to install CCNet as a Windows service (see figure 4.7.). CCNet can work standalone or as a Windows service. If you plan to use CCNet as a production CI server, it should run as a Windows service. Standalone mode is helpful while you're configuring and troubleshooting the server; we'll look at it later in this chapter. Note that the CCNet Windows service won't be started automatically

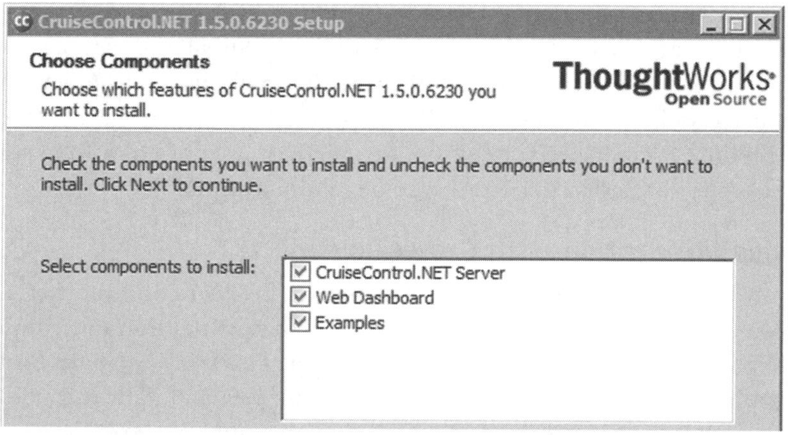

Figure 4.6   **Selecting the CCNet components you need for your server.
CruiseControl.NET Server is the essential part of the installation. Web Dashboard is
a web page that provides build feedback. And Examples provides configuration
examples.**

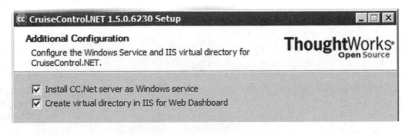

Figure 4.7   You can install CCNet as a Windows service and configure IIS to be ready to serve the Web Dashboard.

after the installation, and you'll be able to start and stop it every time you want to switch to standalone mode.

As shown in figure 4.7, the CCNet installer can prepare everything on IIS for the Web Dashboard. This way, you'll only have to configure your CCNet instance to make it work.

4.3.2   Configuring CCNet

You can access the CCNet configuration file via the Start menu or edit it directly using, for example, Notepad, in %Program Files%\CruiseControl.NET\server\ccnet.config if you installed CCNet in the default location. Immediately after installation, you have an empty configuration file like this:

```
<cruisecontrol xmlns:cb="urn:ccnet.config.builder">
    <!-- This is your CruiseControl.NET Server Configuration file.
    ➥Add your projects below! -->
    <!--
        <project name="MyFirstProject" />
    -->
</cruisecontrol>
```

CCNet lets you define multiple projects. In CCNet nomenclature, a *project* is a separate unit of works that CCNet performs. Define a project for the financial calculator Framework project as shown here.

Listing 4.1   Project configuration in CCNet

```
<project name="Framework">
  <workingDirectory>c:\CI\Framework\</workingDirectory>
  <artifactDirectory>c:\CI\Artifacts.Framework</artifactDirectory>
  <webURL>http://localhost/ccnet</webURL>
  <triggers>
    <intervalTrigger initialSeconds="0" />
  </triggers>
  <sourcecontrol type="svn">
    <trunkUrl>https://HYMIE:81/svn/Framework/trunk</trunkUrl>
    <executable>C:\Program Files\Svn\bin\svn.exe</executable>
    <username>marcin</username>
    <password>password</password>
  </sourcecontrol>
```

❶ Defines interval trigger

❷ Gets source code from SVN

```
<tasks>
  <msbuild>
    <executable>
      C:\Windows\Microsoft.NET\Framework\
      ➥v4.0.20506\MSBuild.exe
  </executable>
    <projectFile>Framework.sln</projectFile>
    <buildArgs>
      /p:Configuration=Release /verbosity:minimal
    </buildArgs>
    <logger>
      C:\[Program Files]\CruiseControl.NET\server\
      ➥ThoughtWorks.CruiseControl.MSBuild.dll</logger>
  </msbuild>
</tasks>
</project>
```

❸ Declares Visual Studio project with default target

After defining a name for your project, you must set some important variables, such as the working directory where the integration will occur. It needs to be a directory solely for CI purposes, so you should prepare an empty one—for example, in c:\CI. CCNet produces various artifacts while integrating. For example, build logs should be stored somewhere; you define this location using the `artifactDirectory` element. If you're using Web Dashboard, define its `webURL`.

The minimal configuration that lets you perform CI consists of three elements. The first is an `intervalTrigger` ❶ which specifies that the integration should occur periodically. This means CCNet will poll the source control system for changes periodically and trigger the build only if something new is found in the repository. Using CCNet, you have to remember that not every change committed to the repository triggers a build. If two commits occur during the wait interval, both of them will be pulled and integrated after the trigger fires.

The second element you must declare is a `sourceControl` ❷ tag. It defines the place from which CCNet should pull the changes to feed the integration. In this example, you're using the SVN server and repository from chapter 2. You need a SVN command-line client on the machine where CCNet is running (you define the path to the client in the `executable` tag). You can get a subversion command-line client at CollabNet (www.collab.net/downloads/subversion/). If you have concerns about the user and password to the SVN repository in the project definition, you should keep a few things in mind. First, in the production environment, the file will reside on a separate machine: the build server. No one else will have access to it. Second, you should have a special SVN user for the CI server with only read rights to the repositories the user is working on.

The last part you have to define is what CCNet should do. In the `tasks` element ❸, you define a task for CCNet. The `MSBuild` task starts the solution file.

Before you start CCNet, you can verify your configuration using the Configuration Validation tool that comes with CCNet; it's available from the Start menu (look for CCValidator). After loading your configuration file, it performs the validation as shown in figure 4.8.

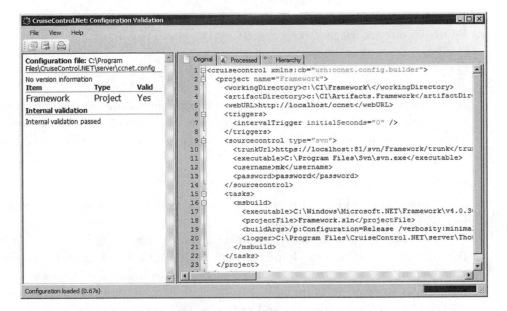

Figure 4.8 The CCNet Configuration Validation can ease the angle-bracket tax you have to pay using this CI server. It lets you check the configuration before you start your server.

When you're sure you've configured everything, you can start the server. You have two options. As mentioned earlier, CCNet can work as a Windows service or as a standalone application. You'll begin with the standalone version. It gives you immediate feedback on screen and is much better to use in the initial phase than the non-UI Windows service version. After starting your CCNet standalone application, you'll see something like figure 4.9.

```
mk;CCNetIntegrationStatus=Unknown;CCNetLabel=1;CCNetLastIntegrationStatus=Failur
e;CCNetListenerFile=c:\CI\Artifacts.Framework\Framework_ListenFile.xml;CCNetModi
fyingUsers=mk;CCNetNumericLabel=1;CCNetProject=Framework;CCNetProjectUrl=http://
localhost/ccnet;CCNetRequestSource=IntervalTrigger;CCNetUser=;CCNetWorkingDirect
ory=c:\CI\Framework\ /p:Configuration=Release /verbosity:minimal Framework.sln /
l:"C:\Program Files\CruiseControl.NET\server\ThoughtWorks.CruiseControl.MSBuild.
dll";c:\CI\Artifacts.Framework\msbuild-results-58504b8a-091d-4d94-8b85-55a9539f5
c5d.xml]
[Framework:DEBUG] Not setting PriorityClass on [C:\Windows\Microsoft.NET\Framewo
rk\v4.0.30319\MSBuild.exe] to default Normal
[7:DEBUG] [Framework C:\Windows\Microsoft.NET\Framework\v4.0.30319\MSBuild.exe]
  CalcCore -> c:\CI\Framework\CalcCore\bin\Release\CalcCore.dll
[7:DEBUG] [Framework C:\Windows\Microsoft.NET\Framework\v4.0.30319\MSBuild.exe]
standard-output stream closed -- null received in event
[6:DEBUG] [Framework C:\Windows\Microsoft.NET\Framework\v4.0.30319\MSBuild.exe]
standard-error stream closed -- null received in event
[3:DEBUG] [Framework C:\Windows\Microsoft.NET\Framework\v4.0.30319\MSBuild.exe]
process exited event received
[Framework:INFO] Task output:     CalcCore -> c:\CI\Framework\CalcCore\bin\Release
\CalcCore.dll

[Framework:INFO] Delete merged file 'c:\CI\Artifacts.Framework\msbuild-results-5
8504b8a-091d-4d94-8b85-55a9539f5c5d.xml'.
[Framework:INFO] Integration complete: Success - 11/3/2010 9:18:31 PM
```

Figure 4.9 CCNet in console mode is best for initial trial-and-error configuration or troubleshooting your configuration. The CCNet console displays a lot of information about what's going on, such as how the integration is going and what the build is saying. It's great for debugging your CI process.

If you get everything right, your software should be integrated. You can of course configure the interval trigger to run as often as you want. You can use another type of trigger, too. Let's look at the possibilities.

4.3.3   *Triggering builds*

If you provide the interval trigger without any parameters, you get the default 60 seconds between the time the last integration ends and when the next cycle begins. By default, the build fires only if something changes in the source repository. You can change the default settings this way:

```
<intervalTrigger seconds="30" buildCondition="ForceBuild"/>
```

This causes CCNet to cycle this project every 30 seconds and build every time regardless of any changes in the repository.

Let's consider a more complicated scenario. In chapter 1, you created a small financial calculator; and in chapter 3, you introduced a build script to integrate it. One section of the calculator is a shared library that contains the mathematical part. It's used in UI projects: Windows and web clients. The shared project is placed in a separate Visual Studio solution and can be referenced from various other projects. What if you want to build projects that are referencing this shared library, and something changes inside it? You can use another type of trigger: a project trigger, as shown in the following listing.

Listing 4.2   Triggering one build with another project build

```
<project name="WindowsCalculator">
  <workingDirectory>c:\CI\WindowsCalculator\</workingDirectory>
  <artifactDirectory>c:\CI\WindowsCalculator.Artifacts</artifactDirectory>
  <webURL>http://localhost/ccnet</webURL>
  <triggers>
    <intervalTrigger initialSeconds="0" />
    <projectTrigger project="Framework">              ◁─┐  Project dependency
      <triggerStatus>Success</triggerStatus>          ❶  trigger
    </projectTrigger>
  </triggers>
  <sourcecontrol type="svn">
    <trunkUrl>https://HYMIE:81/svn/WinCalculator/trunk</trunkUrl>
    <executable>C:\Program Files\Svn\bin\svn.exe</executable>
    <username>marcin</username>
    <password>password</password>
  </sourcecontrol>
  <tasks>
    <msbuild>
      <executable>
        C:\Windows\Microsoft.NET\Framework\
        ➥v4.0.20506\MSBuild.exe</executable>
      <projectFile>build.proj</projectFile>
      <buildArgs>/p:Configuration=Release /verbosity:minimal</buildArgs>
      <logger>
```

```
C:\Pru  ̶ ̶ ̶ ̶  F11 ̶ ̶ ̶  ̶ ̶ ̶ ̶ CUILMI . NUT\server
      ⮡ \ThoughtWorks.CruiseControl.MSBuild.dll
    </logger>
  </msbuild>
 </tasks>
</project>
```

You define the WindowsCalculator project in a fashion similar to the Framework project, but you extend the trigger repository. You're performing an ordinary CI build every 30 seconds and also checking whether a dependent project has completed its build ❶. If so, you fire the build for WindowsCalculator as well.

Think of distributing your projects onto more machines. CCNet lets you distribute projects *indirectly*. This means you don't have one centralized server that is managing build processes; you can couple several CCNet instances (we'll discuss this more in chapter 12). For example, if the Framework project is built on a separate machine, you can provide the additional attribute serverUri to the project trigger like this:

```
<projectTrigger serverUri="tcp://server:21234/CruiseManager.rem"
    project="Core">
   <triggerStatus>Success</triggerStatus>
   <innerTrigger type="intervalTrigger" seconds="30"/>
</projectTrigger>
```

This way, one CCNet instance will ask another instance about the Framework build. In addition, the innerTrigger element lets you define how often it happens. In this case, it will poll the changes from other CCNet servers every 30 seconds rather than the default 5 seconds, which may be too often for a distributed scenario.

What if you have a long-running build that you want to perform once a day, possibly at night? For example, you may need to generate documentation from your source code. This takes a lot of time, and it isn't necessary to generate the documentation whenever the source code changes. You can use the *schedule trigger* to accomplish this. Let's define it:

```
<scheduleTrigger time="03:00" buildCondition="ForceBuild" />
```

In this case, the build will fire every night at 3:00 a.m.

You can limit the trigger further. Let's say you want this build to run once a week, at night, on Sunday. Here you go:

```
<scheduleTrigger time="03:00" buildCondition="ForceBuild">
    <weekDays>
        <weekDay>Sunday</weekDay>
    </weekDays>
</scheduleTrigger>
```

Using triggers, you can fairly easily manipulate the build chain. But this chain has an end: when the build is finished, you have to pass the feedback along. You can do so with *publishers* (we'll talk more about it in the next chapter).

As you can see, there's a lot to configure with CCNet. You can learn about how your CI servers are working by manually configuring CCNet. You have to use the CCNet documentation extensively to do this such that CCNet works the way you want. And it'll take time to learn the configuration basics. If you want get the configuration done more quickly, we have something suitable: another CI server. It's not open source, but it's still free. And you won't have to write a single line of configuration XML to make it work. Meet TeamCity.

4.4 Continuous integration with TeamCity

TeamCity is a CI server that has been gaining popularity in the .NET community for the last few years. It's packed with handy futures that we'll discuss in a minute, and it offers a free version that's suitable for smaller teams.

The free version of TeamCity lets a group of 20 people work with 20 assorted projects. There are a few minor restrictions, such as a lack of more sophisticated login scenarios using Active Directory. If you need support for more developers or projects, you must buy a license for about $1,500. Both versions allow you to set a distributed build grid using *build agents* (specialized build machines). They let you divide your builds over several machines. Basically, you install the agent software on various machines, and TeamCity automatically starts the build on one of the build machines.

TeamCity has a neat feature that lets you forget the manual build technique we discussed earlier in this chapter. It verifies code compiles and passes unit tests before committing your source code into the repository. See figure 4.10 to better understand the difference.

You basically send your changes first to TeamCity and not to your source control system. TeamCity performs the build, tests whether everything is fine, and then commits the changes to the source control system only if everything works fine.

We hope we have your attention and that you're eager to try it for yourself. Let's get started with TeamCity!

4.4.1 Running TeamCity

You can download the TeamCity setup file from the JetBrains website (www.jetbrains.com/teamcity/). It's a large file that contains everything you need to build a CI process. It asks you to install the core features and build agent (see figure 4.11).

Both the Build Agent and Core Server are installed as separate Windows services and automatically hooked together. TeamCity comes bundled with its own web server; all TeamCity configuration and management happen on a web page that's hosted on this server. As shown in figure 4.12, you have to choose a port where TeamCity will be available.

You must choose an account under which to run TeamCity (see figure 4.13). Your choice depends on what you expect to do with the server. Will your build need more rights than a normal system account? It may be possible if you plan to use network shares or have other restrictions on the files on the server. If you aren't sure, run

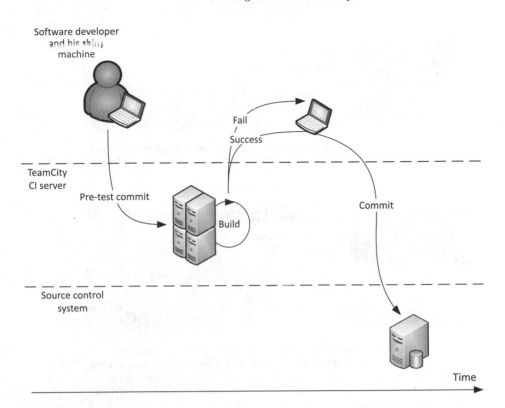

Figure 4.10 TeamCity's pre-test commit feature lets you check your build for correctness before you commit it to the source control repository.

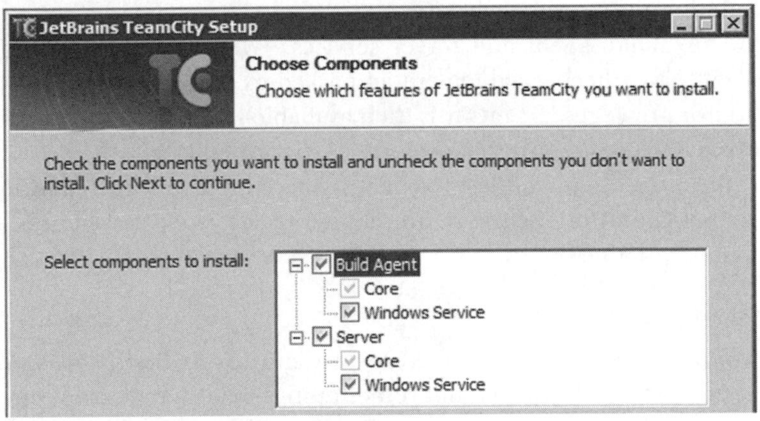

Figure 4.11 To run builds with TeamCity, you need to install at least one Build Agent. You can install more Build Agents on multiple computers to create a build grid.

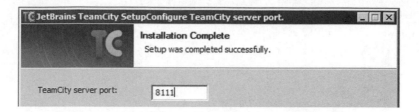

Figure 4.12   TeamCity comes with a bundled web server. If you have IIS or any other application running on a standard HTTP port, you'll have to change the port for TeamCity.

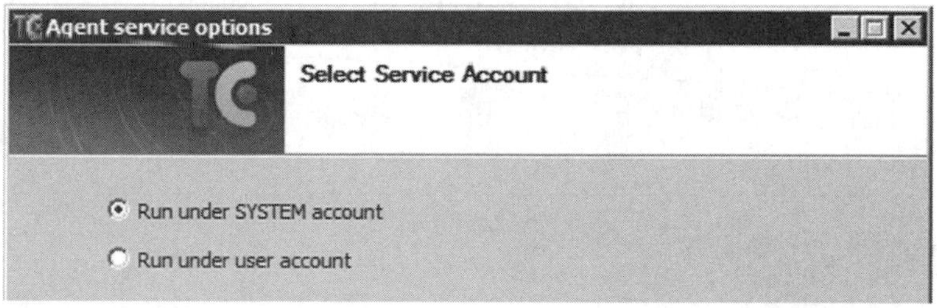

Figure 4.13   If you plan to make TeamCity available outside your intranet environment, don't make hasty decisions here. Run it with the user who has the fewest rights needed for normal usage. If you're a local administrator on the machine, choose the SYSTEM account (you can change it later in the Services Management Console).

TeamCity under the system account—doing so is safer, because your user account is probably an administrator on the machine.

Start both the Build Agent and server services. When the installer is finished, you're presented with a license agreement and asked to create the first user account with administrator privileges. TeamCity is then available for normal work. After initial login, you're asked to create your first project (see figure 4.14).

To make the project run under TeamCity, you must connect TeamCity to the source control configuration, define a runner, and make sure your agent is properly connected. Let's do that next.

4.4.2   Configuring a project

After you've installed TeamCity, you need to configure your first project. You'll go through these steps for each project, but some settings may change from one project to another. Let's walk through setting up the Framework shard library from your financial calculator:

 1   TeamCity needs to know how you'll refer to the project (see figure 4.15). This doesn't have to be the same name as the Visual Studio project. In fact, you probably want to make the name something more understandable, because it'll be

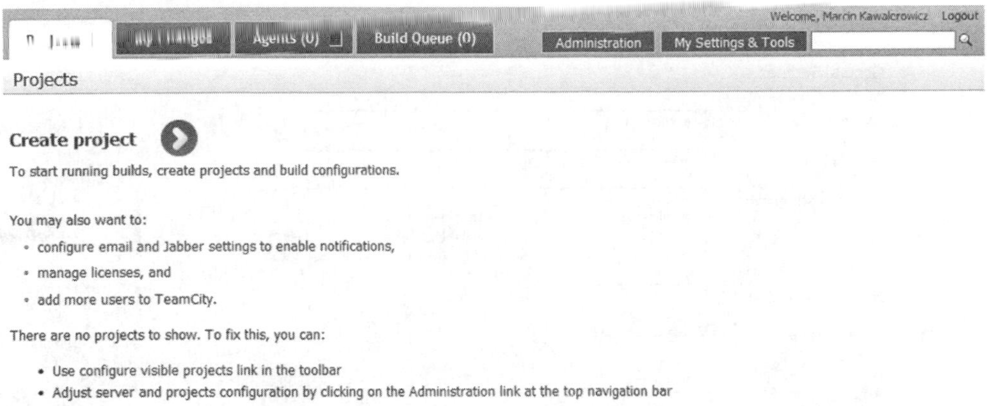

Figure 4.14   When TeamCity is ready to work, the first step is to create a new project.

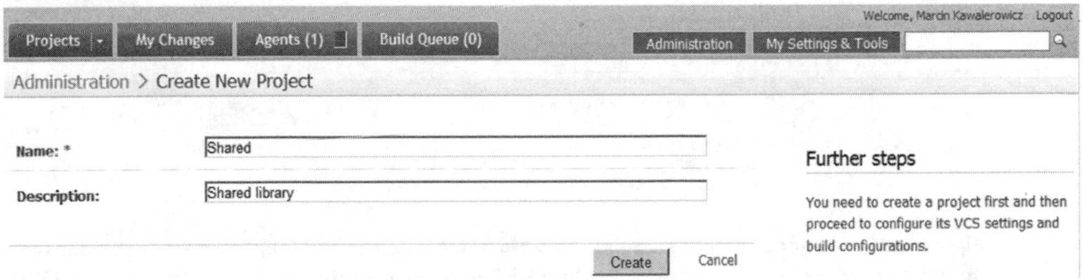

Figure 4.15   TeamCity doesn't impose an angle-bracket tax for most tasks. The entire configuration process runs in a comfortable UI. You're starting with a new project.

used in the feedback mechanism we'll discuss in chapter 5. Enter the name and description for the project, and click Create.

2 You need to configure your TeamCity project (see figure 4.16). Give the build configuration a meaningful name and description. Look at the build-number format (the example takes the revision number and assigns it to the build). The build process doesn't leave any artifacts now, so leave the artifacts paths empty (you'll learn about artifacts in the next chapter). Next, you can decide when to fail a build based on the build exit code, test output, build runner errors, exceeding the maximum build time, lack of system resources, or an unexpected crash. You can decide whether TeamCity will try to detect hanging builds (builds that are running but aren't doing anything). By enabling the status widget, you give external sites the ability to retrieve the build status. The last thing you can decide is the maximum number of simultaneous builds of this type to run.

Notice the Configuration Steps at the right in figure 4.16; they help you keep track of everything you need to do.

Administration > Shared Project > Shared CI Configuration   Run... | Build Configuration Home

General Settings

Name: *	Shared CI
Description:	Shared CI build
Build number format: ⑦ *	{build.vcs.number.1}

Format may include '{0}' as a placeholder for build counter value, for example 1.{0}. It may also contain a reference to VCS changeset number, like {build.vcs.number.1}.
Note: maximum length of a build number after all substitutions is **256** characters.

Build counter: *	0 Reset counter

Artifact paths: ⑦   📝 Edit artifact paths:

Hide

New line or comma separated paths to build artifacts. Support ant-style wildcards like
`dir/**/*.zip` and target directories like
`*.zip => winFiles,unix/distro.tgz => linuxFiles`, where `winFiles` and
`linuxFiles` are target directories.

Fail build if:
☑ build process exit code is not zero
☑ at least one test failed
☑ an error message is logged by build runner
☑ it runs longer than 10 minutes
☑ an out of memory or crash is detected

Build options:
☑ enable hanging builds detection
☐ enable status widget ⑦
Limit the number of simultaneously running builds (0 - unlimited) 0

Configuration Steps

1 General Settings

2 Version Control Settings

3 Runner: sln2008

4 Build Triggering

5 Dependencies

6 Properties and Environment Variables

7 Agent Requirements

Pause	Pause this configuration
Copy	Copy this configuration
Move	Move this configuration
Delete	Delete this configuration and all related data

Figure 4.16   General project settings. Pay close attention to the build-number formatter and the fail conditions. Builds are formatted with the revision number. In this case, you decide to fail if the build exceeds 10 minutes.

3 When you've configured the project's build options, you must configure the connection to the version control system (VCS)—in other words, your source code repository (see figure 4.17). The source root configuration varies depending on the source control system you're using. Because you're using SVN, you must provide at least the SVN URL, username, and password. You have to decide whether to use the default configuration directory (you don't have to change this if you aren't doing anything extraordinary). You can choose to pull the source with all externals (you learned about this in chapter 2). You can leave all the rest of the settings at their defaults.

The newly created source control root will be added to the project configuration.

4 You can also decide what checkout mode you want to use (see figure 4.18). You can do this on the TeamCity server, on the build agent, or not at all if your build script will pull the changes for itself. SVN lets you check out the files on the agent, so do it; this will reduce the load on the main TeamCity server. You can decide where to check out the files or leave it blank for TeamCity to decide. The build folder can be automatically purged before every build

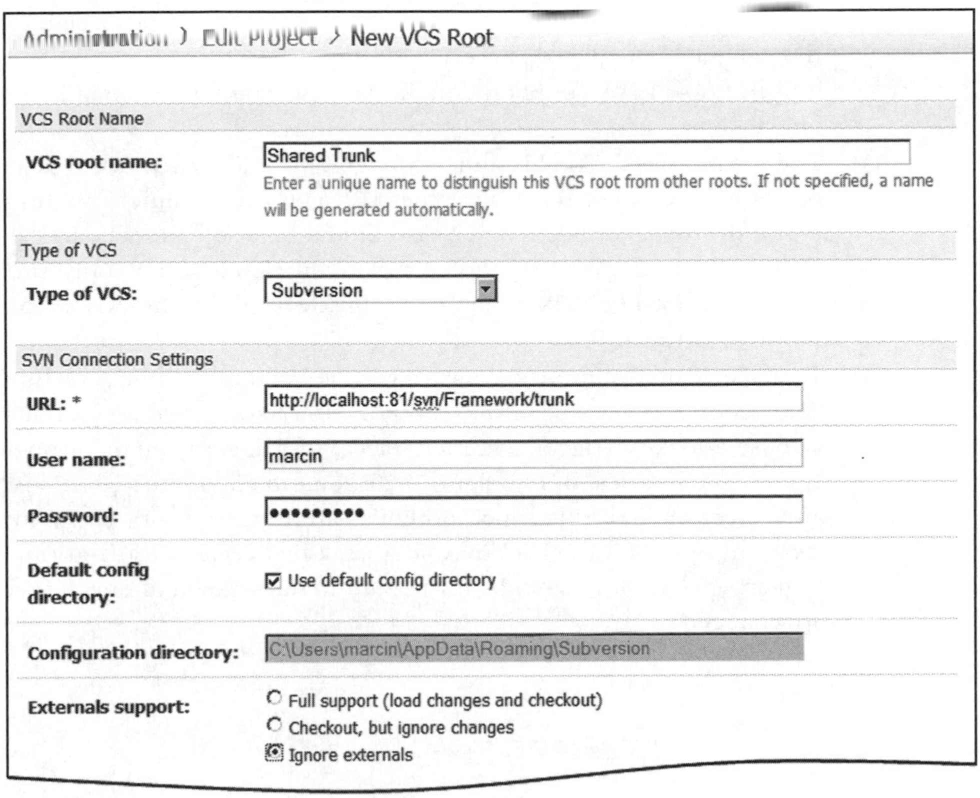

Administration > Edit Project > New VCS Root

VCS Root Name

VCS root name: Shared Trunk

Enter a unique name to distinguish this VCS root from other roots. If not specified, a name will be generated automatically.

Type of VCS

Type of VCS: Subversion

SVN Connection Settings

URL: * http://localhost:81/svn/Framework/trunk

User name: marcin

Password: ●●●●●●●●●

Default config directory: ☑ Use default config directory

Configuration directory: C:\Users\marcin\AppData\Roaming\Subversion

Externals support:
○ Full support (load changes and checkout)
○ Checkout, but ignore changes
◉ Ignore externals

Figure 4.17 Creating a new source control root. You can reuse this configuration in other projects.

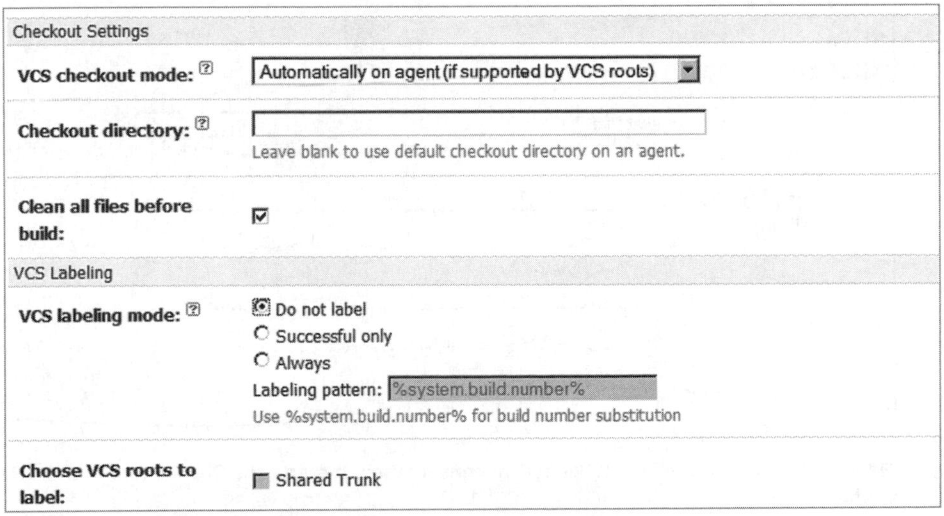

Checkout Settings

VCS checkout mode: ⓘ Automatically on agent (if supported by VCS roots)

Checkout directory: ⓘ

Leave blank to use default checkout directory on an agent.

Clean all files before build: ☑

VCS Labeling

VCS labeling mode: ⓘ
◉ Do not label
○ Successful only
○ Always
Labeling pattern: %system.build.number%
Use %system.build.number% for build number substitution

Choose VCS roots to label: ☐ Shared Trunk

Figure 4.18 Additional source control configuration. Check out on the build agent, choose the default working directory with cleanup, and don't use labeling.

(choose to clean the directory if you aren't doing anything special). Note that you can automatically label every build you make. To do that, you have to dive into additional SVN configuration; in this case, you'll pull the build lever without labeling.

5   The next step is the build runner configuration. The *build runner* is a tool that performs your build. TeamCity comes with a bunch of runners. In this .NET scenario, the MSBuild, NAnt, and Visual Studio Solution runners are handy. Yes, TeamCity can run the solution projects directly and not only through an MSBuild script like CCNet. You'll use this feature for the Shared project, as shown in figure 4.19.

6   To make TeamCity automatically trigger the build every time something new is detected in the source control repository, you have to add a new build trigger. Choose Add New Trigger, and then select VCS Trigger from the drop-down list. You see the screen shown in figure 4.20. You can choose the *quiet period* (a time after every build during which no builds are triggered—it's useful in an environment with a lot of check-ins and a weak build machine). You can also add triggering rules (for example, if you want to start the build only if specific files are changed).

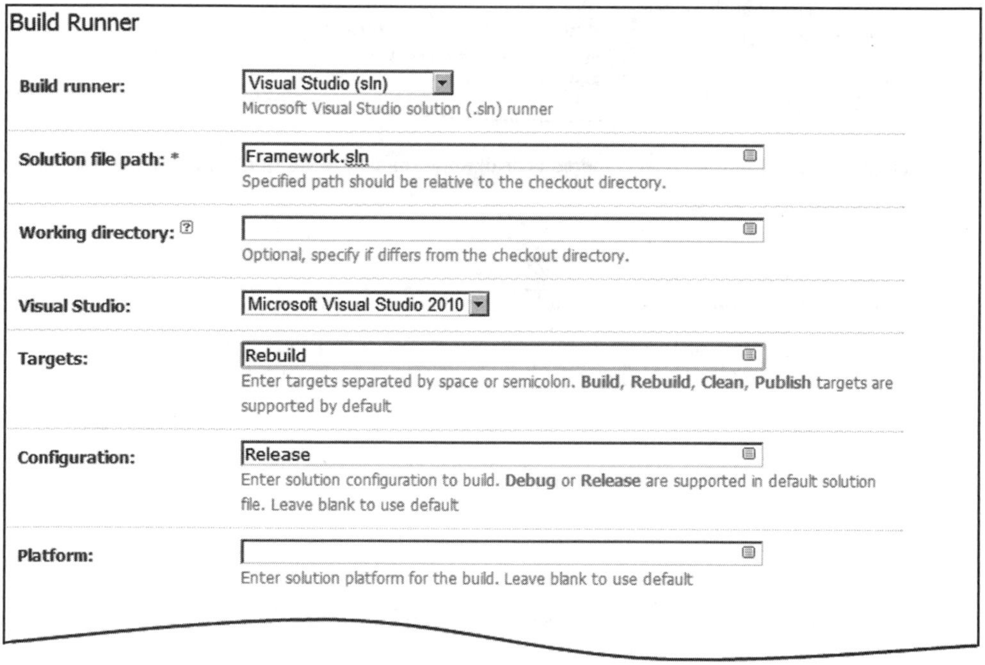

Figure 4.19   Visual Studio Solution runner configuration. It starts the Rebuild target in the Release configuration.

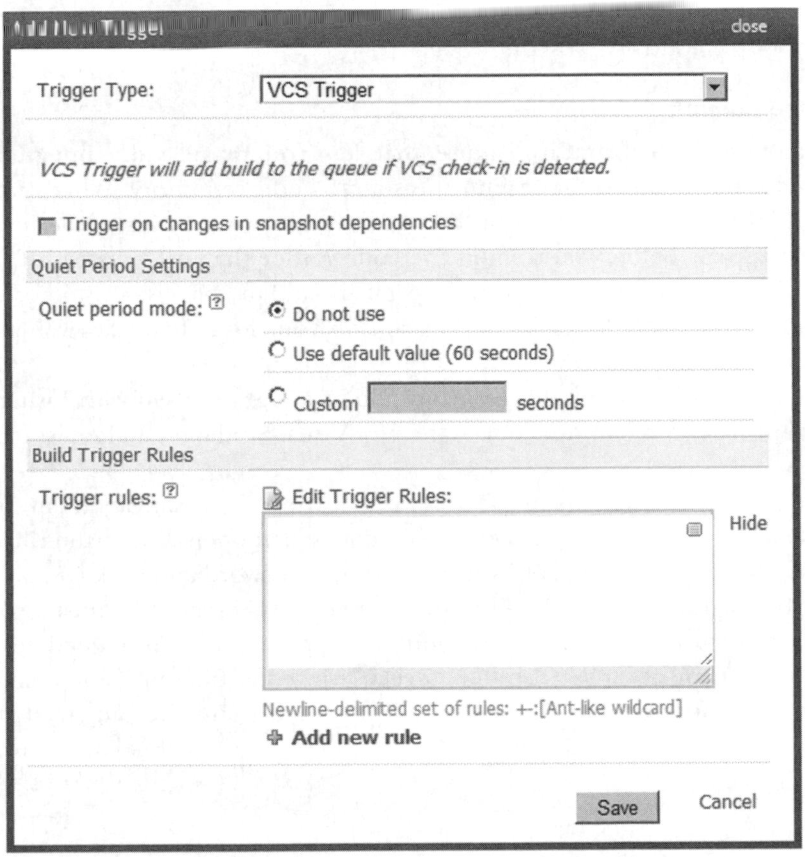

Figure 4.20 Configuring triggers in TeamCity. You can have triggers that fire periodically, or fire based on a dependency.

If you've configured everything correctly, your first continuous build with TeamCity is ready. It should be visible on theuu project overview page (figure 4.21).

We'll pay closer attention to the project feedback page in chapter 5. But now, let's look at a feature we mentioned earlier. It's something that eliminates many broken

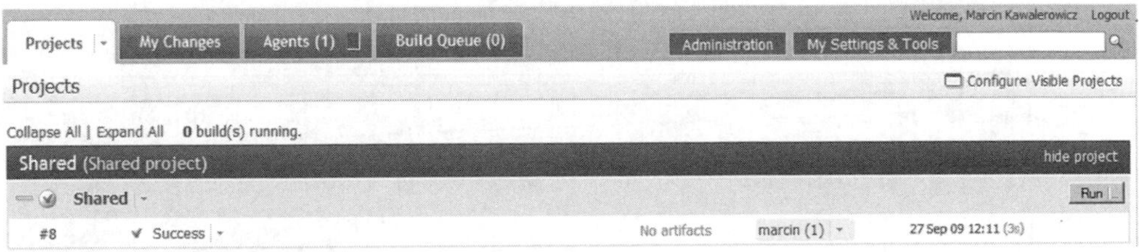

Figure 4.21 Project overview page with one configured project

builds, because it compiles and tests the code before allowing the code to be checked in to the source control repository.

4.4.3   *Pre-tested commit*

Pre-tested commit is a TeamCity feature that lets you make a dry integration run before you check your software into the source code repository. What's important is that the dry run is performed on the integration server, so it's a true integration test that happens before you commit the code rather than after, as with CCNet. To use this feature, you must install the TeamCity add-in for Visual Studio. You can find it under the My Settings & Tools option on your local TeamCity web page (see figure 4.22).

After a successful install, the TeamCity add-in integrates itself with Visual Studio. Open your Shared project, and look at the new Visual Studio menu item shown in figure 4.23.

To use the pre-tested commit feature, run it from the TeamCity menu in Visual Studio. Select TeamCity > Login, and a login dialog box opens. Enter the URL of your TeamCity server and your TeamCity username and password and click OK.

You've now hooked Visual Studio to the TeamCity server. You must also configure the add-in to work with Subversion (see figure 4.24). You need to do this because the TeamCity add-in handles checking in code for you if the compile and tests are successful. Enable Subversion support, and point the plug-in to the SVN

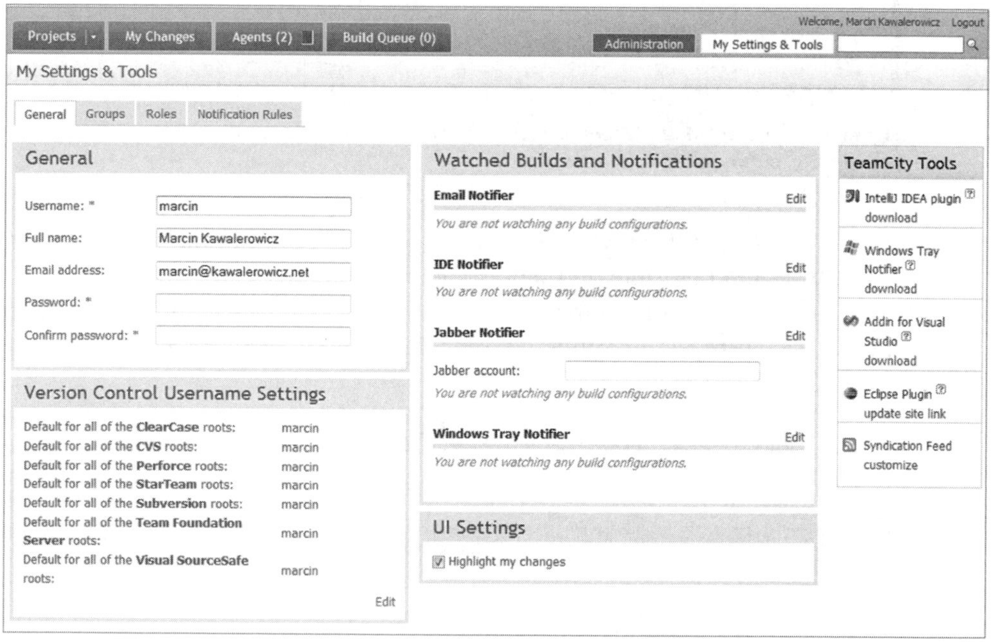

Figure 4.22   Under My Settings & Tools, you can find handy TeamCity additions: a plug-in for Visual Studio and Windows tray notification.

command-line client that you need to install locally on the machine (the Collab-Net client we mentioned earlier is perfect). Enter the SVN credentials, and decide to detect the working copy automatically. Note that in the previous section, you connected the TeamCity server to source control, not the TeamCity add-in.

When everything is set up to perform a test build, introduce an error somewhere in your code so you can see what happens when a build fails. In Visual Studio, select TeamCity > Local Changes. The add-in compares your local files to those in SVN

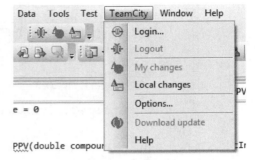

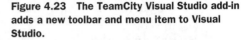

Figure 4.23   The TeamCity Visual Studio add-in adds a new toolbar and menu item to Visual Studio.

and shows you which ones have changed (see figure 4.25). These are the files you need to check in and specifically the ones you need to test.

Figure 4.24   Enabling Subversion support is essential for pre-tested commit.

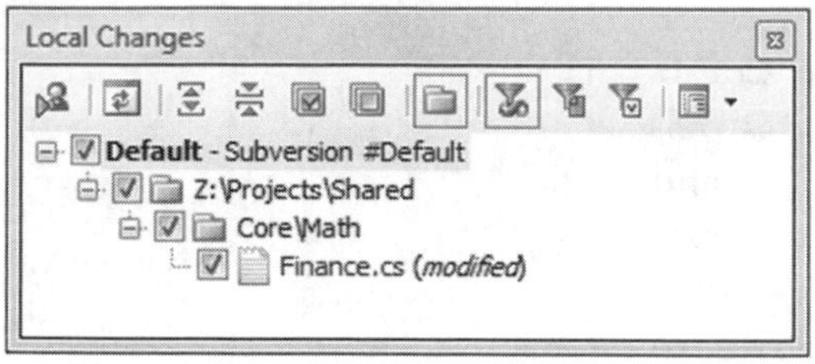

Figure 4.25
The TeamCity add-in for Visual Studio compares the files already in the source code repository with your local copies. If it detects changes, you can choose them for a dry integration run.

Choose the changes you want to pre-test, and click the Remote Run icon 🔍. The window shown in figure 4.26 opens. Choose whether you want to automatically commit the changes if the dry integration run succeeds, and then click Run to build and test the code.

After the pre-test is complete, you're presented with the results (see figure 4.27). Because you purposely had an error in the code, the build and tests failed. But because you told the add-in to check in code only if successful, the bad code wasn't checked in to the source control repository, and other developers on your team and the CI process won't get a broken build due to your error.

TeamCity is a good CI server, no doubt about it. It has a lot of handy features and comes in a free version suitable for small teams. It's definitely worth evaluating as a CI server of choice. Another server you shouldn't omit when evaluating CI solutions for the .NET world is Microsoft Team Foundation Server.

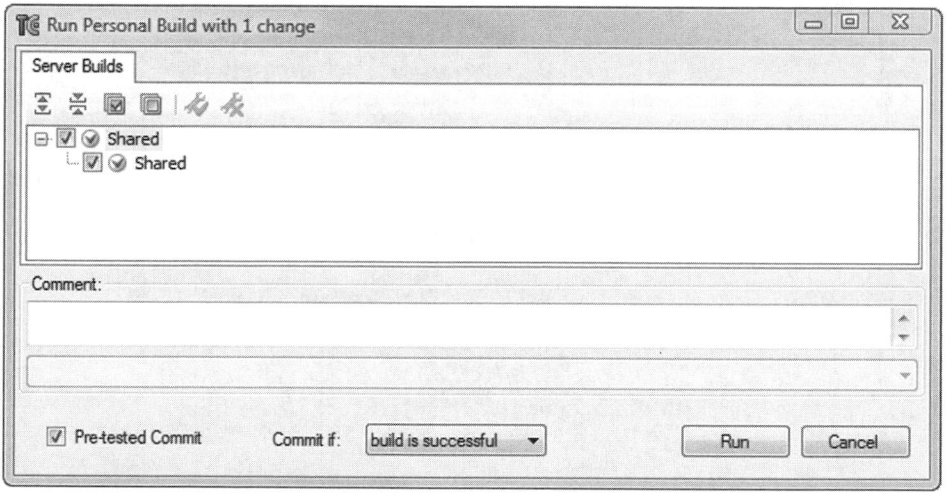

Figure 4.26 You use this pre-tested commit window in Visual Studio to build and test the code before it's checked in to source control.

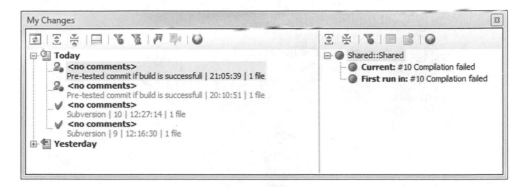

Figure 4.27   The My Changes window shows the results of the last operations. Your pre-tested run failed because the software didn't compile. This way, the broken code stays on your machine to be fixed and never reaches the source control system.

4.5   Continuous integration with Team Foundation Server 2010

Microsoft TFS has been around for some time, but prior to the 2010 release it was cost-prohibitive to many teams. TFS is much more than a CI server. It comes with an integrated source control server, which we discussed in chapter 2. It has extensive work-item tracing tools, and it integrates with SQL Server to provide rich reporting. The feature that's most important for setting up a CI scenario is TFS Team Build. It lets you create a full-blown CI server of your own. It's a grown-up solution for collaborative software development (see figure 4.28).

We're interested in the CI side of TFS 2010. Setting up a CI process with it is straightforward. We're assuming you have the Financial Calculator team project created in TFS source control and that you're connected to it as we described in chapter 2. Now, let's define the build.

4.5.1   TFS and build controllers

TFS 2010 uses a build controller to manage software building tasks. You can install everything onto a single server or split the build process across multiple servers. *Build agents* are services that can be installed on the same or on separate machines to distribute building tasks. A *build-agent pool* is a set of one or more build agents. Figure 4.29 shows a possible TFS build layout.

TFS assigns a build to a build controller. The builds are queued on a given controller and then taken out of the queue one by one or according to a priority and sent to a build agent. A build controller checks in its build-agent pool for a suitable agent to perform the build. After the build is done, the build agent stores the build artifacts and performs notifications.

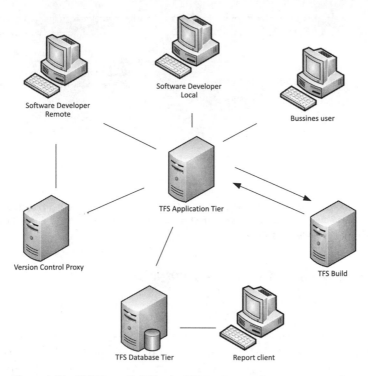

Figure 4.28   TFS Team Build in the TFS landscape. As you can see, the build server is only part of the architecture.

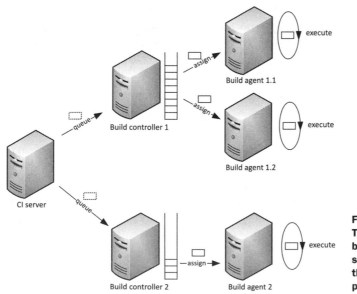

**Figure 4.29
TFS 2010 build layout. A build controller manages a set of build agents, choosing the appropriate one to perform the build.**

4.5.2 Configuring TFS build agents

But first, you need to configure the build agent. You do this on the server side using the Team Foundation Administration Console, which you can run from the Start menu. Choose Build Configuration from the tree beneath your server name, and select Configure Installed Feature. Start the configuration wizard, and follow these instructions:

1 Step through the Welcome screen.
2 On the Project Collection screen, browse for the collection you want to configure, and choose Loan Calculator, as shown in figure 4.30.
3 On the Build Services screen you can leave the default number of 1 build agent to run on the build machine.
4 On the Settings screen, leave the System Account as a user to run the TFS build, and don't change the port (if it's free on your machine).
5 Review the changes that will be made for you, perform the configuration check, and observe the configuration process as it's working. If everything goes well, you're informed about the success on the last wizard screen.

You're finished on the server. Now, switch back to the client and configure the build.

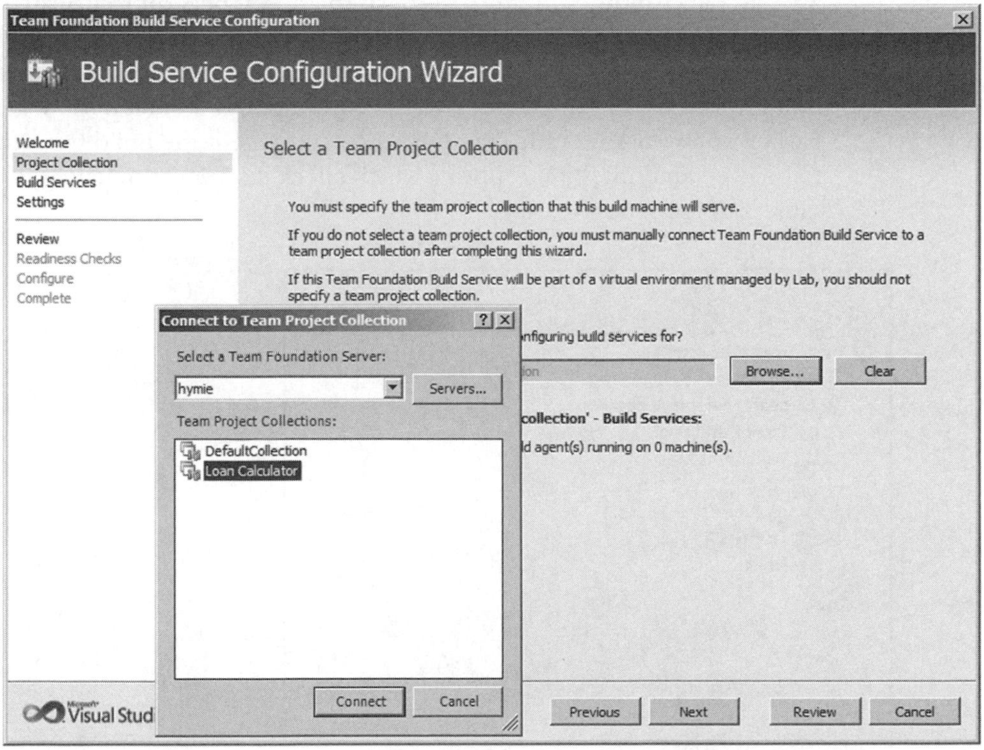

Figure 4.30   While configuring a TFS build agent, you have to choose the project collection that the build machine will serve.

4.5.3 TFS build configuration

Before you can add a build to the build queue, you must define it. You can have as many build definitions as you need. Let's define a CI build for the existing Team project you created in the last chapter (see figure 4.31).

You're by no means limited to a CI kind of build process in TFS 2010. For example, you can have CI builds, scheduled builds, or others. If you create multiple types of builds, we advise using some kind of a prefix like *Ci* for continuous build, *sh* for scheduled, and so on.

After you give the build a name, you can decide what kind of trigger will be used to start the build. See figure 4.32 for the two first steps of the Build Definition Wizard.

You can use five possible build triggers:

- *Manual*—This is in fact not a trigger. It tells TFS not to do anything until the build is submitted manually to the queue.
- *Continuous integration*—This trigger follows the CI principle strictly to build after every check-in.
- *Rolling build*—Rolling builds are suitable if your build is taking longer than the average check-in rate. In other words, if the developers on your team check in more quickly than the build process, you should choose this type of trigger. It accumulates the check-ins and triggers the build after the currently running build finishes. You can also set a rough equivalent of a quiet period, as you saw earlier when working with TeamCity. You can prevent the build from executing for a given amount of time, during which check-ins are accumulated. It isn't the same, but it can do the trick.

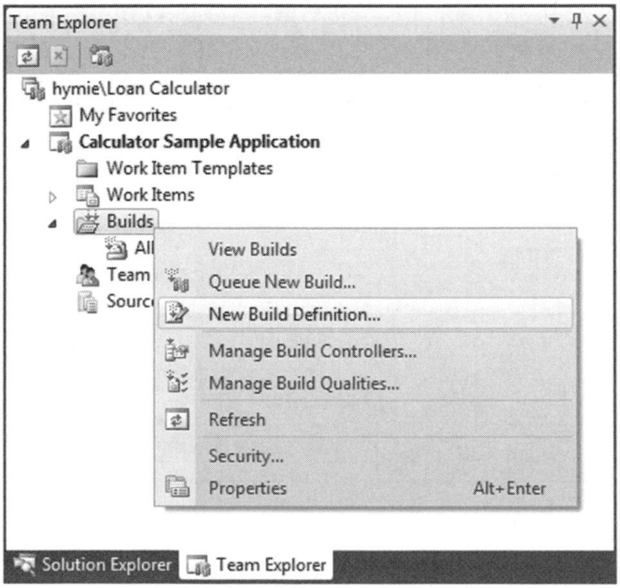

**Figure 4.31
Adding a new build definition to a
Team project in Visual Studio 2010
Team Explorer**

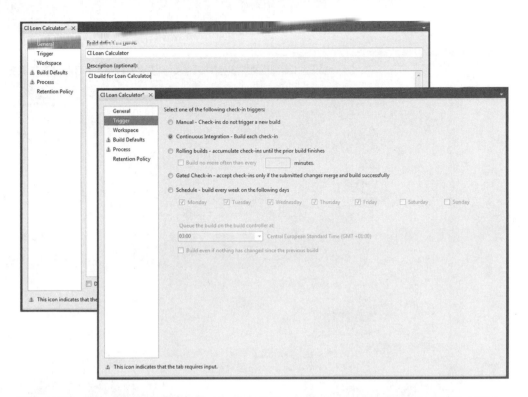

Figure 4.32   Visual Studio 2010 guides you through the creation of a build definition. Assign a name using a convention of some sort that will help you manage a large number of build definitions if you plan to have them. Also choose a trigger type.

- *Gated check-in*—A gated check-in build is a mechanism that prevents bad code from getting into the source code repository. It compiles the code and runs unit tests before check-in. Everything must pass, or the check-in isn't allowed. The gated check-in is similar to the TeamCity pre-tested commit.
- *Schedule*—The scheduled trigger lets you organize your builds; for example, you can do a nightly or weekly build.

In this case, choose a strict CI build. On the Workspace tab, you can define the working folder that the build agent will use and the source control folders it will pull from. Use the defaults unless you have a more complicated source control layout.

On the Build Defaults tab, you choose the Build Controller to be used for this build and the output drop folder where the build agent will copy the build result and the log file. This must be a network share, and you must have enough rights to use it.

A little explanation is needed for the Process tab shown in figure 4.33. The build definition in TFS 2010 is created using XAML and Windows Workflow Foundation. We won't dive into the details in this book; in this case, you'll use the default build template. But if you want to make extensive use of TFS 2010, this is a good opportunity to learn about XAML and Windows Workflow.

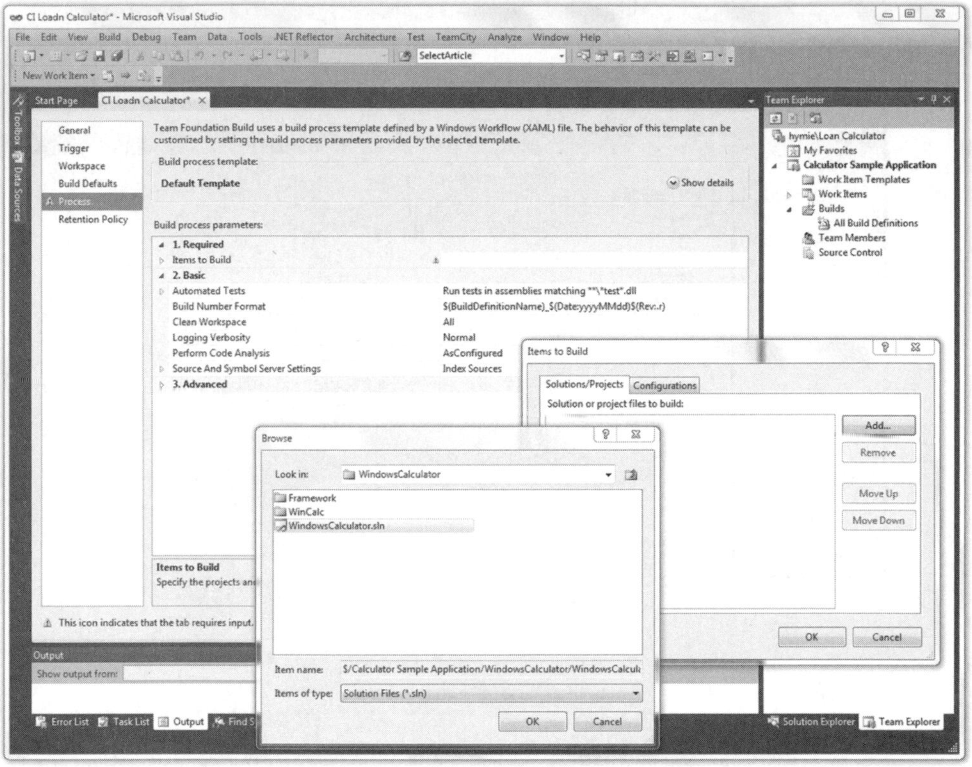

Figure 4.33   When you define a build in TFS, you can use XAML templates. For an ordinary CI process, you can use the default template; but if you want to customize this and that, it's time to get some Workflow Foundation information (you can start at http://msdn.microsoft.com/en-us/vstudio/ aa718795.aspx).

If you stick with the default template, you have to choose the item to be built from the source control repository. It can be a solution file if you wish, or it can be an MSBuild script. Choose Items to Build from the build process parameters (with a small yellow exclamation mark), and click Add on the Solutions/Projects tab. Navigate to the WindowsCalculator.sln file, and choose it. It will be used for the CI build.

The last tab controls the build retention. You define how long build information should be kept for a given build's output.

From now on, your CI build definition runs on the TFS server. Every time you check in something, the build will trigger. To watch the build queue, double-click the build definition in Team Explorer to open the Build Explorer, and choose the Queued tab (see figure 4.34).

You've now defined a CI build process, and it's running on TFS. The build process runs on a build agent and everything is ready for the developers to start work. It's time to move to the next step, defining feedback mechanisms, which we'll look at in chapter 5.

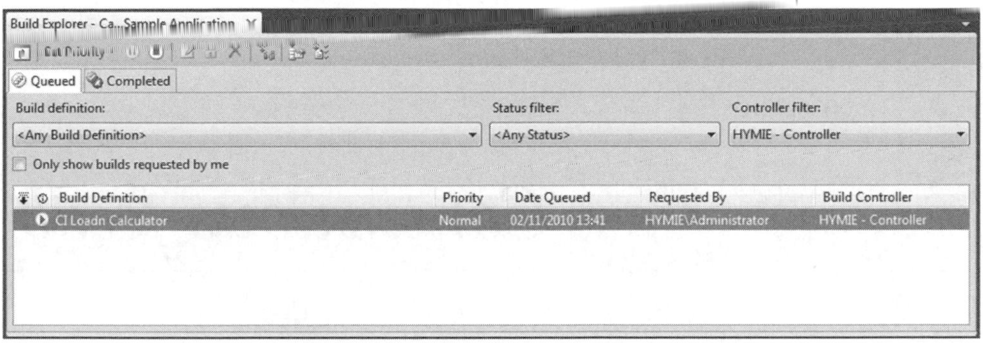

Figure 4.34   You can watch the build queue in Build Explorer. The first build is waiting in the queue.

4.6   Summary

In this chapter, we've talked about using CruiseControl.NET, TeamCity, and TFS 2010 as your CI server. There are others to choose from that we haven't discussed. The market is now in such a state that there's no single obvious tool to use. Some of them are great for small teams and others for enterprise-level development. Some are free; others you must pay for. Some are easy to use, and others put an angle-bracket tax on you. Some are packed with features that solve problems you're not even aware of.

We'll go with a mix of CCNet, TeamCity, and TFS 2010 in the book. We think they're a good ground to lay a foundation under your CI process. CCNet is feature poor, but it's completely open source so you can easily poke around to extend it or to see what's going on inside. It's a good choice for a small team if you like to check things for yourself. TeamCity is free for smaller teams, and it keeps up with the features offered by the Microsoft flagship, TFS.

We know we're throwing a lot of options at you to consider, but you must remember a few important things when considering these CI options. Your CI server shouldn't be a build server. It should provide feedback. It should build quickly and should efficiently give you information whenever the code quality is degrading, there's a problem with your codebase, or your tests are failing. In the next chapter, we'll discuss feedback mechanisms.

Continuous feedback

This chapter covers

- Getting CI feedback from the server
- Getting notifications about the build status
- Using CCNet, TeamCity, and TFS
- Extending build notifications

Picture this. You're about to go on a long-awaited vacation. For months you've planned the best routes for a cross-country trip in your convertible. You've had your car's engine tuned and the oil changed, and you bought new tires for the trip. You should have a smooth drive and a carefree trip. You go to the web for directions, get a map with a detailed route, and study it carefully. One beautiful sunny morning you pack your things, jump in the car, and ... blindfold yourself. Drive carefully!

Do you know what we just described? Your CI process without a feedback mechanism. You seem well prepared. You have your tools ready. You know where you're heading. You seem to know the route, but you don't see the road ahead. You can't see if you drive off the road, and you don't know if you've made a wrong turn. It will be difficult to get to your destination. You're more likely to end up in a ditch or wrapped around a tree.

It's that important to build appropriate controlling mechanisms into your CI process. With continuous feedback, you'll get back the results of every build as soon as it's finished. A well-designed feedback mechanism should do the following:

- Give information about any decrease in code quality
- Be quick
- Provide information in different formats
- Point to the specific place that causes deterioration
- Be accessible to any team member, anytime

You'll probably pack your CI process with tasks that'll examine your code in search of problems. You'll have tests and analysis tasks. They should all be able to produce clear output reports. The reports should be integrated with each other and be available to you on demand.

The process of producing feedback documents and presenting them should be swift. You should be informed about the outcome of the process immediately, so you can react at once.

It's sometimes good to diversify the communication routes from your CI process to the developer. Some people prefer to use tray icons, some want to have the integration feedback within the development environment, and others like to use toys with visual effects. Sometimes it's advisable to diversify the feedback even more; what if you want to be informed about a failing build when you aren't online?

If the build fails, the feedback should be clear about where it failed and why. Information about a problem with the build is useless if you can't see where the problem is so you can react and clean it up.

In this chapter, we'll look at various feedback mechanisms provided by the three CI servers—CCNet, TeamCity, and Team Foundation Server (TFS)—that we've been looking at in this book. The feedback will be provided by web pages, email, and a couple of surprises that we'll save for later in the chapter. We'll show you how to provide immediate feedback mechanisms with tray icons or instant-messaging notifications, and you'll send an email notification. We'll look at detailed build reports to find out why a build failed. You'll make the feedback more visual and send it to developers who are offline. First, let's get the build status.

5.1 Knowing the state of your CI process

Generally, the build process (if it's working) can be in one of three distinct states:

- *Working*—The build is currently doing something. It shouldn't take more than 10 minutes for it to finish its task and transform the state to success or failure.
- *Yet another successful build*—This is the desired state of the integration build. The last integration run was successful. Everything is all right, and everyone can work uninterrupted.

- *Failed*—The last build was interrupted due to a problem. Immediate action is needed to fix something and run another build.

You should ensure that every team member has immediate access to the current build state so that when the build breaks, it can be fixed immediately. One of your goals should be to have as few broken builds as possible, and those that make their way to the CI server should be as loud as possible. The information about broken builds should jump out at the developer. When a team consists of a few developers working together on a few projects, the information should be given to every team member. A broken build should mean

- No one pulls anything from source control. The source is broken, and no one should be interested in broken code.
- Someone should jump in to fix the problem—preferably the person who caused it, but volunteers are welcome.
- All the commits to the repository are withheld until the build is fixed. If you push good code into a spoiled repository, your code may get the smell, too.

In addition to knowing that the build is broken, your team should have easy access to the information about what caused the problem. It'll help them identify the issue and target the effort to fix is as soon as possible.

Software developers should have immediate access to information about what state the process is in. Various tools provide this information; let's examine them.

5.2 Continuous feedback with CruiseControl.NET

CruiseControl.NET, as you may have guessed, is the most difficult of our three CI servers to configure. Build feedback is no exception. The most detailed feedback comes from the CCNet Web Dashboard.

5.2.1 The CCNet Web Dashboard

If you followed our discussion in chapter 4, you should have the CCNet Web Dashboard installed. You can reach it by entering its URL into your web browser. Typically, the URL is something like http://MyServer/ccnet.

The CCNet Web Dashboard (see figure 5.1) is a website that contains information about the state of your CI process. You can install it separately and use it to administer a set of CCNet servers. Web Dashboard works only if the CCNet service or standalone version is running (otherwise, it displays a message about a refused connection). It lists all the projects running on various CCNet servers that are configured to be displayed in a given Web Dashboard installation. The project definitions come from the CCNet configuration file that you learned about in chapter 4.

Next to information about the project's CI state—such as last build state and date, build label, status, and activity indication—are buttons that let you force the build on the server or stop the currently executing integration.

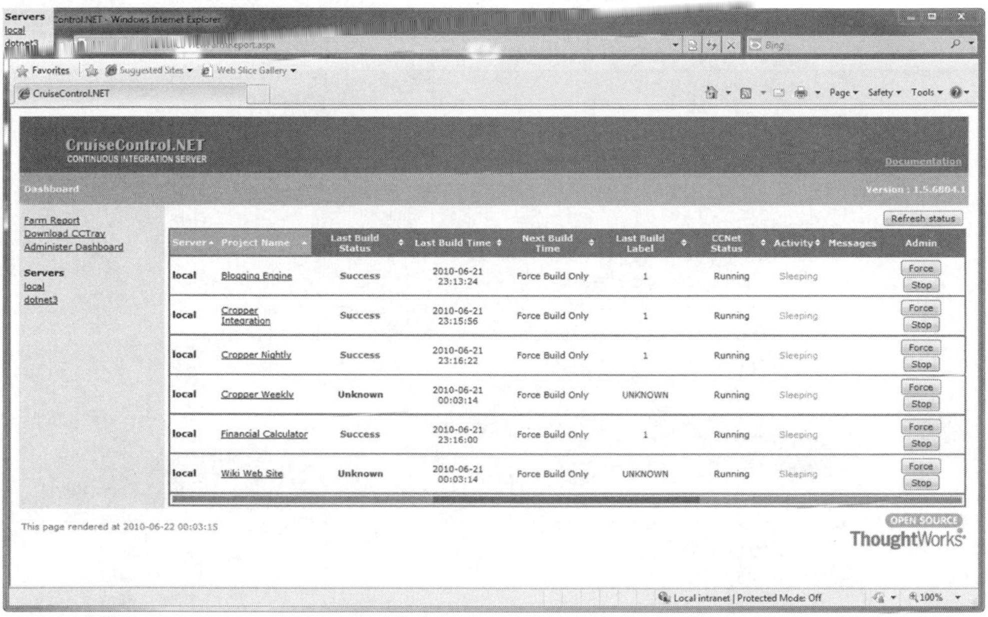

Figure 5.1   The CruiseControl.NET Web Dashboard lets you administer a set of projects. The projects can be hosted on different CCNet servers.

CCNet Web Dashboard information is organized as shown in figure 5.2. At the top is a server farm with all the configured servers connected to the Web Dashboard. You can switch to the server view, which contains information about a given server. If you dig further, you get information about the project; and the most narrow view is of a single build.

Every view is fully configurable and can be extended using plug-ins. You perform the configuration using the dashboard.config file (the default installation places it in the %ProgramFiles%\CruiseControl. NET\webdashboard directory). This is another place where you have to pay the angle-bracket tax: everything is configurable, but you must fight your way through the XML. ThoughtWorks is moving toward web-enabled configuration for CCNet, but the plug-ins aren't ready yet. Until they are, you'll have to look at the plug-ins section of the CCNet documentation (http://confluence.public.thoughtworks.org/display/CCNET/Web+Dashboard). The following listing shows the configuration we're using in this book.

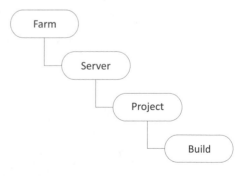

Figure 5.2   The CCNet Web Dashboard is divided into four views. At the top resides the server farm with all the configured servers, and at the bottom is specific build information.

Listing 5.1   A sample CCNet configuration file

```xml
<?xml version="1.0" encoding="utf-8"?>
<dashboard>
  <remoteServices>
    <servers>
      <server name="local"
        url="tcp://localhost:21234/CruiseManager.rem"
        allowForceBuild="true" allowStartStopBuild="true"
        backwardsCompatible="false" />
      <server name="dotnet3"
        url="tcp://dotnet3:21234/CruiseManager.rem"
        allowForceBuild="true" allowStartStopBuild="true"
        backwardsCompatible="true" />
    </servers>
  </remoteServices>
  <plugins>
    <farmPlugins>
      <farmReportFarmPlugin />
      <cctrayDownloadPlugin />
    </farmPlugins>
    <serverPlugins>
      <serverReportServerPlugin />
      <serverLogServerPlugin />
    </serverPlugins>
    <projectPlugins>
      <projectReportProjectPlugin />
      <viewProjectStatusPlugin />
      <latestBuildReportProjectPlugin />
      <viewAllBuildsProjectPlugin />
      <viewConfigurationProjectPlugin>
      </viewConfigurationProjectPlugin>
    </projectPlugins>
    <buildPlugins>
      <buildReportBuildPlugin>
        <xslFileNames>
          <xslFile>xsl\header.xsl</xslFile>
          <xslFile>xsl\modifications.xsl</xslFile>
        </xslFileNames>
      </buildReportBuildPlugin>
      <buildLogBuildPlugin />
      <xslReportBuildPlugin
        description="FxCop Report"
        actionName="FxCopBuildReport"
        xslFileName="xsl\FxCopReport.xsl" />
      <xslReportBuildPlugin
        description="NUnit Details"
        actionName="NUnitDetailsBuildReport"
        xslFileName="xsl\tests.xsl" />
      <xslReportBuildPlugin
        description="NUnit Timings"
        actionName="NUnitTimingsBuildReport"
        xslFileName="xsl\timing.xsl" />
      <xslReportBuildPlugin
        description="FxCop Report"
```

1 Defines servers

2 Farm-level plug-ins

3 Server-level plug-ins

4 Project-level plug-ins

5 Build-level plug-ins

```
          actionName="FxCopBuildReport"
          xslFileName="xsl\FxCopReport.xsl" />
        <xslReportBuildPlugin
          description="NCover Report"
          actionName="NCoverBuildReport"
          xslFileName="xsl\NCover.xsl" />
        <xslReportBuildPlugin
          description="Fitnesse Report"
          actionName="FitnesseBuildReport"
          xslFileName="xsl\fitnesse.xsl"/>
        <xslReportBuildPlugin
          description="MSBuild Report"
          actionName="MSBuildBuildReport"
          xslFileName="xsl\msbuild.xsl"/>
      </buildPlugins>
    </plugins>
</dashboard>
```

⑤ **Build-level
plug-ins**

This configuration file defines two servers ❶: localhost and dotnet3. The Web Dashboard communicates with them using a remoting endpoint. You can define as many servers as you like. You separately configure all the view levels for the server farm ❷, for the servers themselves ❸, for the projects ❹, and for the builds ❺. This example sets up several build reports to be included in the Web Dashboard feedback. If you look closely, you'll see several tools like NUnit, FitNesse, FxCop, and others that we haven't discussed yet. Don't worry about what these tools are and what they do; we'll discuss them in upcoming chapters. Figure 5.3 shows the build-level view at the CCNet Web Dashboard as configured from listing 5.1.

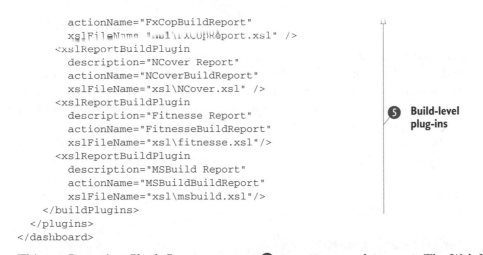

Figure 5.3   All the detail levels of CCNet views in action

When you first install CCNet, none of the build reports from other applications are included. You need to activate them through the Administrator Dashboard. Before the first time you use the Web Dashboard, you have to edit the dashboard.config file (you'll find it in %ProgramFiles%\CruiseControl.NET\webdashboard) and change the initial password in the <administrationPlugin> tag. When you're finished, click the link in the Web Dashboard's main page, enter the Administrator password, and then enable the tool reports you want to include in the Web Dashboard report.

As you can see, you can have full control over the CCNet Web Dashboard. You can write your own plug-ins or obtain plug-ins from the internet. But to have so much control, you have to pay a small administration cost. The Web Dashboard gives you detailed information, and you can use CCTray to get a quick snapshot of what's happening on your build server.

5.2.2   *Getting feedback with CCTray*

CCTray is an application that's installed on each developer's workstation. You can download it from the home page of your CCNet Web Dashboard or directly from the ThoughtWorks website at http://ccnet.thoughtworks.com/. It sits in the Windows Notification area, commonly called the *Task Tray*. It manifests itself with this icon: CC. To configure CCTray, open it (double-click the icon) and choose File > Settings (see figure 5.4).

You need to configure the noise level here as well. You don't want to be interrupted by messages about projects in which you have no interest. Try to keep the noise level as small as possible. Allow only information that's necessary to help you react when the

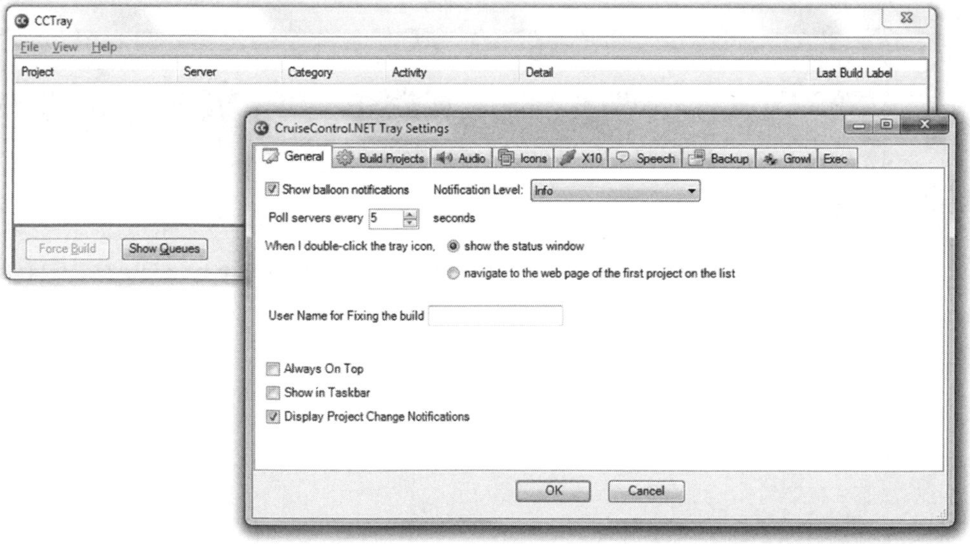

Figure 5.4   When you double-click CCTray, you access CruiseControl.NET and the CCTray configuration settings.

code quality degrades. Choose only the projects you need to see (see figure 5.5). On a fresh installation, you need to add a new CCNet server. To do so, go to settings (File > Settings) and click the Build Projects tab. Click the Add button. In the Project window, click Add Server. The easiest way to connect the CCNet server is over a dashboard: type the CCNet dashboard URL in the window. Keep in mind that if you're connecting to the CCNet server from another machine, you must add a firewall exception (port 80 on a standard IIS installation).

CCTray uses a red/green indicator, similar to what you find in unit test tools. A green tray icon indicates that everything is running fine. A red CCTray icon 🆑 means you have to act. First, you must know where the problem is. The best way to get this information is via Web Dashboard. You can reach the CCNet Web Dashboard directly from CCTray: right-click one of the configured projects, and choose Display Web Page, as shown in figure 5.6.

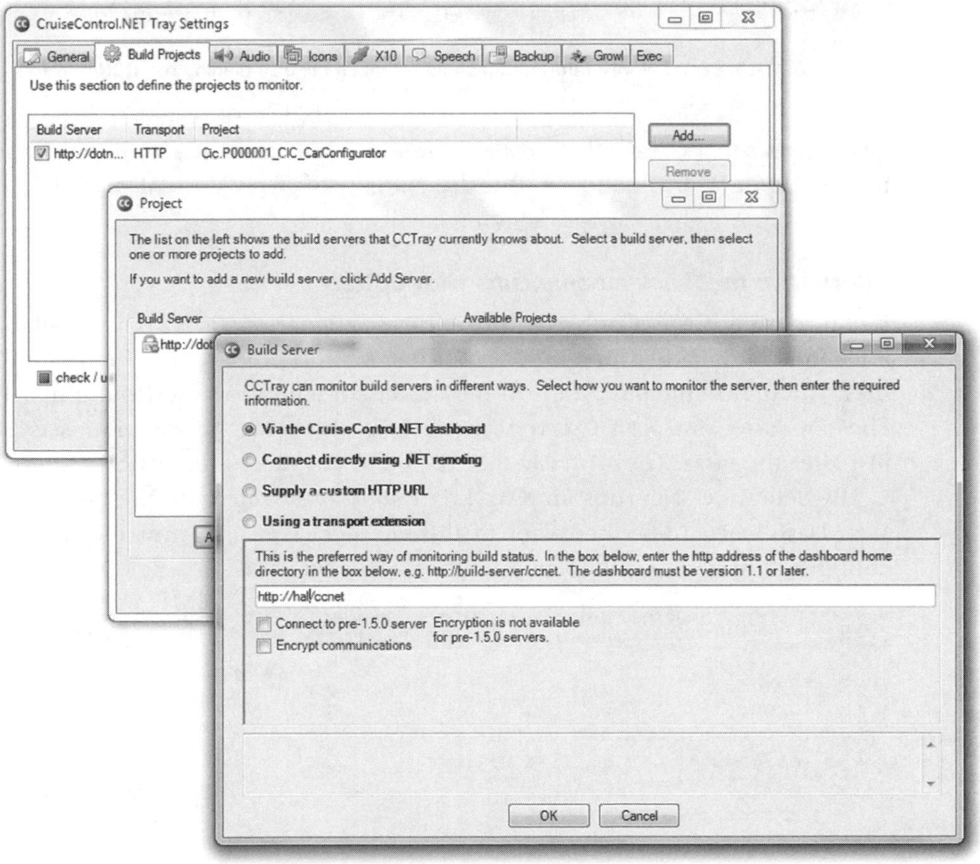

Figure 5.5   Configuring CCTray. One CCTray benefit is the ability to work with more than one CruiseControl.NET server.

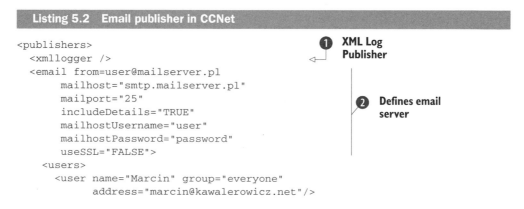

Figure 5.6   Using CCTray with information about a broken build to display the CCNet Web Dashboard

As you can see, CCTray offers lots of power and information without ever connecting to the CCNet Web Dashboard. But these aren't the only ways of providing feedback with CCNet. Another way is to sending email.

5.2.3   *Alternative feedback mechanisms with CCNet*

If you're using CruiseControl.NET, you can configure *publishers*. These publishers run after the build, gather integration information, and prepare it to be presented to the user. You define the publishers in the CCNet configuration file (found in %Program-Files%\CruiseControl.NET\server\ccnet.config—for more information, see chapter 4) just after the tasks. They run whether the build was successful or not.

By default, CCNet runs an XML Log Publisher to integrate the build output with Web Dashboard (described later in this chapter). You can override the publisher's configuration and use an email publisher, as shown next.

Listing 5.2   Email publisher in CCNet

```
<publishers>
  <xmllogger />                                    ❶ XML Log
  <email from=user@mailserver.pl                       Publisher
      mailhost="smtp.mailserver.pl"
      mailport="25"
      includeDetails="TRUE"                        ❷ Defines email
      mailhostUsername="user"                          server
      mailhostPassword="password"
      useSSL="FALSE">
    <users>
      <user name="Marcin" group="everyone"
          address="marcin@kawalerowicz.net"/>
```

```
      <user name="craig" group="everyone"
          address="craig@craigberntson.com"/>
    </users>
    <groups>
      <group name="everyone">
        <notifications>
          <notificationType>Failed</notificationType>
          <notificationType>Fixed</notificationType>
        </notifications>
      </group>
    </groups>
    <subjectSettings>
      <subject buildResult="Broken" value="${CCNetProject}
          broke at ${CCNetBuildDate}
          ${CCNetBuildTime } , last checkin(s)
          by ${CCNetFailureUsers}" />
      <subject buildResult="StillBroken"
          value="Build is still broken for ${CCNetProject}" />
      <subject buildResult="Fixed"
          value="Build fixed for ${CCNetProject}" />
    </subjectSettings>
  </email>
</publishers>
```

If you'll be using the Web Dashboard, you have to integrate the build output with it. Because you're explicitly defining the publishers, you must provide the default XML Log Publisher before any other publisher in your list ❶. Then you define the email publisher ❷, providing all the necessary information about the mail server you want to use. After that, you define the users who will be getting the emails and decide what group they belong to. Depending on the group, you can narrow the information they receive. You can create a group that gets every email, or you can make a group, as in this example, that only receives information about failing and fixed builds. You can even customize the messages' subject lines.

Many predefined publishers are available for you to use. You can clean up your construction site before the next integration, generate an RSS feed to be integrated into the Web Dashboard, send a message to another CCNet instance to start a dependent project, and much more.

Now that you've seen how to get feedback from CCNet, let's discuss how to get the same information from TeamCity.

5.3   *Continuous feedback with TeamCity*

TeamCity, like CCNet, provides detailed build information via a website and a tray application; it also gives you alternate ways to provide feedback. Configuring the different methods is decidedly easier than in CCNet. Let's start with TeamCity's web features.

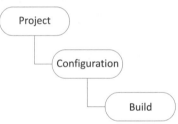

Figure 5.7   The Projects page in TeamCity shows all configured projects.

5.3.1   *TeamCity web feedback*

TeamCity build feedback is merged together with project administration. You do both with a single website that you learned about in chapter 4. All configured projects are visible on the Projects tab (figure 5.7).

As you can see in figure 5.8, TeamCity allows you to create projects with various configurations. For example, you can have a project that builds once as a CI process after every source code change and once as a build runner.

TeamCity provides detailed information about the build. This information is divided into tabs. By default, only a few are available: general and detailed build information, change details, and so on. If you want to integrate additional information with the build page, you can configure additional tabs. If you do so on the server level, the tabs are available for all projects. The tabs configured on the project level are visible only in a given project.

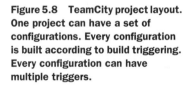

Figure 5.8   TeamCity project layout. One project can have a set of configurations. Every configuration is built according to build triggering. Every configuration can have multiple triggers.

For the purpose of presentation, let's create a (very) hypothetical demand. Let's say you want your build script to generate a file containing all the build parameters listed. To do this, you can use the `echo` command and redirect the output to a file. The following listing shows the MSBuild script that uses this `echo` command to create a file called msbuildvariables.txt that contains some configuration values ($(Configuration) and $(Platform) in this case).

Listing 5.3   Sample TeamCity build script

```
<Project DefaultTargets="Build"
  xmlns="http://schemas.microsoft.com/developer/msbuild/2003">
  <PropertyGroup>
    <Configuration
      Condition=" '$(Configuration)' == '' ">
```

```
      Debug
    </Configuration>
    <Platform Condition=" '$(Platform)' == '' ">"Any CPU"</Platform>
  </PropertyGroup>
  <Target Name="Build">
    <MSBuild Targets="Clean;Rebuild"
      Projects="WinCalculator.sln" ContinueOnError="false" />
    <Exec Command="echo Variables used to in build script:
      ➥Configuration= $(Configuration) Platform= $(Platform)>
    msbuildvariables.txt">
    </Exec>
  </Target>
</Project>
```
Creates file with variables list

Add a new tab to the project information page for this file on the server level (see figure 5.9). The new tab will be visible to all of your projects hosted in TeamCity (provided the build process creates an artifact called msbuildvariables.txt).

If TeamCity runs the script from listing 5.3, a file named msbuildvariables.txt is created in the current working directory. This file will be deleted after the build is finished. That's of course not what you want—you want to see the list of MSBuild variables on a tab in TeamCity. You need to tell TeamCity that the text file you're

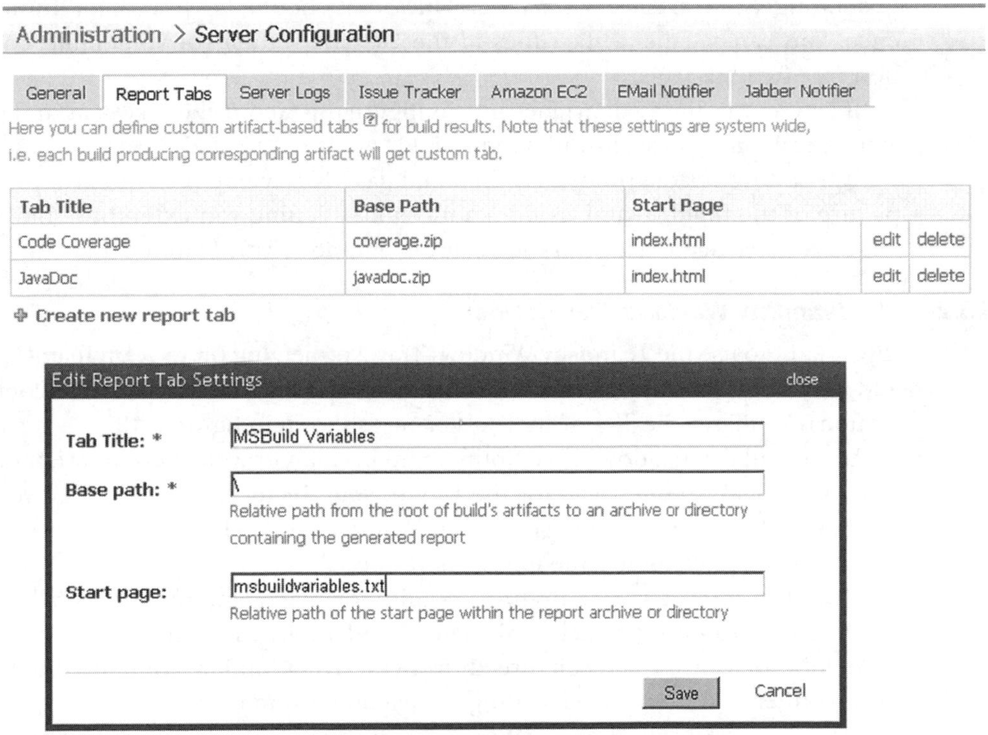

Figure 5.9   Adding a new tab to the build results at the server level. Every time TeamCity finds the file msbuildvariables.txt in the current build directory, it will add a tab containing the file's content.

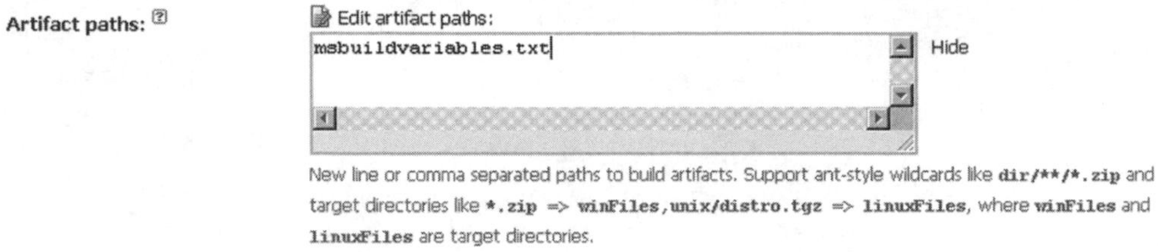

Artifact paths: ⊘

🖉 Edit artifact paths:

```
msbuildvariables.txt
```

Hide

New line or comma separated paths to build artifacts. Support ant-style wildcards like `dir/**/*.zip` and target directories like `*.zip => winFiles,unix/distro.tgz => linuxFiles`, where `winFiles` and `linuxFiles` are target directories.

Figure 5.10   Setting an artifact file in the General settings of a project's configuration in TeamCity

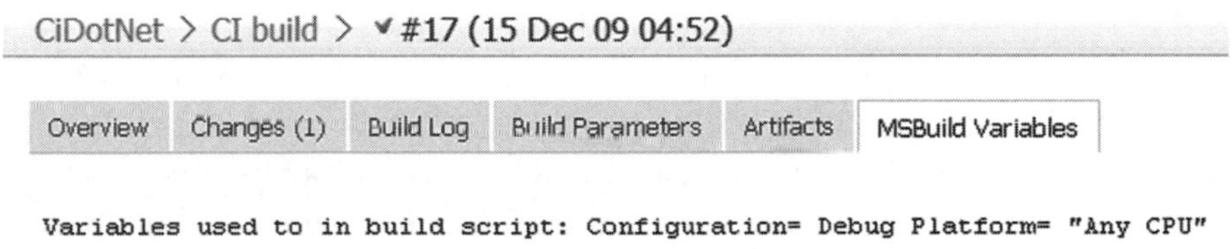

CiDotNet > CI build > ⌄ #17 (15 Dec 09 04:52)

| Overview | Changes (1) | Build Log | Build Parameters | Artifacts | MSBuild Variables |

```
Variables used to in build script: Configuration= Debug Platform= "Any CPU"
```

Figure 5.11   A custom tab on the TeamCity build-report page, containing an artifact text file with a list of MSBuild variables

generating is an artifact. *Artifacts* are files that should be stored for future reference. You can set the artifact files in the General settings of your build configuration (see figure 5.10).

If you set this file as an artifact and configure the tab for the server, as in figure 5.7, you'll get a build tab as shown in figure 5.11.

Integrating custom reports on the build page is very important to give you the big picture of the build. TeamCity does a nice job of letting you extend the build-report pages. Now we need to look at the TeamCity Windows Tray Notifier.

5.3.2   *The TeamCity Windows Tray Notifier*

If you want to use the TeamCity Windows Tray Notifier, log on to your TeamCity server and switch to My Settings & Tools (at the top of the page, beneath the Welcome information). You'll see the TeamCity Tools pane, as shown in figure 5.12.

Download the Windows Tray Notifier and install it on your development machine. The installer will prompt you for the URL to your TeamCity server. When you're finished, you'll see the new icon 🕐 in your Windows Tray. The question mark indicates that you need to configure the notification rule.

TeamCity provides a centralized notification-management site for all feedback mechanisms. To turn it on, click My Setting and Tools, and switch to the Notification Rules tab. You can also select it directly from the Tray Notifier. Configure the Windows Tray Notifier to suit your needs, using the page shown in figure 5.13.

Deciding what kind of notifications to let through is crucial for your reaction time. Remember that letting too much information through the Tray Notifier will most likely blunt your attention span. You should let through only as much information as

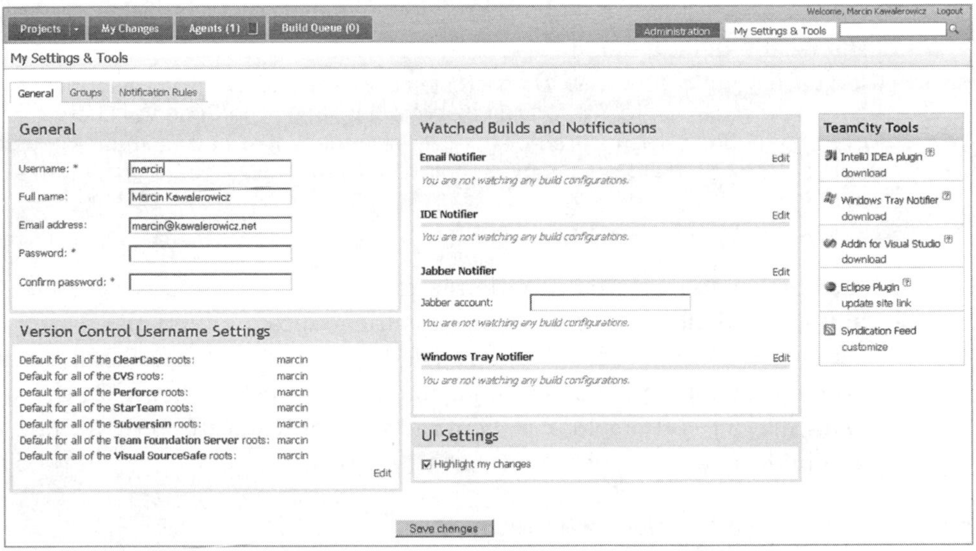

Figure 5.12 The notification possibilities in TeamCity are generous. It provides email, IDE plug-ins, instant messaging, and tray notifications.

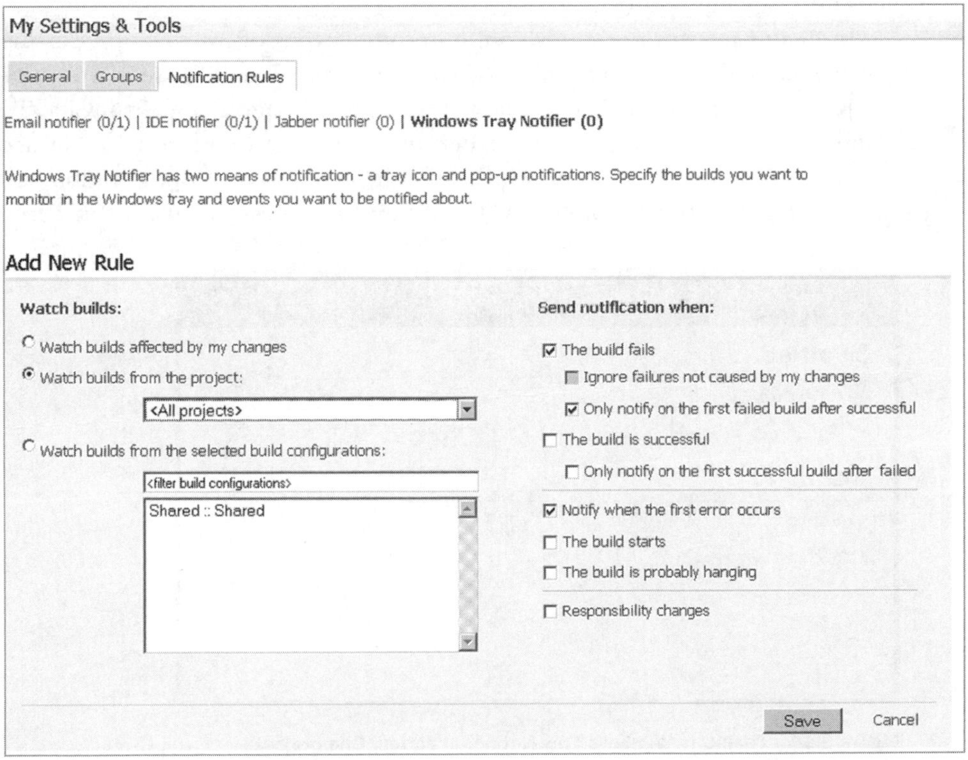

Figure 5.13 Configuring the TeamCity Windows Tray Notifier for the currently logged-in user

> **Blame the build breaker**
>
> It's usually not a good idea to watch only changes caused by your actions. Project health is usually a group effort, and a broken build on the CI server should concern everybody. Some teams are going with crazy ideas like having the last person to cause a broken build wear a funny hat or pay into a piggy bank for a future team activity!

needed for you to react. You're obviously not interested in projects you aren't working with. It's a good idea to let only the first failure notification through.

After you configure the TeamCity Windows Tray Notifier, you can use it to get information about the projects running under TeamCity (see figure 5.14).

This doesn't end our look at notification with TeamCity. Let's see how to send email notifications.

5.3.3   *Alternative notifications with TeamCity*

If you've chosen TeamCity as your CI server, email notification is easy to turn on. Log in to your TeamCity site, go to My Settings & Tools, switch to the Notification Rules tab, and add a new email notification. Voila! Email notification for your account is activated (see figure 5.15).

In TeamCity, you can easily configure other types of information passing. If you use the Jabber-based communicator, you can make TeamCity send you notification on Jabber. Figure 5.16 shows a Jabber success message from TeamCity. To get an instant notification over the Jabber network, you have to assign a Jabber account to the server. To do this, go to Administration, choose Server Configuration, and switch to the Jabber Notified tab. TeamCity will send the messages from this account. You

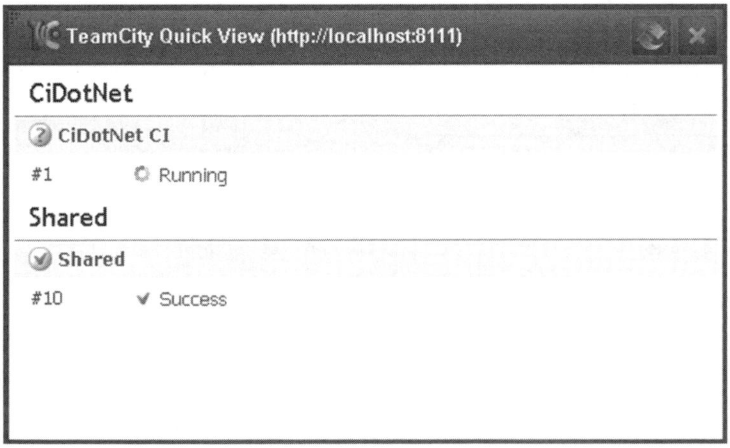

Figure 5.14   TeamCity Windows Tray Notifier in action. One project is currently running while another rests happily in a success state.

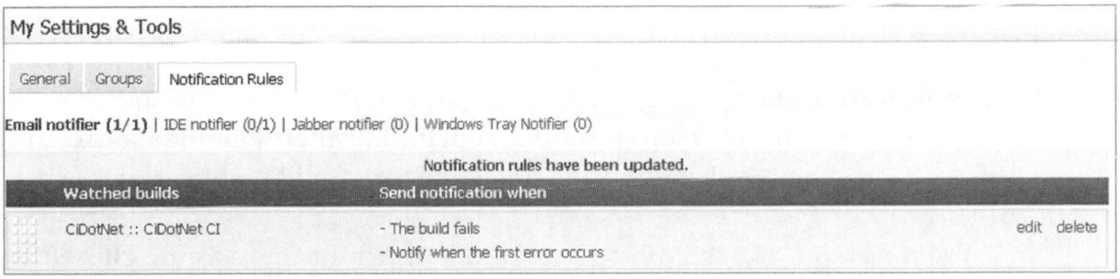

Figure 5.15 TeamCity with configured email notification. You can configure additional notifications just as easily.

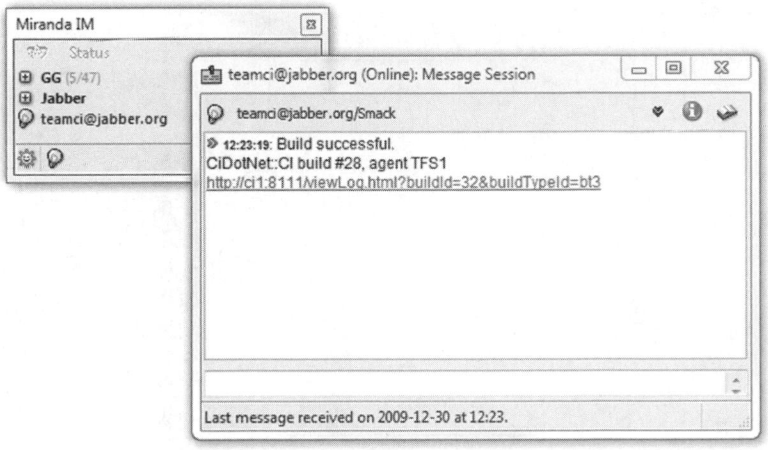

Figure 5.16 Jabber notification from TeamCity in the Miranda IM communicator. The TeamCity server uses its Jabber account (teamci) to send you a notification message.

can provide your account name in the My Setting & Tools section under Notification Rules.

As you can see, TeamCity directly supports several alternative notification methods, and they're easier to configure than with CCNet. Next, let's see how to configure TFS to provide build feedback.

5.4 *Continuous feedback with Team Foundation Server*

As you saw earlier in the chapter, configuring feedback can be easy, as with TeamCity, or more complicated, as with CCNet. TFS is in the easy-to-configure camp—it's even easier than TeamCity.

TFS Basic has a limitation: it doesn't support alternative feedback methods. If you're using the full TFS, you're in luck: it does support them. Let's start our discussion of TFS feedback by looking at tray notification.

5.4.1　*TFS tray notification*

TFS 2010 uses Build Notification, which is installed along with Visual Studio 2010. You can start it from the Start menu. It resides in the Team Foundation Server Tools subfolder. After initial execution, it starts automatically when Windows starts, and displays this icon: ▦. Double-click the icon, and configure Build Notification as shown in figure 5.17.

From now on, TFS Build Notification will display changes to the chosen build definitions (see figure 5.18).

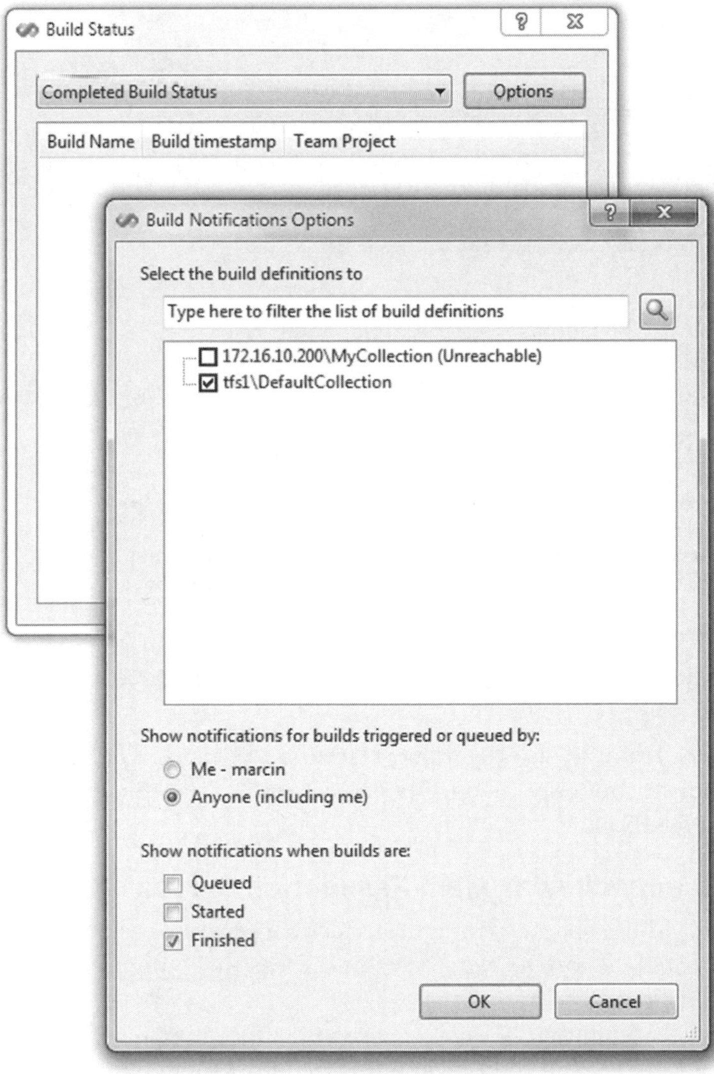

Figure 5.17　Choosing which build definitions to watch in TFS Build Notification

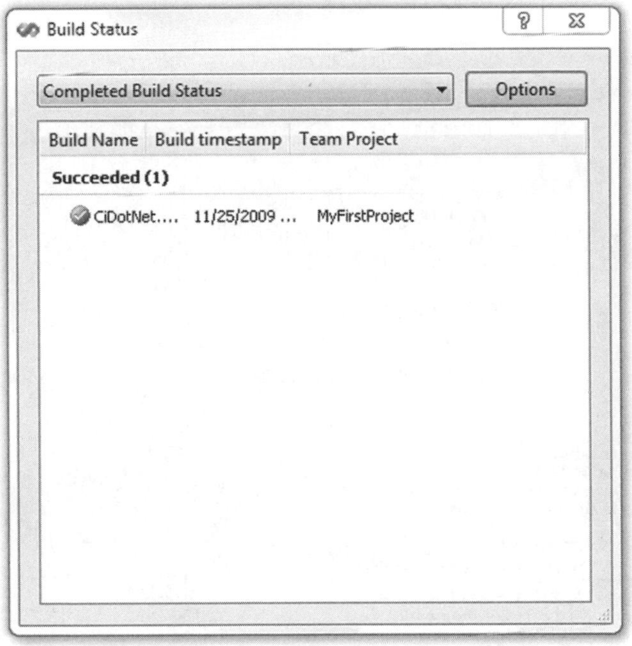

**Figure 5.18
TFS Build Notification
showing build results**

Tray notification is a convenient way to get information about the state of the integration. Let's see how to handle web notification with TFS.

5.4.2 Getting build details from the TFS website

The easiest way to get to the build-details page in TFS is through the Build Notification feature. Double-click the build you're interested in, and you'll get the build report shown in figure 5.19.

That's it! TFS provides full build information for your project without any additional configuration. But what about email notification? It's also supported by TFS.

5.4.3 Alternative feedback mechanisms with TFS

Unfortunately, TFS 2010 in its Basic configuration, which works with SQL Server Express, has no reporting services installed. If you're using this configuration, you can't extend the notification functionality. But if you're using any of the more advanced configurations, you're good to go.

TFS 2010 is extensible with regard to notification. It uses a notification database to manage notification subscriptions. You can subscribe to a set of events using, for example, email or a web service. If the event is raised, the subscriber is notified. You manage subscriptions using the provided API or a command-line tool called BisSubscribe. Let's use the second option to create an email notifier for your build configuration.

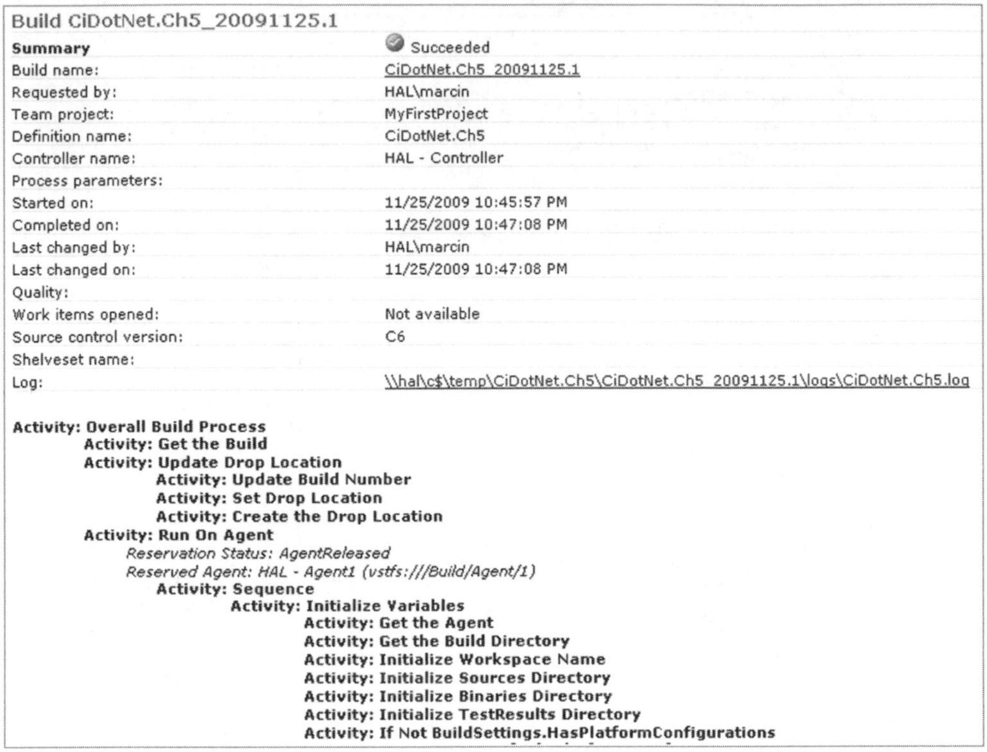

Build CiDotNet.Ch5_20091125.1

Summary	Succeeded
Build name:	CiDotNet.Ch5_20091125.1
Requested by:	HAL\marcin
Team project:	MyFirstProject
Definition name:	CiDotNet.Ch5
Controller name:	HAL - Controller
Process parameters:	
Started on:	11/25/2009 10:45:57 PM
Completed on:	11/25/2009 10:47:08 PM
Last changed by:	HAL\marcin
Last changed on:	11/25/2009 10:47:08 PM
Quality:	
Work items opened:	Not available
Source control version:	C6
Shelveset name:	
Log:	\\hal\c$\temp\CiDotNet.Ch5\CiDotNet.Ch5_20091125.1\logs\CiDotNet.Ch5.log

Activity: Overall Build Process
Activity: Get the Build
Activity: Update Drop Location
Activity: Update Build Number
Activity: Set Drop Location
Activity: Create the Drop Location
Activity: Run On Agent
Reservation Status: AgentReleased
Reserved Agent: HAL - Agent1 (vstfs:///Build/Agent/1)
Activity: Sequence
Activity: Initialize Variables
Activity: Get the Agent
Activity: Get the Build Directory
Activity: Initialize Workspace Name
Activity: Initialize Sources Directory
Activity: Initialize Binaries Directory
Activity: Initialize TestResults Directory
Activity: If Not BuildSettings.HasPlatformConfigurations

Figure 5.19 The TFS build report is produced automatically for you. No additional configuration is necessary.

BisSubscribe.exe is installed along with TFS 2010. You can find it in %Program Files%\Microsoft Team Foundation Server 2010\Tools. To subscribe to an event that notifies you about build completion, issue the following command:

```
BisSubscribe.exe
➥/eventType BuildCompletionEvent
➥/address marcin@kawalerowicz.net
➥/deliveryType EmailHtml
➥/collection http://tfs1:8080/tfs/CiDotNet
```

This command says that when the build of the `CiDotNet` collection is completed, TFS should send an HTML-formatted email to the recipient.

The downside of email notification is that it requires you to be online to receive the information. What if you want to be woken up during the night to be notified about a failing build? Why not text the information to your cell phone? And how about making the notification fun? Let's extend the notification abilities with some other interesting options.

5.5 Extending build notifications

A build notification tells you the results of a build. Did it succeed? Did it fail? And if it failed, why? And which module caused the failure? CI servers have a rich notification repertoire. Windows tray icons, emails, instant messaging, and IDE plug-ins are just some of the possibilities. It's a proof for the thesis that build notification is one of the most important parts of CI.

It's so important that some CI practitioners sacrifice an additional monitor or even a whole machine to provide constant monitoring for the team. It's usually an old computer with an old monitor that stands in a visible place in the developers' room or some place where everybody can see it. The sole purpose of this machine is to provide the team with up-to-date information about the build processes. The dashboard page may refresh every few minutes, or special custom software may monitor the CI server. If your team can benefit from something like this, set it up. Or get geeky and use the following LED message board to provide a broken-build notification.

5.5.1 Providing feedback via an LED message board

An LED message board is a gadget that comes from a big family of crazy USB toys from the China Seas area. The one this example uses is a matrix of 7 x 21 LED lights sealed in a small black plastic casing (sometimes called a *human interface device* [HID]). If you aren't a USB geek, the only thing you have to know is that the HID driver makes it easy to interact programmatically with a HID-enabled device. If you want to buy one, you can search for "USB LED message board" from Dream Cheeky.

Let's write a simple program that checks the state of the builds on a TFS server. If it finds a broken build, it'll display a blinking red circle on the LED message board. This should be hard to miss if the board is in the developers' room.

First, let's find out whether the last build in a given build definition was broken. The following listing shows the details.

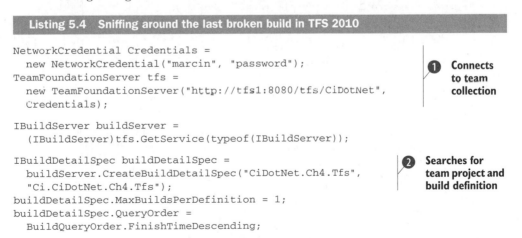

Listing 5.4 Sniffing around the last broken build in TFS 2010

```
NetworkCredential Credentials =
   new NetworkCredential("marcin", "password");           ❶ Connects
TeamFoundationServer tfs =                                    to team
   new TeamFoundationServer("http://tfs1:8080/tfs/CiDotNet",  collection
   Credentials);

IBuildServer buildServer =
   (IBuildServer)tfs.GetService(typeof(IBuildServer));

IBuildDetailSpec buildDetailSpec =                         ❷ Searches for
   buildServer.CreateBuildDetailSpec("CiDotNet.Ch4.Tfs",     team project and
   "Ci.CiDotNet.Ch4.Tfs");                                   build definition
buildDetailSpec.MaxBuildsPerDefinition = 1;
buildDetailSpec.QueryOrder =
   BuildQueryOrder.FinishTimeDescending;
```

```
IBuildQueryResult results =
  buildServer.QueryBuilds(buildDetailSpec);

if (results.Failures.Length == 0
&& results.Builds.Length == 1)
{
  IBuildDetail buildDetail = results.Builds[0];
  if (buildDetail.Status == BuildStatus.Failed)
  {
    MyLedNotify();
  }
}
```

❸ Gets last build

❹ Turns on red light

This example uses the `Microsoft.TeamFoundation` API to sniff for the latest build output. You use the `Microsoft.TeamFoundation`, `Microsoft.TeamFoundation.Client`, and `Microsoft.TeamFoundation.Build.Client` namespaces to first connect to the TFS server and team collection using network credentials ❶. Then you get the build server from the TFS instance and query it for a given team project and build definition ❷. You take only the last build result ❸ and check its state. If it fails, you turn on the big red dot ❹, as shown in the next listing.

Listing 5.5 Using an LED message board to notify you about a broken build

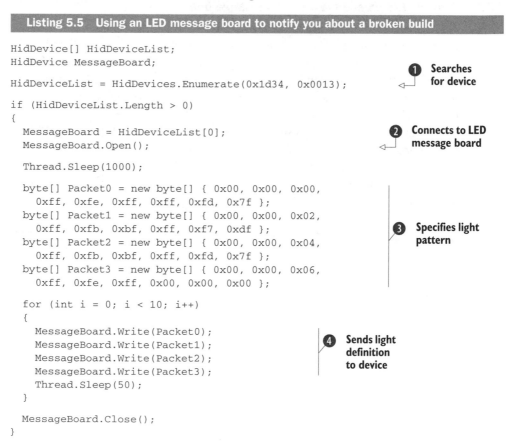

```
HidDevice[] HidDeviceList;
HidDevice MessageBoard;

HidDeviceList = HidDevices.Enumerate(0x1d34, 0x0013);

if (HidDeviceList.Length > 0)
{
  MessageBoard = HidDeviceList[0];
  MessageBoard.Open();

  Thread.Sleep(1000);

  byte[] Packet0 = new byte[] { 0x00, 0x00, 0x00,
    0xff, 0xfe, 0xff, 0xff, 0xfd, 0x7f };
  byte[] Packet1 = new byte[] { 0x00, 0x00, 0x02,
    0xff, 0xfb, 0xbf, 0xff, 0xf7, 0xdf };
  byte[] Packet2 = new byte[] { 0x00, 0x00, 0x04,
    0xff, 0xfb, 0xbf, 0xff, 0xfd, 0x7f };
  byte[] Packet3 = new byte[] { 0x00, 0x00, 0x06,
    0xff, 0xfe, 0xff, 0x00, 0x00, 0x00 };

  for (int i = 0; i < 10; i++)
  {
    MessageBoard.Write(Packet0);
    MessageBoard.Write(Packet1);
    MessageBoard.Write(Packet2);
    MessageBoard.Write(Packet3);
    Thread.Sleep(50);
  }

  MessageBoard.Close();
}
```

❶ Searches for device

❷ Connects to LED message board

❸ Specifies light pattern

❹ Sends light definition to device

NOTE The HID interface isn't a topic of this book. Suffice to say that this example uses a generic .NET HID device library from Mike O'Brien (http://labs.mikeobrien.net/Document.aspx?id=hidlibrary). The library provides a way to connect and use any HID-enabled device. All you have to do is to get a manual for the interface used in this device. The manufacturer of our LED message board is kind enough to provide one when asked.

To connect a HID device, you have to find it ❶ using a unique identifier provided by the manufacturer. After you find the device, you must connect to it ❷ and wait a while for the hardware to snap in. Next, you define the big red dot using a report formatted according to the manufacturer's interface description ❸. For now, you'll have to believe us that the lights form a big red dot on the LED message board. You then send the light definition to the device ❹, after which the device will look like the one shown in figure 5.20. The packets sent to the LED message board light up the device for only a few milliseconds, so you have to refresh the signal to light it up periodically.

It doesn't cost much to provide a new way to notify your team about a problem. Buying a flashing roof light from an emergency vehicle and installing it in the developers' room is an even better idea (of course, including the siren!). But because the Taiwanese LED device is a lot cheaper (around $10 to $20), you can start with it. It's that important to react immediately to a broken build.

Figure 5.20   LED message board blinking with a red eye to tell you about a failed build

What if the blinking lights, emails, and sirens aren't doing the job? How about something more intrusive? Send an SMS message to every team member.

5.5.2   *Providing feedback via SMS notifications*

It's a little scary idea to send someone an SMS message with a build notification. But what if you're on vacation climbing Mount Kilimanjaro, and you want to know if your team is dealing with the broken build fast enough? No problem. You can take the easy route and send yourself an SMS message using Skype and an online computer in your office. Here's how.

Skype provides a COM library to automate some of its tasks. One of the methods provided by this API is `SendSms`, which you'll use here. This method requires you to have Skype installed and some money in your Skype account, because unfortunately SMS isn't free.

> **NOTE**   You can download the Skype library from https://developer.skype. com/. Check the Tools and SDK area.

To do the build-state sniffing, you can use a variation of the program shown earlier in listing 5.4. The hitch is to detect only the change in the state of the build from successful to broken, and then send one SMS message. After such an event, it's a matter of implementing the following code to send the SMS message:

```
Skype Skype = new Skype();
if (Skype.Client.IsRunning)
{
  Skype.Client.Start();
}
Skype.SendSms(PhoneNumber, Message);
```

From now on, you can sleep well, knowing that an SMS message will alert you if something goes wrong with your build. Isn't that comforting?

5.6   *Summary*

Access to immediate and accurate information about the state of your build process is vital to your CI quality. The faster you get the information about a change in the quality of your source code, the more quickly you can react to fix the problem. The faster you fix the problem, the better your team will work. You'll know where you journey is taking you and whether your project is starting to veer off the road.

In this chapter, you learned that you should employ a variety of methods to notify your team about the current build status. The most common technique is a website that reports detailed integration information.

Using a tray notifier is good for providing quick updates to a developer's workstation. At a glance, each team member can know whether a build is broken or things are running smoothly.

Sometimes it's useful to send information about the build status to offline team members. SMS notification may be advisable for mission-critical applications that should build correctly all the time.

You may also want to explore different notification methods such as lights, message boards, RSS feeds, or even messages to team members' instant messaging and Skype accounts.

Now that you've seen how to get feedback to your team, it's time to turn our attention to the last piece of a basic CI process: unit testing. That's where we're heading in the next chapter.

Unit testing continuously integrated code

6

This chapter covers

- Unit testing in a CI environment
- Continuously examining test coverage
- Test mocking

We'll risk the opinion that without automated testing, CI would be obsolete, because CI's main strength is that it shows how the changes you introduce into the code affect the software. The CI process should be designed to show you immediately when a change degrades the code quality. What better way to check for that kind of occurrence than to perform automated testing along with every source code change?

Automated software testing is a broad term. In this chapter, we'll focus on one particular type of automated testing: unit testing. Unit testing lies somewhere toward the bottom of the common automated-test chain. We'll get to the rest of the chain—integration, system, and acceptance testing—in chapter 7. But in this chapter, we'll define what unit tests are and what purpose they serve in the CI process. We'll take two popular testing frameworks, NUnit and Microsoft Unit Testing Framework (MSTest), and incorporate them into the CI process. Then you'll learn how to mock things out to speed up your tests.

6.1   *Unit testing from a bird's-eye view*

Before we jump in to create some unit tests, let's define the term and look at the aspects that are important from the CI perspective. There's a common misunderstanding about unit tests. They're often associated with automated tests in general, but this assumption is incorrect. Unit tests are *part of* automated tests. Figure 6.1 shows the difference. As you can see, there's a lot more to automated testing than just unit tests. (As we mentioned earlier, you'll have to wait until chapter 7 to see the rest.) For now, you'll search for the smallest testable part of the application you're building: a *unit*. Depending on your point of view, it may be a class or a separate method. Unit tests verify this smallest testable part of your application.

A well-designed unit test works with a fully isolated piece of code. It should test the smallest part of your software without dependencies on other classes or external resources. Sometimes unit tests are written by the software developer even before the actual code. They're perfect material for application verification in the CI process. Let's look at how to use them.

When you're designing unit tests for the CI process, you have to keep some simple rules in mind. The most important in the CI context are as follows:

- Make your unit tests fast and unambiguous.
- Have your unit tests rely on as few dependencies as possible.
- Let errors drive your unit tests.

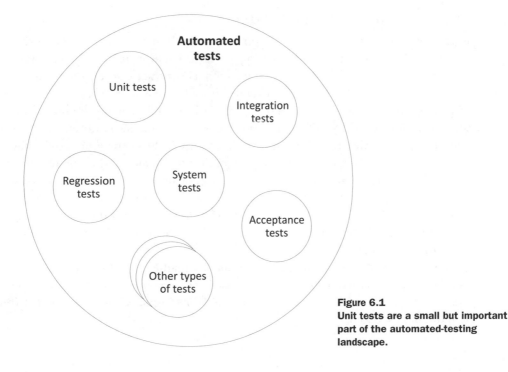

**Figure 6.1
Unit tests are a small but important
part of the automated-testing
landscape.**

Unit test should be fast. One unit test should run in a fraction of a second with no delays and no time-expensive operations. Each small piece of code should be tested in complete isolation, meaning the test shouldn't have any access to external resources. It shouldn't write to the hard drive, nor should it require network connections. If you have code that does that, you'll have to mock it as part of the test. (We'll discuss mocks later in this chapter.)

To illustrate the suspicious-looking rule "Let errors drive your unit tests," we'll revise a Samuel Beckett saying, "Ever tried. Ever failed. No matter. Fail again. Fail better," and say "Ever tried. Ever failed. No matter. Try again. Fail no more." We strongly believe that when it comes to unit tests, you shouldn't fail more than once. This means there's no excuse for not writing a test for every bug. You should be doing *error/defect-driven development.* Every time someone finds a bug in your code, you write a test for it, fix it, and let the test work from then on. It'll function as a regression test in the future. You'll be sure that particular bug is fixed for good, and your build will never again fail because of that bug.

Let's jump right in, take the financial library you've worked with in earlier chapters, and create a simple unit test for it using NUnit and MSTest. You'll integrate the tests with the CI servers. To demonstrate the mocking of functionality in unit tests, you'll extend the financial calculator to perform some I/O operations that you can mock. But before we get into mocking, you need some code to test, and you need to write some tests for the code.

6.2   *First encounters with unit testing*

In chapter 1, we introduced a small application that'll stay with you through your journey with CI. It's your friend the leasing/credit calculator. It can calculate the credit rate according to several input variables such as contract duration and interest. But before we dive into some mathematical details of finance, let's change the calculator a little by flattening the structure. For better clarity, you'll keep all the projects in your solution at one level. If you like the structure with external SVN references, feel free to keep the project that way; but here you'll modify it. From now on, you'll have one solution named CiDotNet with some projects inside, including the calculation core in a project named CiDotNet.Calc (it contains basically what the Framework external SVN reference repository had). The Windows calculator is in the project CiDotNet.WinCalc, the web calculator is in CiDotNet.WebCalc, and the Silverlight calculator is in CiDotNet.SilverlightCalc. The sources provided with this book include a ready-to-use project.

Let's start with the calculation core and its mathematical details. This information isn't necessary from the CI point of view, but it's important to fully understand the unit tests that will follow. If you're a unit testing specialist, please feel free to skip the next section.

6.2.1 The search for perfect unit test material

It's time to add code to the project so you have something to unit test. Open the class library project CiDotNet.Calc and add a new class named FinanceHelper, as shown next.

Listing 6.1 A simple finance mathematical library

```csharp
using System;

namespace Core.Math
{
  public class Finance
  {
    public enum Mode
    {
      BeginMode = 1, EndMode = 0
    }

    private static double CalculateSPPV(double compoundPeriods,
      double periodicInterestRate)
    {
      return System.Math.Pow(1.0 + (periodicInterestRate / 100),
        -compoundPeriods);
    }

    private double CalculateSPFV(double compoundPeriods,
      double periodicInterestRate)
    {
      return System.Math.Pow(1 + (periodicInterestRate / 100),
        compoundPeriods);
    }

    private double CalculateUSPV(double compoundPeriods,
      double periodicInterestRate)
    {
      double uspv = (1 - CalculateSPPV(compoundPeriods,
        periodicInterestRate)) / (periodicInterestRate / 100);
      return uspv;
    }

    private double CalculateUSFV(double compoundPeriods,
      double periodicInterestRate)
    {
      double usfv = (CalculateSPFV(compoundPeriods,
        periodicInterestRate) - 1) / (periodicInterestRate / 100);
      return usfv;
    }

    private static double GetCompoundPeriods(int periods, int ppy)
    {
      return (double)((ppy * periods) / 12);
    }

    private static double GetPeriodicInterestRate(
      double interestRate, int ppy)
    {
```

```
        return (interestRate / ((double)ppy));
    }

    public static double CalculateRate(int periods, int ppy,
        double interest, double presentValue,
        double finalValue, Mode mode)
    {
        int m = (int)mode;
        double compoundPeriods = GetCompoundPeriods(periods, ppy);
        double periodicInterestRate =
            GetPeriodicInterestRate(interest, ppy);
        return -((finalValue * CalculateSPPV(compoundPeriods,
            periodicInterestRate) - presentValue)
            / ((1.0 + ((periodicInterestRate * m) / 100))
            * CalculateUSPV(compoundPeriods, periodicInterestRate)));
    }
}
}
```

Calculates monthly payment

This code seems to include lots of cryptic methods and values, but it's much easier to understand than you can tell at first glance. Single Payment Present Value (SPPV) is the present value of money received in the future at a given interest rate. Single Payment Future Value (SPFV) is the future value of money paid in the future at a given interest rate. Uniform Series Present Value (USPV) is the payment required each period to achieve the future value. And Uniform Series Future Value (USFV) is the future value of a uniform payment.

All of these values are used in the last and most important calculation: the monthly payment, with the public method `CalculateRate()`. It takes as parameters all the necessary data to make the calculation, as shown in table 6.1.

Table 6.1   Parameters to the `CalculateRate()` method

Parameter	Description
periods	Number of periods you want to carry the burden of the loan
ppy	Periods per year—for example, 12 for monthly payments
interest	How much the bank charges you (the interest rate)
presentValue	How much money you need right now
finalValue	How much money you need at the end of the loan
mode	Whether the bank calculates interest income at the beginning of the calculation period or at the end

The `CalculateRate()` method uses the periodic interest rate (annual interest divided over the number of periods in a year) and compound period rate (payments in a month). You may consider the `decimal` data type for use with money-related calculations. You may even want to use your own `Money` type. We won't deal with these issues, to make the case simpler. After all, we're chasing the perfect CI process and not financial issues. This small financial library is a perfect fit for the first test case. You'll test it with NUnit.

6.2.2   *Testing with NUnit*

NUnit (www.nunit.com) is a legend in the unit testing world of .NET. It's one of the oldest automated testing frameworks for .NET and was originally a clone of the Java test library JUnit. NUnit has the responsibility of running unit tests and providing feedback about which tests pass and which ones fail. You'll see that NUnit is easy to use. The easiest way to install it is to download the zip file and extract the core of the testing framework from NUnit-Version\bin\net-2.0\framework into your tools directory.

Next, you have to decide where to put the code you write for the unit test. There are two possible locations for your unit test code: together with the code you're about to test, or in another project. Both approaches have their plusses and minuses. Putting all the code together lets you test the private members, but creates a dependency on the unit testing framework. We prefer using separate library classes for the sake of cleanly separating test and production code. This way, you can easily drop the test DLLs while building the release on the CI server. For this example, you'll go this way.

It's a good idea to use a pattern for the test projects' names. We like to name them after the project they're testing and then add the suffix *.Test*. For the example, this yields the name CiDotNet.Calc.Test.

Further, the test should correspond with the structure of the production code. The same folder structure and of course one test fixture per class is a good way to go. We encourage you to give this some thought; there's no one best pattern for the unit test infrastructure; something else may work better for you. But keep in mind that your test suite will eventually grow to hundreds or thousands of test cases.

Now you need to create the actual unit test. Add a new class library project to your solution, and name it CiDotNet.Calc.Test. Add a reference to the CiDotNet.Calc project and then to the nunit.framework.dll. The Finance.cs class lies in the Math subdirectory of the production project, so create a FinanceTestFixture.cs file in the Math directory of the test project. Add the following code to this new class.

Listing 6.2   A simple unit test for the rate calculation

```
using NUnit.Framework;
using CiDotNet.Calc.Math;

namespace CiDotNet.Calc.Test.Math
{
  [TestFixture]
  public class FinanceTestFixture
  {
    [Test]
    public void CalculateRate()
    {
      int Duration = 12;
      int Ppy = 12;
      double PeriodicInterestRate = 7.5;
```

```
        double presentValue = 30000;
        double finalValue = 0;
        CiDotNet.Calc.Math.Finance.Mode mode =
          CiDotNet.Calc.Math.Finance.Mode.BeginMode;
        double ExpectedRate = 2586.556528260553;
        double ActualRate = Finance.CalculateRate(Duration, Ppy,
          PeriodicInterestRate, presentValue, finalValue, mode);
        Assert.AreEqual(ExpectedRate, ActualRate);
    }
  }
}
```

NUnit uses reflection to dig the test methods from the test library. It uses attributes to find what it needs. First, you need to decorate the test class with the [TestFixture] attribute, which tells NUnit that it's found a class containing tests. All the test methods must be public voids and have the [Test] attribute. In the test code, you can do everything that's possible in .NET. In the CalculateRate() method, you name the calculation parameters in local variables and fill them with values. You then define the ExpectedRate variable and assign it the value that you expect to be returned from the calculation. The ActualRate variable will be set with the actual calculation value from the Finance library.

A test needs something that tells it whether it was a success or a failure. This is called an *assertion*. The Assert.AreEqual method is part of the NUnit framework. It compares the ExpectedRate to the ActualRate. If they're equal, the test passes. If not, the test fails.

You can execute the test a few ways. One of them is to use the GUI test runner that comes with NUnit, nunit-x86.exe. This is a program that lets you interactively run your tests and gives immediate feedback on the results. You'll find it in the NUnit-Version\bin\net-2.0 folder in the NUnit zip archive. Because the CI unit test process needs to run with no user interaction, you won't need it on the CI server. But you'll use it now to demonstrate NUnit's testing capabilities. The source code included with this book contains more unit tests for you to browse and learn from.

Launch the NUnit GUI test runner (see figure 6.2). Select File > Open Project, search for CiDotNet.Calc.Test.dll, and open it. NUnit will load the DLL and prepare everything for the tests.

The left pane shows the assembly and the test methods you've written. You can run all the tests together or mark separate tests to execute them independently. To start the test, click Run. The tests will run, and the results will be displayed in the NUnit GUI (see figure 6.3).

Green means the tests passed and everything is all right. What you don't want to see is red, which means the tests failed; or yellow, which indicates that at least one test wasn't run.

Let's make test results more colorful by creating one failing and one omitted test. In doing so, you'll learn some other NUnit attributes. Copy the CalculateRate() test, paste it into the same class, and change the name to IgnoreTest(). If you decorate it

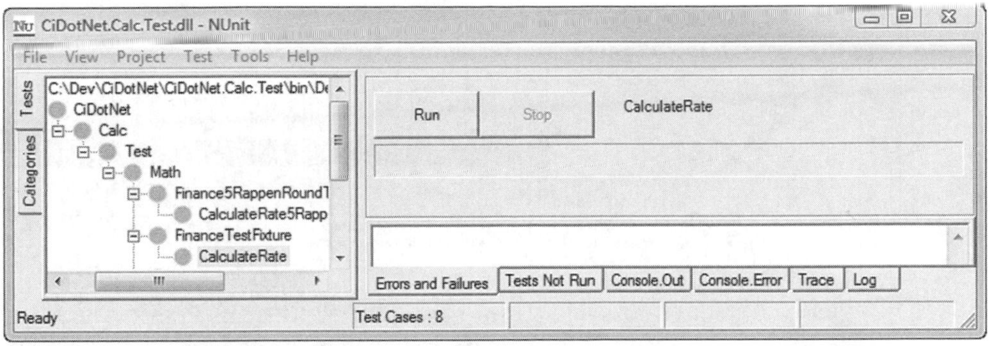

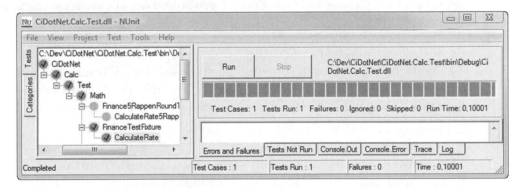

Figure 6.2 The CiDotNet.Calc.Test assembly is loaded into the NUnit GUI test runner and ready to execute.

Figure 6.3 If all the tests pass, you see a green bar in the right pane. The left pane shows a check mark inside a green circle next to each passing test.

with the [Ignore] attribute (in addition to the [Test] attribute), NUnit skips execution and shows a yellow result when you run the test.

Copy the test again, change the name to FailOnPurpose(), and decorate it with the [ExpectException] attribute. This informs the NUnit framework that you expect the tested code to cause an exception. Run the test DLL in the GUI test runner, and you'll get the colorful output shown in figure 6.4.

All the GUI tests are of course useless in the CI environment. The CI server isn't as smart as you are and can't use GUI tools. You need something that you'll be able to start from a build script—something that will perform the tests and save the output in a text file. To do this, you can use a command-line test runner. You'll hook it up to CruiseControl.NET (CCNet).

6.2.3 *Marrying NUnit with CruiseControl.NET*

If you want to integrate the unit tests with your CI server, you'll use a command-line tool and script the process in the build script. NUnit comes with a suitable command-line test

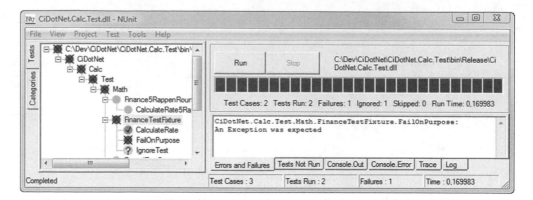

Figure 6.4   If a single test fails, you get a red result in the right pane. The left pane shows an X inside a red circle for failing tests, which bubble up all the way to the top-level assembly. One test, `CalculateRate()`, passed. The `IgnoreTest()` method didn't run, so it displays a question mark inside a yellow circle.

runner. Add the nunit-console.exe file and all the dependencies (nunit-console-runner. dll, nunit-console.exe, nunit.core.dll, nunit.core.interfaces.dll, nunit.framework.dll, and nunit.util.dll) from the NUnit zip file that you downloaded earlier to the tools directory. To execute the tests you created earlier, issue the following command:

```
C:\Dev\CiDotNet>lib\NUnit\nunit-console.exe
➥CiDotNet.Calc.Test\bin\Debug\CiDotNet.Calc.Test.dll
```

The console test runner will perform all the tests, as shown in figure 6.5.

In chapter 3, you chose MSBuild as your build engine of choice. You need NUnit to run from within the MSBuild script. There's an MSBuild Community Task (see chapter 3) to run NUnit that you can use, but you'll now execute it using the exec task as follows.

```
Administrator: Visual Studio 2008 Command Prompt

C:\Dev\CiDotNet>lib\NUnit\nunit-console.exe CiDotNet.Calc.Test\bin\Debug\CiDotNe
t.Calc.Test.dll
NUnit version 2.4.8
Copyright (C) 2002-2007 Charlie Poole.
Copyright (C) 2002-2004 James W. Newkirk, Michael C. Two, Alexei A. Vorontsov.
Copyright (C) 2000-2002 Philip Craig.
All Rights Reserved.

Runtime Environment -
   OS Version: Microsoft Windows NT 6.0.6002 Service Pack 2
  CLR Version: 2.0.50727.4200 ( Net 2.0.50727.4200 )

........
Tests run: 8, Failures: 0, Not run: 0, Time: 0.152 seconds


C:\Dev\CiDotNet>
```

Figure 6.5   NUnit console test runner executing from the command line and performing the tests

Listing 6.3   MSBuild script running the NUnit tests

```
<Project DefaultTargets="Build;Test"
  xmlns="http://schemas.microsoft.com/developer/msbuild/2003">
  <PropertyGroup>
    <Configuration Condition=" '$(Configuration)' == '' ">
      Debug
    </Configuration>
    <TestAssemblies>
      CiDotNet.Calc.Test\bin\$(Configuration)
      ➥\CiDotNet.Calc.Test.dll
    </TestAssemblies>
  </PropertyGroup>
  <Target Name="Build" >
    <MSBuild Targets="Clean;Rebuild" Projects="CiDotNet.sln"
      ContinueOnError="false" />
  </Target>
  <Target Name="Test" >
    <Exec Command="lib\NUnit\nunit-console.exe
    ➥$(TestAssemblies) /xml=NUnitReport.xml"/>
  </Target>
</Project>
```

Launches NUnit and runs tests

As you can see, you start the `Test` target that uses the `exec` task to execute the nunit-console.exe application, providing it with the property that contains the DLL to test. The `/xml` parameter tells NUnit to create an XML report file. You'll use this file on the CI server to integrate the test results within the feedback mechanism.

The build script contains the target named `Build`, which compiles and rebuilds the whole solution. You can use it directly as a build script on the CI server. If your project resides in a revision-control system (we described how to put it there in chapter 2) and you're still using the CruiseControl.NET configuration from chapter 3, then you're good to go. Update the MSBuild script according to listing 6.3, check everything in, and your CI process will snap in and perform the build followed by the test.

Let's quickly glance at the Web Dashboard to see if everything works correctly (see figure 6.6).

You can see a lot on the CCNet Dashboard page. It integrates easily with various test tools. The test tool must be able to produce XML-formatted output; CCNet applies an

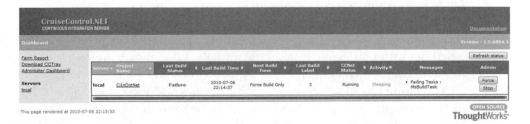

Figure 6.6   CCNet Web Dashboard with a failing project. A red bar under the project is a quick indicator that something's wrong.

XSL transformer to the report to show it on the Dashboard. NUnit can produce XML output. Running NUnit as in listing 6.3 produces a test report called NUnitReport.xml. On the CCNet server, this file needs to be integrated with the overall build report on the Dashboard page. To do so, you'll have to modify the ccnet.config file and the definition for the CiDotNet project by changing the `publishers` tag:

```
<publishers>
  <merge>
    <files>
      <file>NUnitReport.xml</file>
    </files>
  </merge>
  <xmllogger />
</publishers>
```

Don't forget to enable NUnit in the CCNet Dashboard Administrator function and include the `xmllogger` tag in the `publishers` tag. It includes the CCNet logs to the Dashboard page.

The XSL files we've talked about are defined in the dashboard.config file discussed in chapter 5. It's usually located in C:\Program Files\CruiseControl.NET\webdashboard and contains a `buildPlugins` section. This section controls the build-level Dashboard page. To show the NUnit report formatted properly, it should contain this line:

```
<xslReportBuildPlugin description="NUnit Details"
➥actionName="NUnitDetailsBuildReport" xslFileName="xsl\tests.xsl" />
```

The NUnit XSL transformer file is provided with CCNet. Similarly, there's an XSL transformer for NUnit timings. It consumes the same XML report file to display different data.

```
<xslReportBuildPlugin description="NUnit Timings"
➥actionName="NUnitTimingsBuildReport" xslFileName="xsl\timing.xsl" />
```

If you apply the scenario we've just described, you'll get an NUnit report like that shown in figure 6.7.

We'll deal with test analysis and code metrics in chapter 8. But one interesting code metric comes with unit testing: test coverage. Let's look at that next.

6.2.4   *Examining test coverage*

Test coverage is the percentage of your code covered by tests. In this case, it's the unit test. What does "code covered by tests" mean? It's the measurement of how many lines of code are executed by the test code. Some teams strive to cover 100% of their source code lines with tests. Some teams settle for 50%. Covering all the code can be difficult and time consuming; in many cases, a number around 80% is about right.

The mother of all test coverage tools in .NET world used to be NCover. But it went commercial and costs about $200 in its classic version. If you want to do test coverage on the cheap and don't mind a little manual work, a great open source alternative is available: PartCover (http://sourceforge.net/projects/partcover/). After installation, as usual, copy the necessary files to the project tools directory. All it takes to run the

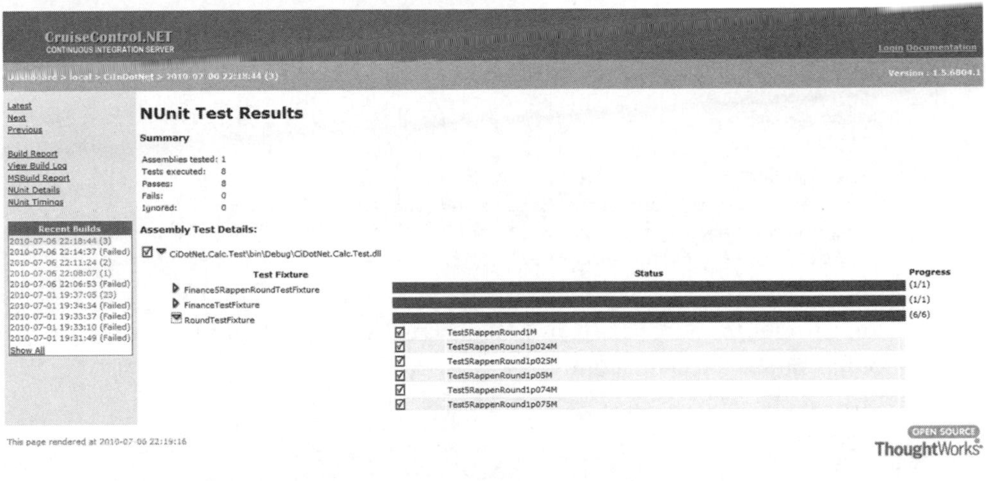

Figure 6.7   An NUnit report transformed from an XML file into a nice web page using an XSL stylesheet, and displayed on the CCNet Dashboard

test coverage with PartCover is starting its command-line tool with the NUnit runner and some test assemblies, like this:

```
<Target Name="Coverage" >
  <Exec Command="tools\PartCover\PartCover.exe --target lib\NUnit\nunit-
  ➥console.exe --target-work-dir CiDotNet.Calc.Test\bin\$(Configuration) -
  ➥-target-args CiDotNet.Calc.Test.dll --output PartCoverReport.xml --
  ➥include [CiDotNet.Calc*]* --exclude [CiDotNet.Calc.Test*]*" />
</Target>
```

This code snippet is a part of an MSBuild script that checks the coverage on the calculator mathematical library, including only the namespace CiDotNet.Calc and excluding CiDotNet.Calc.Test. The output will be saved in the PartCoverReport.xml file. You can call this target in the `DefaultTargets` of your MSBuild project.

The integration of the report file with CCNet works as usual. You have to use an XSLT file on the XML output and integrate it with the CCNet Web Dashboard. Part-Cover comes with some XSLT files. Unfortunately, the files currently must be edited to work with CCNet, because the report file is integrated with the overall build-process report and extracted from there. The original files assume they're working with separate files. We won't discuss the required changes here; we hope the next version of PartCover comes with dedicated XSLT files. To make life easier for you, we've provided the corrected files with this book.

Copy the XSLT files to the xsl folder of your Dashboard installation. Go to dashboard.config, and extend the `buildPlugins` tag as follows.

Listing 6.4   Extending CCNet dashboard.config with PartCover report transformations

```
<buildPlugins>
  <buildReportBuildPlugin>
```

```
    <xslFileNames>
      <xslFile>
        xsl\PartCoverReport.Assembly.xsl
      </xslFile>
    </xslFileNames>
  </buildReportBuildPlugin>
  <buildLogBuildPlugin />
  <xslReportBuildPlugin description="PartCover Report"
    actionName="PartCoverReport"
    xslFileName="xsl\PartCoverReport.Class.xsl" />
</buildPlugins>
```

◁─┐ **Other build report
    plug-ins here**

Don't forget to merge PartCoverReport.xml with the build log in the CCNet project configuration file ccnet.config.

```
<publishers>
  <merge>
    <files>
      <file>PartCoverReport.xml</file>
    </files>
  </merge>
  <xmllogger />
</publishers>
```

You're finished. Get it up and running, run the build, and you'll see a report page similar to figure 6.8.

TeamCity comes with built-in functionality for NCover and PartCover. To use Part-Cover, you have to set it up on the Build Configuration page. First, enable NUnit Tests (mark the flag in New Unit Test Settings). Set it to run the tests from %system.team-city.build. workingDir%\CiDotNet.Calc.Test\bin\Release\CiDotNet.Calc.Test.dll.Go to the .NET Coverage section, choose PartCover from the drop-down list, and provide the path to the executables in the lib directory (%system.teamcity.build.workingDir%\lib\Part-Cover\PartCover.exe). In the Report XSLT test box, provide the following transformation:

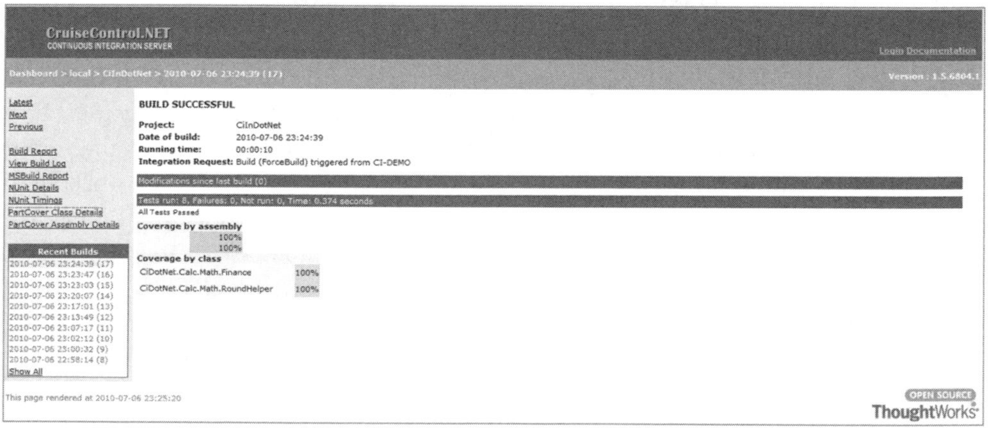

Figure 6.8   The PartCover report in the CCNet Web Dashboard. It shows the assembly test coverage and the coverage divided into separate classes. It's easy to get to 100% coverage with so small a project, but you should try it with one of your own projects.

```
%system.teamcity.build.workingDir%\lib\PartCover\xslt\
➥PartCoverReport.Class.xsl=>PartCover.Class.html
%system.teamcity.build.workingDir%\lib\PartCover\xslt\
➥PartCoverReport.Assembly.xsl=>PartCover.Assembly.html
```

That's it. The next time your project builds, you'll get a nice report about unit tests and test coverage.

NUnit was a big success in the .NET world, so big that Microsoft hired one of NUnit's creators and developed its own unit testing framework.

6.3   *Microsoft unit testing framework*

Since Visual Studio 2003, Microsoft has had its own automated unit testing framework, commonly called MSTest. You'll find it hidden in the Microsoft.VisualStudio.TestTools.UnitTesting namespace. The tools are fully integrated with Visual Studio and are available in all Visual Studio 2010 versions except the Express editions. It's time to try it and see how it works.

6.3.1   *Creating unit tests the Microsoft way*

Let's take the same financial mathematical library you used with NUnit and create unit tests the Microsoft way. Open the Finance.cs file in Visual Studio, right-click somewhere in the text editor, and choose Create Unit Tests from the context menu (see figure 6.9).

Visual Studio browses through the code and finds all the methods worth creating unit tests for. If you don't want to create tests for all the methods in your class,

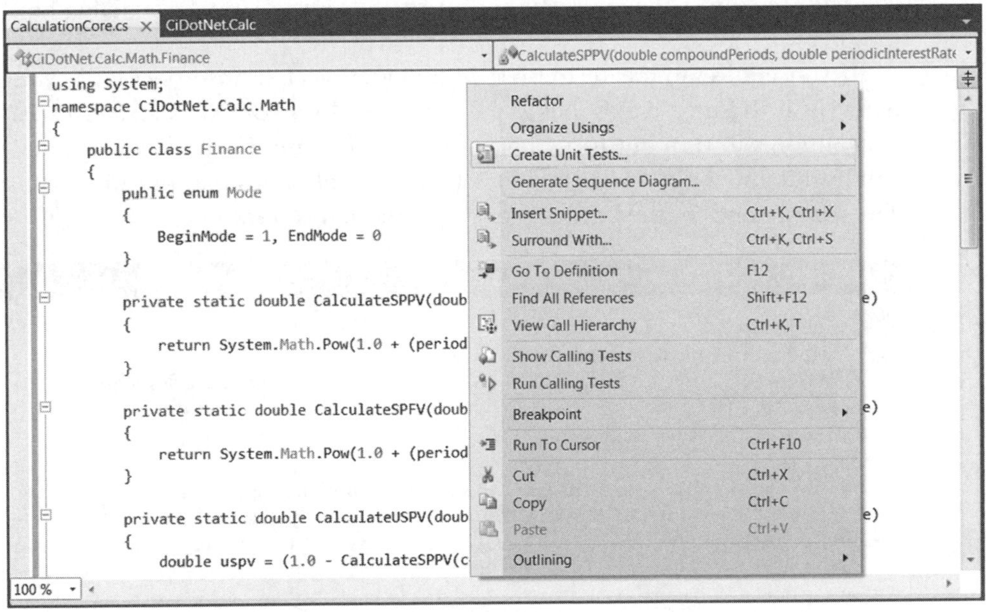

Figure 6.9   Adding a unit test to an existing class in Visual Studio 2010

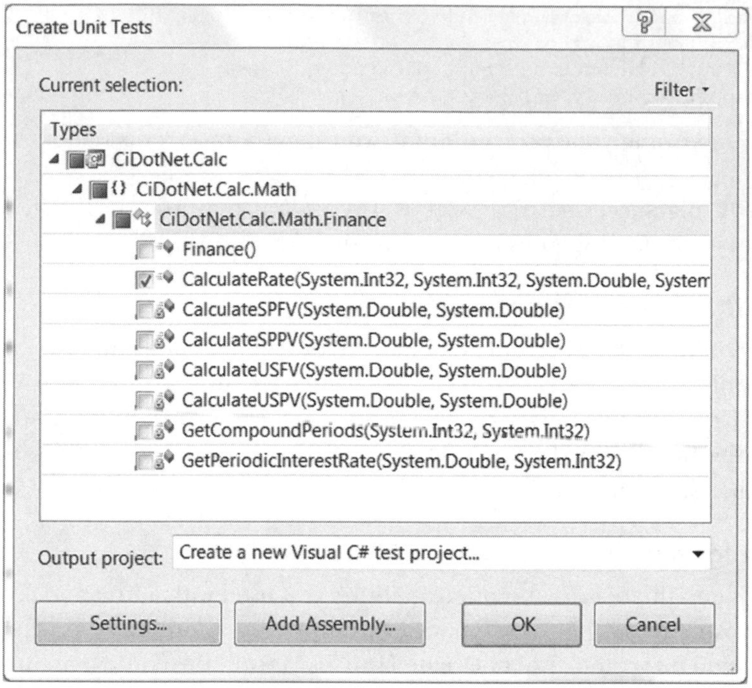

Figure 6.10   To create a unit test from an existing class, choose the methods to test.

you have to choose the ones you want from the Create Unit Tests dialog box (see figure 6.10).

If you choose to create the test in a new project (a wise decision), you need to name it in the next dialog box. In this case, call it CiDotNet.Calc.MSTest; a naming convention will turn out to be important in a minute. In the newly created project, you'll find a new class named after the class it will be testing, but with a `Test` suffix. The test method for the `CalculateRate()` method is shown next.

Listing 6.5   A generated test method

```
/// <summary>
///A test for CalculateRate
///</summary>
[TestMethod()]
public void CalculateRateTest()
{
  int duration = 0; // TODO: Initialize to an appropriate value
  int ppy = 0; // TODO: Initialize to an appropriate value
  double interestRate = 0F; // TODO: Initialize to an appropriate value
  double presentValue = 0F; // TODO: Initialize to an appropriate value
  double finalValue = 0F; // TODO: Initialize to an appropriate value
  CalculationCore.Mode mode = new CalculationCore.Mode(); // TODO:
  ➥Initialize to an appropriate value
```

1 Specifies method is a test

```
double expected = 0F; // TODO: Initialize to an appropriate value
double actual;
actual = CalculationCore.CalculateRate(duration, ppy, interestRate,
  presentValue, finalValue, mode);
Assert.AreEqual(expected, actual);
Assert.Inconclusive(
  "Verify the correctness of this test method.");
}
```

2 Default Assert

As you can see, the test method is given a [TestMethod()] **1** attribute, and the actual test method looks similar to the NUnit test you wrote in the previous section. Now you need to get rid of the TODO comments and set all the variables. Don't forget to erase the line Assert.Inconclusive("Verify the correctness of this test method."); **2**. Even if your assertion passes, this line will make your test yellow.

To start the test, click the Run Tests in Current Context ⚙ button on the toolbar, or choose Test > Run > Test in Current Context from the Visual Studio menu. The test runs directly in the Visual Studio GUI, and the results appear in the Test Results window (see figure 6.11).

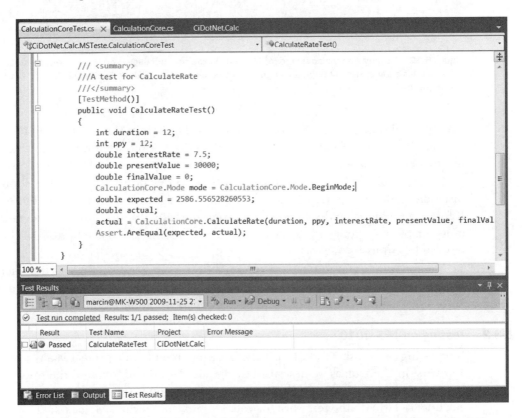

Figure 6.11 MSTest results (bottom pane) for the test code (top pane). As you can see, the test passed.

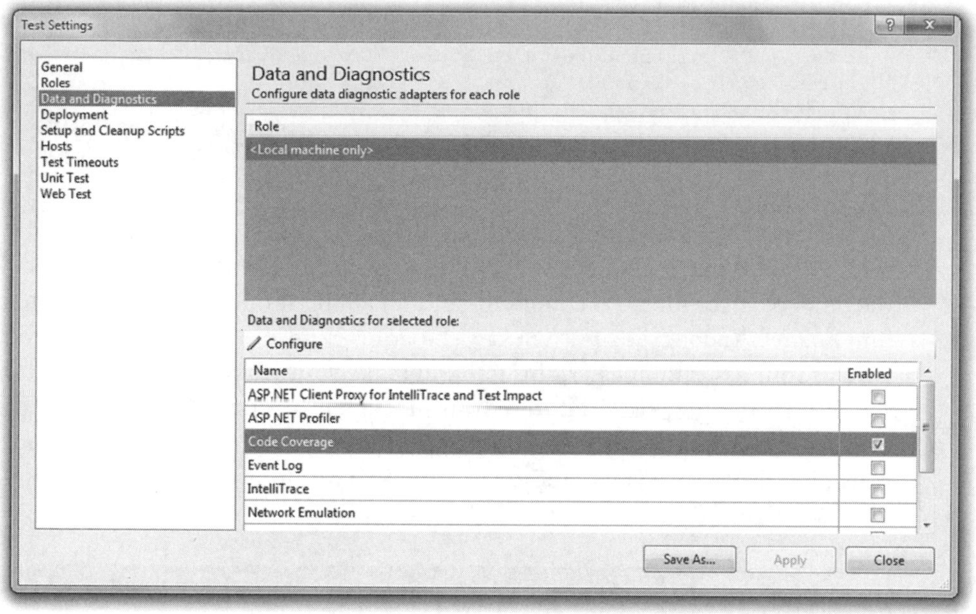

Figure 6.12   Turning on test coverage for MSTest. In the test settings, you have to enable Code Coverage for a given assembly (you can get to the configuration settings by double-clicking the Code Coverage row).

Creating unit tests with MSTest is as easy as it is with NUnit. You can turn on test coverage for MSTest, too. To do so, you have to open the Local.testsettings file in Visual Studio (it's with the solution items); see figure 6.12.

After enabling the test coverage, you have to decide what assemblies should be instrumented. You can do this by clicking the Configure button shown in figure 6.12. If for some reason you decide to strongly sign the assembly that contains the tests, you must enable re-signing. To do so, choose the re-signing key at the bottom of the configuration window.

We encourage you to further explore MSTest. One good resource is the Microsoft Press book *Software Testing with Visual Studio 2010*. But right now, let's see how to add the MSTest test to your continuous build process on Team Foundation Server (TFS) 2010.

6.3.2   *Testing on TFS 2010*

Integrating tests with TFS 2010 is easy. If the source of your project is already under TFS Version Control, as we described in chapter 2, and you followed the project naming convention with the `Test` suffix, you're almost done. You check in your new project, and TFS will do the test work for you. Let's examine why TFS does this.

In Team Explorer in Visual Studio, select your build. Right-click it, and from the context menu, choose Edit Build Definition. In the resulting dialog box, click the Process tab; you'll see a definition like that shown in figure 6.13.

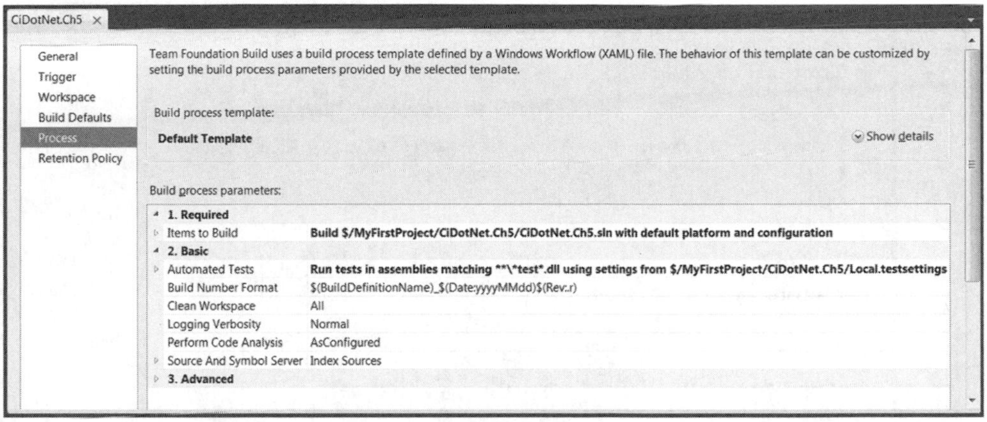

Figure 6.13 The build definition with the Automated Tests assembly matching pattern in the Basic area. All assemblies containing the word *test* search for automated tests.

In the Basic area of the Process tab is an Automated Tests property. This property tells TFS the assemblies from which to run the automated tests.

By default, the definition is "Run tests in assemblies matching ***test*.dll using settings from $/MyFirstProject/CiDotNet.Ch5/Local.testsettings." If you followed the pattern and named the test project to contain the Test suffix, your tests will be performed. Your continuous build should execute all the tests from your test library because it matches the pattern ***test*.dll.

To see the build results from the context menu of your build definition, choose View Builds from the Builds folder of your team project in Team Explorer, and open the last-performed build (see figure 6.14). At the bottom of the report is the executed test count. Click it, and you'll see the detailed test report.

Integrating MSTest with other CI servers isn't as straightforward as with its natural habitat, TFS. Let's see how can you do so with CCNet and TeamCity.

6.3.3   *MSTest in non-TFS environment*

Sometimes you need to go against the flow and integrate MSTest with a third-party CI server. You have to go against the flow because, unfortunately, MSTest isn't a framework—it's part of Visual Studio and the TFS environment. This means you can't take only the MSTest executables and run them friction-free on the build server. You have to install Visual Studio on the build server, do a lot of manual hacking to make it work without Visual Studio, or use third-party test runners for MSTest. By installing Visual Studio on the build machine, you're going against the rule of a vanilla server that has as few external dependencies as possible. It also means you must purchase an additional license for Visual Studio, which increases your costs.

If you want to go the hacker way and make MSTest run without Visual Studio, you can use an external tool such as Gallio.

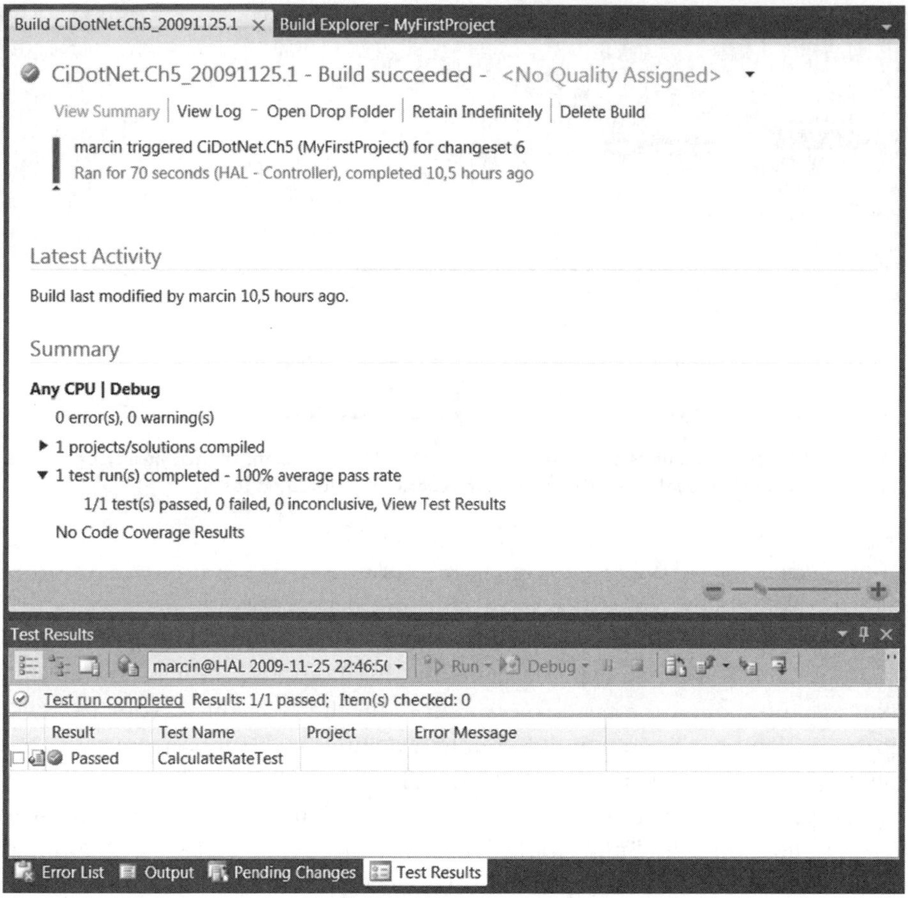

Figure 6.14   The TFS 2010 build report with test results at the bottom

We'll assume that you got your tests running on the build machine one way or another, and show you how to integrate MSTest with CCNet and TeamCity. As usual, you begin by extending the MSBuild script, as shown here.

Listing 6.6   An MSBuild target for running MSTest

```
<Project xmlns="http://schemas.microsoft.com/developer/msbuild/2003">
  <PropertyGroup>
    <MSTestPath Condition=" '$(MSTestPath)' == ''
    ➥">%ProgramFiles%\Microsoft Visual Studio 10.0\Common7\IDE
    </MSTestPath>
    <TestAssemblies>
      CiDotNet.Calc.Test\bin\$(Configuration)\CiDotNet.Calc.Test.dll
    </TestAssemblies>
  </PropertyGroup>

  <Target Name="Test">
    <Delete Condition=
```

❶ Path to MSTest

```
       "Exists('MSTestReport.trx')" Files="MSTestReport.trx">
    </Delete>
    <Exec Command="&quot;$(MSTestPath)\MSTest.exe&quot;
    ➥/testcontainer:$(TestAssemblies) /resultsfile:MSTestReport.trx"/>
  </Target>
</Project>
```

Performs test ❷

All you do is use the command line to run the MSTest runner ❷ installed on the build agent ❶ to produce an MSTestReport.trx file. The .trx file is nothing more than an XML file. To add the test results to CCNet, you apply an XSLT file and configure the Dashboard to show the results. You already know the drill, so we won't discuss it here. More interesting is the integration with TeamCity, which gives us the opportunity to discuss TeamCity service messages.

Service messages in TeamCity are commands you can pass from the build script to TeamCity itself. For example, you can tell TeamCity that you have a .trx file with an MSTest report for it to transform and show on the build page. You send a service message to TeamCity by outputting it to the standard output in the build script. If you're using MSBuild, you use the simple line

```
<Message Text="##teamcity[importData type='mstest'
➥path='MSTestReport.trx']"></Message>
```

TeamCity can interpret this message and has the built-in ability to process the MSBuild report files. So if it gets an importData command of type mstest, it searches a given path for the report to transform and then displays the results. Make sure you add the .trx file to the project artifacts. Add the previous message line to your build script, and you'll get a TeamCity Test Details page as shown in figure 6.15.

Figure 6.15   The standard TeamCity Test Details page showing the results of the MSTest run on the build server

As you can see, integrating unit tests with the CI server is a straightforward task. It should be. Getting the unit tests to run every time the project is integrated is essential for a good CI process. Now it's time to wrap up our discussion of unit testing.

6.4   *Summary*

We've covered a lot of ground in this chapter. Congratulations for making it all the way through! Writing good unit tests is an art of its own, and we've merely glossed over the surface. If you want to go deeper and master unit testing, look at Roy Osherove's great book, *The Art of Unit Testing* (Manning, 2009).

You've written a simple unit test and seen how to isolate the tests from external resources. But most important, you know why you need unit tests in the CI process and how to incorporate them into your CI server of choice.

Unit tests are the fastest way to ensure that the code you're producing maintains some given level of excellence. Writing tests and running them inside your CI process lets you discover every fault as quickly as possible. Unit tests must run quickly—running a single unit test should take a fraction of a second. Remember that the entire test run, together with other CI activities, shouldn't last longer than 5 to 10 minutes.

Together with unit tests comes a very useful software metric called *test coverage*. You saw how test coverage can show you how much of your code is tested. The more code you test, the higher the code quality.

Depending on your CI server, you can incorporate unit tests into the build script as you've done using MSBuild and CruiseControl.NET, or use built-in features of the CI server, like the CI setup in TFS 2010. We tend to believe that controlling everything in the build script is a better way to do it. We like to have total control over the build process, and MSBuild lets us do so. Of course, TFS relies on MSBuild under the hood, and you can take control; but it isn't as obvious as using the build script from the beginning.

The general output from the suite of unit tests is always binary. All the tests pass, or the entire CI process is broken. This information, although important, is only part of the story. You can run many other tests—integration, acceptance, and system tests, for example—to check whether your code is operating properly. Those tests are the subject of the next chapter.

Part 2

Extend it

Can you develop software without testing? Sure you can. Can you float without knowing how to swim? Sure you can—for about 20 seconds.

Software development involves constantly striving to produce code that's as bug-free as possible. And that means testing—starting at the lowest level and ending at the highest. In a modern software development company, the lowest level is usually unit testing, which you learned about in part 1. It's followed by a happy crowd of other types of testing including, but not limited to, integration, regression, and load testing, ending with end-user acceptance testing. You can accomplish this in the CI process by making the testing and analysis happen constantly. In part 2 (chapters 7 and 8), we discuss how to extend your test repertoire beyond unit testing and incorporate other types of testing into the CI process. Finally, you'll learn how to perform code analysis on the source and at the intermediate code level.

After reading this part of the book, you'll be able to extend your CI process's testing, add static code analysis, and take total control over CI feedback.

Performing integration, system, and acceptance testing

This chapter covers

- Integration testing and mocking
- Automating UI testing of Windows, web, and Silverlight applications
- Acceptance testing with FitNesse

In chapter 6, you learned how to unit test continuously integrated source code. A unit test is the most basic form of test that a software developer can create, and this type of test should be done first. It's like adding sauce to pizza dough. But you can use a lot of other tests too, just as you can add pepperoni, mushrooms, and extra toppings to a pizza. And you can get tests from other sources. Many tests can be automated and integrated into the CI process. We'll deal with other types of tests and how to integrate them into your CI process in this chapter.

But first, let's try to answer the following question: what other types of tests are there? Unit tests are only the tip of the iceberg. The answer to the question depends on your point of view. Tests are categorized in various ways. Who performs the test? Do you need a person to manually test the software, or can the process be automated? Who creates the test—a developer, test personnel, or the domain expert? Do you know the source code you're testing (white-box testing), or does a module seem to magically perform some functionality (black-box testing)? What parts of your software are you testing, and where? Is it an integration test or regression test? You must consider many variables, and these questions are also relevant from the CI point of view.

In chapter 5, we compared continuous feedback to a cross-country road trip. In this chapter, we'll focus on additional testing techniques. Think of each testing technique as an important stop on your cross-country journey. We'll introduce integration, system, and acceptance testing. And you'll see a lot of tools in this chapter; table 7.1 gives a quick overview of the tools we'll talk about.

Table 7.1   Tools to extend your test repertoire

Tool	Purpose
NUnit	Performing integration tests
Mocking framework	Simulating the behavior of some objects while unit testing others
White	Testing Windows Forms and Silverlight applications
Selenium	Testing web applications
FitNesse	Performing acceptance testing in a highly sophisticated manner

We'll show you how these tools can become a part of your CI process. But before we get there, it's important to understand the entire testing process so you can see how these tools and techniques fit in.

7.1   *Extending your CI test repertoire*

In this chapter, we'll focus on tests that can be automated. Without automation, test activities wouldn't play a valuable role in CI because they'd have to be done manually. Manual tests are important as another means to improve software quality, but they tend to be difficult to perform continuously. It's hard to imagine test personnel performing tests after every check-in to the repository, don't you think?

The developer isn't the only person who can write tests. In many scenarios, domain experts create their own tests. Of course, they need a different set of tools to write tests than developers use. We'll deal with one of these tools, FitNesse, in this chapter.

When you know what you're testing, and your tests are based on the actual code, you're doing *white-box testing*. If the inner workings of a piece of software you're testing are unknown to you, that's *black-box testing*. Unit testing is most definitely a white-box test methodology. Regardless of whether you do test-driven development (TDD), you know the implementation details of what you're testing. We'll focus in this chapter on black-box testing. Usually, black-box tests are functional tests—they don't care how the software works as long it meets the requirements.

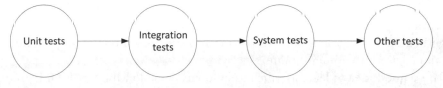

Figure 7.1 The testing timeline. First, you do the unit tests. Then, you take a bigger piece of software and test how it integrates with other pieces. After that, you test how the software behaves in the production environment with a system test.

The test process that begins with unit testing usually continues with integration tests (see figure 7.1). Integration tests usually involve testing the interoperability between a few modules. The modules are usually thoroughly covered with unit tests, and integration testing lays the groundwork for the next step: system testing. System tests are roughly equivalent to the functional tests we mentioned earlier. They occur in fully integrated software, preferably in the deployment environment, and ensure that the software works as designed and meets all the requirements.

From the system and functional tests emerges yet another interesting aspect of software testing in the CI environment: acceptance testing. This type of test can be designed and performed by an end user or a domain expert. Usually, a system test doesn't require programming skills. In this chapter, we'll investigate acceptance tests that you can automate.

Various testing frameworks let you automate integration and system tests. We'll look at three of them in depth throughout this chapter:

- *White*—Tests a WinForms or Silverlight application
- *Selenium*—Tests an ASP.NET application
- *FitNesse*—Performs acceptance tests

As you can see, there's a lot more to testing than just unit tests. Let's look at these additional tests from the CI angle.

7.1.1 Beyond unit tests in CI

Unit tests are merely the first step in the long testing journey. Think of this journey as a road trip: each state border you cross requires a different type of test. You start at the state of unit tests, and as you continue on the trip, you find a series of more complex testing scenarios.

- Integration tests
- System, functional, and acceptance tests
- Performance, load, and stability tests

As you enter the state of each test, you look for road signs to help you understand what each test is and why you're interested in it. Let's see what these signs have to say.

INTEGRATION TESTS

Integration tests usually take multiple pieces of functionality and test how they behave together. Such tests can involve two or more classes, assemblies, components, or even small programs that interoperate.

It's a good idea to leave as much isolation as possible while you're integration testing. What does this mean? When you unit test your software, the goal is to mock every external activity the code is performing. There's no database connection present, no reading or writing to files, no network connectivity—not even the configuration matters. Integration tests are allowed to interact with the system, but they should stay as small as possible. The tests should be fast and give you immediate feedback if there's a problem. Integration tests are perfect to use in a CI environment.

FUNCTIONAL TESTS

Functional tests, on the other hand, are sometimes associated with integration tests and sometimes with system tests. You extract functional tests from other types of tests to support your CI scenario.

Let's say your functional tests extend your integration tests. Code tested in this manner has no interfaces stubbed. You don't use mocking to isolate your functionality.

There's one important thing to remember if you want to integrate functional tests in your CI process: the CI tests should be fast. If you rely on a database connection or other external resources, the tests tend to take longer. If you're able to fit the tests into a 10-minute run, you're good to go. If the functional tests take longer, you should think about dividing your build process into smaller chunks.

ACCEPTANCE TESTS

Acceptance tests take fully integrated software with all its dependencies and test it against a normal environment. This means no mocking—only the real deal. You should test I/O, network, and database operations with specific configurations.

Acceptance tests can be designed by the customer or domain specialist. This kind of test usually takes longer to run. These tests won't break your build, so they're usually not included in the CI build, but they're great material for periodic builds, such as the nightly or weekly build.

SYSTEM TESTS

System tests are also performed on fully integrated software, but the environment tends to mimic a production environment more than it does during acceptance tests. This kind of test is hard to integrate within your build process; these tests tend to rely on specific hardware and software configurations. But if you strain a little, some system tests can be included in your automatic build and test schedule.

Software that passes system tests can be tested in various other ways. For example, you can test how it performs under high load. During this kind of test, you try to stress your software in various ways. For instance, you may issue thousands of requests to a website or take your software through the mill with your database.

STABILITY TESTS

You may also want to test the stability of your software. Stability tests answer such questions as whether there are any memory leaks in your Windows service, whether your program can restore the database connection after hibernation, and so on. Although in most cases it's possible to automate these tests, they usually have no place in CI the process. They take too much time. You need hours to properly test your software under stress or to make sure it's stable. We won't deal with this kind of test in this book.

These test techniques build a kind of pyramid (see figure 7.2). It's a good idea to start at the bottom of the test pyramid with unit testing and build up from that. You should test the integration of software that's covered with good unit tests. You should start functional tests as soon as you're ready with your integration tests, and so on.

As you can see, unit testing is the foundation or base of your different types of tests. Without it, the other tests collapse and are less meaningful. Additional tests build on unit tests and then on each other. Many of the tests you run involve the customer, and that's what we talk about next.

7.1.2 *Involving the customer or domain expert in the CI testing process*

With the rise of agile software development methodology, the role of the customer in the software development cycle has skyrocketed. Maybe it's time you acknowledge that and give the customer limited access to the CI process.

If you get cold shivers at the thought of letting the customer get so close to the process, it's understandable. It takes a special relationship to let the customer mess with your CI process. But think about a domain specialist or product owner. Most likely they aren't programmers, but they can have a positive influence on your process. Why not give them tools to write their tests?

Of course, you don't want to make them program the tests. There are other ways to classify tests. The first type, *code-facing tests*, focuses on the technical part of the software equation. This kind of test tells you whether the software is written the right way. Does everything work as you, the developer, expect it to work? Are the data flows correct? Does the UI respond the right way? And so on.

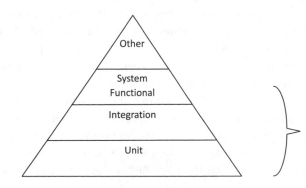

Figure 7.2
The software testing pyramid shows how to lay a good base with unit tests and then build up. In the CI scenario, you'll probably cut the peak off the pyramid because some types of tests take too long to run.

The second type is *customer-facing tests*. These answer such questions as, is what the developer wrote what the customer needs? Does it fulfill customer expectations? Will it be of value to generate return on investment?

Customer-facing tests tend to fall into another category that's relevant in the CI scenario: *user-acceptance tests*. Such tests are roughly the equivalent of the functional testing you do, which we described in section 7.1.1. They let the customer, the domain expert, or even the project manager set acceptance boundaries on the software that's developed for them.

Some user-acceptance tests are good material to include in the CI process. You have to remember that this kind of test must follow the normal rules for CI tests: it needs to be automated and run fast.

You can't use manual tests in the CI process. And if the tests aren't quick enough, they'll introduce unnecessary friction in your day-to-day work. If the user-acceptance tests aren't fast enough, it may still be a good idea to include them in the nightly build. As more and more user-acceptance tests pass, your feeling of being on the right path will strengthen.

Wait a minute: "As more and more user-acceptance tests pass"? Does that mean not all tests need to pass? It's time to look at this interesting problem.

7.1.3 *Right timing, right failing*

When you're designing tests for the CI process, you should keep this golden rule in mind: "Fail fast." This means you should design your test suite so that in case of a problem, you'll detect it as soon as possible. In order to do that, you should

- Perform quick tests at the beginning.
- Break the build after the first failing test.

If you perform the quick tests earlier in the CI process, you'll get the potential fail more quickly. It's a waste of resources to perform time-consuming tests if some of the quick ones can potentially fail earlier. In addition, you should break the entire build after the first failing test. (OK, it may be the first test suite or group, but be sure to break your build.)

Unit tests are definitely the quickest. They should be designed to focus on details: test one specific thing, and don't rely on external resources. After that, testing complexity grows, as does execution time. Figure 7.3 shows roughly how the typical execution time of a test depends on the test's detail level.

There may be situations when you don't want to break your build on a failing test—for example, if the test is written by a customer. Consider the following scenario. You've written the code and created a set of acceptance tests. These tests define a product with full functionality. Acceptance tests should break the build if they fail. But what about user-created acceptance tests? If such tests are part of your CI process, they shouldn't break the build, because acceptance testing comes long after the build is finished. A broken build should indicate that the code either doesn't compile or that unit and integration tests fail.

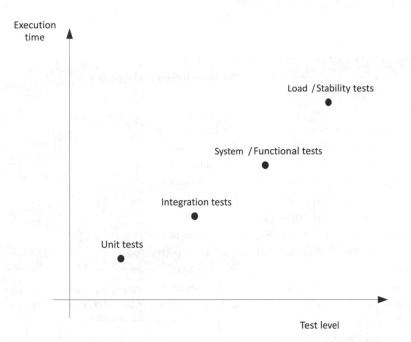

Figure 7.3 **This diagram shows that the further from the code and closer to the functionality (test level) you are, the longer a test takes to run. (If you have rich testing scenarios, the execution time of the entire test suite may vary.)**

Try to be specific. Group the tests that you don't expect to pass just yet in another test suite, and move them into your main test suite when the code functionality is ready for them.

Now that we've covered the concepts, let's dive deep into extended testing in CI.

7.2 Up close and personal with integration tests in CI

As we said earlier, integration tests are one step higher than unit tests in the complex testing hierarchy. Elements that were previously tested in isolation are now tested together. Integration tests check how the individual pieces of code behave collectively. In addition, integration tests are allowed to interact with external resources: they can read or write from the database or from the hard drive. Integration tests also tend to take more time; when you're designing a CI scenario with integration tests, you have to take this into consideration. How do you perform integration testing?

7.2.1 Performing integration testing

To perform integration testing, use a testing framework you're familiar with. It can be NUnit or MSTest. You'll just organize your tests a different way this time.

First, you have to separate the integration tests from your normal unit tests—you shouldn't mix them. Unit tests should run quickly, because they have to run in every CI iteration. Integration tests can run in every CI iteration, but they take longer, and the test execution time may eventually exceed acceptable CI execution time. You should keep as many tests as possible in every CI build, but sometimes it's a good idea to move some of the tests into a periodic or nightly build.

Let's dig out the leasing calculator project that you used earlier in the book. It's small, slick, and easy to use. You can enter the credit amount, interest, duration, and other variables, and it will calculate your rate (see figure 7.4). Using this example, you've set the revision-control system, developed a build process, and performed some unit tests.

Let's extend this calculator. Suppose you're selling it to a customer in Switzerland. It's a custom in Switzerland to round prices to 5 rappen, which is 1/100 of a Swiss Franc. It's also a custom in Switzerland that no payable amount of money should be less than 5 rappen. So Swiss bankers invented the so-called *5-rappen round*. Look at this helper class to see how to perform the 5-rappen round:

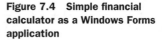

Figure 7.4   Simple financial calculator as a Windows Forms application

```
public class RoundHelper
{
  public static decimal Round5Rappen(decimal price)
  {
    return Math.Round(price * 20,
    MidpointRounding.AwayFromZero ) / 20;
  }
}
```

This calculation is easy enough. You take the price, multiply it by 20, and round away from zero (it's called the *accountant method*). Thanks to that, if you multiply again by 20, you get the price rounded to exactly 5 rappen.

The 5-rappen-round method should be unit tested. Here's an example:

Listing 7.1   An ordinary unit test for the 5-rappen-round method

```
[Test]
public void Test5RappenRound1p024M()
{
  decimal Price = 1.024M;
  decimal ExpectedPrice5RappenRound = 1M;
  decimal ActualPrice5RappenRound =
    CiDotNet.Calc.Math.RoundHelper.Round5Rappen(Price);
  Assert.AreEqual(ExpectedPrice5RappenRound,
    ActualPrice5RappenRound);
}

[Test]
```

```
public void Test5RappenRound1p025M()
{
  decimal Price = 1.025M;
  decimal ExpectedPrice5RappenRound = 1.05M;
  decimal ActualPrice5RappenRound =
    CiDotNet.Calc.Math.RoundHelper.Round5Rappen(Price);
  Assert.AreEqual(ExpectedPrice5RappenRound,
    ActualPrice5RappenRound);
}
```

You're testing the individual pieces of software separately. The rate-calculation method was unit tested in chapter 5. Your new 5-rappen-round method is unit tested in listing 7.1. Now, let's test them together by performing your first integration test. In this case, the easiest approach is to take the unit testing framework and set it to work as an integration testing framework. Follow along as you do it.

Remember that you want to keep your unit tests and integration tests in separate places. So create a new class library project called CiDotNet.Calc.IntegrationTest. Reference your favorite unit testing framework from it (this example uses NUnit), add a new class, and add the following test.

Listing 7.2   Testing the rate calculation and the 5-rappen round

```
[Test]
public void CalculateRate5RappenRound()
{
  int Duration = 12;
  int Ppy = 12;
  double PeriodicInterestRate = 7.5;
  double presentValue = 30000;
  double finalValue = 0;
  CiDotNet.Calc.Math.Finance.Mode mode =
  CiDotNet.Calc.Math.Finance.Mode.BeginMode;

  double ExpectedRate = 2586.556528260553d;
  double ActualRate = Finance.CalculateRate(Duration, Ppy,
    PeriodicInterestRate, presentValue, finalValue, mode);

  Assert.AreEqual(ExpectedRate, ActualRate);

  decimal ExpectedRate5RappenRound = 2586.55M;
  decimal ActualRate5RappenRound =
    RoundHelper.Round5Rappen((decimal)ActualRate);

  Assert.AreEqual(ExpectedRate5RappenRound, ActualRate5RappenRound);
}
```

This is a simplified integration test, but it shows the idea well. It uses a bottom-up approach, which means you first test the lower-level functionality and build up from there. In this case, you first test the simple rate calculation and then use the outcome as input for a second test with the 5-rappen round. This way, you test all the functionality together.

As you can see, the border between unit tests and integration tests is often only semantics. This integration test case isn't much different than the unit test. But because of its structure, it's beyond our definition of a unit test. Let's look at something more complicated: an integration test that touches I/O.

7.2.2 *From mocking to integration testing*

Integration tests, unlike unit tests, aren't bound by the rule to have as few external dependencies as possible. To demonstrate, let's take the financial calculator and extend it with the ability to export the calculation values to a file. The exported data can be imported into an accounting tool to create an invoice or used by an external tool to create a document. For your purposes, let's say you want to append the calculations to a comma-separated value (CSV) file somewhere on the disk, which contains all the calculation data. It will have one row and one calculation.

First, to make everything testable, you need to abstract the file operations. Let's do this by defining an interface called IFileWrapper. You need the new functionality to check whether the file exists, to create it if it doesn't exist, and then to append a line of text to it:

```
public interface IFileWrapper
{
  bool FileExists(string path);
  void CreateFile(string path, string text);
  void AppendLine(string path, string text);
}
```

You use an interface because you need to substitute a fake for the actual implementation. The implementation uses the System.IO namespace to check whether the file exists, create it, and append a line to it. This is the functionality you'll test in your integration tests. But before that, you should test your piece of functionality. This way, you can observe the difference between unit tests and integration tests.

Use the IFileWrapper from the CsvFileProvider class, as follows.

Listing 7.3 `CsvFileProvider` using `IFileWrapper` to save a CSV file

```
public class CsvFileProvider
{
  private IFileWrapper fileWrapper;

  public CsvFileProvider(IFileWrapper fileWrapper)
  {
    if (fileWrapper == null)
    {
      throw new ArgumentNullException("fileWrapper");       Injects I/O
    }                                                        interface
    this.fileWrapper = fileWrapper;
  }

  #region ICsvFileProvider Members
  public bool Append(string path, string[] values)
  {
```

```
       bool Success = true;
       string CvsLine = string.Join(",", values);

       if (path == null || path.Length == 0)
       {
           throw new ArgumentException("Path is null or empty", "path");
       }

       if (!this.fileWrapper.FileExists(path))
       {
           this.fileWrapper.AppendLine(path,
             "Duration, Ppy, InterestRate, PresentValue, FinalValue, Mode");
       }

       try
       {
         this.fileWrapper.AppendLine(path,
           System.Environment.NewLine);
         this.fileWrapper.AppendLine(path, CvsLine);
       }
       catch
       {
         Success = false;
       }
       return Success;
    }
#endregion
}
```

The `CsvFileProvider` takes the `IFileWrapper` in the constructor. This way, you can inject any custom functionality you want. The heavy lifting is performed in the `Append` method, which uses `IFileWrapper` to insert something into the file.

Let's write a unit test that uses the mock framework.

Listing 7.4   Unit test with mocked file operations

```
[Test]
public void UnitTest()
{
  DynamicMock fileWrapper =
    new DynamicMock(typeof(IFileWrapper));
  fileWrapper.ExpectAndReturn("FileExists", true,
    new object[] { "path" });

  CsvFileProvider csvFileProvider = new
    CsvFileProvider((IFileWrapper)fileWrapper.MockInstance);
  Assert.IsTrue(csvFileProvider.Append("path",
    new string[] { "test" }));
}
```

This test uses the mocking framework that comes with NUnit. Many other good mocking frameworks are available, such as Rhino Mocks, Moq, and Typemock Isolator. This example uses the one that comes in NUnit.Mocks because you already have it in your tools directory.

DynamicMock is a fake object created using the IFileWrapper interface. You tell the mocking framework that you expect the method FileExist to return true. The last parameter is the path to the file, which is irrelevant because you're faking. After that, your CsvFileProvider object is created using the fake IFileWrapper object. Finally, you assert that the Append operation on csvFileProvider returns true, which indicates success. This way, you're fulfilling all of the unit tests' criteria and not touching the filesystem.

How does the integration test differ? Remember that our definition of integration tests lets the tests interoperate with external resources, such as the filesystem. You don't need to mock anything. You can use the real implementation for IFileWrapper, shown here.

Listing 7.5 System.IO implementation of the file wrapper

```
public class FileWrapper : IFileWrapper
{
  #region IFileWrapper Members
  public bool FileExists(string path)
  {
    return System.IO.File.Exists(path);
  }
  public void CreateFile(string path, string text)
  {
    AppendLine(path, text);
  }
  public void AppendLine(string path, string text)
  {
    System.IO.File.AppendAllText(path, text);
    System.IO.File.AppendAllText(path, System.Environment.NewLine);
  }
  #endregion
}
```

Every test should function against a system that's in a known state. This means that in order to get repeatable results, you have to set the test variables to a known state. Unit tests do this by definition. But this isn't the case with integration tests. If your tests rely on data in a database, you must make sure you have the data in the database. If you rely on a system variable, it's a good idea to check that the variable exists or to re-create it every time the test is executed.

If your tests change anything in the system, you should clean up those changes after the tests run. This way, your tests will have less influence on the system itself and will be more repeatable. The following listing shows the CSV file integration test.

Listing 7.6 CSV file integration test

```
[TestFixture]
  public class CsvFileIntegrationTestFixture
  {
    private string _path = @"c:\temp\export.csv";
```

```
[SetUp]
public void SetUp()
{
    CleanUp();
}

[TearDown]
public void TearDown()
{
    CleanUp();
}

[Test]                                                          Integration
public void IntegrationTest()                                   test
{
    FileWrapper fileWrapper = new FileWrapper();
    CsvFileProvider csvFileProvider =
        new CsvFileProvider(fileWrapper);
    Assert.IsTrue(csvFileProvider.Append(_path,
        new string[] { "test" }));
}

[Test]                                                          Integration test 2:
[ExpectedException]                                             gets exception from
public void IntegrationTest2()                                  code being tested
{
    FileWrapper fileWrapper = new FileWrapper();
    CsvFileProvider csvFileProvider =
        new CsvFileProvider(fileWrapper);
    Assert.IsTrue(csvFileProvider.Append(null,
        new string[] { "test" }));
}

private void CleanUp()
{
    if (System.IO.File.Exists(_path))
    {
        System.IO.File.Delete(_path);
    }
}
    }
}
```

Integration tests done in this fashion are still pretty code-centric. But they're as important for the health of your software as unit tests. You should definitely use them in your CI setup. Pay close attention to the execution time, and separate slow-running tests. Put the latter in a separate process, such as a periodic build. Be aware that the tests may change the environment, and try to set it back to a known state every time you run the tests.

What if you want to go even higher with your tests' detail level, closer to system or functional tests? You can do this by using the UI testing framework with your application. You can even integrate it into your CI process. Let's look at how to do that.

7.3   *Testing the user interface*

If you're lucky enough to have a QA department, you're probably familiar with the process it typically follows:

1 Pull test scenarios for the day's tests
2 Read the description
3 Do exactly as described
4 Observe the output
5 Compare the output with the description
6 Assert

Repetitive and boring, isn't it? But how about automating the process? Is it possible to make the machine read and perform UI tests automatically? Yes; and there are tools you can use to do that.

The tools are called *GUI testing tools*. They comprise a broad set of tools that basically pretend they're a real user. They need a formal description of what to do, and they do it. You provide steps such as *start the application, enter this field, click that button, check whether the text box gets the proper value,* and so on. One of these GUI test tools is called *White*. Let's look at it.

7.3.1   *Testing Windows Forms with White*

White is an open source tool developed by ThoughtWorks. It lets you automate a bunch of technologies including old-style Win32, Windows Forms, and Windows Presentation Foundation (WPF). And here's something cool: it works with Silverlight, too. You'll see how to use it with both WinForms and Silverlight before you're finished.

Underneath the hood of White sits the Microsoft UI Automation (UIA) framework. This framework makes programmatic access to the UI possible. The UIA framework is a set of APIs that allow programs to interact with various Windows GUI elements. White adds a layer of abstraction to UIA, making it easy to automate testing the UI.

Let's automate the testing of the financial calculator. The Windows Forms version looks like figure 7.5.

To use White, download it from www.codeplex. com/white and put it in your project's tools directory. It's probably a good idea to separate the GUI tests from the rest, so create a new class library project. Add a reference to the `White.Core` assembly, which contains White's basic functionality. Now you need something to run the test cases: NUnit will work great for this.

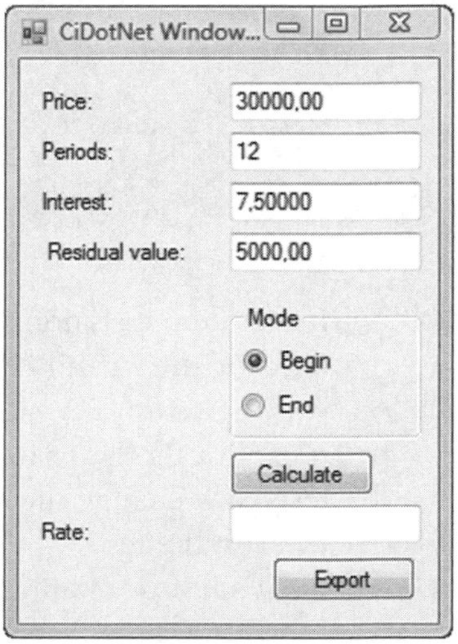

Figure 7.5   The WinForms financial calculator against which you'll run UI tests

Writing a White test works like writing an NUnit test. Decorate the testing class with a `TestFixture` attribute and a public void method with a `Test` attribute. The following listing shows how to set up GUI testing with White.

Listing 7.7 Basic Windows GUI test performed with White

```
using System;
using NUnit.Framework;
using White.Core;
using White.Core.UIItems.WindowItems;
using White.Core.UIItems;

namespace CiDotNet.WinCalc.Test
{
  [TestFixture]
  public class AcceptanceTests
  {
    private string _path =
      @"..\..\..\CiDotNet.Win\bin\Debug\CiDotNet.WinCalc.exe";

    [SetUp]
    public void SetUp()
    {
      _application = Application.Launch(_path);       ❶ Starts
    }                                                      application

    [TearDown]
    public void TearDown()
    {
      _application.Kill();                            Shuts down
    }                                                 ❷ application

    [Test]
    public void Test()
    {
      Window Window =
        _application.GetWindow("CiDotNet Windows Calculator");

      TextBox TxtPrice = Window.Get<TextBox>("txtPrice");
      TextBox TxtPeriods = Window.Get<TextBox>("txtPeriods");
      TextBox TxtInterest = Window.Get<TextBox>("txtInterest");
      TextBox TxtResidualValue =
        Window.Get<TextBox>("txtResidualValue");
      RadioButton RbModeBegin =
        Window.Get<RadioButton>("rbModeBegin");

      TxtPrice.Text = "10000,00";
      TxtPeriods.Text = "36";
      TxtInterest.Text = "7,50";
      TxtResidualValue.Text = "1000,00";
      RbModeBegin.Click();
      string ExpectedRate = "284,45";

      Button Button = Window.Get<Button>("btnCalculate");
      Button.Click();
```

```
        TextBox rateTextBox = Window.Get<TextBox>("txtRate");
        Assert.AreEqual(rateTextBox.Text, ExpectedRate);
    }
  }
}
```

You use the `SetUp` and `TearDown` methods to initialize ❶ and close ❷ the application under test, respectively. White is able to attach to a working application process or to start a new one. You start the application using a relative path (in production you should consider copying the exe and tests to one directory and performing the tests from there—it will make the relative path obsolete). The test begins by getting a `Window` object—in this case, by searching for the window title—then gets the controls from the window, using their names. The controls can be manipulated on demand. You set the `Text` properties to provide calculation values. You deal with the Radio button by executing the `Click()` method on the control instance. When you're finished with the initial values, you get the instance of the Calculate button. Click it: `Assert.AreEqual` then verifies that you get the value you expected.

Integrating test results with CI is easy. White generates an ordinary XML NUnit report file that you can integrate with your CI feedback mechanism (see chapters 5 and 6). But you must keep one issue in mind if you want to perform the GUI tests in the CI environment: the CI server process usually works as a Windows service under a system account. This means that, normally, there's no chance the service can start and use something with the UI. You'll have to deal with that and make the appropriate changes to the CI server's service properties by selecting the Allow Service to Interact With Desktop check box (see figure 7.6). You can get to the service properties by choosing Start > Control Panel > Administrative Tools > Services, and selecting Cruise-Control.NET Server Properties.

This way, your CI process can start and test your Windows application automatically. But WinForms programs aren't the only type of application that White deals with. You may want to automate an old Win32 application or a new WPF app. But what makes White exceptional is its ability to automatically test Silverlight applications.

7.3.2 *Silverlight test automation*

Silverlight has a gained considerable momentum in the .NET world. It's an exceptional technology that mixes web availability and Windows responsiveness. It lets .NET developers use the knowledge they already have to build a web application to create a Windows style application. Figure 7.7 shows the financial calculator as a Silverlight application. We won't walk you through the creation of this application, but we provide full source code with this book.

Testing a Silverlight application in White is as easy as testing a Windows application. You again use NUnit to perform the test. The following listing shows how to set up White to test your Silverlight application.

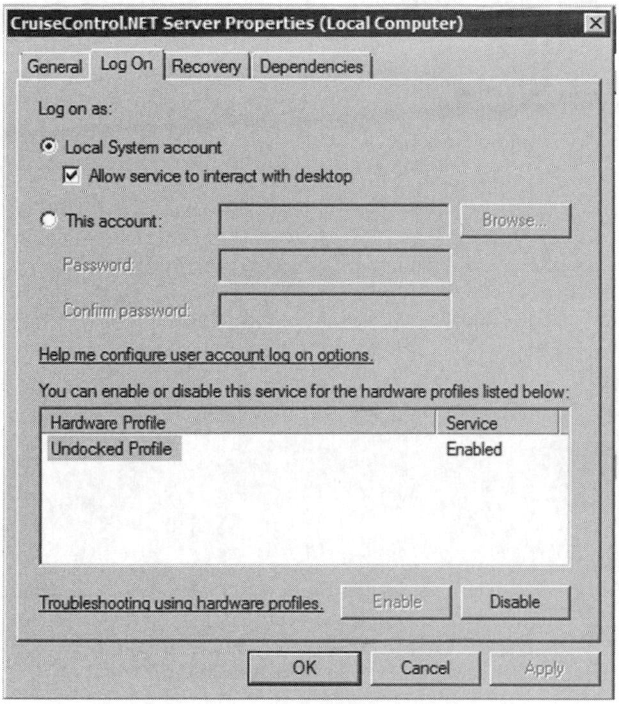

Figure 7.6
If you want your CI server to be able to test the Windows GUI, you have to allow it to interact with the desktop.

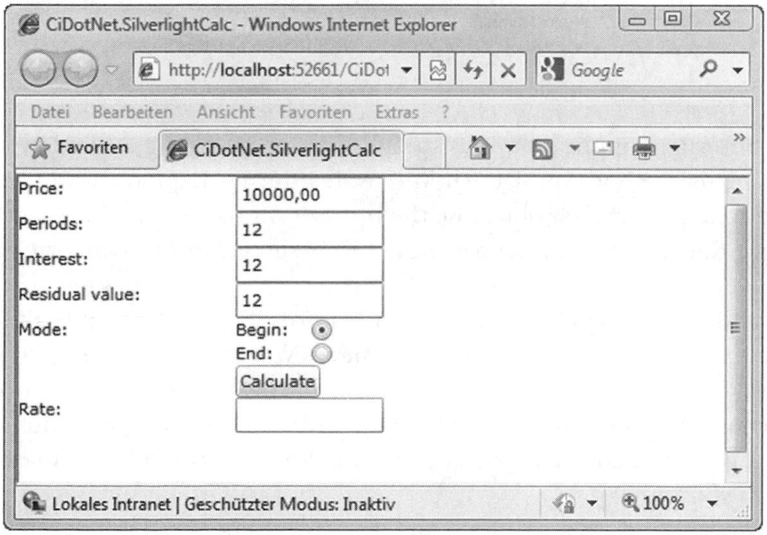

Figure 7.7   The example financial calculator running as a Silverlight application

Listing 7.8 Automating UI testing of a Silverlight application

```
[TestFixture]
public class SilverlightCalcUiTestFixture
{
  InternetExplorerWindow _browserWindow;

  [SetUp]
  public void SetUp()
  {
  _browserWindow = InternetExplorer.Launch("http://localhost:52661/
  ➥CiDotNet.SilverlightCalcTestPage.aspx",
  ➥"CiDotNet.SilverlightCalc - Windows Internet Explorer");
  }

  [TearDown]
  public void TearDown()
  {
    _browserWindow.Dispose();
  }

  [Test]
  public void Test()
  {
    SilverlightDocument document =
      _browserWindow.SilverlightDocument;
    Button button = document.Get<Button>("btnCalculate");
    button.Click();

    System.Threading.Thread.Sleep(5000);

    TextBox rateTextBox = document.Get<TextBox>("txtRate");
    Assert.AreEqual(rateTextBox.Text, "878,754159722056");
  }
}
```

Testing the Silverlight application is as straightforward as testing a Windows application. In the SetUp method, you launch Microsoft Internet Explorer with your Silverlight application. In TearDown, you close the browser. In the test method, you first get the Silverlight document from the page; the test is similar to the WinForms app you tested earlier.

White comes with a ton of neat additional features. For example, it has the ability to reuse a test in multiple test scenarios. This means you don't have to search the controls on the GUI using the Get() methods. The controls are generated and provided to you in strongly typed fashion. Detailed usage of White isn't a topic of this book, so we won't cover the extended features any further, but we encourage you to explore it. It's well worth your time!

You've tested a Windows application and a Silverlight-powered website. How about an ordinary website? White won't help you there. But you can use another tool, Selenium, to test websites.

7.3.3 *Testing a web application with Selenium*

Selenium is a web application testing framework that originally came from Thought-Works. It's a set of tools, including the Selenium IDE, which is a Firefox plug-in that helps to record and play the test, and Selenium RC, a remote control to perform tests for various browsers from various languages. You can get Selenium from http://seleniumhq.org/. It automatically installs; after a restart, you'll have one additional item on the Tools menu: Selenium IDE.

Let's automatically test the web financial calculator, shown in figure 7.8.

You'll do exactly the same test you did with the Windows and Silverlight applications, but you'll use Selenium IDE to record the test. First, get the Firefox web browser (www.firefox.com/) if you don't already have it. You'll only need it on your development machine because the Selenium IDE is a Firefox plug-in. To install it, use Firefox: go to http://seleniumhq.org/, browse to the download, and click the link to an .xpi file. This is the plug-in file for Firefox. When you click it, Firefox prompts you to allow the installation. Do so, and restart Firefox. Run the web financial calculator from Visual Studio. Doing so launches the ASP.NET development server. Now, launch Firefox, and navigate to the URL of your application. Start the Selenium IDE from the Firefox Tools menu. You'll get the empty test suite shown in figure 7.9.

Be sure the 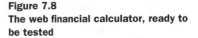 button is selected, and you're good to go. Enter some values into the calculator, and click the Calculate button. Selenium, by default, records all your clicks and keystrokes and places them in a table (see figure 7.10).

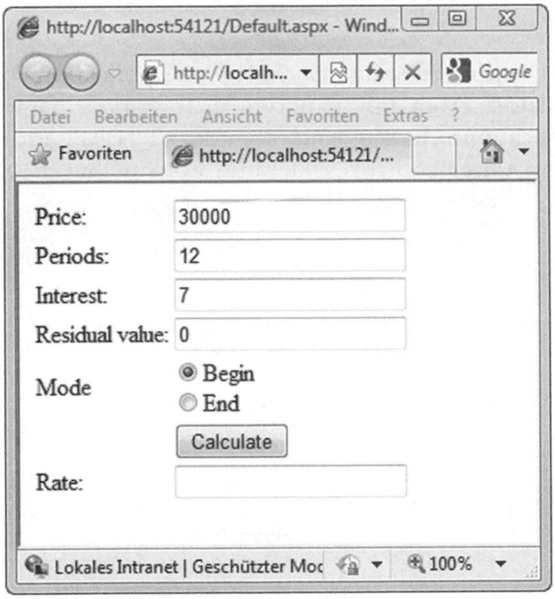

Figure 7.8
The web financial calculator, ready to be tested

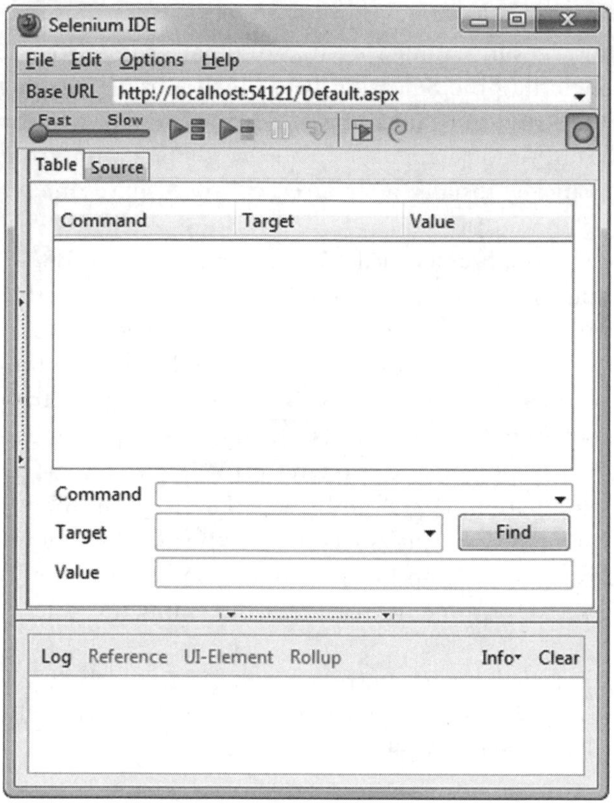

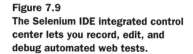

Figure 7.9
The Selenium IDE integrated control center lets you record, edit, and debug automated web tests.

NOTE You may be wondering how Selenium performs on applications bigger than the simple calculator. From our experience, it works fine with modern business web applications. In the end, they're all HTML with a bunch of links, buttons, and other controls. Selenium even manages Ajax and similar technologies.

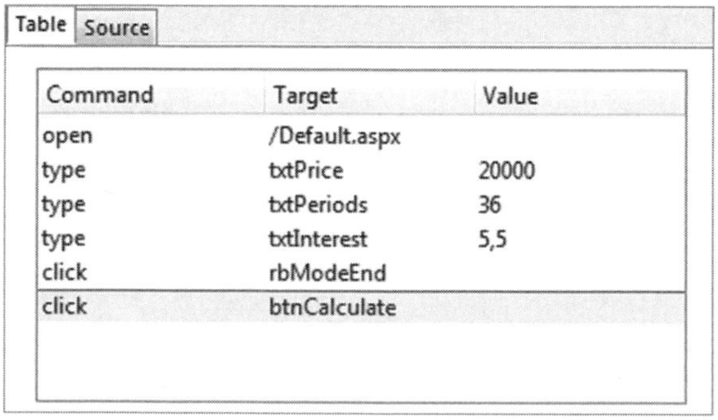

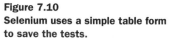

Figure 7.10
Selenium uses a simple table form to save the tests.

| Table | Source |

Command	Target	Value
open	/Default.aspx	
type	txtPrice	20000
type	txtPeriods	36
type	txtInterest	5,5
click	rbModeEnd	
click	btnCalculate	
waitForPageToLoad		3000
assertValue	txtRate	603,90

Command assertValue

Target txtRate   Find

Value 603,90

Figure 7.11
Although Selenium can record your clicks and keystrokes, you have to manually add additional commands to complete the test.

The table consists of three columns: Command, Target, and Value. A *command* is a Selenium instruction that defines what the testing framework should do. For example, open directs the browser to open the document specified in the Target column; type enters text specified in the Value column into the field specified in Target; and click clicks a control specified in Target.

To complete the test, you have to do an *assertion*. To do that, click the Record button again to stop the recording. Go to the empty line at the end of the test steps, and add two more commands, as shown in figure 7.11.

You add the waitForPageToLoad command with a value of 3000 milliseconds because your application does a postback after you click the Calculate button. The test suite has to wait until the page is loaded; after that, you assert the output rate value. You then issue an assertValue command to the target txtRate (the name of the field on the website) and check that the value is correct.

Your first automated test is ready. Click the Play button 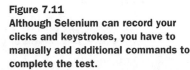 to run it. Selenium executes the entire test suite (which consists of only one test) and displays the output (see figure 7.12).

As we said earlier, the default table-style test layout isn't the only input Selenium accepts. You can easily change the format to C# so that you can run the test as an NUnit test. In the Selenium IDE window, choose Options > Format > C# - Selenium RC. You'll get the code shown next.

| Log | Reference | UI-Element | Rollup | Info | Clear |

```
[info] Executing: |type | txtPrice | 20000 |
[info] Executing: |type | txtPeriods | 36 |
[info] Executing: |type | txtInterest | 5,5 |
[info] Executing: |click | rbModeEnd | |
[info] Executing: |click | btnCalculate | |
[info] Executing: |waitForPageToLoad | 3000 | |
[info] Executing: |assertValue | txtRate | 603,90 |
```

Figure 7.12
Selenium executes the commands in the script sequentially and detects the correct value. It looks like everything works.

Listing 7.9   Selenium test case as a C# NUnit test fixture

```
using System;
using System.Text;
using System.Text.RegularExpressions;
using System.Threading;
using NUnit.Framework;
using Selenium;

namespace SeleniumTests
{
  [TestFixture]
  public class Untitled
  {
    private ISelenium selenium;
    private StringBuilder verificationErrors;

    [SetUp]
    public void SetupTest()
    {
        selenium = new DefaultSelenium("localhost", 4444,
          "*chrome",
          "http://change-this-to-the-site-you-are-testing/");
        selenium.Start();
        verificationErrors = new StringBuilder();
    }

    [TearDown]
    public void TeardownTest()
    {
      try
      {
        selenium.Stop();
      }
      catch (Exception)
      {
        // Ignore errors if unable to close the browser
      }
      Assert.AreEqual("", verificationErrors.ToString());
    }

    [Test]
    public void TheUntitledTest()
    {
      selenium.Open("/Default.aspx");
      selenium.Type("txtPrice", "20000");
      selenium.Type("txtPeriods", "36");
      selenium.Type("txtInterest", "5,5");
      selenium.Click("rbModeEnd");
      selenium.Click("btnCalculate");
      selenium.WaitForPageToLoad("3000");
      Assert.AreEqual("603,90", selenium.GetValue("txtRate"));
    }
  }
}
```

❶ Defines Selenium RC server proxy

This test can only be run against a Selenium RC server that's able to play the test remotely. It starts and closes one of the supported web browsers and acts as a proxy between the test case and that browser. On the test case side, Selenium RC is a set of assemblies that allows communication with the Selenium RC proxy server.

Let's prepare the client test case side of the browser-automation test suite. First, from http://seleniumhq.org/, download Selenium RC. It contains the server and the client-side libraries. Take the libraries from the selenium-dotnet-client folder and copy them to your tools folder.

We've put a ready-to-use project in the source codes accompanying the book. Reference the ThoughtWorks.Selenium.Core.dll in the test project, and copy the Selenium-generated code from listing 7.9 into a new test fixture class. Modify the namespace and class name to suit your needs. The Selenium client connects to the RC server over a proxy server. This server is specified in the test fixture `SetUp` method ❶.

Selenium RC server is a Java-based application that comes with the Selenium RC archive. Extract the contents of the selenium-server directory. Then go to the command line, navigate to the directory with your server, and issue a command to start the server from the JAR file:

```
java -jar selenium-server
```

By default, the Selenium RC server starts on port 4444. If it doesn't collide with any of your network services, it can stay this way. If not, change it and edit ❶ to use the new port number. The first parameter in the `DefaultSelenium` constructor is the Selenium RC server address, the second is the port number where it listens, and the third is the browser to automate (you can change this to `*firefox` or `*iexplore` if you don't have Google Chrome). The last parameter is the URL to the site you're about to test. In this case, the constructor can be

```
selenium = new DefaultSelenium("localhost", 4444,
➥"*firefox", " http://localhost:54121");
```

Start the test with your favorite NUnit tool. Selenium RC server starts the browser (see figure 7.13), performs the test, and then closes everything.

Now that you know how to test the UI of your application, let's see how to integrate those UI tests into your CI process.

7.3.4 *Integrating UI tests into the CI process*

The answer to the question of whether to include UI testing in your CI suite comes from the "it depends" series. Are the tests fast enough to complete in 10 minutes? Are the tests reliable enough not to introduce unnecessary tension by breaking some dependency?

SPEED

Tests that involve the UI are often slow. You have to start the application. If it's an ASP.NET application, that can mean starting a web server, compiling the application on the server, and starting a browser with which to perform the test. If your program

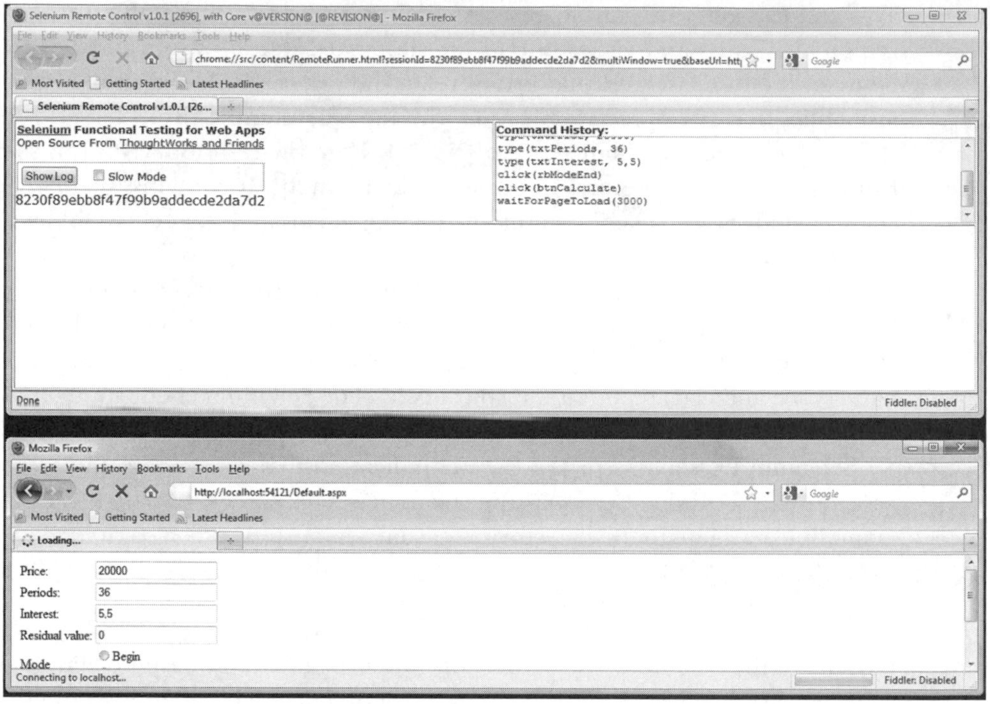

Figure 7.13   Selenium RC performing the test in Firefox

makes a connection to the database, you have to go all the way to the database server to reach it. This can mean the test execution time is unacceptable.

You can fight that issue in various ways. A good solution for accelerating your web test is to deploy your application to a preconfigured web server and test it on that server. We'll deal with this in chapter 11. Another good idea is to prepare a special database for this kind of test, with less data and faster query-execution times.

RELIABILITY

Are the tests reliable enough? You have to pay closer attention to the fact that the functional UI tests depend on the environment in which they're executing. If you're developing and testing on the same database, you're likely to introduce data that will interfere with your test suite. If your tests depend on the company's network architecture, you'll get a false alarm if your network administrator decides to replace an old switch in the server room.

You can minimize this kind of problem by using a separate test database for development, manual testing, and automated testing. It may even be a good idea to set up the database every time, as with integration tests. You can minimize network dependency by setting up your hardware test architecture yourself. If it's physically impossible, how about using a virtual server? If all else fails, think about putting the UI tests in a periodic-build scenario—say, every 2 hours or every night.

SELENIUM

Working with Selenium in a CI environment has its own issues. Starting the Selenium RC server every time to run a test is a bad idea. It takes time; and if you're working with several projects that use Selenium, you'll quickly reach the point where two projects want to start the Selenium RC server on the same port, and the second project is out of luck.

The best way to use Selenium RC server is to install it on a machine and let it work constantly. You can start Selenium RC server as a Windows service. That way, it's always ready to perform the tests.

To install Selenium RC server as a Windows Service, follow this quick guide:

1 Make sure you have Java installed on the server where you want to run Selenium RC server.

2 Extract Selenium RC server to the destination server: for example, c:\tools\seleniumrc directory.

3 Get Non-Sucking Service Manager (NSSM) and copy it to your tools folder. Issue `nssm.exe install SeleniumRC` from the command line. You're asked what program you want to start as a service (see figure 7.14).

> **NOTE** The Non-Sucking Service Manager is a service-helper program that handles the failure of an application running as a service. You can download it from http://iain.cx/src/nssm/.

4 Open the Windows Services console. Search for your new SeleniumRC service.

5 Go to Properties. On the Log On tab, select Allow Service to Interact With Desktop (as shown earlier in figure 7.4).

6 Start the service.

7 The last thing you'll most likely have to deal with is an exception on your firewall. If you start the Selenium RC service on the default 4444 port, you must define a hole in the firewall for this port.

8 From now on, you don't have to run Selenium RC server on your local machine. All you have to do is direct your test to the server where it's running as a service (see listing 7.10 ❶).

GUI tests are a great extension to your test repertoire. With tools like White and Selenium, you can design and write high-level tests for your applications. But can you

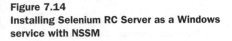

Figure 7.14
Installing Selenium RC Server as a Windows service with NSSM

imagine someone else doing at least part of this testing for you? How about a customer? Yes, it's possible, and that's what we'll talk about next.

7.4   *Acceptance testing with FitNesse*

FitNesse is a highly sophisticated acceptance test tool. Essentially, it's a web server that hosts wiki-style web pages you can use as tests for your software. It's a direct descendant of Framework for Integrated Test (Fit) by Ward Cunningham.

The basic idea of Fit and FitNesse is to give nontechnical users, such as end users and domain experts, the ability to write acceptance tests. The tests can be expressed in a table form that can be understood and managed by a customer or a domain specialist. The table-form tests are executed against a test runner, and the output is presented to the user. There's no better way of learning than doing, so let's jump in and try out FitNesse.

7.4.1   *Preparing the FitNesse framework*

FitNesse is written in Java, so make sure you have the Java Runtime environment installed (you can get it from http://java.com/en/). Download FitNesse from http://fitnesse.org/, and copy the fitnesse.jar file to your directory of choice—for example, c:\tools\fitnesse. To start FitNesse, issue `java -jar fitnesse.jar` from a command window.

By default, FitNesse runs on port 80. It's a standard HTTP server; so if a web server is present on the machine, this port is most likely taken. To start FitNesse on another port, use the `-p` switch: for example, `java -jar fitnesse.jar -p 8888`.

Open a web browser, and navigate to http://localhost:8888, substituting your host name or IP address in place of localhost. The FitNesse home page opens, as shown in figure 7.15.

Figure 7.15   The FitNesse home page. FitNesse is a wiki-style service that allows nontechnical users to write and perform acceptance software tests.

The next step is to prepare FitNesse to run .NET code. Download fitSharp from www.syterra.com/FitSharp.html. You'll have to tell FitNesse where the .NET files are installed; to make the relative path short, copy the contents of the zip file to a dotnet folder next to your fitnesse.jar file. FitNesse.NET contains the files needed on both the client test side and on the FitNesse server side.

Let's say you want to give the financial calculation specialists the ability to test your financial calculation library. It's the core of your calculator application. The library lets you calculate the rate for a given lease or credit amount with various parameters. You've covered this code with your unit tests, but it would be nice for nontechnical people to be able to write their own tests. In order to do that, you have to prepare a class that will be an interface between the code you're about to test and the FitNesse wiki site.

Drop the content of FitNesse.NET into the tools folder in your project, and reference a test project with fit.dll and fitSharp.dll. This assembly contains the fit.Column-Fixture class, which will be the base class for your test fixture.

Listing 7.10   A class that hooks up the financial library with FitNesse

```
namespace CiDotNet.Calc.Test.Math
{
  public class FinanceColumnFixture : fit.ColumnFixture
  {
    public int duration;
    public int ppy;
    public double periodicInterestRate;
    public double presentValue;
    public double finalValue;
    public CiDotNet.Calc.Math.Finance.Mode mode;

    public double CalculateRate()
    {
      return CiDotNet.Calc.Math.Finance.CalculateRate(
        duration, ppy, periodicInterestRate,
        presentValue, finalValue, mode);
    }
  }
}
```

First, you inform FitNesse that you'll be using the most common fixture that maps the test's columns to the appropriate properties. You define the available properties and do the work. The input values from the test columns are passed to the financial library implementation.

You're good to go on the client side. Now, let's define a test in FitNesse. To create a new wiki site with FitNesse, you must navigate to the application test page on your Fit-Nesse server, such as http://localhost:8888/CalcTest (this test suite is included with the book's source code). This page will host a test suite. You can have as many test suites as you wish; you just have to navigate to a new URL like http://localhost:8888/AnotherTestSuite. When the page opens in your browser, you're presented with a new wiki site (see figure 7.16) that you can use to enter the FitNesse test.

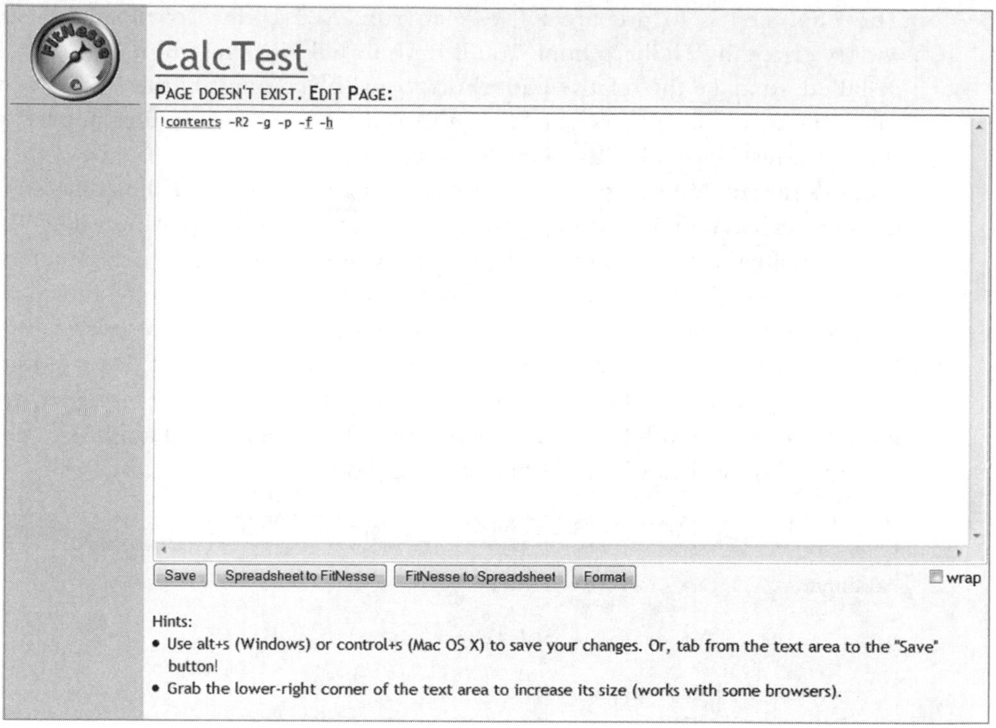

Figure 7.16   Blank wiki test page in FitNesse. This page is where you enter the instructions for FitNesse to test your application.

Let's say that the assembly with the `FinanceColumnFixture` is called CiDotNet.Calc. Test.dll. The simplest test looks like this:

```
!define COMMAND_PATTERN {%m -r
➥fitnesse.fitserver.FitServer,dotnet\fit.dll %p}
!define TEST_RUNNER {dotnet\Runner.exe}
!path ..\..\CiDotNet.Calc.Test\bin\Debug\CiDotNet.Calc.Test.dll

!|CiDotNet.Calc.Test.Math.FinanceColumnFixture|
|duration|ppy|periodicInterestRate|presentValue|finalValue|
➥mode|CalculateRate?|
|12|12|7|30000|0|1|2580,75|
|24|12|7|30000|0|1|1335,40|
|36|12|7|30000|0|1|920,95|
```

You first define the test environment, starting from `COMMAND_PATTERN` and continuing through to `TEST_RUNNER` and the path to the test library. The *test runner* is a tool that takes the wiki test definition and performs the test; it's part of FitNesse.NET, which you downloaded earlier. It uses the command pattern specified earlier.

If you're familiar with wiki syntax, the test definition is straightforward. It's a table with a header containing the test fixture class name. The table is enclosed with | bars and prefixed with ! to prevent the wiki engine from interpreting the CamelCased name as a link to another page. The columns are defined between the | bars. The column values will be mapped to the test fixture class properties, one line after another, one each time.

After you enter the test information into the wiki page, click the Save button. The test page looks like figure 7.17.

You can easily switch back to edit mode using the side toolbar. At the top of this toolbar is a Test button that launches the test runner to perform the wiki-defined test. Click Test; the output is shown in figure 7.18.

This is only the tip of the iceberg when it comes to acceptance tests with FitNesse. It isn't easy to involve domain experts in the testing like this. It's even harder to involve the customer. But it's certainly worth trying. This is the best way to get the people with the best domain knowledge as close to development as possible.

To deepen your FitNesse knowledge, Gojko Adzic has a great book about FitNesse, *Test Driven* .NET *Development with FitNesse.* If you want to extend your test repertoire, look at it. We'll deal now with something more important to us: FitNesse integration into your CI process.

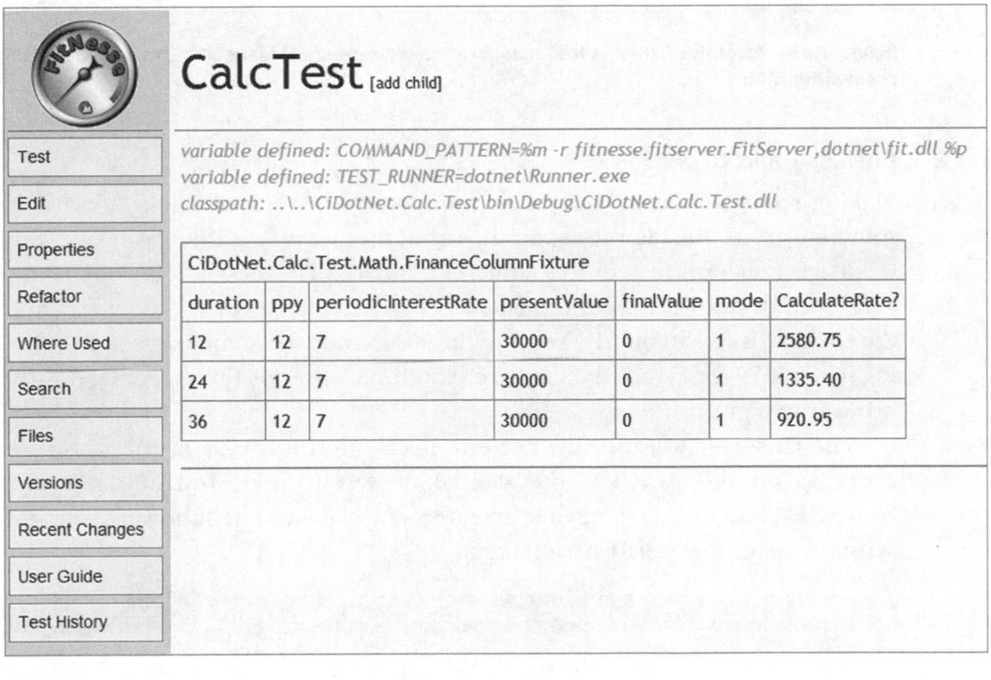

CalcTest [add child]

Test	*variable defined: COMMAND_PATTERN=%m -r fitnesse.fitserver.FitServer,dotnet\fit.dll %p*
Edit	*variable defined: TEST_RUNNER=dotnet\Runner.exe*
	classpath: ..\..\CIDotNet.Calc.Test\bin\Debug\CIDotNet.Calc.Test.dll

CiDotNet.Calc.Test.Math.FinanceColumnFixture

duration	ppy	periodicInterestRate	presentValue	finalValue	mode	CalculateRate?
12	12	7	30000	0	1	2580.75
24	12	7	30000	0	1	1335.40
36	12	7	30000	0	1	920.95

Side toolbar items: Test, Edit, Properties, Refactor, Where Used, Search, Files, Versions, Recent Changes, User Guide, Test History

Figure 7.17   A simple FitNesse test page after the test instructions have been entered

CiDotNet.Calc.Test.Math.FinanceColumnFixture						
duration	ppy	periodicInterestRate	presentValue	finalValue	mode	CalculateRate?
12	12	7	30000	0	1	2580.75
74	12	7	30000	0	1	1335.40
36	12	7	30000	0	1	920.95

Figure 7.18   After the FitNesse test runs, everything is green. It looks like the financial library has passed the test.

7.4.2   FitNesse and CI

Making FitNesse play in your CI environment can be a little tricky because it involves someone from outside the team; in addition, integrating the test result with your CI feedback mechanism requires some extra work. The best way to deal with the first issue is to install FitNesse on a machine that's available for the domain expert (keep the security issues in mind). You can do this exactly the same way you install Selenium RC server. FitNesse runs as a service; you'll have to tell the customer to direct their browser to a given URL.

The CI server will use this FitNesse installation to perform the tests remotely. In order to do this, you use the standalone test runner, TestRunner.exe, from FitNesse.NET. You can use it against an external test page. The following listing shows the MSBuild script that performs a test run.

Listing 7.11   MSBuild using `TestRunner` to perform an acceptance test

```
<Project DefaultTargets="FitTest"
  xmlns="http://schemas.microsoft.com/developer/msbuild/2003">

  <PropertyGroup>
    <FitNesseServer>localhost</FitNesseServer>
    <FitNessePort>8888</FitNessePort>
    <FitNesseTest>CalcTest</FitNesseTest>
  </PropertyGroup>
```

```
<Target Name="FitTest" >
  <Exec Command="tools\FitNesse\dotnet\Runner.exe
    ➥-r fitnesse.titserver.TestRunner,Tools\FitNesse\dotnet\fit.dll
    ➥-results FitNesseLog.html -format html
    ➥$(FitNesseServer) $(FitNessePort) $(FitNesseTest)" />
</Target>
</Project>
```

You execute `TestRunner` with the `Exec` command. You start TestRunner.exe from the dotnet folder while the working directory is set to the FitNesse directory. This way, the relative file paths in the test will be correct. The results file is saved under the name FitNesseLog.txt. The server name, port number, and test page name are saved in MSBuild properties.

The test results that FitNesse produces are simple HTML documents. Integration with TeamCity is straightforward. As you learned in previous chapters, add the FitNesseLog.html file to your project artifacts, and define a new FitNesse project tab. After the next test run, you see the tests results on the TeamCity webpage.

To integrate the test runner results with Cruisecontrol.NET you must use the fitSharp and XML results (change `-format` in the listing 7.11 to `text`) it produces or transforms the html output of the test runner to XML. After that, apply a proper XSLT transformation to it like this:

```
<xslReportBuildPlugin description="Fitnesse Report"
  ➥ actionName="FitnesseReport" xslFileName="xsl\fitnesse.xsl"/>
```

You'll have to integrate it into your CI server feedback mechanism. And there you have it: customer testing, integrated into your CI system.

7.5 Summary

Extending a test repertoire into your CI process is worthwhile. Different tests reveal different problems. Unit tests live close to the code and aim for different issues than integration or functional tests. The latter have broader scope; they target interactions within the code or beyond it, to external resources. With the broader scope comes complexity. Integration and functional tests tend to take longer and to be harder to isolate. You can no longer rely on mocked objects—you have to deal with interactions and a real environment. Nevertheless, it pays to integrate as many tests as possible into your CI process.

The more you test, the more certain you can be that you aren't breaking anything. As long as you can keep your integration and functional tests quick and reliable, you're good to go with CI. If not, think about putting these tests in periodic builds. Keep in mind that you need to organize your tests in any CI process from the quickest to the longest running; this way, you'll get feedback as soon as possible.

Sometimes it's a good idea to involve a client or a nontechnical person with domain knowledge into the test process. Acceptance tests have their place in CI too. They probably won't break the build if they fail, and they're better indicators of being on the right track. The art is to use them as a kind of specification and to gradually make them more and more green. There is no better feeling than being sure the work you've done delivers what the customer wants.

Various tests ensure that the software works as designed. This is important. But these tests say little about how maintainable the software is. Will it be easy to extend with new features? Is the code readable to others besides the developer who wrote it? Is it properly commented and understandable? Does it follow the rules? To answer all these questions, you may consider doing the static code analysis automatically and integrating it into the CI process. This is the topic of the next chapter, "Analyzing the code."

Analyzing the code

This chapter covers

- Using FxCop and StyleCop for static code analysis
- Integrating FxCop and StyleCop into the CI process
- Extending the CI process with custom rules
- Using NDepend

Have you ever taken over a project to fix a bug or code a feature? In such a situation, did you feel uncertain, lost, or upset? How many times have you wanted to find the person who originally wrote the piece of code you're working on and simply ... thank them warmly? If you're living in the same world we are, this has happened to you at least a few times (see figure 8.1).

Did you ever wonder why you felt like this? Was it because the code didn't do what it was supposed to do? If it wasn't a bug, it was probably something else: the software *smelled*. And nothing is worse than smelly code. In this chapter, we'll discuss what you can do about smelly code and how to enforce clean code using CI. We'll look at a few tools that make this possible: FxCop, StyleCop, NDepend, and a TeamCity tool that checks for code duplication.

Figure 8.1
Always code as if the person who will maintain your code is a violent psychopath who knows where you live (picture courtesy of http://kkphoto.art.pl/).

These tools do static code analysis against the code you're writing and tell you where you could do better. The testing methods we showed you in the previous two chapters are called *dynamic analysis*. That is, you run the code to determine its correctness. With *static analysis*, you don't run the code: you check it for other types of issues. Each tool checks for a different type of issue, something we'll explain as we look at each tool.

Two of the tools, FxCop and StyleCop, are appropriately named because they enforce rules for good coding. They have your back when the psychopath comes lurking. In this chapter, we'll look at how to enforce obedience to good coding rules and how to define your own rules for these tools. You'll also integrate everything into your CI process. You'll do all this so you don't anger the psychopath who knows where you live. Let's get started by looking at FxCop.

8.1   Analyzing object code with FxCop

FxCop is a free Microsoft tool for code analysis. It examines compiled .NET assemblies for things like performance, naming conventions, library design, globalization, and security.

FxCop started as a standalone program that enforced the rules from Design Guidelines for Class Library Developers (http://msdn.microsoft.com/en-us/library/czefa0ke(VS.71).aspx), a document that contains good coding practices for developers writing .NET code. FxCop was incorporated into Visual Studio Team System 2008 and Visual Studio Premium 2010 as Code Analysis. The good news is, it's also still available as a standalone program, and it's helpful as part of CI. Let's look at FxCop in action.

8.1.1   Using Visual Studio Code Analysis

If you have an edition of Visual Studio 2010 that includes Code Analysis, using it is straightforward. Go to your project's properties, click the Code Analysis tab, and select the Enable Code Analysis on Build check box (see figure 8.2).

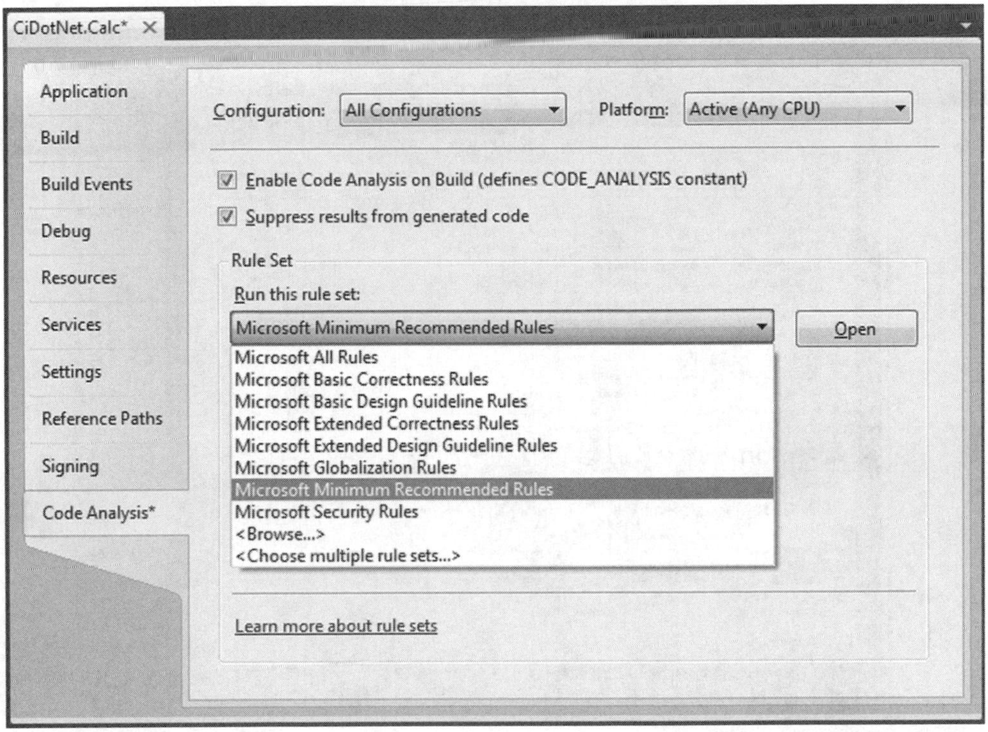

Figure 8.2 FxCop is built in to Visual Studio 2010's Premium and Ultimate editions as Code Analysis.

Microsoft suggests that by default you use the Microsoft Minimum Recommended Rules. It's up to you what set of rules to use; you can even define your own. Keep in mind that the rules come from a document that contains the word *guidelines* in its title. What's important is that you're making a conscious decision about using the rules. To see the rules that are working, click Open next to the Run This Rule Set drop-down list. You can modify the list according to your needs and save the output file for future use in other projects (see figure 8.3).

You can decide which rules will break your build and which will only cause compiler warnings. After you turn on Code Analysis, every time your project compiles, the analysis is finished.

But what about situations when you feel you have to make an exception to a rule you chose to obey? To do this, you can use *suppressions*. You can suppress FxCop messages directly in the code where they occur, or you can use a global suppression file. Visual Studio comes with neat functionality to make this easier. To suppress a particular issue, right-click it in the Error List window, and select Suppress Message(s) (see figure 8.4). You can suppress the messages either in the source code or in a special suppression file. The way we do it is to give developers a free hand in suppressing the particular message. Of course, they should be able to support their decisions, but we

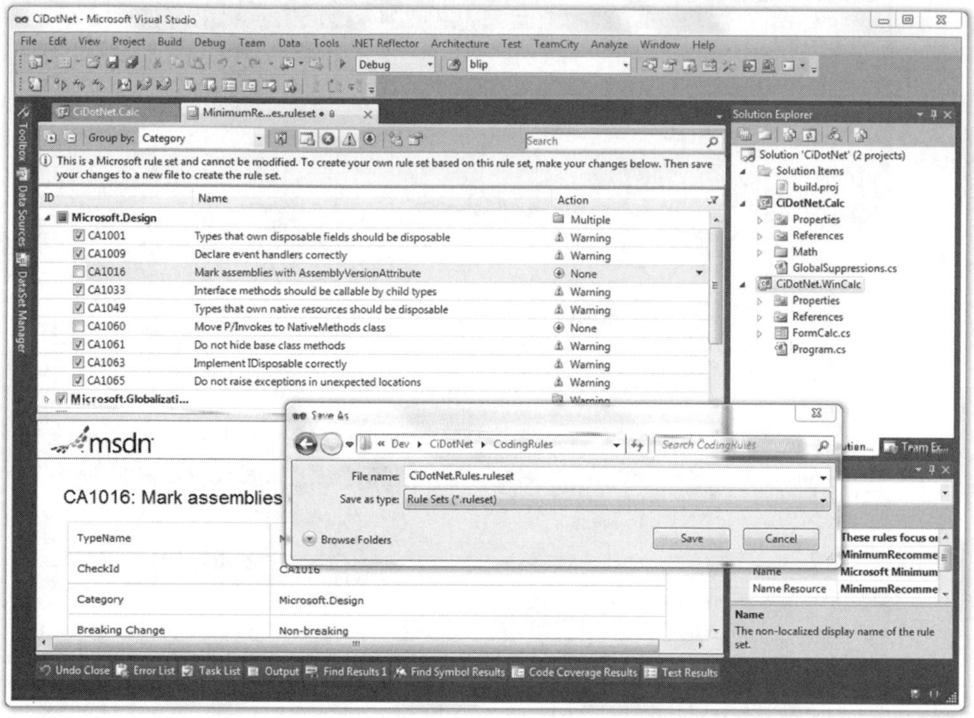

Figure 8.3 **When you define a set of Code Analysis rules in Visual Studio 2010, you can save them to a rule-set file so you can apply them to projects.**

don't want to handicap development (peer code review is a good time to discuss suppressions). On the other hand, the project suppression file should be treated with respect. The records it contains should be carefully chosen by senior members of the team.

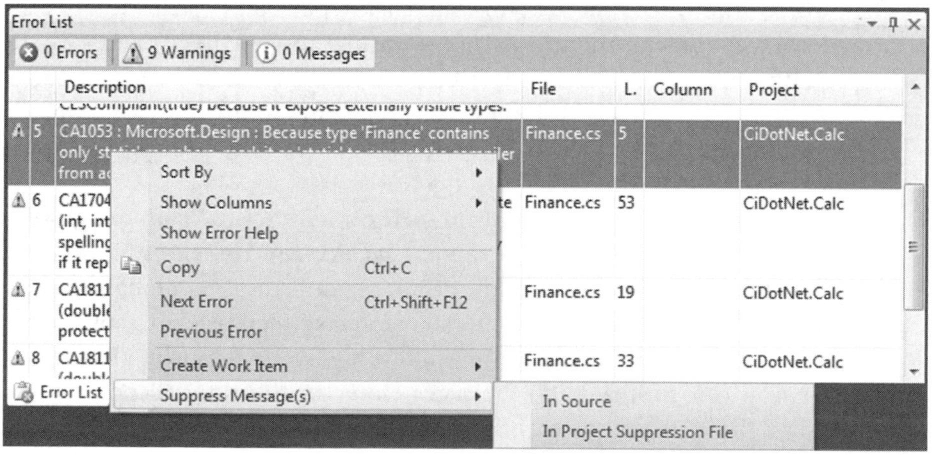

Figure 8.4 **Suppressing a Code Analysis message in the Error List window in Visual Studio 2010**

You should approach static code analysis with caution. Turning on all the rules for an old project can be painful. You'll probably get hundreds of errors (especially if you're threading warnings as errors). From experience, we know that one reasonable solution is to go through the available rules, think about them, and turn on only the ones you're convinced are right for you. Keep in mind that, in most cases, you aren't writing something that must be as clean as .NET Framework. You want to get your job done as well as you can without generating too much additional cost.

Using Code Analysis is fine, but what if it isn't included in your edition of Visual Studio, or you need it to run automatically on your CI server? The answer is to use FxCop.

8.1.2   *Setting up continuous FxCop code analysis*

As you've seen, FxCop has been dressed up nicely as Code Analysis and migrated to Visual Studio. Fortunately, the FxCop source project didn't die: it's still actively supported. Even if you don't have the full-blown Visual Studio, you can still use FxCop; you just have to download it from http://code.msdn.microsoft.com/codeanalysis and install it. Of course, using it won't be as friction-free as using Visual Studio Code Analysis; but with standalone FxCop, you can customize your CI process as you wish. And using the FxCop GUI (see figure 8.5), you can do basically everything that is possible with Code Analysis in Visual Studio.

FxCop stores information about the assemblies that it needs to analyze in an FxCop project. You can recognize a project by its .FxCop extension. The project is created automatically as you add your .NET assemblies to the FxCop GUI—just remember to save the FxCop project in the same directory as your .NET solution

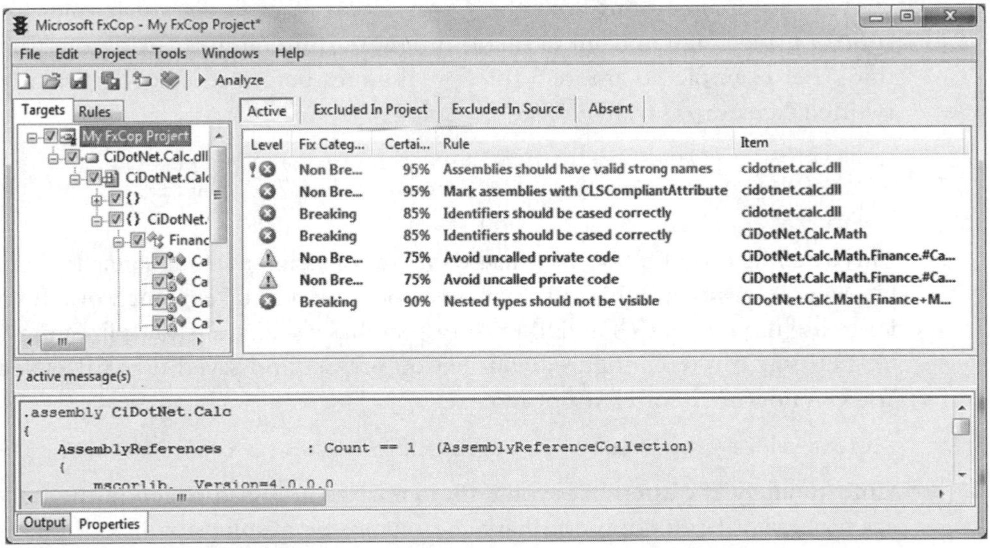

Figure 8.5   Standalone FxCop performs the same analysis as Code Analysis in Visual Studio and allows you to create FxCop project files for use in your CI process.

so it can be checked in to your source code repository, where the CI process can grab it.

Let's configure the CI server to analyze your code. First, copy the contents of the standalone FxCop tool to the tools subdirectory. One important file is the FxCop command-line tool, FxCopCmd.exe.

Next, you need to extend the MSBuild project file with a new code-analysis task. You can use the MSBuild Exec task with FxCopCmd.exe. In addition, an MSBuild Community Task automates the usage of command-line FxCop (if you want to know how to use it, refer to chapter 3).

When you run FxCop as part of your CI process, you must consider two issues. First, if you're picky about the rules you're using, it's better to manage them visually in the FxCop GUI. Second, getting information about rules violations isn't as straightforward as it could be.

The command-line tool, FxCopCmd, can take either the list of assemblies to analyze and the list of rules to be checked or the FxCop project as an input parameter. If you aren't picky about the rules you want to check, the command to check your assembly is pretty clear:

```
tools\FxCop\FxCopCmd.exe /f:CiDotNet.Calc/bin/Debug/CiDotNet.Calc.dll
➥/r:tools/FxCop/Rules /console
```

This takes the financial library you created earlier in the book and runs in through FxCop using all the rules from the tools/FxCop/Rules directory. The /console switch tells FxCopCmd to output everything to the console. If you want to write the output to a file, you need to specify the filename with /o:FxCopReport.xml.

If you're choosier about what rules to use and what to leave out, you can use the /ruleid parameter along with the +/- notation to indicate which rules to include (put a plus (+) sign in front of them) or ignore (put a minus (-) sign in front of the rule). For example, to ignore a rule, put a minus before its category and id number (written Category#Id), like this:

```
tools\FxCop\FxCopCmd.exe /f:CiDotNet.Calc/bin/Debug/CiDotNet
➥.Calc.dll /r:tools/FxCop/Rules /ruleid:-Microsoft.Design#CA2210
➥/console
```

This example turns off the rule that says you must assign a strong name for your assembly. You can customize this call as you wish, but doing so takes some work. It's a lot easier to use the FxCop GUI and filter the assemblies visually, as shown in figure 8.6.

Let's say you've configured your FxCop project and saved it as CiDotNet.FxCop. You can now use it with FxCopCmd.exe:

```
tools\FxCop\FxCopCmd.exe /project:CiDotNet.FxCop /out:FxCopReport.xml
```

Unfortunately, the assemblies you want to analyze are hard coded in the FxCop project file. Even if you choose to have the relative or absolute path to the targets and you're using the standard Debug or Release scenario, you'll end up with one of the output directories being written into the FxCop project file:

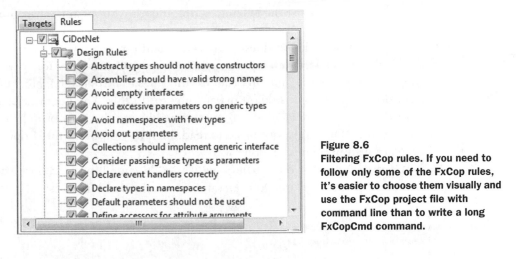

Figure 8.6
Filtering FxCop rules. If you need to follow only some of the FxCop rules, it's easier to choose them visually and use the FxCop project file with command line than to write a long FxCopCmd command.

```
<Target Name="$(ProjectDir)/CiDotNet.Calc/bin/Debug/CiDotNet.Calc.dll"
➥Analyze="True" AnalyzeAllChildren="True" />
```

One way to resolve this is to have two FxCop project files: one for Debug and one for Release. If you want to vary the analysis for both scenarios (not recommended from our experience, because Release tends to be neglected by developers), it should work for you. If not, you have to use a different solution.

MSBuild comes with a possible answer: the Community Tasks we examined in chapter 3 include a FileUpdate task. You can use it to change the assembly directory in the FxCop project file in a CI scenario, as shown in the following listing.

Listing 8.1   FxCop run from the command line using a manipulated project file

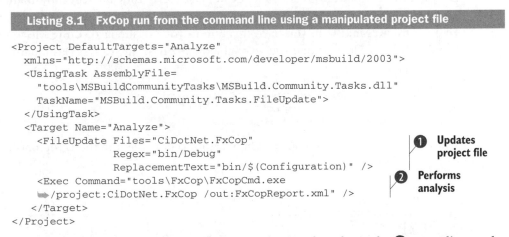

```
<Project DefaultTargets="Analyze"
  xmlns="http://schemas.microsoft.com/developer/msbuild/2003">
  <UsingTask AssemblyFile=
    "tools\MSBuildCommunityTasks\MSBuild.Community.Tasks.dll"
    TaskName="MSBuild.Community.Tasks.FileUpdate">
  </UsingTask>
  <Target Name="Analyze">
    <FileUpdate Files="CiDotNet.FxCop"                          ❶ Updates
                Regex="bin/Debug"                                  project file
                ReplacementText="bin/$(Configuration)" />
    <Exec Command="tools\FxCop\FxCopCmd.exe                     ❷ Performs
    ➥/project:CiDotNet.FxCop /out:FxCopReport.xml" />             analysis
  </Target>
</Project>
```

First you import the Community Task to use it to update the paths ❶ according to the current configuration. You then call FxCopCmd ❷ to perform the analysis.

We generally recommend that you incorporate all the rules provided and then exclude specific rules that you think aren't important. Nevertheless, if you're picky, you can use our solution.

But as you'll see by starting the MSBuild script, it ends without any errors or warnings even if there are rule violations in your code. This isn't acceptable, because you can bet that if the rule violation doesn't break the build, no one will bother to obey the rules. You can't expect developers to check the FxCop results for a working build—you have to break the build in order for the rules to be obeyed. Unfortunately, FxCopCmd doesn't provide a straightforward way to do this. The `ContinueOnError` property in the `Exec` task reacts only on exceptions during the FxCopCmd run and not to broken rules. One of the options is to read the XML output from FxCopCmd to find the violations. But there's an easier way.

FxCopCmd produces an output file only if there's something to report, such as broken rules. So, if the file exists, you can safely break the build like this:

```
<Target Name="Analyze">
  <Delete Condition="Exists('FxCopReport.xml')"
    Files="FxCopReport.xml">
  </Delete>
  <Exec Command="tools\FxCop\FxCopCmd.exe /project:CiDotNet.FxCop
    /out:FxCopReport.xml"/>
  <Error Condition="Exists('FxCopReport.xml')"
    Text="FxCop found some broken rules!" />
</Target>
```

You're now fully prepared to integrate your code analysis with your CI server of choice. Let's find out how to do this.

8.1.3   *Integrating FxCop with CI servers*

As you know from previous chapters, CCNet takes XML files and can show them on the Dashboard page. Fortunately, it comes with an XSD file to perform a transformation to HTML format. Make sure you have this line in your dashboard.config file to include the FxCop XSD file, and that you've enabled FxCop on the CCNet Dashboard Administrator screen:

```
<xslReportBuildPlugin description="FxCop Report"
  actionName="FxCopBuildReport"
  xslFileName="xsl\fxcop-report_1_36.xsl" />
```

You also need to merge the FxCopCmd output report file into the Dashboard:

```
<publishers>
  <merge>
    <files>
      <file>FxCopReport.xml</file>
    </files>
  </merge>
  <xmllogger />
</publishers>
```

After you check everything into your source code repository, it should work fine. You can see the FxCop report, as shown in figure 8.7.

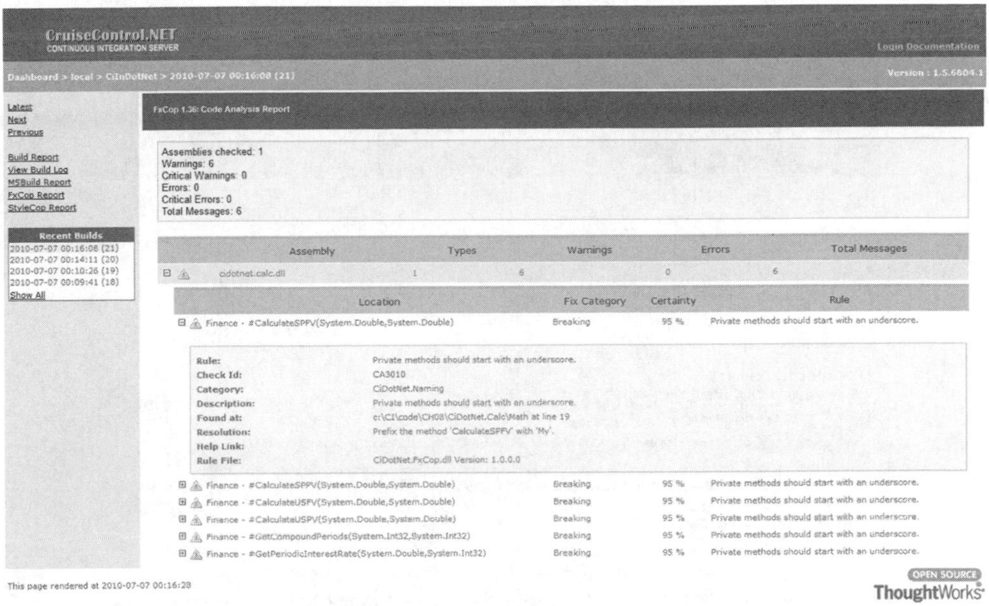

Figure 8.7 FxCop analysis report on the CCNet Dashboard page. The output from FxCopCmd is formatted using the XSD file supplied by CCNet to provide an easily readable report.

Integration with TeamCity requires an HTML file to merge with the TeamCity web page. FxCopCmd can produce an HTML file instead of the standard XML file. You only have to modify the call:

```
tools\FxCop\FxCopCmd.exe /project:CiDotNet.FxCop /out:FxCopReport.html
➥/axsl
```

The `axsl` parameter tells FxCopCmd to apply the XSL style sheet and produce HTML output. When that's finished, you're ready to add a new tab to the TeamCity website. Remember from earlier in the book that you have to define a new artifact FxCop-Report.html and a new tab server configuration. You'll end up with this page being part of the TeamCity build report (see figure 8.8).

If you're using TFS 2010 as your CI server, you're probably using the built-in code-analysis tools. You can turn on Code Analysis even without the Visual Studio 2010 Premium Edition. It's just a matter of adding a line to the project file:

```
<RunCodeAnalysis>true</RunCodeAnalysis>
```

You can also optionally specify the rule set to use:

```
<CodeAnalysisRuleSet>AllRules.ruleset</CodeAnalysisRuleSet>
```

You can't benefit from Code Analysis right away on your development machine, but TFS 2010 will snap in and perform the check for you when it performs a build. Figure 8.9 shows the TFS build report.

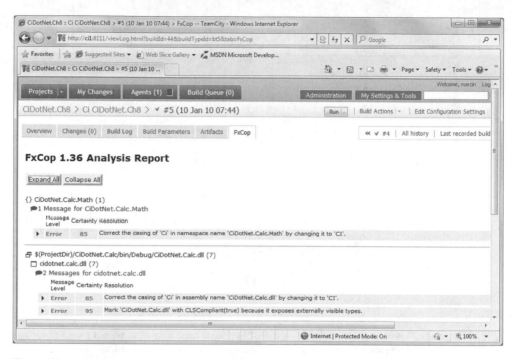

Figure 8.8   An FxCop analysis report in TeamCity.

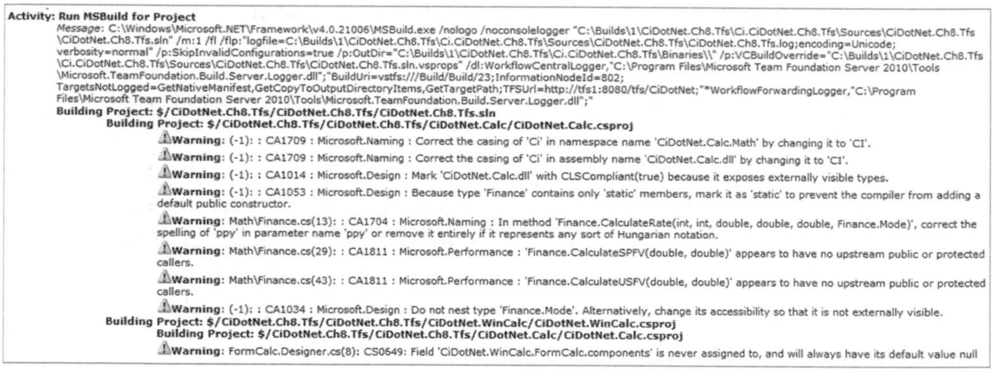

Figure 8.9   The TFS build report with Code Analysis output on the Build summary page. If you want to break the build on a given violation check, change the action to Error.

FxCop does a great job of checking the conformance of your assemblies to the Microsoft .NET Framework Design Guidelines. Because it checks assemblies and not actual code, it has some limitations. What if you want to check *everything*? Here comes StyleCop.

8.2 Analyzing C# with StyleCop

StyleCop is a static code-analysis tool that works with the actual C# source code, rather than assemblies. It checks for things like class, variable, and namespace naming; maintainability, readability, spacing, documentation, and ordering. Unfortunately, if you're a VB.NET or F# developer, you're out of luck, because StyleCop supports only C#.

StyleCop is a useful and complementary tool to FxCop. Together they'll guard your code cleanliness like watchdogs. But beware! You may get into a clinch with those two tools. If you run two conflicting rules, one on your C# code and one on the intermediate language it produces, the issue will be difficult to fix. Keeping this in mind, let's make StyleCop work.

8.2.1 Using StyleCop

StyleCop is a separate product that you need to download on its own (http://code.msdn.microsoft.com/sourceanalysis). It's installed as a Visual Studio plug-in. Don't forget to install the MSBuild files; you'll use them to work with CCNet and TeamCity.

After installation, StyleCop is available from the Tools menu in Visual Studio. Let's start with the settings. Choose StyleCop Settings from the project's context menu in Solution Explorer. A window opens, like the one shown in figure 8.10.

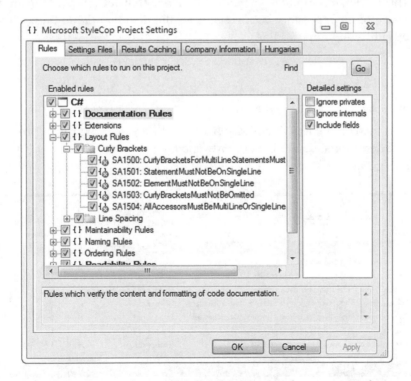

Figure 8.10 You can choose which StyleCop rules to enforce on your project.

You can turn the rules to be used on and off by selecting the check boxes. When you're finished, look inside the project folder. You'll find a new file: Settings.Style-Cop. It'll control how StyleCop performs on your local Visual Studio project or later on the server.

To perform the analysis, right-click the project in Solution Explorer, and click ⟨⟩ Run StyleCop. It may take a while to analyze your project, especially if it contains lots of files. When it's finished, you'll get list of errors (see figure 8.11).

Unfortunately, StyleCop isn't integrated with Visual Studio the way Code Analysis is, so you can't suppress rules from the context menu in the Error List window. You have to disable the rule you don't want to obey, using the dialog box shown in figure 8.10. But the integration with your CI process should be even simpler than the FxCop integration, as you'll see in the next section.

8.2.2 *Continuous StyleCop analysis*

If you don't mind editing your project file by hand, you can get StyleCop to work with TFS 2010 without any problem. Just as with the other scenarios, take the StyleCop components, make a folder in your project called tools/StyleCop, and check it in to your source control repository. The files you need are in the StyleCop installation directory (probably %ProgramFiles%\Microsoft StyleCop) and in the MSBuild targets directory (probably %ProgramFiles%\MSBuild\Microsoft\StyleCop\ plus version number). If the size of the repository is an issue, leave the documentation files. Go to the build's project file, and find this line:

```
<Import Project="$(MSBuildToolsPath)\Microsoft.CSharp.targets" />
```

Just after it, add a new line:

```
<Import Project="..\tools\StyleCop\Microsoft.StyleCop.targets" />
```

This line tells the compiler to import the `Microsoft.StyleCop.targets` project and run the StyleCop target defined there. We encourage you to look inside to know exactly what's going on.

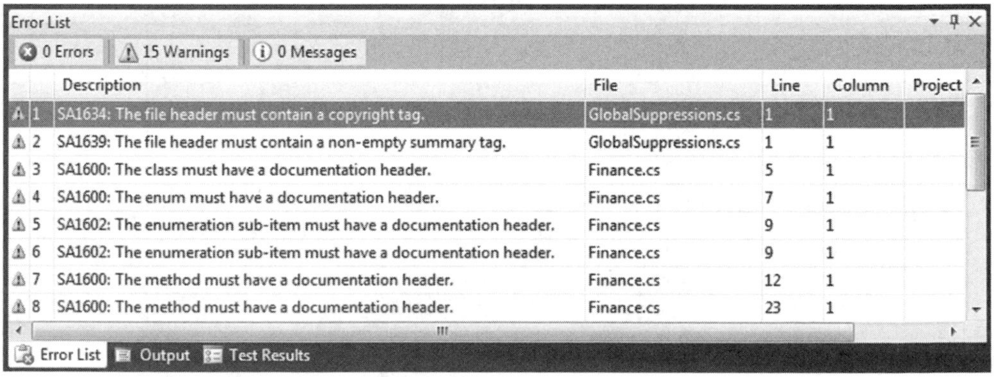

		Description	File	Line	Column	Project
⚠	1	SA1634: The file header must contain a copyright tag.	GlobalSuppressions.cs	1	1	
⚠	2	SA1639: The file header must contain a non-empty summary tag.	GlobalSuppressions.cs	1	1	
⚠	3	SA1600: The class must have a documentation header.	Finance.cs	5	1	
⚠	4	SA1600: The enum must have a documentation header.	Finance.cs	7	1	
⚠	5	SA1602: The enumeration sub-item must have a documentation header.	Finance.cs	9	1	
⚠	6	SA1602: The enumeration sub-item must have a documentation header.	Finance.cs	9	1	
⚠	7	SA1600: The method must have a documentation header.	Finance.cs	12	1	
⚠	8	SA1600: The method must have a documentation header.	Finance.cs	23	1	

Error List   ⊗ 0 Errors   ⚠ 15 Warnings   ⓘ 0 Messages

Error List   Output   Test Results

Figure 8.11   A StyleCop analysis displays its errors in the Visual Studio Error List window.

Figure 8.12 TFS build report with StyleCop Code Analysis reporting

By default, all StyleCop rule violations are only compiler warnings, but they can easily break your build if you define a new property in the main property group in your csproj file:

```
<StyleCopTreatErrorsAsWarnings>false</StyleCopTreatErrorsAsWarnings>
```

That's everything you have to do to run StyleCop analysis in the TFS 2010 context. Check everything in, and wait for your CI process to start. The project build report should look like figure 8.12.

If you're using MSBuild as your build platform, you can use the StyleCopTask that comes with StyleCop. The usage isn't complicated.

Listing 8.2 MSBuild project for StyleCop analysis

```
<Project DefaultTargets="Analyze;"
  xmlns="http://schemas.microsoft.com/developer/msbuild/2003">
  <UsingTask AssemblyFile="tools\StyleCop\Microsoft.StyleCop.dll"
    TaskName="StyleCopTask"/>
  <Target Name="Analyze">
    <CreateItem Include="**\*.cs">
      <Output TaskParameter="Include" ItemName="StyleCopFiles"/>
    </CreateItem>
    <StyleCopTask
      ProjectFullPath="$(MSBuildProjectFile)"
      SourceFiles="@(StyleCopFiles)"
      ForceFullAnalysis="true"
      TreatErrorsAsWarnings="false"
      OutputFile="StyleCopReport.xml"
      CacheResults="true" />
  </Target>
</Project>
```

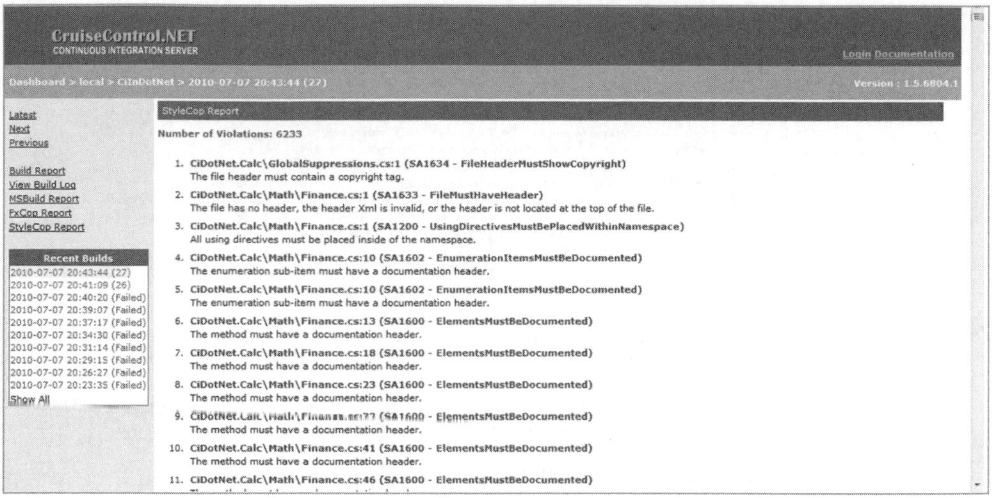

Figure 8.13   The default StyleCop report in CCNet

To use the task that comes with StyleCop, you first have to import it. It takes the list of .cs files as input and produces a StyleCopReport.xml file.

Unfortunately, CCNet doesn't come with a good XSL transformer for StyleCop. A better StyleCopReport.xsl file is provided with this book; copy it to the dashboard/ xsl folder on the CCNet server, and add this line to the <buildPlugins> tag in the d=Dashboard.config file:

```
<xslReportBuildPlugin description="StyleCop Report"
  actionName="StyleCopBuildReport" xslFileName="xsl\StyleCopReport.xsl" />
```

After you restart the Dashboard, you'll see a new menu option that should contain the formatted StyleCop page (see figure 8.13).

You need a ready-made HTML file to combine the analysis report with TeamCity. You have to transform the XML to HTML using the XSL. The best way to do it is in the MSBuild script. As usual, MSBuild Community Tasks can help. The following listing shows an MSBuild script.

Listing 8.3   MSBuild StyleCop script for TeamCity

```
<Project DefaultTargets="Analyze;"
  xmlns="http://schemas.microsoft.com/developer/msbuild/2003">
  <UsingTask AssemblyFile=
    "tools\MSBuildCommunityTasks\MSBuild.Community.Tasks.dll"
    TaskName="MSBuild.Community.Tasks.Xslt" />
  <UsingTask AssemblyFile=
    "tools\MSBuildCommunityTasks\MSBuild.Community.Tasks.dll"
    TaskName="MSBuild.Community.Tasks.XmlRead" />
  <UsingTask AssemblyFile=
```

```
      "tools\StyleCop\Microsoft.StyleCop.dll"
      TaskName="StyleCopTask"/>

  <Target Name="Analyze">
    <CreateItem Include="CiDotNet.Calc\**\*.cs">
      <Output TaskParameter="Include" ItemName="StyleCopFiles"/>
    </CreateItem>

    <StyleCopTask
      ProjectFullPath="$(MSBuildProjectFile)"
      SourceFiles="@(StyleCopFiles)"
      ForceFullAnalysis="true"
      TreatErrorsAsWarnings="true"
      OutputFile="StyleCopReport.xml"
      CacheResults="true" />

    <Xslt Inputs="StyleCopReport.xml"
      RootTag="StyleCopViolations"
      Xsl="tools\StyleCop\StyleCopReport.xsl"
      Output="StyleCopReport.html" />
    <XmlRead XPath="count(//Violation)"
      XmlFileName="StyleCopReport.xml">
      <Output TaskParameter="Value"
        PropertyName="StyleCopViolations" />
    </XmlRead>
    <Error Condition="$(StyleCopViolations) > 0"
      Text="StyleCop found some broken rules!" />
  </Target>
</Project>
```

① Transforms StyleCop report to HTML

② Counts violations

③ Conditionally fails build

The first part of the script works like previous scripts. The script then does three new things at the end. It doesn't fail the build in StyleCopTasks, but goes further. It performs an XSLT transformation **①** and counts the violations **②** using the XmlRead task and some XPath query language. Finally, it fails the build **③** if the number of violations is greater than zero.

To show the StyleCop build report in TeamCity, you have to do the same thing as in FxCop: add the artifact file, and a new tab appears in the build report page (see figure 8.14).

You've used both the FxCop and StyleCop static code-analysis tools with the rules provided with them. Most of those rules are well thought out and worth following. But what if you want your own set of rules? Can you write custom FxCop and StyleCop rules? Of course. The next section will show you how to do it.

8.3 Custom FxCop and StyleCop rules

Both FxCop and StyleCop are fairly extensible. If you aren't satisfied with the rules they provide, you can always define your own set of rules. When you're planning your rules for FxCop and StyleCop, keep in mind the small but substantial difference between them. Although both are used for static code analysis, FxCop works on compiled assemblies, whereas StyleCop works on the source code. Some things may be checked for all .NET languages and some only for C#. Let's define some rules.

Figure 8.14   The StyleCop report in TeamCity

8.3.1   *Developing a custom FxCop rule*

As an example of a custom FxCop rule, let's say you want to visually distinguish all the private methods in your classes. You've decided to name them all using a `My` prefix. (This isn't the time or place to deliberate the usefulness of this rule—this is the time to implement a custom FxCop rule to enforce it.) The easiest way to extend FxCop is to extend the Microsoft.FxCop.Sdk.BaseIntrospectionRule class and override the `Check()` method. Copy the FxCopSdk.dll and Microsoft.Cci.dll files to the lib folder in a new project named CiDotNet.FxCop, and add a reference to the project that points to the two DLLs. Then look at the following listing for implementation details.

Listing 8.4   FxCop rule: private methods should start with `My`

```
namespace CiDotNet.FxCop.NamingRules
{
  using System;
  using Microsoft.FxCop.Sdk;

  public class PrivateMethodsShouldStartWithMy          ❶ Inherits base
    : BaseIntrospectionRule                                 rule class
    {
    public PrivateMethodsShouldStartWithMy():
      base("PrivateMethodsShouldStartWithMy",
      "CiDotNet.FxCop.NamingRules",
      typeof(PrivateMethodsShouldStartWithMy).Assembly){}
```

```
public override ProblemCollection Check(Member member)        ◁┐  Performs
{                                                             ❷  rule check
  Method Method;
  string Name;
  Method = member as Method;

  if ((Method != null) && (Method.IsPrivate))
  {
    if (!RuleUtilities.IsEventHandling(Method))
    {
      Name = Method.Name.Name;
      if (!Name.StartsWith("My",StringComparison.Ordinal))
      {
        this.Problems.Add(new                              ❸  Submits rule
          Problem(this.GetResolution(Name)));                  violation
      }
    }
  }
  return this.Problems;
}
}
}
```

BaseIntrospectionRule provides ❶ a suitable extension point for FxCop rules. All you need to do is override the Check() method ❷ that works on the class members. It's called every time the member is found during the analysis. The Check() method reads the method name and, if it's private, conducts the actual check. If the method name doesn't conform to the My prefix rule, a new problem indicator is added ❸.

To fully prepare the new CiDotNet.FxCop assembly to work as an FxCop rule, you have to define an XML definition file as shown next.

Listing 8.5   XML definition for a custom FxCop rule

```
<?xml version="1.0" encoding="utf-8" ?>
<Rules FriendlyName="CiDotNet Naming Rules">
  <Rule TypeName="PrivateMethodsShouldStartWithMy"        ❶  Defines
    Category="CiDotNet.Naming" CheckId="CA3010">               new rule
    <Name>Private methods should start with My.</Name>
    <Description>Private methods should start with
    ➥My</Description>
    <Url></Url>
    <Resolution>Prefix the method '{0}' with 'My'.</Resolution>
    <MessageLevel Certainty="95">Warning</MessageLevel>
    <FixCategories>Breaking</FixCategories>
    <Email></Email>
    <Owner></Owner>
  </Rule>
</Rules>
```

The Rule tag ❶ is the most important line in the definition file. It tells the FxCop framework what type the new rule has and in what category it appears, and it defines the code by which the rule will be called. The rest is a description in which you should provide as much information as needed to identify the rule and the violation.

Set the XML definition file as an embedded resource in the project. Compile everything, and copy the output assembly to the FxCop rules folder in the project you want to check. We'll deal with build-process integration in a moment; first, let's define a custom StyleCop rule.

8.3.2   *Developing a custom StyleCop rule*

StyleCop works on a different level than FxCop. It can do some of the checks that FxCop is unable to do because the translation process erases or changes some of the source code information. For example, the length of each line in the source file doesn't carry over to the compiled assembly. The information will be lost, but some developers like to have a maximum line length for their source files. You can easily check this using StyleCop.

Prepare a new project named CiDotNet.StyleCop. Copy the Microsoft.StyleCop.dll and Microsoft.StyleCop.CSharp.dll files to the lib directory of the project. Add a reference for each DLL to the project. Then examine the following listing for implementation details.

Listing 8.6   StyleCop rule: line length must not exceed a set number of characters

```
namespace CiDotNet.StyleCop.ReadabilityRules
{
  using Microsoft.StyleCop;
  using Microsoft.StyleCop.CSharp;

  [SourceAnalyzer(typeof(CsParser))]                    ① C# parser attribute
  public class LineLengthMussNotExceedNumberCharacters
    : SourceAnalyzer                                     ② Defines analysis extension point
    {
      private const int MAXLINELENGTH = 60;

      public override void AnalyzeDocument(CodeDocument document)
        {
          Param.RequireNotNull(document, "document");

          CsDocument CsDocument = (CsDocument)document;

          // TODO: check if generated code should be checked
          if (CsDocument.RootElement != null &&
           !CsDocument.RootElement.Generated)
           {
             foreach (CsToken TokenLoop in CsDocument.Tokens)
               {
                 if (TokenLoop.CsTokenType == CsTokenType.EndOfLine)
                   {
                     if (TokenLoop.Location.StartPoint.IndexOnLine - 1
                       > MAXLINELENGTH)
                     {
                       this.AddViolation(CsDocument.RootElement,
                         TokenLoop.Location.StartPoint.LineNumber,
```

```
                        "LineLengthMussNotExceedNumberCharacters",
                        MAXLINELENGTII);
                    }
                }
            }
        }
    }
}
```

Because the class contains a StyleCop rule, it needs to be decorated with [Source-Analyzer(typeof(CsParser))] ❶. The easiest way to extend StyleCop is to overload the SourceAnalyzer class ❷. It provides all the basic functionality, including an AnalyzeDocument() method that you can override. Inside, you're working on code *tokens*: parts of a parsed C# source file. You iterate through them all in search of a newline token. If the new line occurs too late in the line, after the MAXLINELENGTH limit, you add a violation.

Similar to FxCop, you need an XML definition file for the custom StyleCop rule.

Listing 8.7 StyleCop XML definition file for a custom rule

```xml
<?xml version="1.0" encoding="utf-8" ?>
<SourceAnalyzer Name="CiDotNet Rules">
  <Description>CiDotNet Rules extensions</Description>
  <Rules>
    <RuleGroup Name="CiDotNet Readability Rules">
      <Rule Name="LineLengthMussNotExceedNumberCharacters"
        CheckId="EX1001">
        <Context>Line length</Context>
        <Description>Line schould not be longer than a
        ➥given number of characters.</Description>
      </Rule>
    </RuleGroup>
  </Rules>
```

The Rule tag defines a new rule: it specifies the Rule Name and CheckId. The rules are gathered into groups, which correspond with the StyleCop settings tree in Visual Studio. The XML definition file should be an embedded resource.

Your StyleCop rule is ready. Let's try to integrate it, together with the custom FxCop rule, into your CI process.

8.3.3 *Incorporating custom rules into the CI process*

If you're using the FxCop GUI for code analysis, as we described earlier in this chapter, you're one step away from incorporating your custom FxCop rule into the CI process. Copy the CiDotNet.FxCop.dll file into the tools/FxCop/Rules directory, open the FxCop project file in the FxCop GUI, and then switch to the Rules tab and make sure your new rule is selected (see figure 8.15).

Figure 8.15
Adding a custom FxCop rule to the project in the FxCop GUI

Save the project. You can test it in the FxCop GUI; but, more important, from now on, if you point to the FxCop project in your MSBuild file as shown in the following code snippet, the rule will be checked:

```
<Exec Command="tools\FxCop\FxCopCmd.exe /project:CiDotNet.FxCop
  /out:FxCopReport.xml"/>
```

When it comes to StyleCop, the trick is to get the rule description into the StyleCop settings file Settings.StyleCop. The easiest way is, as you may have suspected, through the StyleCop GUI. Copy the assembly with the new rule into the StyleCop installation directory (which is something like C:\Program Files\Microsoft StyleCop 4.x.x.x). Go to Visual Studio, open the StyleCop Project Settings window (see figure 8.16), and make sure your new rule is selected.

If you're using the configuration we've proposed in this chapter, you only have to make sure the MSBuild task is using the correct Settings.StyleCop file, and you're good to go. The new StyleCop rule will be checked.

8.4   Extending code analysis

If you feel that your code isn't getting enough attention from FxCop and StyleCop, you can always extend your analysis repertoire. One of the best static code-analysis tools is NDepend. TeamCity also provides another kind of code analyzer that can detect code duplications. Let's look at these two tools.

8.4.1   Static analysis with NDepend

NDepend (www.ndepend.com) is a powerful static code-analysis tool that comes with a free noncommercial version. The professional commercial license costs about $410 and is more customizable than the free version. If you're interested in the large number of different code metrics that are built in to NDepend, it should be a tool for you. You can write your own metrics using the built-in Code Query Language (CQL). It's time to run NDepend and integrate it with the CI process.

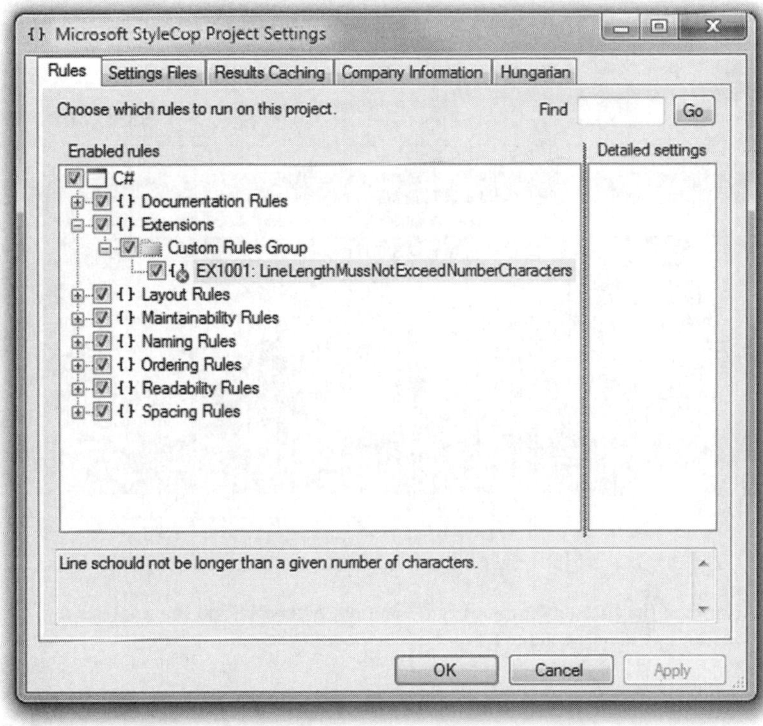

Figure 8.16 StyleCop Visual Studio project settings with the new custom rule

NDepend completely integrates itself with any non-Express edition of Visual Studio from version from 2005 to 2010. After downloading the tool and installing the add-in in Visual Studio (you can do so from VisualNDepend.exe), you can attach the NDepend project to your current solution by using the new NDepend menu item (see figure 8.17).

After you attach the NDepend project, the new plug-in will perform the default analysis and show it to you. You'll get immediate access to all the CQL rules and analysis diagrams. You can configure the project by choosing Edit > Project Properties. Figure 8.18 shows the analysis results and NDepend project properties.

Leave all the options set to their defaults, and let's get right into the CI integration. You'll use MSBuild to automate the NDepend analysis. You have two options for integration: you can use the provided NDependTask or run the console version of NDepend using the Exec task. For now, go the command-line way. The NDepend analysis target in MSBuild may look like this:

```
<Target Name="NDependAnalyze">
  <Exec Command="tools\NDepend\NDepend.Console.exe
    $(MSBuildProjectDirectory)\CiDotNet.NDepend.xml"/>
</Target>
```

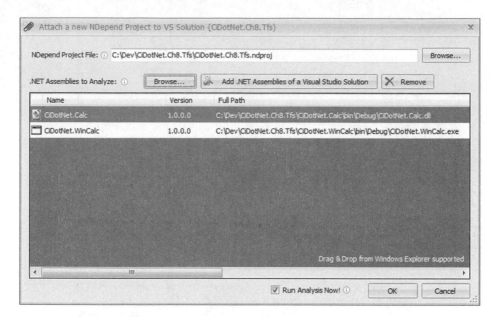

Figure 8.17   Attaching the NDepend project to a solution. Afterward, all the analysis and configuration possibilities of NDepend are available in Visual Studio.

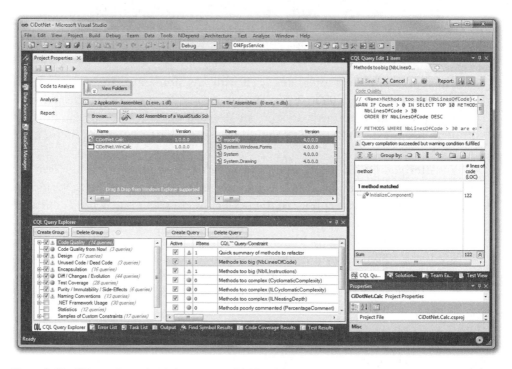

Figure 8.18   NDepend completely integrates with Visual Studio and comes with a handy Visual NDepend tool in which you can configure the project you'll use on the CI server.

If you run the MSBuild project using this task, you'll get a detailed NDepend report in the NDependOut folder. Let's try to integrate it with TeamCity. You'll integrate the NDepend report only for pure informational purposes. You haven't yet defined any build-breaking rules in the NDepend project file. The perfect place to show the analysis report is on the project page, not on the build page. You're getting the HTML report, so you're ready to integrate it with TeamCity. First, you have to define new artifacts on the General Settings page (see section 5.3.1 to learn how to do this). You can go with `NDependOut/*.* => NDependOut`.

> **NOTE** Some rules are more important than others. You may consider some rules so important that they must break the build so the CI process will stop and inform the team that something is wrong. To define the build-breaking rule in NDepend, you have to decorate it with the Critical Rule attribute. To do so, go to the CQL Query Editor and click the ⊗ button.

TeamCity takes all the files from the NDependOut folder and copies them to the same-named NDependOut folder as artifacts. Remember that each and every build will contain the data; this can result in a lot of files if you do the analysis continuously. Consider choosing only the files you need or running NDepend in the nightly build.

In TeamCity, you can add custom reports at the server level to make them visible for the build in any project, or you can do it at the project level where they're visible only in a particular project. Figure 8.19 shows the second approach. To reach this dialog box, select Administration on the main TeamCity page, edit the project properties, and add a new tab on the Report Tabs page (see section 5.3.1 to learn how to do this).

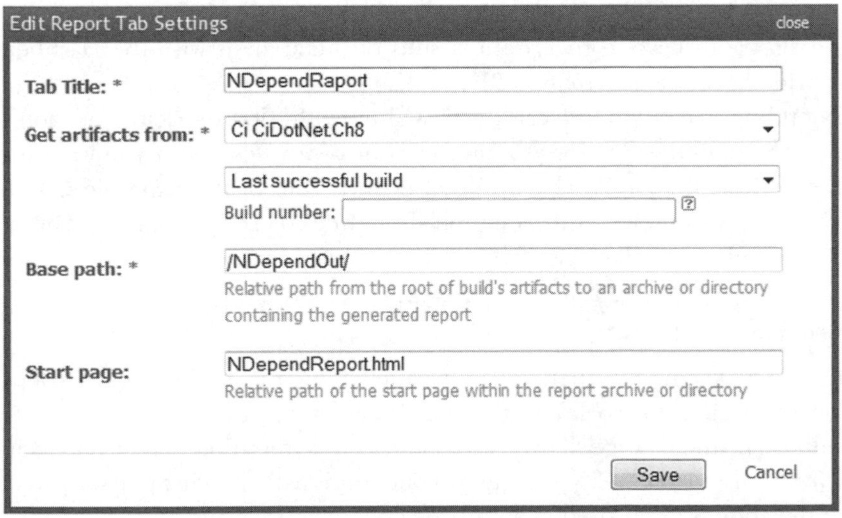

Figure 8.19   Adding a new project-level tab in TeamCity. It contains the NDepend report from the last successful build.

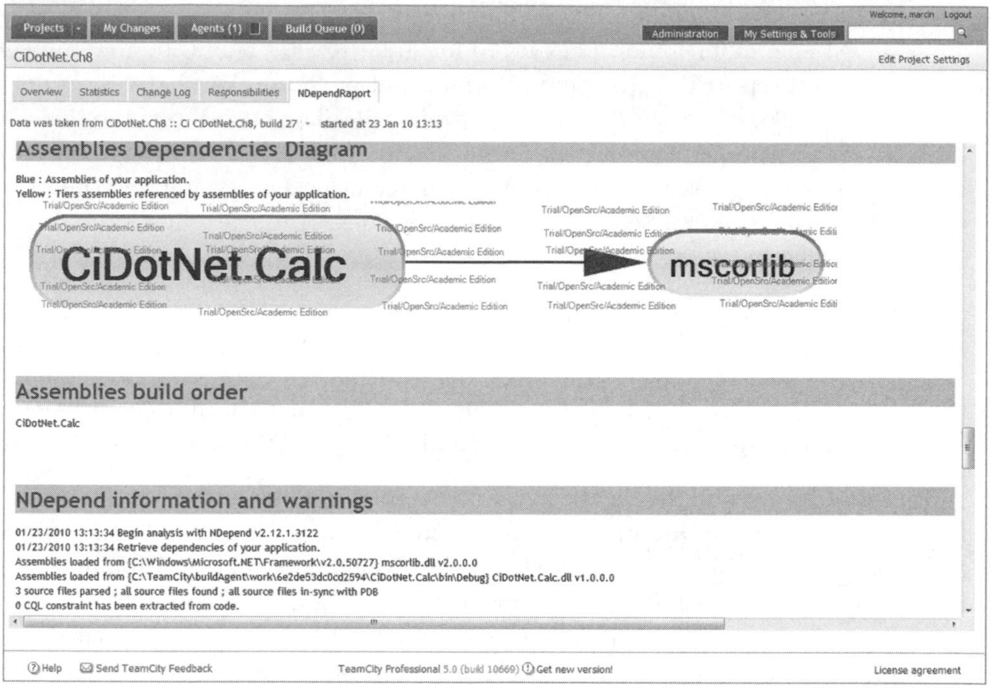

Figure 8.20   A project-level NDepend report in TeamCity

From now on, the project page will always include the last NDepend report from the last successful build (see figure 8.20).

NDepend integrates just as easily with other CI servers like CCNet. If you're using this server, you'll have to merge the results of the analysis with the Dashboard using the provided XSL transformation file.

Extending the NDepend rules is easy due to the handy CQL. You don't have to write any NDepend extensions to enforce your own rules; but if you want to, you can do this in the commercial version of NDepend. One of the example CQL rules says that the number of lines in the method shouldn't be greater than 30. The query that checks this rule looks like this:

```
WARN IF Count > 0 IN SELECT TOP 10 METHODS WHERE NbLinesOfCode > 30 ORDER
➥BY NbLinesOfCode DESC
```

If you don't like the number, you can easily change it. Open Visual NDepend, and choose Reset Views to Work with CQL Language. In the CQL list, choose Methods Too Big, edit CQL, and change `NbLinesOfCode > 30` to something bigger. That's it!

If you're using TeamCity, you can do one more useful code analysis: you can check where the code is duplicated in your projects.

8.4.2 *Analyzing code duplication with TeamCity*

TeamCity includes the JetBrains Duplicates Finder for .NET. Its purpose is to find the places in your code where your team has duplicated the code. These places are obvious candidates for refactoring. Having too much duplicated code in the project can be dangerous: a bug in one piece of code may exist somewhere else in the code base, but you can't detect it if you don't check for code duplication.

The Duplicates Finder is a separate build runner in TeamCity. You can reuse the existing project and define an additional build configuration to quickly get TeamCity to analyze your code for duplications.

To do this, you can reuse some of an existing project's settings. Go to Administration, and, in the project, choose Create Build Configuration. Name the build configuration—for example, CiDotNet Duplication Finder. You can reuse the existing version control system configuration you created earlier. In the build-runner configuration, choose Duplicates Finder (.NET). If you choose CI Trigger for the build configuration, you'll always get the duplication analysis. Figure 8.21 shows an example.

Finding similar code fragments is one of the TeamCity features we recommend you use in a continuous manner. The more you reuse your code, the better. Code duplications aren't desirable. Analyze, detect, and get rid of them!

Figure 8.21 TeamCity can report on duplicate code found in a project.

8.5   *Summary*

From experience, we know that projects tend to grow. Developers have a tendency to add new lines of code to their projects. They sometimes even change old lines to fix something. Some projects exist for many years and are modified by many developers. They usually want to know what's going on in the project. But when they change the code, they add to the project's growth.

But what if you're handed a project that looks like a big ball of mud? One class may have been developed with Cobol influence and look like functional programming. Some lines may be 1,000 characters long; or a previous developer may have used one-character variable names. It's a pain to work with smelly code. The only way out is to enforce some rules. Many software shops have written coding guidelines, but having rules doesn't mean they'll be obeyed. Developers are human—they're working under time pressure, and sometimes they neglect or don't even understand the rules. Only if the coding rules are enforced will they be obeyed. Keep in mind that you should adjust the number of rules you want to obey to the project you're working on. FxCop and StyleCop offer hundreds of rules, and some may be more important to you than others (see Krzysztof Cwalina's and Brad Abrams' book *Framework Design Guidelines* for more on that topic).

There's nothing better than static code analysis to check the rules. Tools like the ones you've used in this chapter—FxCop, StyleCop, NDepend, and Team City's Duplicates Finder—are great guards against bad coding habits. Static code analysis as part of your CI process will effectively fight any smell in the code. You can even write your own rules, to guard yourself against that violent psychopath who may work on the code next.

It's especially important to have clean code if you're moving toward the next part of our CI journey: code documentation. As we've gone through the chapter, you've probably seen StyleCop rule violations that tell you parts of the code aren't documented. It's time to obey this rule, too, as you'll find out in the next chapter.

Part 3

Smooth and polish it

Every business has room for improvement. Skyscrapers can be taller, cars can be faster—even grass can be greener. CI isn't any different. There's always room to do it better—an opportunity for smoothing and polishing.

In the last part of this book (chapters 9 through 12), you'll squeeze even more from the CI process. You'll extend it with automatically documentation generation, using the .NET XML documentation feature to build readable technical documentation right from the source code. We'll continue the discussion with deployment and delivery techniques in CI. You'll learn how to sleep well, knowing that your software is always ready to be deployed. We'll look at continuous database integration. And in the last chapter, we'll peek into high-scale CI setups.

CI can be extended *ad absurdum*. The key is, as usual, to maintain balance—to include everything you need and nothing else. You shouldn't try to pack everything into the CI process: remember that you need the build feedback as soon as possible. The entire CI process should take less than 10 minutes, so choose wisely what you include. Leave the rest for regular nightly or weekly builds. In this section of the book, we'll help you choose.

After reading this part, you'll be able to produce nice-looking technical documentation out of the comments in your code during the periodic CI build. You'll have enough know-how to automate the software deployment in various scenarios. You'll know how to bind CI with database management and how to scale CI.

If you want to make your CI process shine, keep reading: we'll teach you how to polish it!

Generating
documentation

9

This chapter covers

- Using XML documentation tags to comment code
- Creating rich technical documentation with Sandcastle

Every developer knows another developer who doesn't like to write documentation. Most of them see this fellow developer every day morning in the mirror; some see the other developer a little later, in the office. Even if you're in the second group, you probably wouldn't mind a little help on the documentation side, right?

There's no magical way to produce documentation. It has to be written. But you can do this the smart way. How about documenting your code inside your source files and generating the documentation from there? You can do so by adding special XML comments to the code. The specially formatted tags, which you'll learn to use in this chapter, are extracted during the build to a separate XML file. An external tool called *Sandcastle* can take this file and transform it into nice-looking technical documentation. Figure 9.1 illustrates the process.

In this chapter, we'll look at how to document your code using XML notation. To do this, you'll use Sandcastle to generate an HTML and Compiled

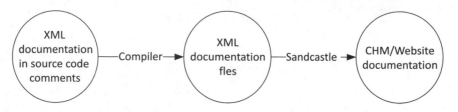

Figure 9.1   Generating documentation: from source code to XML, and finally to technical documentation

HTML Help (CHM) format documentation. Then you'll integrate everything into your CI process.

9.1   XML documentation

A normal comment in C# looks like this

```
// This is
// comment.
```

or like this

```
/* This is:
Comment */
```

There is a third kind of comment:

```
/// This is
/// comment.
```

This type of comment is threaded specially by the compiler. It can be extracted to a particular kind of XML file that can be used for two main purposes:

- As a source for any kind of documentation formatting
- By Visual Studio in IntelliSense highlighting

We're obviously interested in the first purpose, because we want to generate nicely formatted documentation during the CI process. But let's not forget about the IntelliSense side effect, shown in figure 9.2, which you'll get when you're finished.

If you're using Visual Basic, you get the same functionality with the ``'''`` comment. Let's examine the commenting techniques you can use.

9.1.1   Common XML documentation tags

We'll show you the most common XML tags used for XML documentation. For the source code, you'll use the financial library project. It's a perfect target for documentation, because it's used across multiple projects as the central point for lease and loan calculations.

Let's use the `Finance` class from the `CiDotNet.Calc.Math` namespace (it resides in `CiDotNet.Calc`). The XML tag you'll use the most is shown in the following listing.

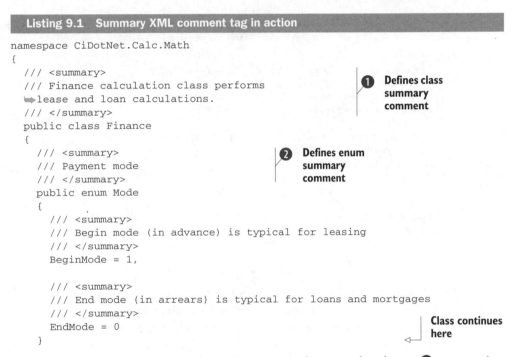

Figure 9.2   The Visual Studio IntelliSense mechanism is based on XML documentation.

Listing 9.1   Summary XML comment tag in action

```
namespace CiDotNet.Calc.Math
{
  /// <summary>
  /// Finance calculation class performs
  ➡lease and loan calculations.
  /// </summary>
  public class Finance
  {
    /// <summary>
    /// Payment mode
    /// </summary>
    public enum Mode
    {
      /// <summary>
      /// Begin mode (in advance) is typical for leasing
      /// </summary>
      BeginMode = 1,

      /// <summary>
      /// End mode (in arrears) is typical for loans and mortgages
      /// </summary>
      EndMode = 0
    }
```

❶ Defines class summary comment

❷ Defines enum summary comment

Class continues here ⟵

You can use the <summary> tag for various parts of your code: classes ❶, properties, methods, enumerators ❷, fields, constants, delegates, and so on.

If you want to comment a method or delegate in addition to using <summary>, you can use the <param> and <returns> tags, as shown here.

Listing 9.2   Commenting methods with XML comments

```
/// <summary>
/// Calculates the present value of an amount of
➡money received in the future at a given interest rate..
/// </summary>
```

```
/// <param name="compoundPeriods">Compound periods</param>
/// <param name="periodicInterestRate">Periodic interest rate</param>
/// <returns>SPPV</returns>
private static double CalculateSPPV(double compoundPeriods,
➥double periodicInterestRate)
{
  return System.Math.Pow(1.0 + (periodicInterestRate / 100),
  ➥ -compoundPeriods);
}
```

The <param> tag requires a name attribute, which links the description with the parameter name. The <returns> tag defines the description for the return parameter.

   Some methods may throw an exception. It's a good habit to document the possible exceptions using the <exception> tag. Doing so makes it easier for someone using this method to track down possible problems. The following listing shows an example of the <exception> tag.

Listing 9.3   Describing an exception with the `cref` attribute

```
/// <summary>
/// Gets the compound periods.
/// </summary>
/// <param name="duration">The duration.</param>
/// <param name="ppy">The ppy.</param>
/// <returns></returns>
/// <exception cref="CalcArgumentException">
➥if <paramref name="duration"/> or
➥<paramref name="ppy"/> &lt; 1.</exception>
public static double GetCompoundPeriods(int duration, int ppy)
{
  if (duration < 1)
    throw new CalcArgumentException();
  if (ppy < 1)
    throw new CalcArgumentException();
  return (double)((ppy * duration) / 12);
}
```

The description of the exception uses the cref attribute to create a link in the documentation to CalcArgumentException. You can also use cref attributes in other parts of your documentation. In addition, you provide some information about when the exception will be thrown. Using a <paramref> tag with a name attribute creates a link in the documentation to a given parameter.

   The next commonly used XML documentation tag is <remarks>. You can apply it to classes, methods, properties, and so on. This tag usually contains additional data that's important for the use of a given element.

   Other useful tags include <example>, which is used for usage examples; and <value>, which describes a property value. Finally, the <see> tag creates a link from some text to another XML comment. The following listing contains examples of these tags.

Listing 9.4 Using `<remarks>`, `<example>`, and `<see>`

```
/// <summary>
/// Calculates leasing or credit rate
/// </summary>
/// <param name="periods">for how long do you want
to carry the burden of loan</param>
/// <param name="ppy">periods per year
(for example 12 for monthly payments)</param>
/// <param name="interestRate">how much will the bank
charge you (interest)</param>
/// <param name="presentValue">how much money do you need</param>
/// <param name="finalValue">will you be paying something
after the payoff period (especially for leasing)</param>
/// <param name="mode">how the bank calculates the interest
income <see cref="Mode"/></param>                        ⟵┐  References
                                                        ❶  another element
/// <returns>rate</returns>
/// <example>
/// CiDotNet.Calc.Math.Finance.CalculateRate(
36, 12, 7.5, 30000, 500, Calc.Math.Finance.Mode.BeginMode)
/// </example>                                           ⟵┐  Gives
                                                        ❷  example
/// <remarks>
/// Implements the so-called HP method.
/// </remarks>                                           ⟵┐  Defines additional
                                                        ❸  remarks
public static double CalculateRate(
int periods, int ppy, double interestRate,
double presentValue, double finalValue, Mode mode)
{
    int m = (int)mode;
    double compoundPeriods = GetCompoundPeriods(periods, ppy);
    double periodicInterestRate = GetPeriodicInterestRate(interestRate, ppy);
    return -(
      (finalValue * CalculateSPPV(compoundPeriods,
      periodicInterestRate) - presentValue)
      /
      ((1.0 + ((periodicInterestRate * m) / 100)) *
      CalculateUSPV(compoundPeriods, periodicInterestRate))
      );
}
```

The <see> tag ❶ creates a link to the Mode enumerator. The examples at ❷ and ❸ give a little more information about the commented code. They contain simple text, but you can customize the documentation by formatting the text inside the elements. Let's look at how to do this.

9.1.2 *Formatting text in XML comments*

If you think the XML comments aren't readable to a normal human being, you aren't alone. XML tagging doesn't make the comments people-friendly. Fortunately, tools are available to create comments that are easier to read. One of them is a Visual Studio plug-in called GhostDoc (http://submain.com/GhostDoc/). You press Shift-Ctrl-D, and it reads the names of classes, methods, and parameters and automatically creates or updates the XML comments. Try it: it's free and worth using, especially if you go a level higher and format the text inside the comments. But keep in mind that with great power comes great responsibility: it's easy to overuse GhostDoc. You should treat the generated comments with caution. Most of them need to be edited.

For example, to format part of the text in an XML comment as code, you can use <c> (inline) and <code> (multiline), as shown here (this listing extends listing 9.4.).

Listing 9.5   Highlighting code portions in comments

```
/// <example>
/// Let's say you want to lease a car for 36 moths (<c>periods</c>)
/// that costs 30000 $ (<c>presentValue</c>)
/// by 7.5 interest (<c>interestRate</c>)
/// and 500 $ residual value (<c>finalValue</c>).
/// <code>CiDotNet.Calc.Math.Finance.CalculateRate(
///         36,
///         12,
///         7.5,
///         30000,
///         500,
///         Calc.Math.Finance.Mode.BeginMode)</code>
/// Calculation mode for leasing is
➥(<c>Calc.Math.Finance.Mode.BeginMode</c>)
/// </example>
```

Both kinds of code element will be nicely formatted in the output document.

You can also introduce lists into your documentation with the <list> tab. Lists can be bulleted or numbered, or can appear in a table, as shown next.

Listing 9.6   Extended summary with a bulleted list

```
/// <summary>
/// Finance calculation class performs lease and loan calculations.
///
/// <list type="bullet">                          ◁┐ Declares
/// <listheader>                                     bulleted list
///     <term>term</term>
///     <description>description</description>
/// </listheader>                                 ◁┐ List header
/// <item>
///     <term>SPPV</term>
///     <description>present value of a money amount received
➥in the future at a given interest</description>
/// </item>                                       ◁┐ List item
/// <item>
///     <term>SPFV</term>
///     <description>value of an amount of money paid in the
➥future at a given interest rate </description>
/// </item>
/// <item>
///     <term>USPV</term>
///     <description>payment required each period to
➥achieve future value</description>
/// </item>
```

```
/// <item>
///     <term>USFV</term>
///     <description>future value of a uniform future payment</description>
/// </item>
/// </list>
/// </summary>
```

As we mentioned, you can use the `<list>` tag to create a table, but you'll quickly reach the limit of this functionality—it only lets you create a simple table. The other option is to use the HTML `<table>` tag, as shown next.

Listing 9.7 Remarks for the payment mode enumerator

```
/// <summary>
/// Payment mode
/// </summary>
/// <remarks>
/// <div class="tablediv">          ⟵┐ Contains
/// <table>                                 │ HTML-style table
/// <tr valign="top">
/// <th>Term</th>
/// <th>Description</th>
/// <th>Example</th>
/// </tr>
/// <tr valign="top">
/// <td>In advance</td>
/// <td>Begin mode is typical for leasing</td>
/// <td><c>Calc.Math.Finance.Mode.BeginMode</c></td>
/// </tr>
/// <tr valign="top">
/// <td>In arrears</td>
/// <td>End mode is typical for loans and mortgages</td>
/// <td><c>Calc.Math.Finance.Mode.EndMode</c></td>
/// </tr>
/// </table>
/// </div>
/// </remarks>
```

As you can see, you can declare HTML-style tables inside the XML documentation.

That's nice, you say. It's a lot of XML code in my source files. IntelliSense is handy in Visual Studio, but that's hardly real documentation. But what if we tell you that you can generate from the XML documentation like that shown in figure 9.3?

You can create this MSDN-style documentation using Sandcastle.

9.2   *Sandcastle*

Sandcastle is a set of free tools from Microsoft that you can use to transform XML documentation into a formatted document. It contains a bunch of command-line programs that you can automate to create documentation, but this technique would take too long to discuss here. There's a much quicker and more pleasant way: you can use Sandcastle Help File Builder (SHFB), which is also free. Both are available

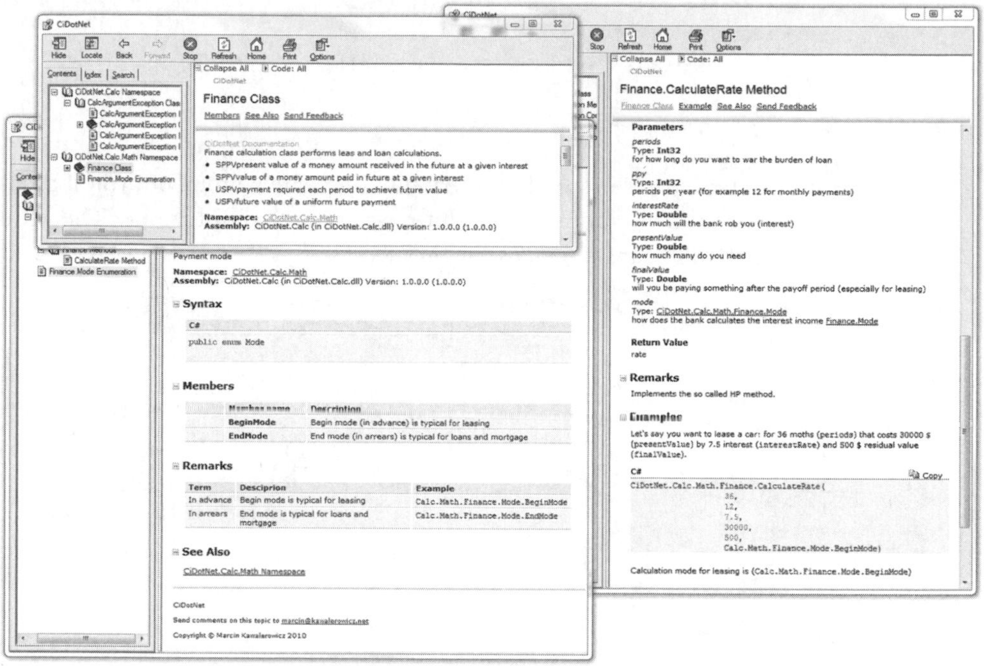

Figure 9.3   Readable documentation that's been transformed from XML documentation

from CodePlex: Sandcastle at www.codeplex.com/Sandcastle and SHFB at http://shfb.codeplex.com/. Install both on your development machine.

Before you start, make sure Visual Studio is extracting all of your XML documentation into a single XML file. You can check this XML Documentation File setting in your project properties (see figure 9.4.).

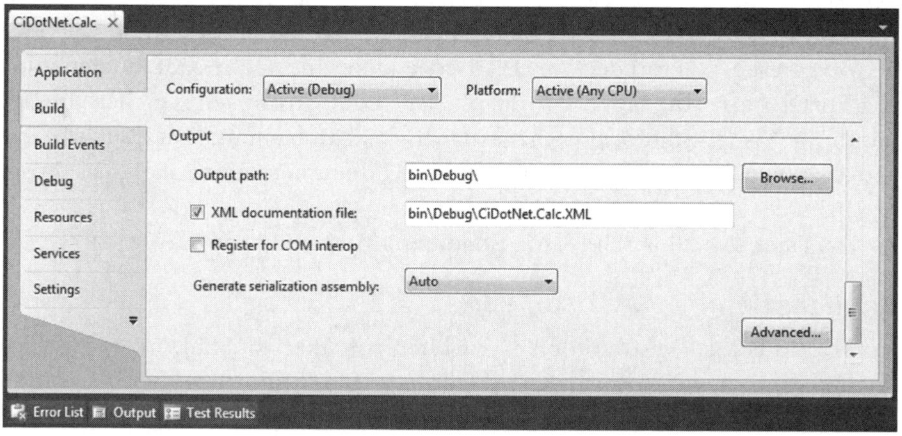

Figure 9.4   Select the XML Documentation File check box in your project properties to make Visual Studio extract the XML documentation into a given XML file.

Visual Studio 2010 is so clever that it makes this change for you as soon you add the first /// comment to a project (provided you've selected the option Tools > Options > Text Editor > C# > Advanced > Generate XML Documentation Comment for ///). In earlier versions, you'll have to select the option manually.

9.2.1 *Building with Sandcastle*

Start SHFB, which is essentially a GUI for Sandcastle. Using this tool, you'll create a project file with all the necessary settings. At the end, you'll take this file for a ride with MSBuild.

You want to be able to create documentation even on a machine that doesn't have Sandcastle and SHFB installed. So take both installed tools and copy them to the tools directory in your project folder: put Sandcastle in tools\Sandcastle and SHFB in tools\SHFB. Remember to put in the tools directory only what's needed—don't clutter the project directory with unnecessary files. What you need depends on what template you'll use to format the documentation. You can delete all the readme and help files—you don't need them in the repository.

Start SHFB by running tools\SHFB\SandcastleBuilderGUI.exe. Add the compiled DLL and accompanying XML file to Documentation Sources in Project Explorer. Specify the obvious project properties, such as `FooterText`, `HeaderText`, `HelpTitle`, `CopyrightText`, and so on. Then get to the not-so-obvious but important properties that are important from the CI point of view; see figure 9.5 for details.

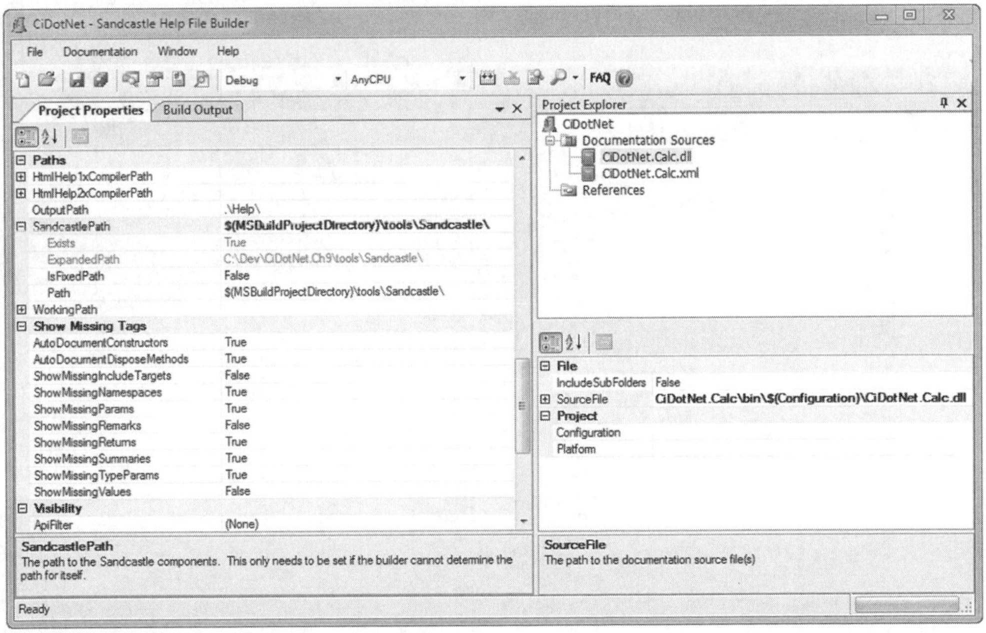

Figure 9.5 Customizing the SHFB project file

If you're building using the Debug/Release configuration, go to the DLL and XML properties and replace the configuration name with the $(Configuration) MSBuild variable. You can use the MSBuild variables because the SHFB project files are in fact MSBuild scripts. One important project property you have to set is SandcastlePath: set it to $(MSBuildProjectDirectory)\tools\Sandcastle\. It'll use the MSBuild pre-defined variable to build an absolute path to the Sandcastle binaries.

You need to set one more property in order for the documentation process to work on a machine that doesn't have Sandcastle installed. In Project Properties, locate UserDefinedProperties, and click the ... button. Figure 9.6 shows the dialog box that opens.

Thanks to the SHFBROOT variable, MSBuild tasks can locate the SHFB installation for any necessary files.

There's no way to document the namespace using the XML documentation. Even if you use the <summary> tag on a namespace, it'll be ignored by the compiler, and it won't be added to the XML file. You can close this gap by documenting the namespace in the SHFB GUI. In Project Properties, locate the Namespace Summaries property, and open it. Figure 9.7 shows the dialog box in which you can add the summaries.

You can browse the other properties, such as HelpFileFormat. By default, you're generating an HtmlHelp file. But you can change it to a website if you want to deploy the documentation to a web server for immediate viewing. And look at the PresentationStyle property: you can dress up your documentation in various ways. Visibility lets you choose which filters to use on the documentation elements.

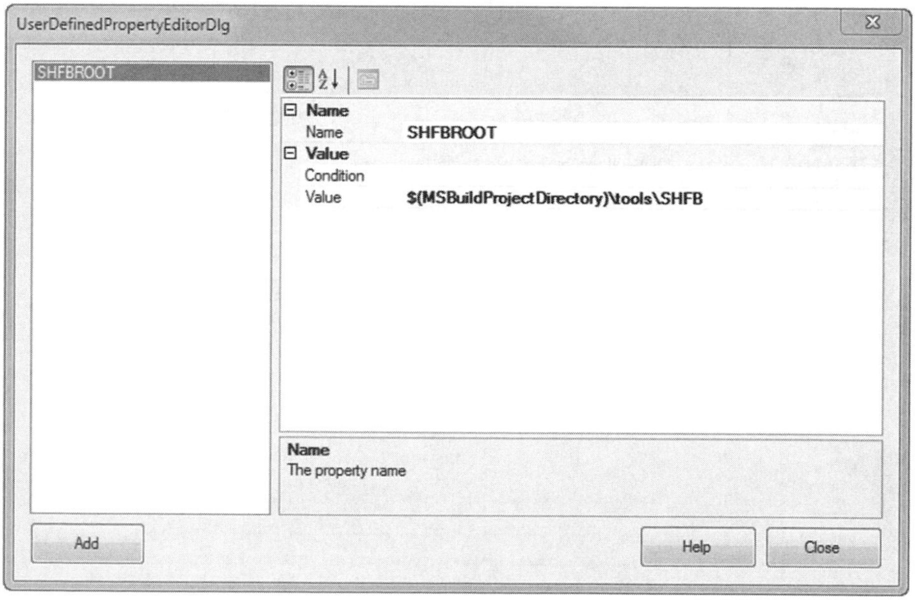

Figure 9.6   Setting the SHFBROOT **variable in the SHFB user-defined properties dialog box**

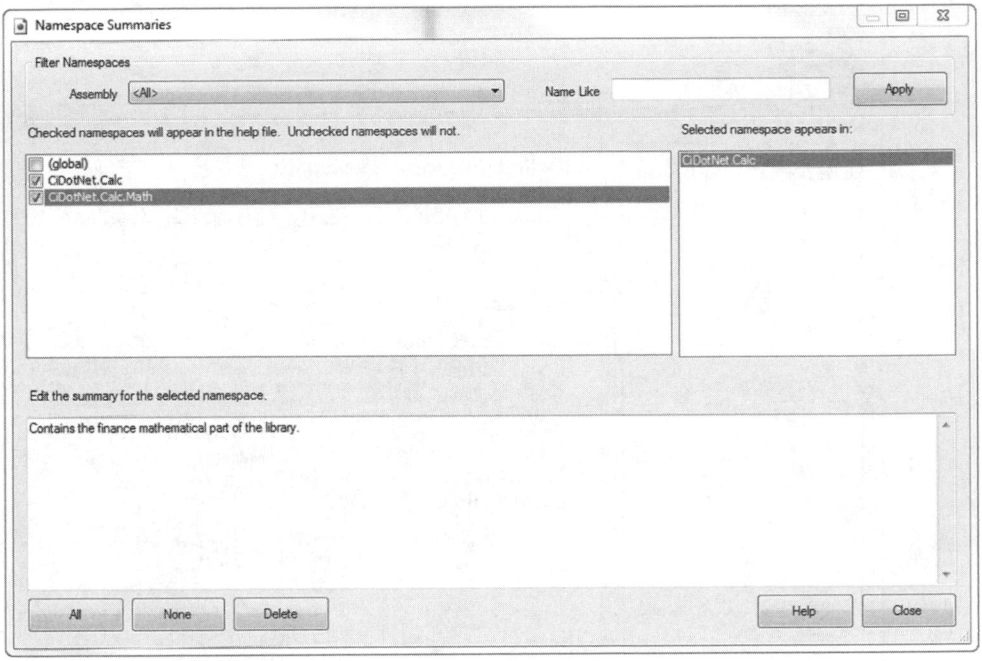

Figure 9.7 Editing summaries on namespaces. To include them in your documentation, you have to use SHFB.

When you're ready, click the Build the Help File icon on the SHFB toolbar to make a test run. SHFB will switch to the Build Output window and create the documentation. You can look in the Help directory for a Documentation.chm file (figure 9.8 shows the file's content).

You now have nice-looking HtmlHelp documentation. You're ready to make documentation creation part of your CI process.

9.2.2 *Sandcastle in CI*

Before you add Sandcastle documentation generation to the CI server, you have to automate it. This task is easy. As we said earlier, an SHFB project file is in fact an MSBuild script. All you have to do to create documentation is add a task like this to build.proj:

```
<Target Name="Document" >
  <MSBuild Projects="CiDotNet.shfbproj"/>
</Target>
```

That's it. If you hook up the new target to run during an automated build and check everything in to the repository, your build server should snap right in. You'll get the CHM file on the server. Now you need to do something useful with it: send it over email, copy it to a location where it'll be available for everyone, or add it to the deployment package (we'll deal with deployment in the next chapter).

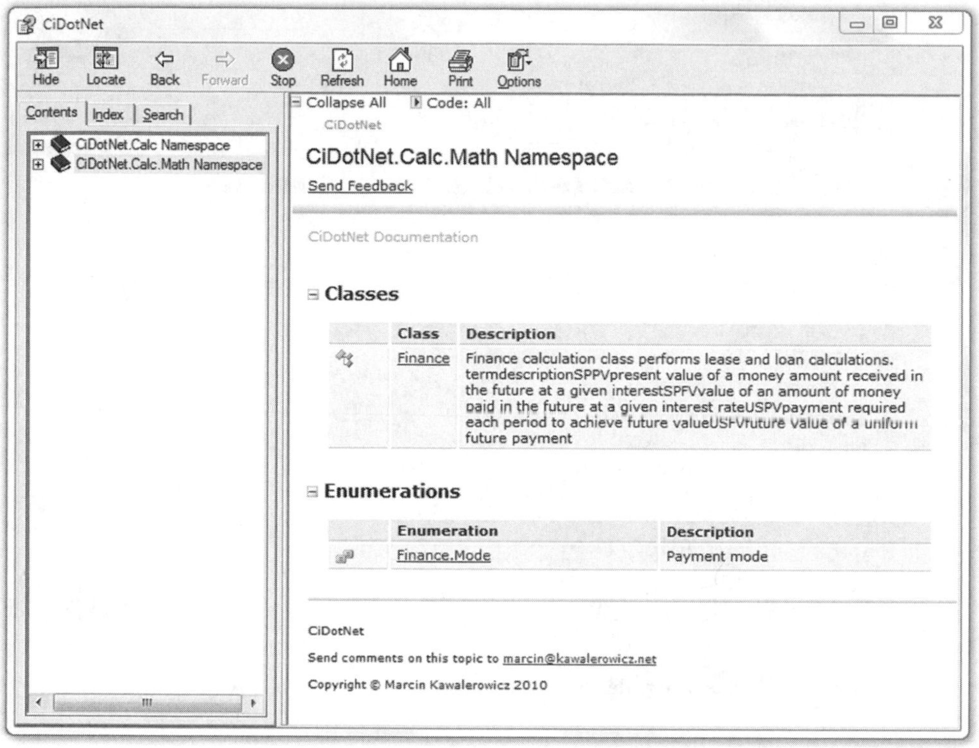

Figure 9.8   A CHM file created from XML documentation using Sandcastle

But here, let's do something different. How about generating the documentation and integrating the results with the TeamCity CI server? Change the type of generated documentation to Website (the `HelpFileFormat` property in SHFB Project Properties).

Getting the documentation to be visible on the build-information page in Team-City is straightforward. Go to your TeamCity project's General Settings, and set the Artifacts path to

```
Help/**/* => Help
```

This causes all the Help folder content from the current build to be copied to the Help artifacts folder. To make the documentation visible on the build-report page, add a new tab in the server configuration, pointing to /Help/Index.html. After a successful build, you should see something like figure 9.9.

You should consider two things when you incorporate Sandcastle into CI. First, as you can see, generating documentation files with Sandcastle takes time. Even for a tiny project, it can take a few minutes. If you feel it's taking too long, consider moving the documentation build out of CI and into the daily build.

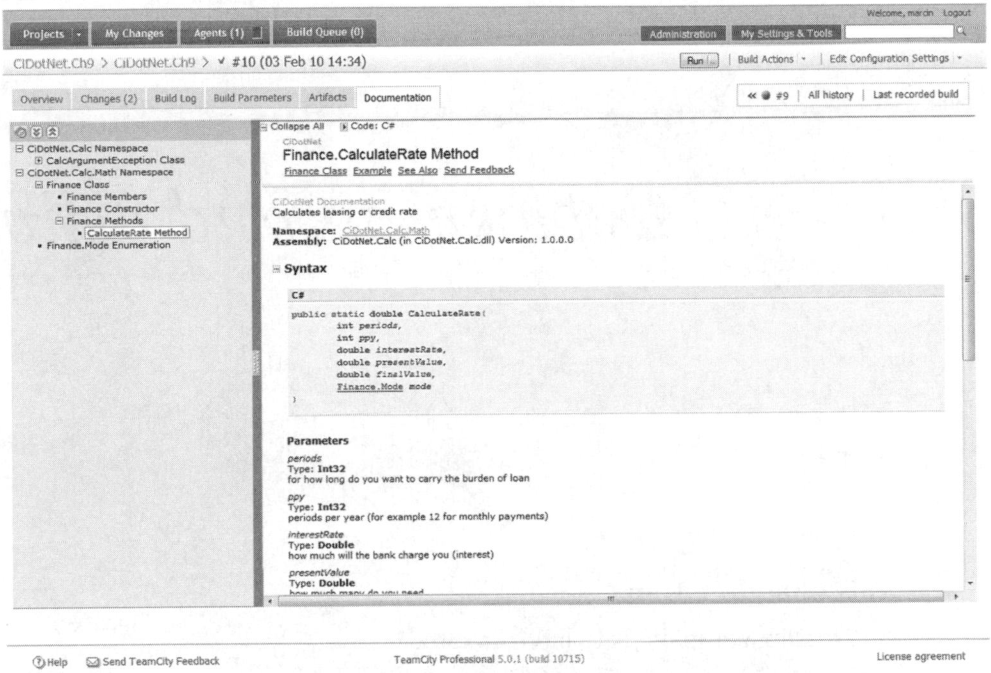

Figure 9.9 Sandcastle-generated documentation integrated with TeamCity build report page

The second issue is the size of the artifacts. If you store every documentation drop, you'll need to consider the amount of hard drive space required.

9.3 Summary

It's maybe a truism, but well-documented code is more valuable and more maintainable than code with neglected documentation. Knowing the reason code was written one way and not another way makes a difference. Good documentation will make it easier for you or anyone else to understand the code later and to fix bugs. And by commenting your code, you can get help such as IntelliSense in Visual Studio, which means you can develop more quickly.

Using tools like Sandcastle, you can generate nice-looking, readable documentation in the form of Windows Help files or a website. The process can be automated and incorporated into CI. This way, you'll always have up-to-date, code-level documentation available.

You can add documentation generated this way to your software, in a step we'll look at in the next chapter: deployment.

Deployment and delivery

This chapter covers

- Creating setup projects in Visual Studio
- Using WiX to create installation routines and incorporate them into CI
- Using MS Deploy with web applications

If you've been following along with us chapter by chapter, your software is continuously built, tested, analyzed, and documented. After every check-in to the version control system, you're creating a piece of bulletproof software. Some developers make rules that every act of sending software to the repository must be associated with a feature. Other developers strive to have potentially shippable software after it's been continuously built. If you fall into the latter group, you're fully prepared to include new elements in the CI process: deployment and delivery. Even if you don't have such high goals, you should have your software deployed to a test site or create an installer.

CI deployment and delivery target a few important aspects, such as what to do with continuously built software at the end of the CI process, how to prepare it for various tasks like manual testing and presentation, and how to deal with deployment targets. In this chapter, we'll give you a taste of several types of deployment candy. We'll look at different aspects and discuss tools that may help you with deployment and delivery. You may like the taste of the MSI installer using Visual Studio and learn why other tools such as WiX are sweeter and better tasting. You'll script ClickOnce deployment using MSBuild. Then we'll look at the wrappings of how to deploy web software using some new and tasty Visual Studio 2010 technologies like Web Deployment and how to use it in the CI process. Let's get started with Windows delivery.

10.1 Creating an installer for your Windows application

The common scenario for Windows applications delivery is the build of an installation package that can be installed on a target machine. It may be a good idea to incorporate the installation package creation into the CI environment. This way, your software will always be ready for eventual delivery and deployment. Let's say your boss wants to see where your team is with development of your application, or you want the test team to be able to get the newest version, without your involvement, every time they need it. This is easy to do. We'll show you by creating the installation package for the financial calculator.

10.1.1 Creating a Microsoft Installer package in Visual Studio

The easiest way to create the installation package is to use built-in Visual Studio features. If you want to do it and eventually incorporate the installation package creation into your CI process, you have keep in mind that you'll need to install Visual Studio on the build server. We'll deal with this issue in a moment. But first, let's make the setup project. Open the solution where you have the Windows version of the financial calculator. Right-click the solution, choose Add > New Project, select Other Project Types > Setup and Deployment > Visual Studio Installer, and choose Setup Project (see figure 10.1).

In the Solution Explorer, you'll get a new setup project. Right-click it, and choose Add > Project Output. In the Add Project Output Group window (see figure 10.2), choose Primary Output from the project CiDotNet.WinCalc. Doing so adds all the files that are needed to run the calculator. As your project grows, you may want to add other types of files, such as documentation files (if you have any) or content files (if you have files marked as content that are needed by the application). More details about every file group are provided at the bottom of the window.

For a project as simple as the financial calculator, that's all you have to do. If you wish, you can make the setup project prettier. To do so, in the setup project's properties, specify the Manufacturer, ProductName, and Title. You can change the setup user interface (right-click the project and select View > User interface). You can also add the icon on the desktop or an item in the Start menu (in View > File System, right-click the primary output, choose Create Shortcut, and drag it to the user's desktop or user's Programs menu).

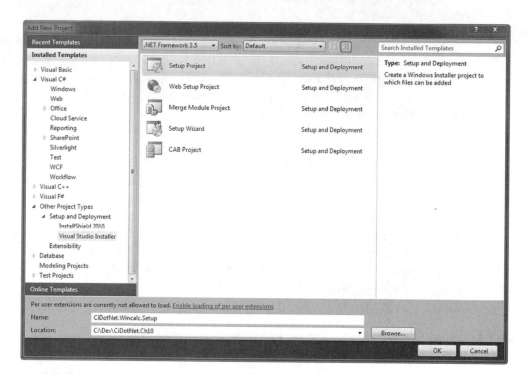

Figure 10.1   If you want to use the standard Setup Project from Visual Studio in your CI process, you'll have to install the entire development environment on the build server.

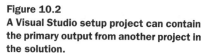

Figure 10.2
A Visual Studio setup project can contain the primary output from another project in the solution.

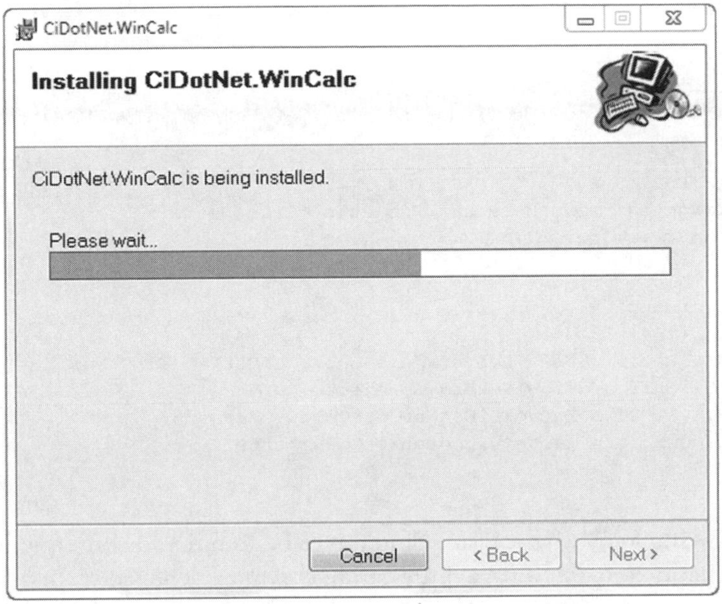

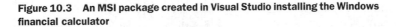

Figure 10.3   An MSI package created in Visual Studio installing the Windows financial calculator

After you build the project, you should test the installation package. To do so, right-click the setup project in Solution Explorer, and choose Install. Visual Studio starts the installation wizard (see figure 10.3).

The MSI package is created in the Setup Project directory. It can be taken from there and given to anybody interested in it. You can incorporate the entire setup process into the CI process.

10.1.2 *Continuously creating installation files*

The creation of the MSI package with Visual Studio can be scripted into an MSBuild file. Unfortunately, the creation of setup files designed using setup projects can be performed only using Visual Studio. This means you'll need to use the Visual Studio devenv.exe file from the command line. The script that shows how to do this is shown next.

Listing 10.1   Creating setup files in MSBuild using Visual Studio

```
<Project DefaultTargets="Build;Setup;" xmlns="http://schemas.microsoft.com/
    developer/msbuild/2003">
  <PropertyGroup>
    <!--Default Configuration-->
    <Configuration Condition=" '$(Configuration)' == ''">
      Debug
    </Configuration>
```

```
<!--Default Platform-->
<Platform Condition=" '$(Platform)' == '' ">"Any CPU"</Platform>
<!--Visual Studio path-->
<VSPath Condition=" '$(VSPath)' == '' ">
➥%ProgramFiles%\Microsoft Visual Studio 10.0\Common7\IDE</VSPath>
</PropertyGroup>

<Target Name="Build" >
  <MSBuild Targets="Clean;Rebuild" Projects="CiDotNet.sln"
  ➥ContinueOnError="false"/>
</Target>

<Target Name="Setup" >
  <Exec
    Command="&quot;$(VSPath)\devenv.exe&quot; CiDotNet.sln /build
    ➥&quot;$(Configuration)&quot; /project
    ➥CiDotNet.WinCalc.Setup\CiDotNet.WinCalc.Setup.vdproj"
    ➥ContinueOnError="false" IgnoreExitCode="true" />
</Target>
</Project>
```

Defines Visual Studio path ❶

Creates setup files ❷

You have to tell MSBuild ❶ where Visual Studio is to be found and consequently use it from the command line ❷ with a little strange syntax. The code first specifies devenv.exe, and then the solution file name, build configuration, project, and setup project file name. This script can create the MSI setup packages.

As we mentioned earlier, this entire procedure has one fault: you must install Visual Studio on the build machine. You have to be able to configure the build on the build server and substitute the $(VSPath) MSBuild property for the actual path on the server. If you're using CCNet, it can be something like this:

```
<tasks>
  <msbuild>
    <executable>
      C:\WINDOWS\Microsoft.NET\Framework\v4.0.21006\MSBuild.exe
    </executable>
    <projectFile>build.msbuild</projectFile>
    <buildArgs>/p:VSPath="C:\Program Files (x86)\Microsoft Visual Studio
    ➥ 10.0\Common7\IDE\"</buildArgs>
  </msbuild>
</tasks>
```

Installing Visual Studio on the build server isn't always a good idea. Remember the CI rule that says the environment where the CI occurs needs to have as few dependencies as possible. Visual Studio is a big breach of this rule. Not to mention licensing: you'll need an extra license for this Visual Studio installation. But have no fear! There's a way to deal with it using WiX.

10.2   *Windows Installer XML toolset*

Windows Installer XML (WiX) is a free Microsoft tool for creating Windows installation packages. The WiX scripts are XML files, and you can use WiX from the command line. It's easy to incorporate into the CI process.

10.2.1 *Creating an installer using WiX*

Download and install the WiX package (if you're using Visual Studio 2010, use at least version 3.0) from http://wixtoolset.org/. In the next couple of pages, you'll do the usual drill and install WiX on the development machine for day-to-day work and then extract and put in the tools subdirectory what's needed on the build server for CI.

Open your solution and add a new project. Locate Windows Installer XML templates, and choose Setup Project (see figure 10.4).

WiX is a giant mine of functionality. We won't discuss the full functionality of this toolset; we'll only dive into it enough to produce a simple install file for the Windows calculator. WiX stores all the information it needs to produce the installation file inside one or more XML files. If you want to penetrate WiX capabilities you'll surely have a lot to do with the angle brackets. Listing 10.2 shows a simple WiX file.

NOTE You can find the complete WiX documentation on the WiX website at http://wix.sourceforge.net/.

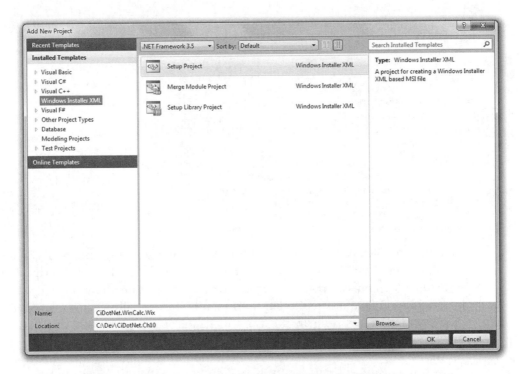

Figure 10.4 A WiX setup project doesn't require Visual Studio on the build server.

Listing 10.2   WiX script file for Windows financial calculator

```xml
<?xml version="1.0" encoding="UTF-8"?>
<Wix xmlns="http://schemas.microsoft.com/WiX/2006/wi">
  <Product Id="4c50dba3-f33d-41a2-bc25-8a983e4fe398"
    Name="CiDotNet.WinCalc" Language="1033" Version="1.0.0.0"
    Manufacturer="CiDotNet"
    UpgradeCode="3dbf5cd7-bda4-46a5-bb99-53c7df6a3bad">
    <Package InstallerVersion="200" Compressed="yes" />
    <Media Id="1" Cabinet="media1.cab" EmbedCab="yes" />
    <Directory Id="TARGETDIR" Name="SourceDir">
      <Directory Id="ProgramFilesFolder">
        <Directory Id="INSTALLLOCATION" Name="CiDotNet.WinCalc">
        <Component Id="Calculator"
          Guid="b01b0452-7507-4b06-acef-9e7f693599b8">
          <File Id="exe" Name="CiDotNet.WinCalc.exe" DiskId="1"
          Source= "..\CiDotNet.WinCalc\bin\$(var.Configuration)
          ➥\CiDotNet.WinCalc.exe" KeyPath="yes">
            <Shortcut Id="desktopIcon" Directory="DesktopFolder"
              Name="WinCalc" WorkingDirectory="INSTALLDIR"
              IconIndex="0" Advertise="yes" />
          </File>
        </Component>
        <Component Id="FinancialLibrary"
          Guid="ada092ce-5e6d-4ba7-a986-a8cabb895cb8">
          <File Id="dll" Name="CiDotNet.Calc.dll" DiskId="1"
          Source="..\CiDotNet.WinCalc\bin\$(var.Configuration)
          ➥\CiDotNet.Calc.dll" KeyPath="yes" />
        </Component>
      </Directory>
    </Directory>
    <Directory Id="DesktopFolder" Name="Desktop" />
  </Directory>

  <Feature Id="ProductFeature" Title="CiDotNet.WinCalc.WiX" Level="1">
    <ComponentRef Id="Calculator" />
    <ComponentRef Id="FinancialLibrary" />
  </Feature>
  </Product>
</Wix>
```

Creating complex installation files with WiX is a topic for a separate book. So let's discuss it just enough for you to understand the example file. The WiX script defines a `Product`. It contains a `Name`, `Manufacturer`, and information about the `Language`. WiX installers are fully translatable. This information is essentially what you see in the Programs and Features pane in the Control Panel of your Windows installation. The `Product` tag also contains the `Package` and `Media` values. You'll leave default values.

Inside the `Product` is a `Directory` definition. It contains the directory tree where the product will be installed. WiX uses a set of predefined identifiers. What's important is that the software will be installed inside the Program Files folder in the CiDotNet.WinCalc directory. This directory will contain two components: the executable and the financial library.

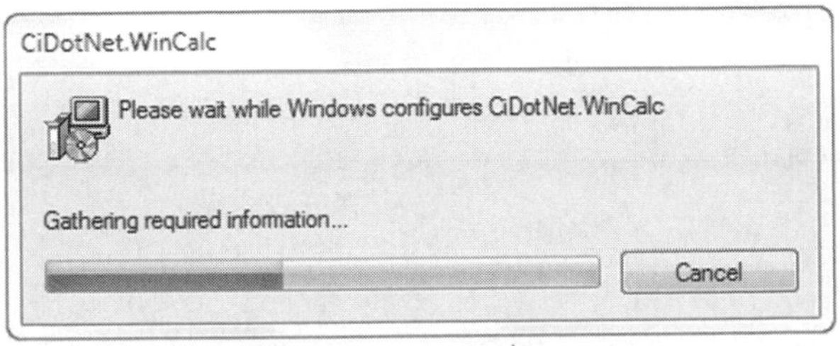

Figure 10.5
The WiX installation running without any UI defined

Inside every `Component`, you can define any number of files or even other types of resources, such as registry keys. Inside the `Component` tag, you define the executable file. Look at the `$(var.Configuration)` macro: it's used to pass variables into the WiX script, in this case the build configuration.

The executable file contains a shortcut named WinCalc that's created inside the `DesktopFolder`. The shortcut points to the executable defined in the `Component` tag. The second component contains the DLL file with the financial calculation library. Everything is put together with the `Feature` tag. If you compile the project in Visual Studio, you'll get the MSI package in the WiX Setup Project folder. Give it a try, and install the software (see figure 10.5).

You have to be observant to catch the WiX installer you've created when you run it. Because you didn't define any UI components, it's a message box with a progress bar. But as you can see, it gets the job done. An icon is installed on the desktop, and the software can be uninstalled from the Programs and Features snap-in. WiX is now tamed; let's combine it with the CI process.

10.2.2 *Automating WiX with CI*

WiX can easily be combined with the CI process. Take the content of the WiX installation bin folder (usually inside your Program Files folder in Windows Installer XML v3.5), and copy it to the tools\WiX folder in your project directory. You'll use MSBuild to automate the WiX process, so you need to get the MSBuild bits of WiX (usually in the Program Files folder in the MSBuild\Microsoft\WiX\v3.5 subdirectory). Copy the DLLs (containing the MSBuild tasks and the .targets files) into the same directory in your project folder.

Take a peek into the .WiXproj file. Does it look familiar? It should, because it's an MSBuild script. Look at the `WiXTargetsPath` property: it defines the WiX installation path. By default, it resides on your development machine. You have to pass the path to tools/WiX, instead. The best way to do this is from the build script, as shown in the following listing.

Listing 10.3   Starting WiX MSBuild .WiXproj file

```
<Project DefaultTargets="Build;Setup;"
   xmlns="http://schemas.microsoft.com/developer/msbuild/2003">
  <PropertyGroup>
    <!--Default Configuration-->
```

```
    <Configuration Condition=" '$(Configuration)' == ''">
      Debug
    </Configuration>
    <!--Default Platform-->
    <Platform Condition=" '$(Platform)' == '' ">
      "Any CPU"
    </Platform>
  </PropertyGroup>

  <Target Name="Build" >
    <MSBuild Targets="Clean;Rebuild" Projects="CiDotNet.sln"
      ContinueOnError="false"/>
  </Target>

  <Target Name="Setup" >
    <MSBuild
      Projects="CiDotNet.WinCalc.WiX\CiDotNet.WinCalc.WiX.WiXproj"
      Properties="WiXTargetsPath=$(MSBuildProjectDirectory)
      ➥\tools\WiX\WiX2010.targets;"/>
  </Target>
</Project>
```

❶ Calls external MSBuild script

In the `Setup` target, you use the `MSBuild` task to call the .WiXproj file and pass the `WiXTargetsPath` property ❶ into it. The property points to the local tools folder. If you check everything in to your repository and configure your build server to start this MSBuild script, the MSI is created after every commit. You can then copy it to a location or send it using email. You can even remotely install it on a machine if you want. But there's a simple way to make a Windows application available over the internet without using installation files: it's called ClickOnce. Let's use it in the CI process.

10.3   *ClickOnce deployment*

ClickOnce is a Microsoft technology that lets you easily deploy a Windows application, whether it's a Windows Forms or Windows Presentation Foundation (WPF) application, via a web page. An application deployed in this manner is sometimes called a *smart client*.

This application is installed in a sandbox on the client machine and has fewer rights than a normally installed application. One limitation is that the application has no access to local files. It isn't installed in the Program Files folder but in the private folder of the user who installs the application. The advantage of ClickOnce deployment is that whenever a new version of the application is available on the website, the user can decide whether to install the upgrade.

If you like this approach, you can easily incorporate it into your CI process and make the new version available after every check-in. Interested? Let's see how to do it.

10.3.1 *Creating a ClickOnce deployment*

You'll make the Windows calculator available with ClickOnce. In order to do this, go to the CiDotNet.WinCalc's project properties, and switch to the Publish tab (see figure 10.6).

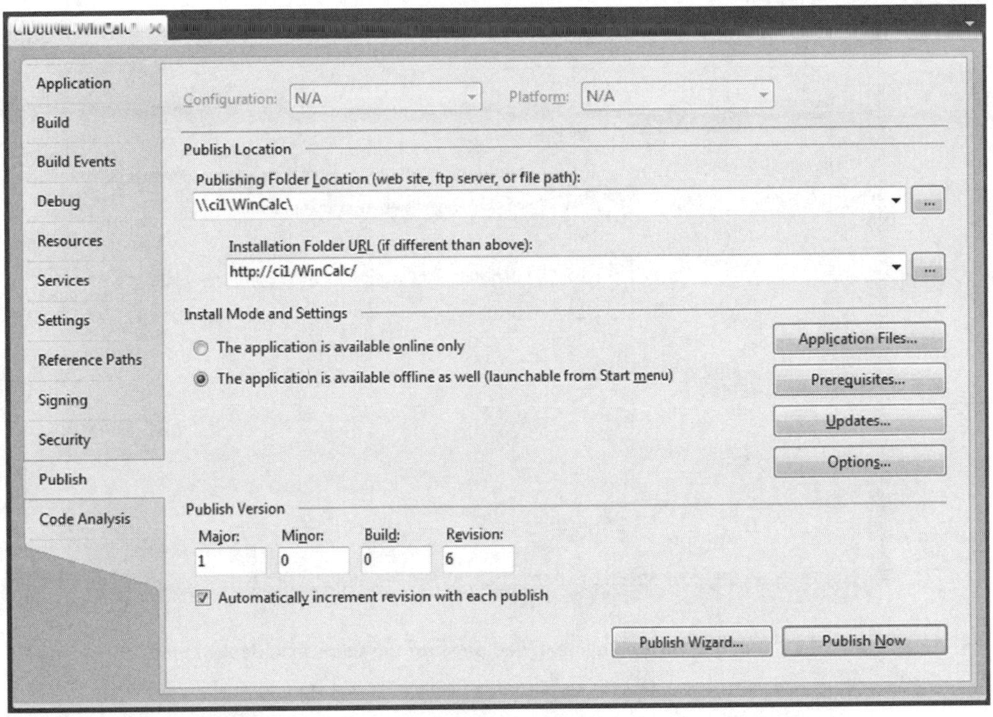

Figure 10.6 **The Publish tab for a Windows application. The install is deployed to a share in the local network that is available over HTTP.**

You need a web server (IIS works) to host your ClickOnce-published applications. Figure 10.6 shows a publishing target somewhere in the local network. In the test setup, IIS is installed on the ci1 server, sees the WinCalc folder, and is able to immediately host the WinCalc application. If you have FrontPage Server Extensions installed on the remote IIS server, you can publish onto it right away. This technology was designed to allow Microsoft FrontPage to communicate with the web server. In this case, you'll use the publishing features of FrontPage Server Extensions.

To make the published version look nice, you should define the deployment web page. Click the Options button. Fill in the Description, and then select Deployment from the list box (see figure 10.7.)

It's time for a test publication. Click the Publish Now button or use the publishing wizard. Then launch Internet Explorer and open the remote location (see figure 10.8). Be advised that Firefox and other browsers don't support ClickOnce without special plug-ins.

Now, if you click Install, WinCalc is installed on your computer. The entire process works like a charm from Visual Studio. With a command line (and eventually CI), it isn't so easy, as you'll see next.

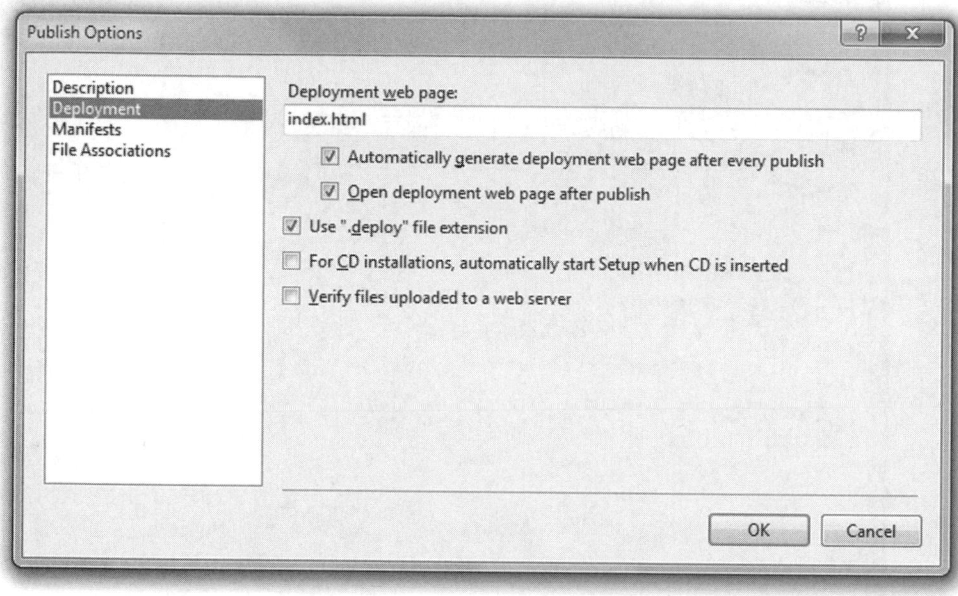

Figure 10.7 Defining the Deployment web page for the ClickOnce deployment

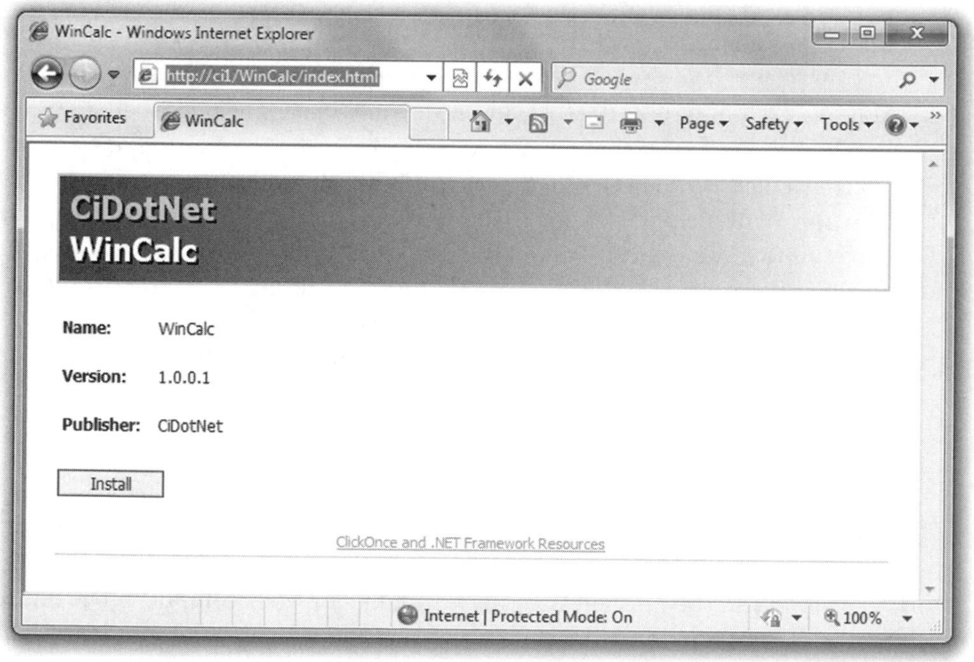

Figure 10.8 A published ClickOnce application on a web page

10.3.2 *ClickOnce in a CI scenario*

Publishing a ClickOnce-based application in Visual Studio is easy, as opposed to the automated deployment. But it's still tricky, and if you want to do it, you can either use a command-line tool like mage.exe or have MSBuild do the work for you. You're a master of MSBuild now, so you'll use this build tool.

You can generate the publication files with MSBuild by using the Publish target on the solution file like this:

```
msbuild CiDotNet.sln /t:Publish
```

There are several problems with this approach:

- The version number isn't incremented.
- The publication files are created in the bin\$(Configuration)\app.publish folder and not on the destination location.
- The website HTML file isn't generated at all.

Let's deal with these issues one at the time. You can set the version number from outside by providing the `ApplicationVersion` property on the MSBuild command line:

```
Msbuild CiDotNet.sln /t:Publish /p:ApplicationVersion=1.0.0.3
```

But how do you get the version number on the build server? Visual Studio takes it from the `ApplicationRevision` property inside the .csproj file, and it isn't a good idea to mess with it on the server. But how about combining the `ApplicationVersion` number with the revision number? You did something similar in chapter 3 when you got the revision number to update the project version number. You'll use the same method here.

First, make sure the MSBuild community tasks have been copied into the tools directory. Next, get the svn.exe file, and copy it to the svn subdirectory in the tools folder. You'll use them both, as shown in the next listing.

Listing 10.4 Publishing an application versioned with an SVN revision number

```
<Project DefaultTargets="Publish"
    xmlns="http://schemas.microsoft.com/developer/msbuild/2003">
  <UsingTask
    AssemblyFile="tools\MSBuildCommunityTasks\MSBuild.Community.Tasks.dll"
    TaskName="MSBuild.Community.Tasks.Subversion.SvnInfo"></UsingTask>
  <PropertyGroup>
    <ApplicationVersion Condition=
    " '$(ApplicationVersion)' == '' ">
    </ApplicationVersion>
    <RevisionNumber Condition=" '$(RevisionNumber)' == '' ">
      0
    </RevisionNumber>
  </PropertyGroup>

  <Target Name="Publish">
    <SvnInfo RepositoryPath="http://ci1/svn/CiDotNetCh10/trunk"
      Username="user" Password="password" ToolPath="tools\svn">
```

❶ Defines immutable version part

❷ Defines mutable version part

```
      <Output TaskParameter="Revision" PropertyName="RevisionNumber" />
    </SvnInfo>
    <MSBuild Targets="Publish" Projects="CiDotNet.sln"
      ContinueOnError="false" Properties=
      "ApplicationVersion=$(ApplicationVersion)$(RevisionNumber)"/>
  </Target>
</Project>
```

After importing the `SvnInfo` MSBuild Community Task (see chapter 3), you define the immutable ❶ and mutable ❷ version-number parts. In the `Publish` target, you get the `RevisionNumber` using the `SvnInfo` task and apply it to the `ApplicationVersion` property. Problem one, setting the version number, is now solved.

The second problem is that the files aren't copied to the target location. The Click-Once files are created in bin\\$(Configuration)\app.publish. They need to be copied to the web server. The easiest way is to define the target location:

```
<DeploymentFolder>\\ci1\WinCalc\</DeploymentFolder>
```

Then, gather the source files:

```
<ItemGroup>
  <DeploymentSourceFiles
  ➥Include="CiDotNet.WinCalc\bin\$(Configuration)\app.publish\**\*.*" />
</ItemGroup>
```

After the publishing files are created, you can copy them:

```
<Copy
  SourceFiles="@(DeploymentSourceFiles)"
  DestinationFiles="@(DeploymentSourceFiles->'
  ➥$(DeploymentFolder)\%(RecursiveDir)%(Filename)%(Extension)')"/>
```

The last problem is the lack of the HTML website. There is no elegant way to deal with that. The best solution is to take the created index.html website and create a kind of template with it. Let's copy the index.html file to the solution project folder and change the current version to a string stored in the `ApplicationVersion` variable. You'll use the `FileUpdate` task from the MSBuild Community Tasks. Here's the file-update usage:

```
<Copy SourceFiles="index.htm"
  DestinationFiles="$(DeploymentFolder)\index.htm"/>
<Copy SourceFiles="wincalc.png"
  DestinationFiles="$(DeploymentFolder)\wincalc.png"/>
<FileUpdate Files="$(DeploymentFolder)\index.htm"
  IgnoreCase="true"
  Multiline="true"
  Singleline="false"
  Regex="ApplicationVersion"
  ReplacementText="$(ApplicationVersion)$(RevisionNumber)"/>
```

Using the HTML template gives you one more opportunity to customize the ClickOnce website to suit your needs. For example, you can provide additional information to the

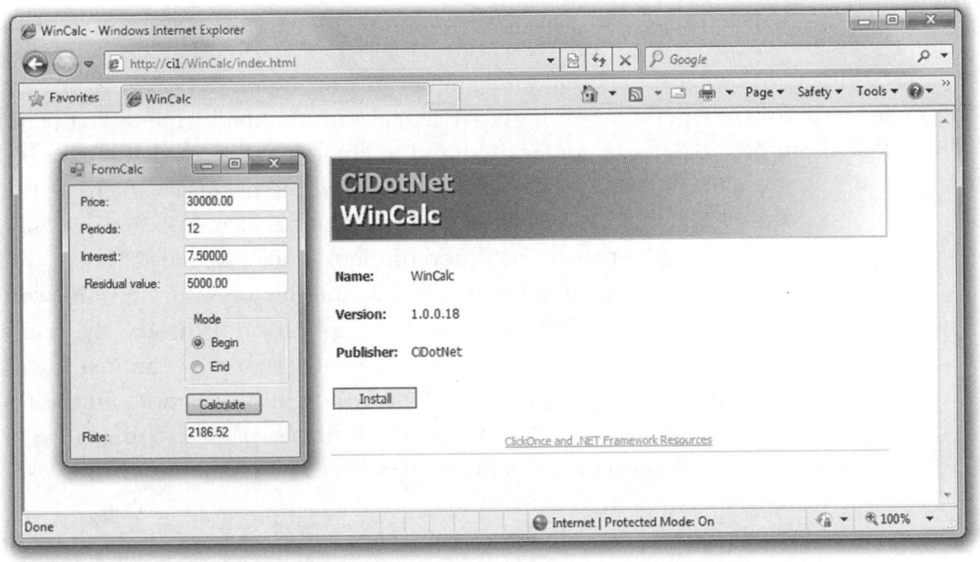

Figure 10.9   A customized ClickOnce website generated directly from the build server

user. First you take the custom-made HTML template file together with an application screenshot and copy it to the destination folder. Afterward, you apply the `FileUpdate` task, search for the `ApplicationVersion` string, and replace it with the version number. Don't forget to import the `FileUpdate` task from MSBuild Community Tasks. Your ClickOnce website may look like the one in figure 10.9.

You can make your CI server use this build script to deploy a brand-new application every time something changes in the repository.

Deployment and delivery of Windows applications is a completely different beast than web applications, which is the topic of the next section.

10.4 Web Deployment Tool

Deploying web applications in .NET has always been an adventure. .NET web apps aren't interpreted files like PHP or Ruby on Rails. Part of the application is compiled; another part may not be or is only precompiled. There are sophisticated techniques like handlers and modules, and configuration and databases must be dealt with. An easy thing became complex, so Microsoft had to came up with an idea for how to deal with that.

Earlier versions of Visual Studio had Web Deployment projects. You had to install them separately, and unfortunately they addressed only part of the problem. In Visual Studio 2010, Microsoft went the extra mile and introduced a set of Web Deployment Tools that interoperate with IIS MS Deploy. Let's look at how to use it and how to incorporate it into the CI process.

10.4.1 *Visual Studio 2010 and MS Deploy*

Microsoft Web Deployment Tool (MS Deploy) is a tool that provides support for deployment, synchronization, and migration to a newer IIS version. It can do a lot more than you'll get to know here. We'll deal with the deployment part of MS Deploy. Visual Studio 2010 uses it under the hood to create so-called *web packages*. It's nothing more than a compressed zip file containing everything necessary to create the application on the IIS server. The process of creating the package is called *publishing*. You'll create a web package for the web edition of the finance calculator.

To use the full packaging/publishing capabilities of Visual Studio, you have to install IIS on the local machine and run the application using IIS. By default, Visual Studio uses a small development server to host the web applications. It differs from full-blown IIS, where your application will be hosted in production. To use IIS settings, you have to run Visual Studio 2010 with administrator rights. Using IIS as your local test server, go to the web project's properties; on the Web tab, select the Use Local IIS Web Server option (see figure 10.10).

After you do that, you can use all the features of packaging/publishing, including IIS settings. This is a huge improvement over previous versions, because it makes your local IIS settings migrate to the package and eventually to the target environment. The package contains, for example, information about the application pool, authentication method, and error handling. It makes it easier to migrate application-specific settings to the server.

The settings for packaging/publication are available in the web application properties on the Package/Publish Web tab (see figure 10.11).

The general idea is to create a package that contains everything necessary for deployment on a remote machine, beginning with the files that constitute the application, through the database files and IIS settings. Choose to deploy only the files needed to run this application. You can leave the program database (PDB) files and the App_Data folder. You don't have a database, so we don't need to choose Include All Databases Configured in Package/Publish SQL Tab. Include the IIS settings without the application pool (you don't do anything special, so you

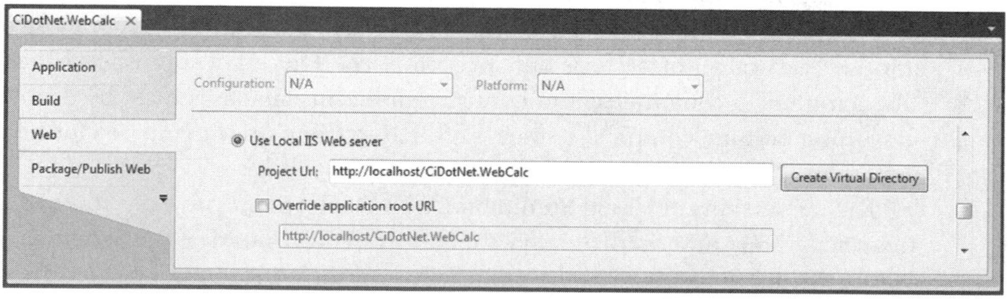

Figure 10.10   Running a web application under a local IIS web server

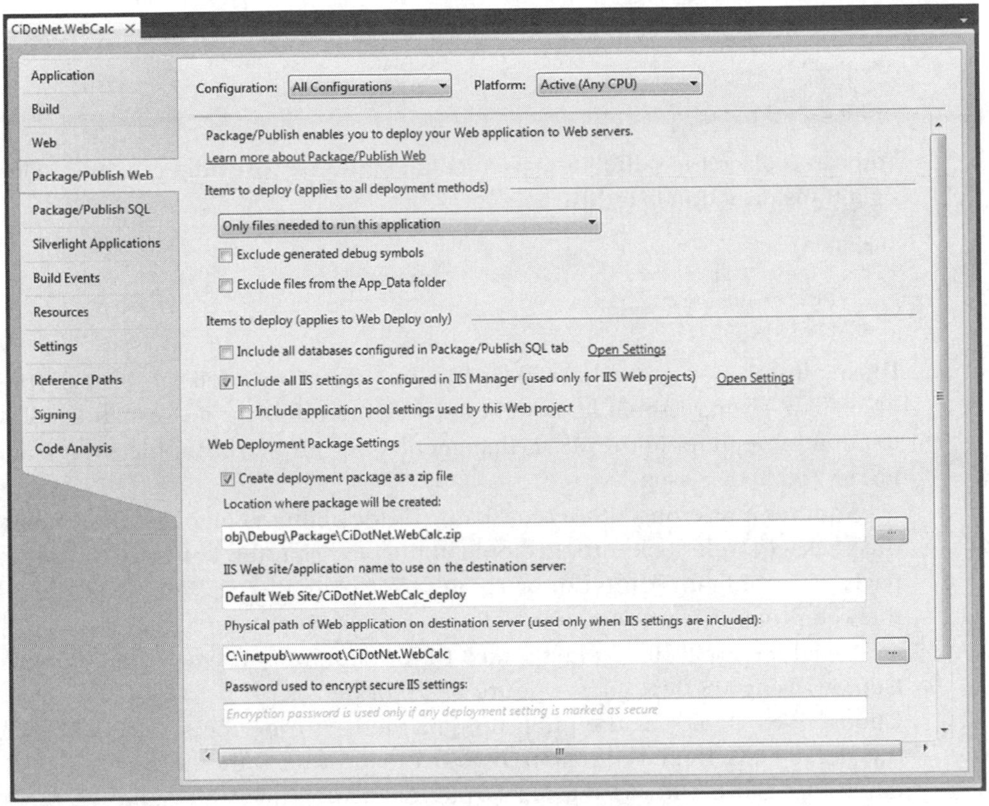

Figure 10.11 The packaging/publication settings of a web application

don't need it). Finally, create the deployment package as a zip file (you can leave the default paths).

Web Deployment in Visual Studio 2010 addresses the configuration files too. If you look at the web.config file, you'll notice the dependent files shown in figure 10.12.

Issues with managing configuration files are severe especially for automatic packaging and deployment. Your goal is to separate the configuration and installation issues. Visual Studio 2010 lets you use simple XML transformations with your web.config files. Let's say you want to identify the installed version of the web calculator by providing a name in the browser title. You want to pull the title in Default.aspx from your configuration file:

Figure 10.12 Configuration management in Visual Studio web applications. The dependent config files are transformations for the standard web.config file.

```
<title><%= ConfigurationSettings.AppSettings
➥["Title"]%></title>
```

And in web.config, an `appSettings` value contains the title:

```
<appSettings>
  <add key="Title" value="Welcome to developement!"/>
</appSettings>
```

You can replace the value for a given configuration by providing in Web.Release.Config a transformation like this

```
<appSettings>
  <add key="Title" value="Welcome to production!"
    xdt:Transform="Replace"/>
  </appSettings>
```

During installation, the value will be replaced with a provided value. MS Deploy developers have given reasonable thought to configuration file transformations. If you want to know more, refer to the MSDN documentation (http://msdn.microsoft.com/en-us/library/dd394698.aspx).

Another interesting MS Deploy feature is the ability to manage the database out of the package. We'll look into this topic in the next chapter. For now, you're ready: the package is configured and can be created. To create the package, select Publish from the web project context menu in Solution Explorer.

Visual Studio 2010 provides a nice UI for deployment. One of the options is Web Deploy (using MS Deploy); see figure 10.13 for details.

Choose Web Deploy as the publishing method. Provide the service URL (if you use the default MS Deploy installation, you can provide only the server name; if not, enter the entire URL to the MS Deploy service). Enter the name of the site and application (for example, Default Web site/CiDotNet.WebCalc). You don't have to delete the files prior to deployment and provide the physical path for the files. At the bottom, provide the credentials of the user who is allowed to use the deployment service.

The Visual Studio 2010 publishing window, however nice, is useless in a CI scenario. Fortunately, the MS Deploy developers thought about automated deployment, too. Let's look at how to incorporate MS Deploy into the CI process.

10.4.2 *MS Deploy on the build server*

In the previous section, you saw how to create an MS Deploy package in Visual Studio. Now you want to create the package from within the MSBuild project and deploy the package on the test/staging server. Here's how to do it.

First, gather everything you need to build the project inside the repository. In this case, you need all the MSBuild targets and DLLs with tasks to compile and create packages for web applications. The files you're looking for are in the folder %ProgramFiles%\MSBuild\Microsoft\VisualStudio\v10.0\ when you install Visual Studio 2010. You need the Web and WebApplications folders in the tools folder. Copy the folders to the subdirectory tools\Microsoft\VisualStudio\v10.0\ in your project. This is important

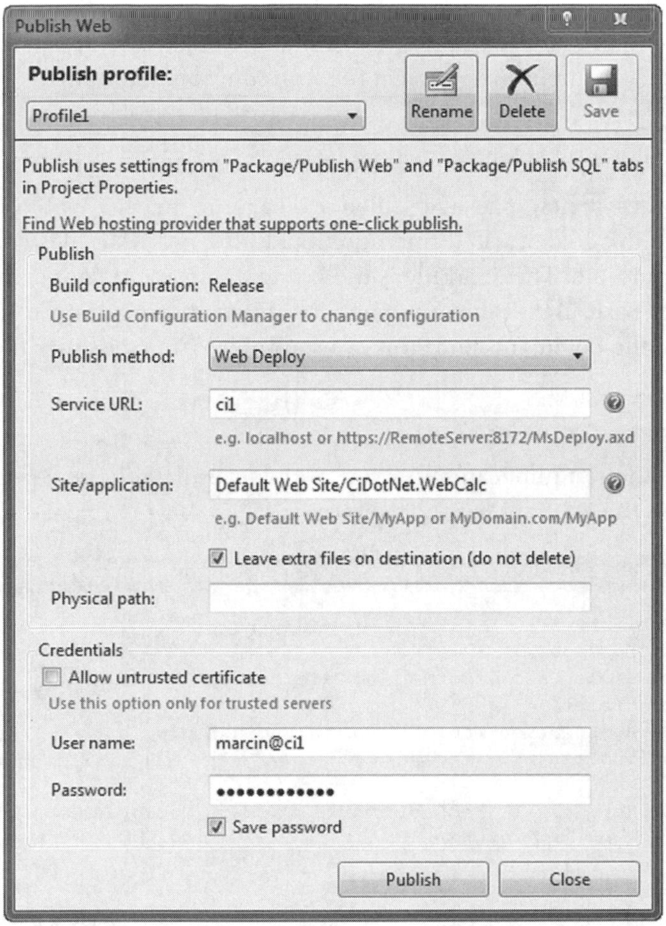

Figure 10.13
Publishing the web application from Visual Studio 2010, made easy. Provide a URL to a server with MS Deploy installed. Give the application a name, and click Publish.

because of the way the path is created in the .csproj script. Look in the CiDotNet.Web-Calc.csproj file, and you'll find this import:

```
<Import
Project="$(MSBuildExtensionsPath32)\Microsoft\VisualStudio\v10.0\
➥WebApplications\Microsoft.WebApplication.targets" />
```

This tells you that you have to pass the $(MSBuildExtensionsPath32) parameter in the MSBuild task in the script:

```
<Target Name="Build" >
  <MSBuild Targets="Clean;Rebuild"
    Projects="CiDotNet.sln"
    ContinueOnError="false"
    Properties="MSBuildExtensionsPath32=..\tools" />
</Target>
```

This way, MSBuild knows to look in the tools folder for the web application–specific targets and tasks. Using the same path, you tell MSBuild to create the web package. It's as easy as starting the web application project file from the command line:

```
msbuild CiDotNet.WebCalc.csproj /t:Package
➥/p:PackageLocation=WebPublication\Package.zip
```

This command creates a new package called Package.zip in the WebPublication folder. If you look in this folder, you'll find additional files: two XML files containing manifests and one .cmd file. The .cmd file is the key to deployment. You can use it to perform publication. Basically, it's the same functionality as shown in figure 10.13, but made available from the command line. You can start a dry run by issuing the following command:

```
WebPublication\Package.deploy.cmd /T
```

This command does the test publication for you. You encapsulate the real publication inside a new target in the MSBuild script, as shown next.

Listing 10.5   Creating a web package and installing it in the MSBuild script

```
<Target Name="WebPublish" >
  <MSBuild Targets="Package"
    Projects="CiDotNet.WebCalc\CiDotNet.WebCalc.csproj"
    ContinueOnError="false"
    Properties="PackageLocation=WebPublication\Package.zip;
    ➥MSBuildExtensionsPath32=..\tools"/>             Creates
                                                      package
    <Exec
      Command="CiDotNet.WebCalc\WebPublication\Package.deploy.cmd
      ➥/Y /m:ci1 /u:marcin /p:password"
      ContinueOnError="false"
      IgnoreExitCode="true"
    />                                          Deploys package on
</Target>                                       remote machine
```

One more thing you have to deal with before you can use this technique properly is installing MS Deploy on the deployment target machine (it's available at www.iis.net/expand/WebDeploy) and starting the Web Deployment Agent Service.

   If you're deploying to a local machine, you can use filesystem deployment and not worry about any Windows services running on the machine. You can now pass the source code to the CI sever and configure it to process the build script. If you've done everything right, you should have a package ready and deployed.

10.5   *Summary*

Automating delivery and deployment and incorporating them into the CI process is a natural thing to do. It feels right to take the compiled, tested, analyzed, and documented code and wrap it up like a delicious candy. You've created this colorful wrapping for your Windows application using Visual Studio and WiX. You've sent the candy to a remote server for immediate delight. You've taken a web application and used new Visual Studio 2010 features to create a professional casing. You've dealt with configuration issues. You've used MSBuild to automate the packaging. And you're able to deploy your software to various locations using a single command.

The delivery and deployment scenarios you've seen are only the tip of the iceberg. You can extend them based on your needs. You can, for example, provision virtual PC setups just like physical ones. You may want to add the automatically generated documentation to the package. You may also need to take into account laws, such as Sarbanes-Oxley (SOX) in the U.S., which prohibit development from touching QA or production servers. In this case, you can use agents on QA and production servers to get the latest build. You may want to create safety-net functionality in your build script to redo changes if something goes wrong. You should now be equipped with enough knowledge to do what you want with your deployment process.

Did you ever think about combining the deployment process with database creation or preparation, or how to manage and version schema and stored-procedure changes? All these things are possible. Read on to the next chapter to learn how.

Continuous database integration

11

This chapter covers

- The basics of database CI
- How Visual Studio helps you maintain the database
- Database-level testing

We've spent the last 10 chapters discussing various parts of the continuous integration process. All these parts involve the source code, assemblies, or the actual application. But one part of CI is often overlooked and is just as important as the code and application. We're talking about dealing with the database.

In this chapter, you'll use Microsoft SQL Server. Even though the Northwind sample database no longer ships with SQL Server, you'll use it because it's well understood and has almost everything needed for the examples.

> **NOTE** All SQL Server sample databases are available via download from various Microsoft websites. You can find the Northwind database at www.microsoft.com/downloads/details.aspx?FamilyID=06616212-0356-46A0-8DA2-EEBC53A68034.

You can use many tools for database maintenance. We'll look at some of them, including SQL Server Management Studio (SSMS), the open source tool RoundhousE, and

Visual Studio. We won't look at higher-end solutions such as those from Red Gate that provide tools for dependency tracking, documentation, data and schema comparisons, and so on, but we highly recommend that you evaluate these tools to see if they fit your database maintenance needs and budget.

We'll get into the tools in a moment, right after we define *continuous database integration* and discuss some best practices.

11.1 *What is continuous database integration?*

As developers, we're aware of the importance of source code control, automated testing, and easily rolling out application changes. We stressed these topics earlier in the book. But do you put your database under source control? Do you have a way to track changes to the schema, stored procedures, functions, and so on? Do you fully test each stored procedure? Can you easily update databases not only in your development and test environments, but also in production? Can you do this without causing data loss?

Don't overlook the importance of good database-management processes. This is just as important as handling changes to the application source code. In fact, the database schema, stored procedures, and other database objects should be considered part of your application source code. After all, you can't run your program without both the code and the database.

Every object in your database should be scripted. This means you'll have to learn T-SQL. Don't let that scare you—T-SQL isn't that difficult. It's another programming language, albeit one that is procedural rather than object-oriented. Yes, newer versions of SQL Server support CLR objects, but you shouldn't use them for database-maintenance issues because T-SQL provides better performance and maintainability over CLR objects.

Scripting allows you to reliably reproduce the database at any time. This adds confidence to the database operations. Haven't we already told you about increasing confidence in your application through CI? If you answer, "No," go back to chapter 1 and start reading the book again.

Scripts are stored in .sql files, which are text files. This makes it easy to add them to source control. You check them in like any other source file.

Every change to the database schema should be handled via a script. If you create a database or table, set security, create a stored procedure, add a constraint, add a column, drop a table, or whatever, you should do it via a script.

Each developer should run a local copy of SQL Server. It can be the free SQL Server Express or SQL Server Developer Edition, which is available for a small fee. When you keep things local, if one developer makes a schema change, it causes problems for other team members. It also makes it easier to test the application. Can you imagine the problems created by using a database on the server when you test that data-update routine only to find that another developer has deleted the row you need to update as part of your test?

Having local copies of the database brings up additional questions such as, should each developer be allowed to make schema changes? That depends on your environment, but if you think of schema changes the same way as source code changes, your automated test system will catch issues that it creates.

Another question that is raised from local data is how to handle conflicts and merges. But again, the same answer applies. Bring down changes from the server as source code changes.

Database configuration changes, such as connection strings, can be handled by having the automated test system modify the connection strings (most likely stored in your app.config file) before running tests.

But, there is one rule that should apply here. If you have a DBA or data architect as part of your team, you should push schema requests through them and let them handle them.

Your CI system should also have its own copy of the data so that tests can be run from the server.

SQL Server stores the data in a file with a .mdf extension; the log file has a .ldf extension. If your test database is small enough, you should also keep the database files under source control. It's difficult to determine what "small enough" really means because each application has different requirements, but a good rule of thumb would be a few hundred records. Databases zip down to a very small size, so they don't require much disk space. Storing the database this way makes it quick and easy to get your test database back to a known state. Often it's faster to get the latest version, unzip it, and then attach it than it is to run the database script.

Now that you have an idea what continuous database integration is all about, let's try it, starting with doing it all yourself.

11.2   *Rolling your own continuous database integration*

One of the easiest ways to get started with continuous database integration is to use SSMS. After you install it, it gives you everything you need to write scripts to maintain your database.

Start by logging in to your SQL Server. Right-click the Pubs database, and select Script Database As. You can save the script into a file or open it in SSMS for editing (see figure 11.1). After you've created a script file for the database, you should create one for each table and other database objects so they can be created programmatically.

You should create a new table from scratch, one that doesn't exist in the database. How about a States table to use as validation? Make sure the Database drop-down in the toolbar is set to Pubs, and click the New Query button. Enter the script in the next listing into the script editor.

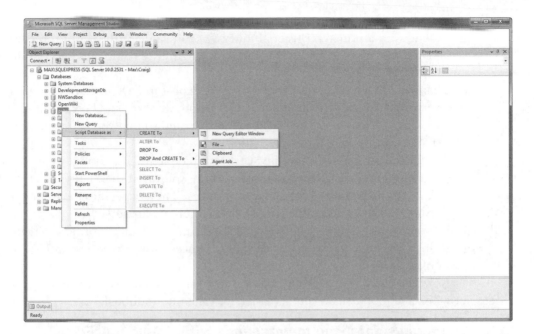

Figure 11.1   You can create a script file for each object in your database. This is an easy way to get started with database scripts.

Listing 11.1   SQL script to create the States table

```
USE [pubs]
GO
```
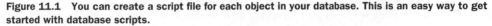
Selects ① **database**

```
SET ANSI_NULLS ON
GO

SET QUOTED_IDENTIFIER ON
GO

SET ANSI_PADDING ON
GO
```

Creates table ②

```
CREATE TABLE [dbo].[states](
  [states_id] [char] (4) NOT NULL,
  [abbrev] [char](2) NOT NULL,
  [state_name] [varchar](40) NULL,
  CONSTRAINT [UPK_statesid] PRIMARY KEY CLUSTERED
  ( [states_id] ASC )
  WITH (PAD_INDEX = OFF, STATISTICS_NORECOMPUTE = OFF,
  IGNORE_DUP_KEY = OFF, ALLOW_ROW_LOCKS = ON, ALLOW_PAGE_LOCKS = ON)
  ON [PRIMARY])
ON [PRIMARY]

GO

SET ANSI_PADDING OFF
GO
```

The script first ensures that the proper database is selected ❶. The table is created along with a primary, clustered index ❷. You can run the script directly inside SSMS: click the Execute button on the toolbar. After it completes successfully, save the script.

That was fun, wasn't it? But you can hardly expect to have to run the script manually every time you want to create the table. Before we show you how to automatically run the script, delete the States table you just created so that you can re-create it outside of SSMS.

To run the script, you'll use the SQL Server command-line utility. Launch a command prompt, and navigate to the folder where you saved the States.sql script. Type `sqlcmd -S[database server name] -iStates.sql`. The `-i` specifies the input file. The script runs, and the States table is added to the Pubs database.

All you need to do to create the database is run the scripts in order or create a single script that does everything. Inside your CI process, you run `sqlcmd` with the proper script files as input.

Now that you have an idea how to automatically run database-maintenance scripts, let's look at a tool to make all this easier. It's called RoundhousE.

11.3   *Continuous database maintenance with RoundhousE*

If you've ever seen a Chuck Norris movie, you know what a roundhouse is. Chuck is known for his roundhouse kicks. In fact, his blurred image is used as the logo for the RoundhousE project. According to Wikipedia.org, a roundhouse is "a kick in which the attacker swings his leg around in a semicircular motion, striking with the front of the leg or foot."

What does this have to do with database maintenance? The RoundhousE home page (http://code.google.com/p/roundhouse/) says RoundhousE "is an automated database deployment (change management) system that allows you to use your current idioms and gain much more. It seeks to solve both maintenance concerns and ease of deployment." In other words, it provides a knockout kick for database maintenance. And because it's an open source project, you can use it free of charge.

You should be aware that RoundhousE isn't as feature-rich as Visual Studio. It doesn't support database unit testing or creating test data. What RoundhousE *will* do is help you with database migration, which means upgrading and making changes to the database. It does this through Windows batch files and SQL scripts.

After you download and unzip RoundhousE, you're ready to get started. A good place to begin is the sample apps that ship with RoundhousE. But take note that many of the samples use NAnt to show you how to integrate with your CI solution.

If you drill down to the RoundhousE\Sample\Deployment folder, you'll find several .bat files. LOCAL.DBDeployment.bat is a good one to start with.

Listing 11.2 LOCAL.DBDeployment.bat sample file from RoundhousE

```
@echo off

SET DIR=%~d0%~p0%

SET database.name="TestRoundhousE"
SET sql.files.directory="%DIR%..\db\TestRoundhousE"
SET server.database="(local)"
SET repository.path="http://roundhouse.googlecode.com/svn"
SET version.file="_BuildInfo.xml"
SET version.xpath="//buildInfo/version"
SET environment=LOCAL

"%DIR%Console\rh.exe" /d=%database.name% /f=%sql.files.directory%
➥/s=%server.database% /vf=%version.file% /vx=%version.xpath%
➥/r=%repository.path% /env=%environment% /simple

pause
```

Note the server name specified (`local`): you'll need to change this if you're using SQL Server Express or not using a local server. After you've made the change, you can run the batch file from the Windows command prompt. RoundhousE runs several .sql scripts from the db\TestRoundhousE folder to create the TestRoundhousE database.

If you run RoundhousE without any switches, you get a list of command-line switches. One that's important for CI is `/ni` or non-interactive mode. This tells RoundhousE not to display any input prompts when it runs.

To set up RoundhousE to handle database changes in the CI process, you first need to create your .sql scripts. You can do this in Visual Studio, SSMS, or any text editor. When you have the scripts, you need to save them into a SQL Scripts folder and check them into source control.

You then need to run an external program from your MSBuild script. Here's how to do this with the RoundhousE sample you saw earlier:

```
<Target Name="Database" >
    <Exec Command="lib\rh.exe /ni
    ➥/d="TestRoundhousE"
    ➥/f=..\SQLScripts\TestRoundhousE
    ➥/s=(local)
    ➥/vf=_BuildInfo.xml
    ➥/vx=//buildInfo/version
    ➥/r=http://roundhouse.googlecode.com/svn
    ➥/env=LOCAL /simple" />
</Target>
```

RoundhousE is still a work in progress and lacks some needed functionality, but the people behind it are dedicated to making it feature complete. It doesn't have unit-test or test-generation abilities, but it can solve some database-maintenance issues for you.

Perhaps you're interested in a more robust or feature-complete tool. Hang on: we're heading into the territory of Visual Studio Data Dude.

11.4   *Continuous database maintenance with Visual Studio*

One of the least-known features of Visual Studio is its great tooling for database maintenance. Originally released as Visual Studio 2005 Team Edition for Database Professionals (wow, what a mouthful), it was more commonly called Data Dude. One reason it wasn't well-known is that Data Dude started as a special version of Visual Studio that most developers didn't own and didn't want to purchase. Luckily, Microsoft later rolled Data Dude features into Visual Studio 2010 Premium and Ultimate Editions. It's time for us to introduce you to the Visual Studio 2010 version of Data Dude.

11.4.1   *Getting started with database projects*

In order to see what continuous database integration does for you, you need to learn how to use it in Visual Studio. Let's jump right in:

1   Launch Visual Studio, and create a new SQL Server 2008 Database Project named NWSandbox (see figure 11.2). Store it wherever you want on your disk; don't add it to source control at this time.

2   Right-click the NWSandbox project in the Solution Explorer, and select Import Database Objects and Settings from the context menu. The Import Database Wizard is displayed (see figure 11.3). Create a connection to the Northwind

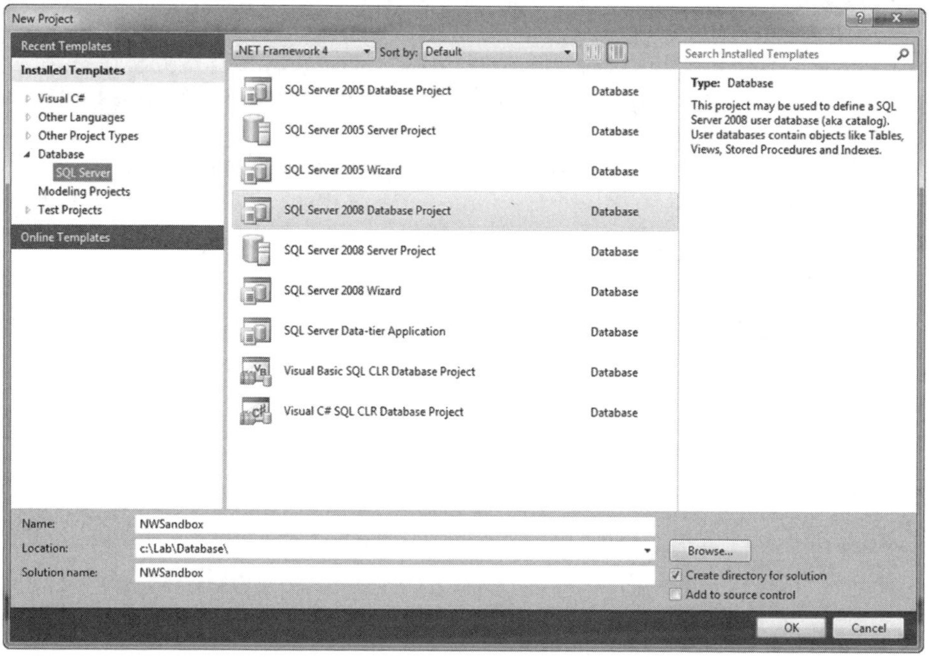

Figure 11.2   Visual Studio includes several database project templates.

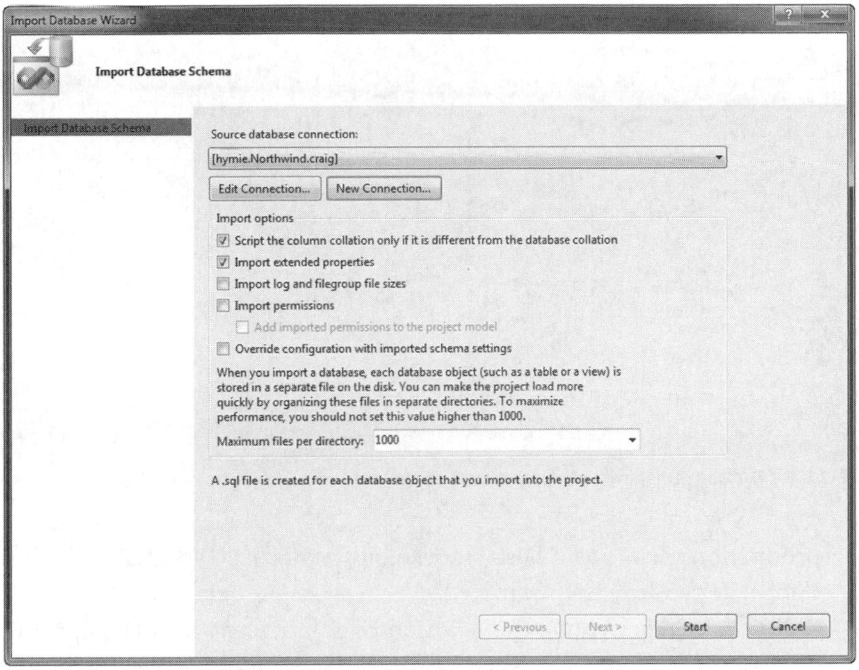

Figure 11.3   You use the Import Database Wizard to connect to an existing database and create .sql scripts to import into the project.

database you installed from the download. Typically, you'll import a production database to get started.

3   Click Start to begin the import process. This process examines your database schema and creates SQL scripts for creating the database, tables, fields, indexes, stored procedures, and other objects in your database. It doesn't import any of the data.

4   When the import process is complete, go out to Windows Explorer and drill down to the folder where you stored the project; you'll see that each script is saved in its own file. This makes it easy to place your database under source control: follow the same process that we outlined in chapter 2 for your application files.

5   Go back to Visual Studio, and double-click one of the .sql files. It opens in the T-SQL Editor. This is a fantastic way to edit SQL scripts, because you're already familiar with Visual Studio.

6   Build the project.

7   Open the project properties, and navigate to the Deploy tab (see figure 11.4). Change the Deploy action to Create a Deployment Script (.sql), and deploy to the database. Also set up the target connection. This target should never be a

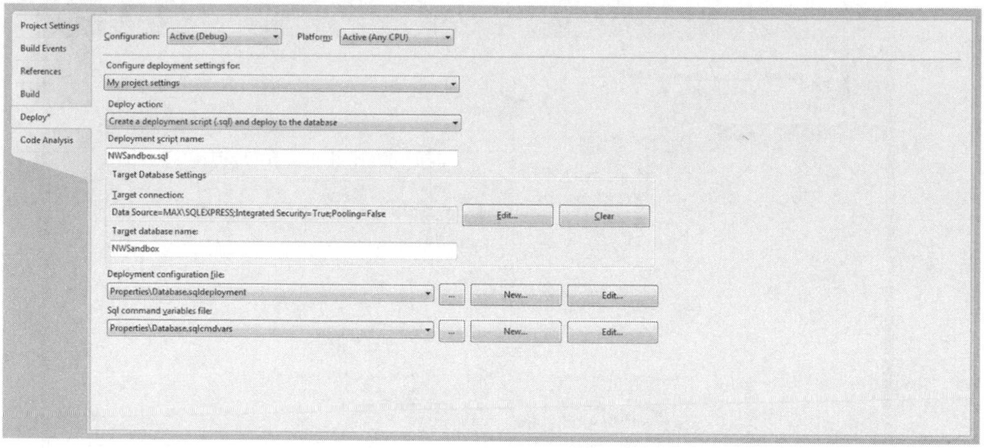

Figure 11.4   Database deploy options are part of the database project properties.

production server; as a best practice, always target a local SQL Server installation such as SQL Server Express.

8 Right-click the project in the Solution Explorer, and select Deploy. If you watch the Output Window, you'll see Visual Studio generate a SQL script that is then sent to the target database and run to create the NWSandbox database.

You can generate the deployment script without specifying the target database, but it won't run because there are variables in the script that specify the target and are left empty. It's a simple matter to load the script into SSMS Studio, validate it, find these places, and manually enter the needed values.

Now that you've created the database, you need to add some test data. You'll learn how to do that in the next section.

11.4.2 *Generating test data*

Have you ever tried to test an application, only to find that another developer on your team is using the same database and has changed the data in a way that causes your tests to fail? If you're manually testing your application, this isn't too big of a problem; but imagine how this will cause automated tests to fail in a CI process.

You can take two steps to resolve this issue. First, you should always use a local copy of the database rather than a shared server. Second, you can generate test data when you need it. Normally, generating test data sounds like a big job, but Visual Studio makes it easy:

1 In the NWSandbox project in the Solution Explorer, right-click Data Generation Plans and select Add > New Item.

2 In the Add New Item dialog box (see figure 11.5), select Data Generation Plan, and then click Add.

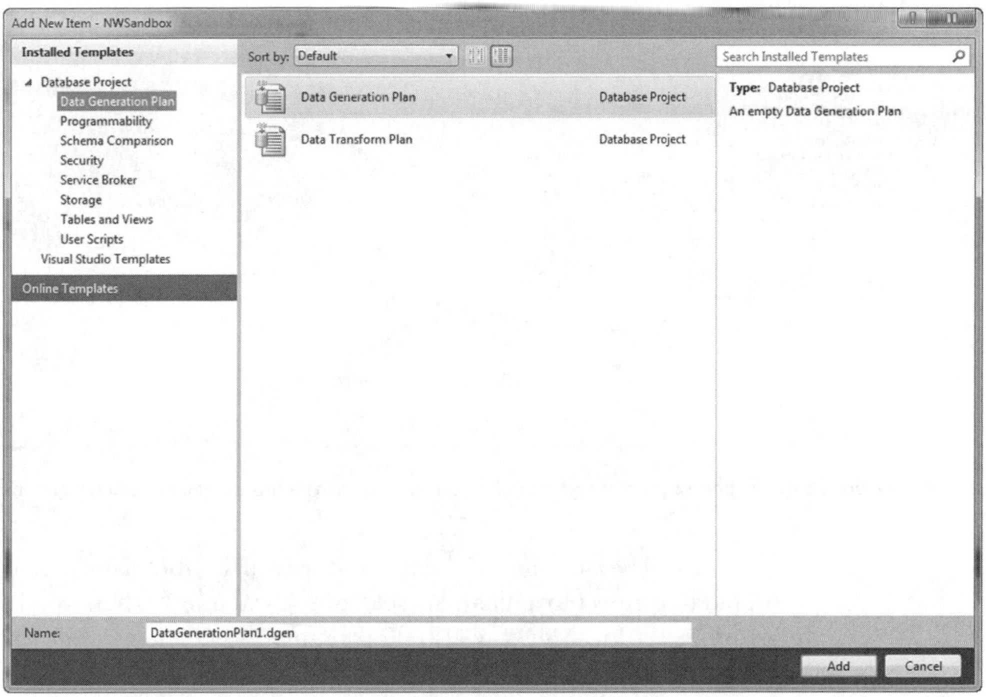

Figure 11.5 Add a data-generation plan to create test data for your database.

3   On the Visual Studio menu, select Data > Data Generator > Include All Tables from Data Generation (see figure 11.6). You can generate data for a single table if you want to, but you'll need additional test data later to unit test a stored procedure.

The top pane of the Data Generation Plan window shows the tables from the database. The bottom pane shows the fields for the selected table. You can choose the generator to use to create the data. One generator, Data Bound Generator, lets you generate data from the results of a query. You do this by checking the columns you want to include in the query.[1] You can change the output for each column based on the generator. In this case, use the default settings for each column.

4   Select Data > Data Generator > Preview Data Generation from the Visual Studio menu. The generated data is displayed in a preview window. You may be shocked, because the data looks like random characters and dates. We never said the data was perfect, but it will work for some purposes.

---

[1]   Creating a test data query can be a complex process depending on how you want to process each column, the number of records to include, and other details. Complete instructions are available on the MSDN website at http://msdn.microsoft.com/en-us/library/dd193257.aspx.

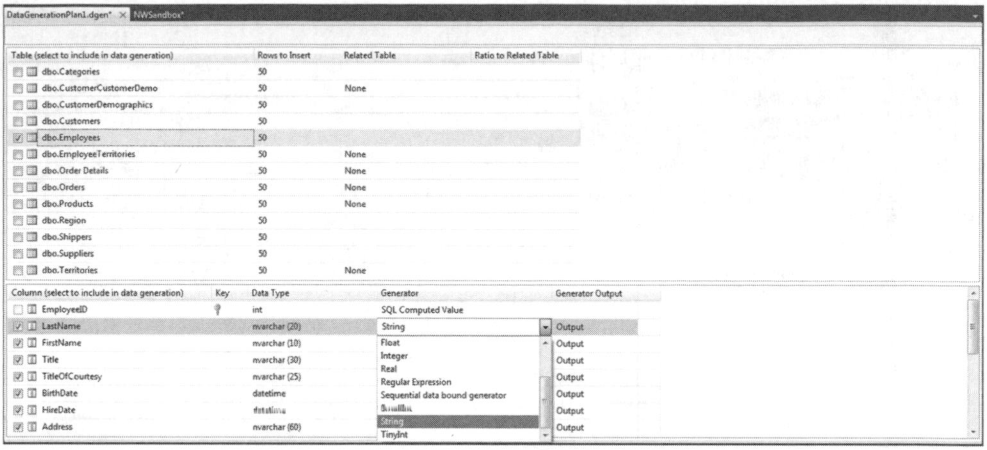

Figure 11.6   As part of generating test data, you can specify the tables, columns, and a generator to use.

5   Press F5 to generate the test data and populate the database. If you're prompted to connect to a database, select the local test database you created in the previous section. You may also be prompted to delete current test data in the selected tables.

Visual Studio inserts the data into the selected tables. You may see warnings about data in other tables being deleted; this is because of referential integrity rules set up in the database.

One drawback to automatically generating test data is that the data is basically unreadable (see figure 11.7). If you need readable data, you can have Visual Studio

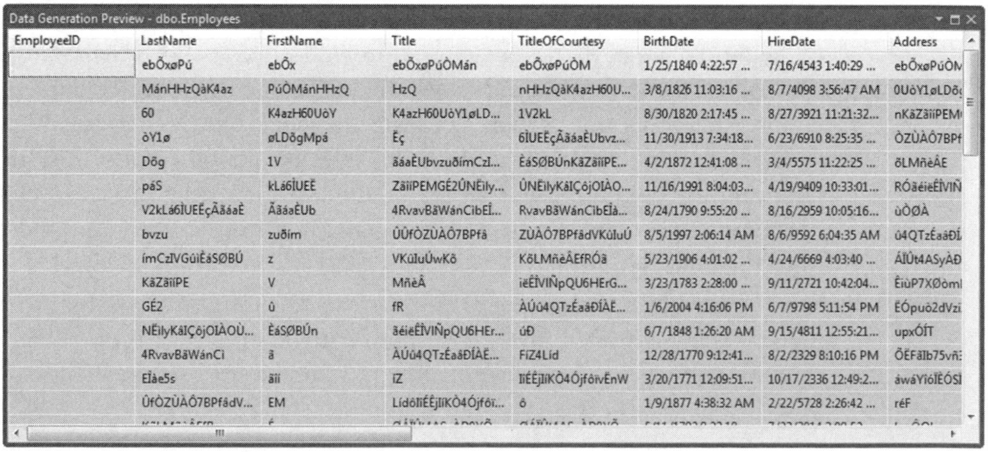

Figure 11.7   When you generate test data, you get gobbledygook, but it's good enough for many of the tests you need to run.

gencrate data from an existing data store, or you can create your own data and either load it through a SQL script or bulk-insert it from a text file.

You've generated the schema, stored procedures, and so on from the existing database, and created test data. Next up, you'll unit test a stored procedure.

11.4.3 *Unit testing stored procedures*

Back in chapter 6, we talked about the importance of unit testing your code and showed how to do it manually with different unit test tools. You then integrated unit testing into the CI process.

When you think about it, a stored procedure is no different than code in your application. For this reason, you should unit test your stored procedures, just like your C# or VB.Net code.

Before testing a stored procedure, let's look at the one you're going to use: Ten Most Expensive Products. To open it in the T-SQL Editor, double-click it in the Solution Explorer. Here it is:

```
create procedure "Ten Most Expensive Products" AS
SET ROWCOUNT 10
SELECT Products.ProductName AS TenMostExpensiveProducts, Products.UnitPrice
FROM Products
ORDER BY Products.UnitPrice DESC
```

To run this stored procedure and see its results, open the Server Explorer in Visual Studio, and drill down to the NWSandbox database until you find the stored procedure you want. Right-click it, and select Execute. The query will run against your Northwind database and the results appear in the Output window (see figure 11.8).

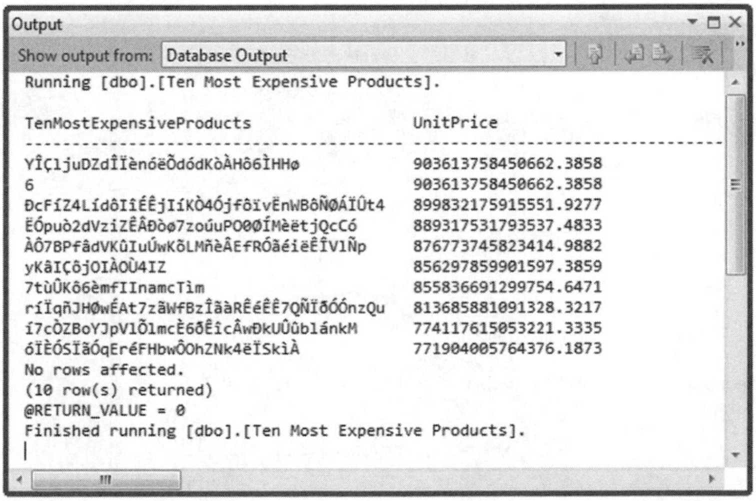

Figure 11.8   The results of the Ten Most Expensive Products stored procedure

The question is, how do you test this? The following steps show you how:

1 In Visual Studio, select Test > New Test. The Add New Test dialog box opens (see figure 11.9).

2 Name the test TenMostExpensiveProductsTest, and click OK.

3 If you don't have a test project in the solution, you're asked to add one. Name it NWTests. Click Create.

4 In the Project Configuration dialog box shown in figure 11.10, select the NWSandbox database. We won't deal with the other configuration options; click OK.

5 The Database Test Designer opens. Click the link in the middle to create your first test.

6 Click the Rename button, and name the test RowCountIs10.

7 Remove the comments in the editor, and replace them with the following snippet:

```
EXEC [dbo].[Ten Most Expensive Products]
```

8 In the bottom pane, click the X to remove the current test.

9 Select Row Count in the Test Conditions drop-down.

10 Click the + to add a new test.

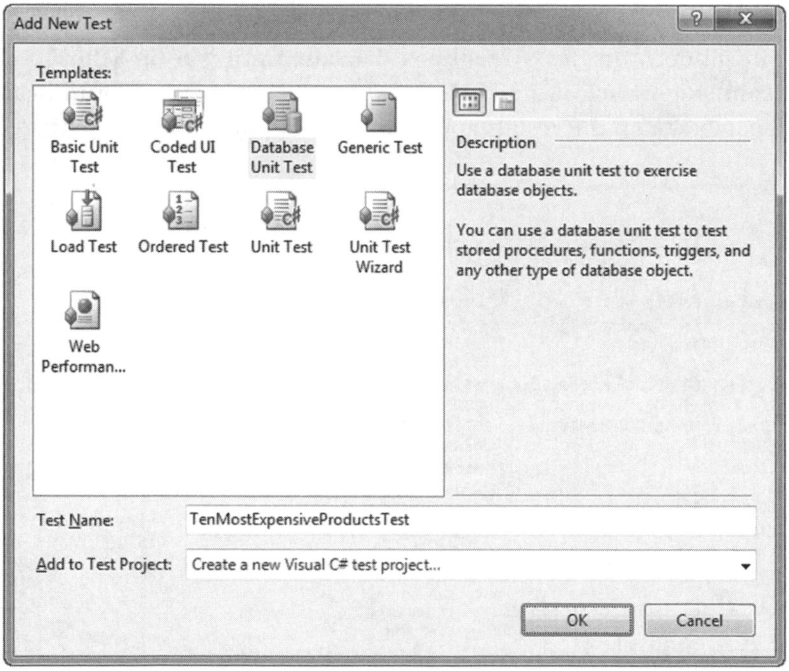

Figure 11.9   Visual Studio can unit test database objects. You create a new test in the Add New Test dialog.

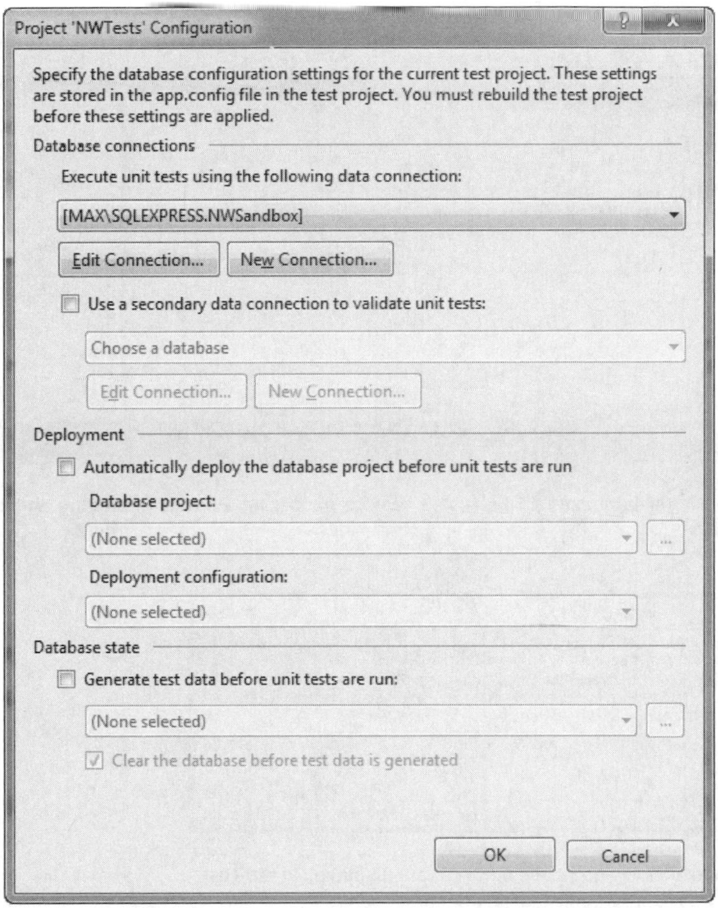

Figure 11.10 When you create a new database test, you need to specify which database you want to use.

11 In the property sheet, set the name to RowCountIs10 and Row Count to 10. Visual Studio should look something like figure 11.11.

12 Select Test > Run > Tests in Current Context to execute the test. Visual Studio builds the project, runs the test, and displays the results in the Test Results window (see figure 11.12).

You can create database tests against the schema, procedures, triggers, and functions, and even compare table values between one database and another. Along the way, you can test for several conditions including data checksum, empty resultset, execution time, expected schema, not empty resultset, row count, scalar value, and inconclusive results, or create your own tests.

Now that you've seen some of the database functionality in Visual Studio, you need to learn how to integrate it into your CI environment.

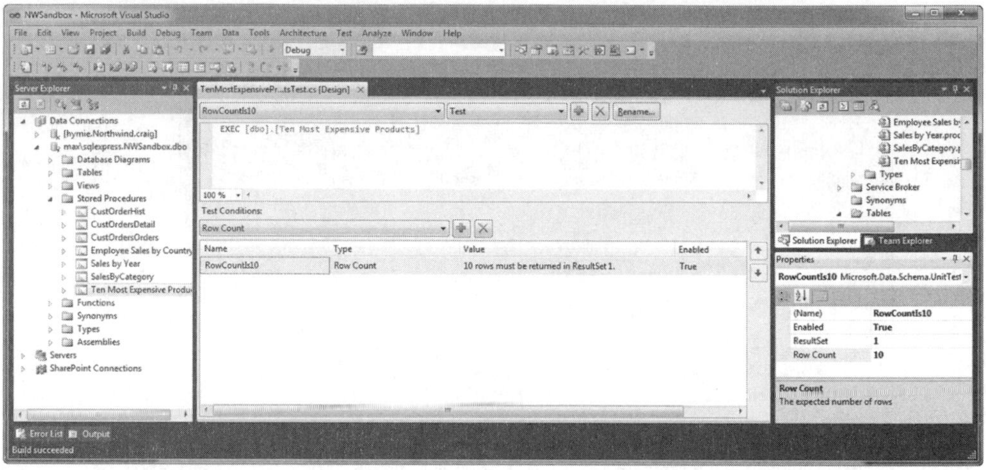

Figure 11.11 Creating a database unit test is as easy as executing a stored procedure and checking its return value.

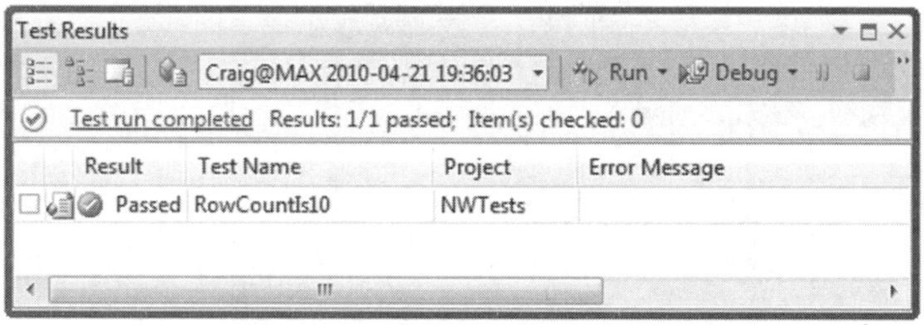

Figure 11.12 The results of a database unit test are displayed in the Test Results pane, just as when you unit test application code.

11.4.4 *Putting Visual Studio database maintenance into CI*

Did you pay attention to the projects you created earlier? You have NWSandbox.dbproj and NWTests.csproj. These are both MSBuild files, so they aren't any different than the projects we've been looking at until now.

But there are settings that you probably want to change. In figure 11.9, you saw how to set up the connection to your database. You won't want automated testing done on the same database because it's local to your development PC. So you need to change the database connection string. You can do this by configuring the MSBuild command line in your build script:

```
<MSBuild
  Projects = "$(SolutionRoot)\NWSandbox.dbproj"
  Properties = "Configuration=Debug; TargetDatabase=NewDBName"
  Targets = "Deploy"/>
```

Handling database maintenance and creation through Visual Studio adds lots of power to your development process. But testing a database is part of MSTest, so to use it from something other than TFS requires that you install Visual Studio on your build server or use a trick described in 6.3.3.

We've only scratched the surface of database maintenance in Visual Studio. You can add more unit tests, refactoring, and much more. But as you can see, Visual Studio lets you do much more than rolling your own or roundhouse.

11.5 Summary

In this chapter, we've provided an introduction to continuous database integration. Ideally, you'll follow the same concepts you do for your program source code: that is, you should store your SQL scripts in source code control; have a way to unit test your stored procedures, functions, and so on; and have a way to easily deploy your database changes.

We also showed you how to use Visual Studio to deal with database changes; and we introduced you to a free tool, RoundhousE, that can help with maintenance issues.

Coming up in chapter 12, we conclude our CI coverage by discussing issues such as large and/or many projects and teams, how to grow your CI system, and other issues you may encounter along the way.

Extending continuous integration 12

This chapter covers

- Dealing with slow builds
- Scaling the CI process
- Measuring the maturity of the CI process

Now that you have your CI process up and running and you've added some capabilities, you may have found that not everything is a bed of roses. Some things don't work as you expect or become slower as you add more capabilities. You may also have found political or legal issues that cause you pain.

This chapter will help you. We'll wrap up our discussion of CI by talking about extending your process and how to overcome some of these obstacles. The topics we'll present in this chapter aren't necessarily directly related to each other, but they're important enough that we need to discuss them. You'll learn how to work with large projects, lots of projects, large and geographically separated teams, and legal roadblocks, and see where your CI process should be headed to make it more efficient and able to handle more of your software pipeline.

We'll discuss the seven deadly sins of slow software builds and how to receive absolution. You'll tweak the MSBuild scripts. We'll look at how to technically scale the TeamCity server builds. And after dealing with Sarbanes-Oxley, we'll examine the Enterprise CI Maturity Model. Let's begin with team and project problems.

12.1 Speeding up CI

How many times have you started a project and, when it was finished, found that it required no enhancements, no bug fixes, and no more work? We're guessing rarely, if ever. It's inevitable that projects become bigger and more complex over time. Additional functionality means that more is happening in your CI process, which slows it down. You may be creating more and more projects. It's rare to have a single project in your shop. And what happens when you're working in California and the rest of your team is in New York?

The solutions to all these problems are pretty much the same. Let's talk about the not-so-obvious first. You can remove code. Yes, you read that correctly: *remove code*. At some point, all projects have old code that's no longer needed. Why do you carry around the old code? Because you *might* need it someday? Delete the old code from the source. You won't lose anything. It's still in your source control system, so you can always get it back. After you strip out the old code, your compile time should drop; the difference may only be a few seconds, but it may be a minute or more if the codebase is large.

Did you take out the unit tests with the old code? That will save even more time during your build process.

Now for the more obvious: you can get a bigger, faster build box. That should speed things up. You can also spread out the build to multiple machines. Most CI servers support build agents running on more than one machine. When you do this, one machine controls the build process and farms out the actual build to other machines; then it aggregates the results into the feedback mechanism. In other words, you're working with parallel builds. We'll have more to say about this in a moment, when we discuss the seven deadly sins of slow software builds.

You can also set up a different build machine for each project. We don't recommend this: it makes feedback more complicated because you'll need multiple feedback mechanisms or have to do some fancy configuration to pull all the build results into a single reporting tool. We also don't recommend running geographically separated build servers. But there are other things you can do without spending money on more hardware.

Do you need to run all those unit or integration tests with every check-in? Remember, the build time is ideally less than ten or five minutes. Separate the unit and integration tests. Typically, integration tests take longer to run than true unit tests. Run the integration tests at night when you can afford the time for longer tests.

Next, you can look for other steps in your CI process that don't need to run at every check-in. You may be doing additional testing or different types of statistical analysis on the code. These items can wait until the nightly or even weekly build.

One other thing you may want to do for geographically separated teams it use a distributed source control system such as Git. Doing so allows developers to work locally, without check-in/checkout wait times.

Table 12.1 describes your options for dealing with slow builds.

Table 12.1   Having problems with slow builds? Use one of these techniques.

Problem	Solution
Slow compile time	Delete old code.
Slow build machine	Scale using multiple build agents.
Slow tests	Categorize your tests, and don't run them all every time.
Overall slow build	Categorize your builds.

Now you know the obvious solutions for speeding up the build. But how about darker lore? Let's examine the seven deadly sins of slow builds.

12.2   *Seven deadly sins of slow software builds*

When you get right down to it, serialized builds, where one step has to complete before the next begins, are slow. When your build runs slowly, you may have one or more of the *seven deadly sins of slow software builds*. This is a term coined by Usman Muzaffar of Electric Cloud,[1] a company that provides high-end build-management and build-analysis software. The seven deadly sins lead to serialized processes. Why not speed up that large project or multiple projects by running things in parallel as much as possible? Table 12.2 lists the seven deadly sins and contrasts them with good guidelines.

Table 12.2   The seven deadly sins of slow builds

Deadly sin	Good guideline
Make at the bottom	Let make drive your build.
Targets with side effects	Update only one file in a make rule.
Multiple updated files	Write each file only once during a build.
Pass-based builds	Visit each directory once.
Output in the source directory	Write output to its own directory.
Monoliths	Split long jobs into multiple targets.
Bad dependencies	Specify relationships in a make file.

Now that you've been introduced to the seven deadly sins, let's dig into them to understand what they mean and how you can counteract them with the good guidelines. We'll paraphrase Usman's explanations of the seven deadly sins.

---

[1] Electric Cloud Commander provides functionality similar to TeamCity and CruiseControl.NET. For more information, visit www.electriccloud.com.

12.2.1 *Making a build script drive your build*

Throughout this book, we've looked at MSBuild. Have you enjoyed spelunking into the XML that makes MSBuild run? We didn't think so. You may think it would be easier to wrap MSBuild in a cool PowerShell or Python script and have it call MSBuild multiple times. The problem is, you're not letting MSBuild do the things it does best, such as comparing timestamps on files and dealing with dependencies.

MSBuild is designed to understand what you want to happen, and then go back and figure out how to do it. When externally scripted, you make multiple calls to MSBuild. You're telling it not only what you want, but how to get there. This causes unnecessary serialization. The external script is at the top of the process, not MSBuild. You want MSBuild to drive the actual compile, not have some external script do it.

There are two ways to fix this. First, you can remove the external scripts and put MSBuild back at the top. But this approach can lead to *monoliths*, where you have one big job; or it can create bad dependencies. These are two of the seven deadly sins. Don't have a single target in the MSBuild script; use multiple targets to break things up.

The second approach is a much better solution. It's called *separation of powers*. Don't have MSBuild do everything for you; if you need to do some setup work, such as checking out code or cleaning up folders from a previous build, do so outside of your MSBuild script. If you've followed us through this book, that's exactly what we've done.

Now that the first sin has been resolved, let's look at the second: targets with side effects.

12.2.2 *Getting rid of build-script targets' side effects*

Do you need to pass data from one build target (see chapter 3 for details) to another? For example, does one target get the new version number and then pass it to another? Or does a target figure out if you're doing a debug or release build, only to send that information to another target? This sounds innocent enough, doesn't it?

The problem is that you have serialization, where one build target implicitly calls another. To make it worse, this serialization is hidden. And even worse, it's often impossible to tell if it isn't working properly. But wait: there's more bad news. If the two targets run in parallel, things can fail unpredictably. In this case, you should introduce serialization with an explicit dependency. Or, even better, merge the multiple targets into a single target.

The next sin occurs when you update a file more than once.

12.2.3 *Multiplying updated files*

The build process updates many files, some of them more than once. Examples include build logs, program database (.pdb) files, and updated zip files. The problem is that if a file is updated multiple times (see figure 12.1), it takes longer to create multiple input files than to create the final file one time (see figure 12.2).

Figure 12.1 shows a serialized process that updates an output file more than once. Source file 1 is processed, and the result placed in the output file. A second source file

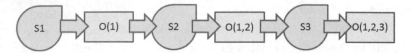

Figure 12.1   A serialized process that updates the output file after each step in the process

is processed, and the output from that process updates the output file. Depending on how the output code is written, the output for source 2 can do a simple append to the output file, or it can cause the output file to be completely rewritten. This process gets even more lengthy when source file 3 is added.

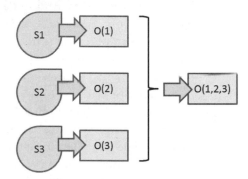

Figure 12.2   Multiple output files that are combined only once to create the final output can be significantly faster than updating the output file multiple times.

Figure 12.2 shows an alternative process. Each source file produces its own output file after processing. Each separate output file is then combined one time to create the final output file. This way of updating a file only once can provide significant speed increases, especially if the source files can be processed in parallel.

In the case of the .pdb file, you can compile each source file separately. Use the /pdb switch on the compiler (either csc or vbc) command line to specify that each source file gets its own .pdb file. Don't worry about combining them at the end of the build. You don't debug on the build server, so why take the extra step to combine the .pdb files?

Next we turn to pass-based builds.

12.2.4   *Pass-based builds*

Pass-based dependencies occur when you have to build things in a particular order or you say, "We have cyclical dependencies, so we have to control the order of the build." This completely serializes your build.

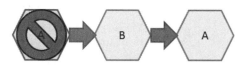

Figure 12.3   Project A compiles and fails. We then compile project B, which succeeds. We then compile A again. Because it's successful, we assume we have a cyclical dependency.

First, there's no such thing as a cyclical build. MSBuild doesn't allow it. If you think you have one, you don't. Analyzing this more closely, we get figure 12.3.

In this figure, we know that project B depends on project A; but when we compile A, we get errors, and it doesn't actually build. We then build B, and it succeeds. If we then build A again, we assume that we have a cyclical dependency. But what's really happening is depicted in figure 12.4.

The reality is that B relies on only part of A. That part builds. The other part of A relies on B, so A fails the first time. Because it's partially built, B can now build, and then A can build properly when the build is run a second time. The solution is to break A into two parts and serialize them. There's always a serialization that works.

Figure 12.4 What really happens is that part of A builds, and then B. Then, the remainder of A that relies on B can build.

Now we move on to where to place output from the build process.

12.2.5 *Output in the source directory*

When you build your Visual Studio project, where does the output go? By default, it goes in either the bin\debug or the bin\release folder under the project directory. You can then manually or automatically copy the generated assemblies to some other folder for unit testing. The additional copy takes time.

Do you clean out the generated files before each build? If you have to specify each individual file, it takes more time to delete these generated files. What if you have to clean the output folders for multiple Visual Studio projects?

The solution is obvious: point all the generated output from the build to a single folder. This way, you'll have one output folder for the compiled assemblies and a second output folder for the build artifacts, such as the build log, unit test results log, and so on. Also, if you put this output on the local disk instead of a server drive, you'll get better performance.

Next, we look at monoliths.

12.2.6 *Monoliths*

Monoliths exist when you have a single, large build target or a build target that performs many tasks. This can get tricky. It's fairly easy to identify monoliths, but it can be difficult to break them up. Where they occur in the build process can make a difference. You may have one at the beginning of your build that identifies dependencies. At the end, you may have many file copies or copy a large file.

The bad news is, monoliths are often unavoidable. You have to use them. But if you do have a monolith, you can ask several questions to try to break it up:

- Is it necessary?
- If it's necessary, is there a faster way?
- Can it be rewritten as MSBuild targets?
- Can it be pushed later in the build process?
- Can it be made optional?
- Should it be run locally (on the build server) rather than on a file server?
- Can it be cached?
- Is it really part of the build or the setup?
- Can it be broken into smaller steps, each one a separate target?

After you've asked these questions, you may be able to break down the monolith, making it faster and more manageable.

There's one more sin to cover: bad dependencies.

12.2.7   *Bad dependencies*

Dealing with bad dependencies is another tricky area. It's almost impossible to resolve all dependencies so that everything builds cleanly. The problem is that sometimes dependencies build correctly, and other times the build fails. Even worse, you may not know exactly why the build failed. Things may build correctly when you run the build serially but fail on a parallel build. Or the build may not fail every time, only when race conditions are just right. A race condition exists when the output of one process is dependent on other processes completing in a specific sequence, but they run in parallel, thus completing in an unexpected order.

How do you deal with this issue? First, you can run parallel builds often. The more you run them, the more often the race conditions are likely to show up. This will alert you to where the errors are so you can fix them.

Second, whenever possible, add the missing dependency. Make sure it exists. Maybe you can serialize that part of the build process and run the rest in parallel.

Finally, you can centralize build rules. Doing so helps eliminate mistakes. Don't copy the same build code into multiple build files for the same project; this increases the chances that one build script will be changed and another won't. In other words, follow the same rule for your build scripts that you would for source code: don't copy and paste code into multiple files. Put things in one place and one place only.

We've covered a lot of ground discussing ways to speed up your build. We've talked about things as simple as adding more hardware and as varied as the seven deadly sins of slow builds. But you may have to deal with other issues as your CI process grows. Next, let's scale.

12.3   *Scaling CI*

Your CI setup grows. You have more and more projects working on the build server. You've done your best to minimize the time the build takes to run, but the CI server is overloaded. You have many projects, and you work with many developers. The changes are pouring in more quickly than the build server can process them. One option is scaling up (in other words, scale vertically) by buying more memory for the server, switching the processor for a better one, or adding disk space. It's easy, but you may bump the ceiling. What if you can't scale higher? Try scaling out.

12.3.1   *Build-agent theory*

Most modern build servers can scale vertically. This means you can add more physical machines. We touched on this topic briefly in chapter 4 when we discussed Microsoft Team Foundation Server. Let's dig a little deeper.

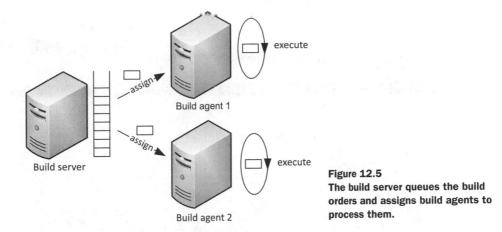

Figure 12.5
The build server queues the build orders and assigns build agents to process them.

The theory is simple. There's one central CI server and a bunch of build agents. The server is responsible for build management. The server doesn't process any builds itself; it passes the order to build to one of the build machines. The server checks whether there's something to do, and if so, it queues the build or chooses the build agent to do the work (see figure 12.5).

The algorithm to assign jobs to build agents is a science in itself. It's based on measuring the build-agent workload. You can measure the workload by analyzing the build results. Does one particular agent take longer and longer to build or is it sitting idle most of the time?

When using an agent, the CI server assigns a job to the build agent that is least used or one that's idle. It can also direct a build to a given build agent because of the build agent's characteristics; for example, it may have the proper operating system to perform the build. The server can start builds simultaneously on different machines—for example, to test the software under various environments and give feedback more quickly. Build agents are often categorized, and builds are marked to check for compatibility.

Build agents often don't need to communicate with the source repository. The CI server deals with getting the last version to build.

12.3.2 *Scaling TeamCity*

TeamCity lets you set up a *build grid*. It's a TeamCity server with a farm of build agents. Setting up such a farm is easy; you'll build one now. Follow these steps:

1 Prepare a separate machine onto which to install a build agent.
2 Go to the TeamCity website on your server, and switch to the Agents tab. You'll see something like figure 12.6.
3 In the upper-right corner is an Install Build Agent link. Click it, download the install file, and execute it.

   If the machine you want to install on uses Windows, you're asked whether to install the build agent as a Windows service (if you want to use it productively,

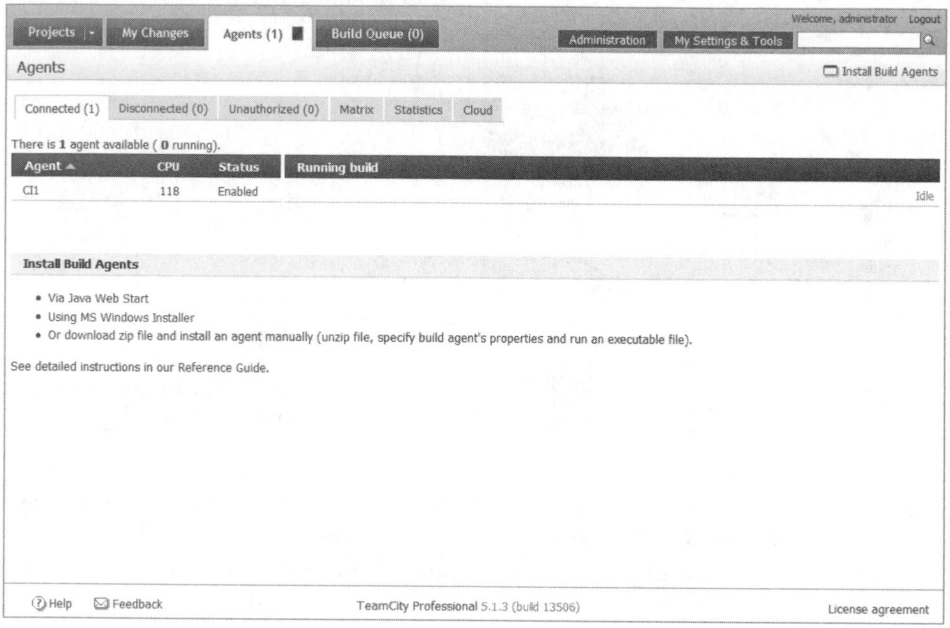

Figure 12.6   Default build agent running together with the TeamCity server. From here, you can install a new build agent.

you should choose to install it as a service). On other operating systems, you can use Java Web Start or take care of the installation yourself (a zip package of shell scripts is available to help you).

4 When you're finished with the installation, you're given the opportunity to configure the newly installed build agent; figure 12.7 shows the details.

You can change the configuration variables using this window. The build agent comes with its own Java Runtime Environment, and the path is set to it by default. TeamCity is installed on the current machine using port 9090 by default. Remember to open the port on the firewall to make communication possible. Change the `serverUrl` variable to match your TeamCity server installation. You can change the temporary and working directories if you like. You can always change the variables later by editing the XML configuration file.

5 After installing, you're finished on the build-agent side. Go back to the server website. On the Agents tab is a new Unauthorized agent. Click its tab, and click the Unauthorized link to authorize the build agent (see figure 12.8).

You have one build agent installed, together with the TeamCity server and an additional build agent. If both your machines use Windows and all the projects are .NET projects, you have no compatibility issues, and TeamCity will always assign builds to the build agent that is least occupied. As a result, TeamCity can execute more builds simultaneously. You've achieved horizontal scaling, as you can see in figure 12.9.

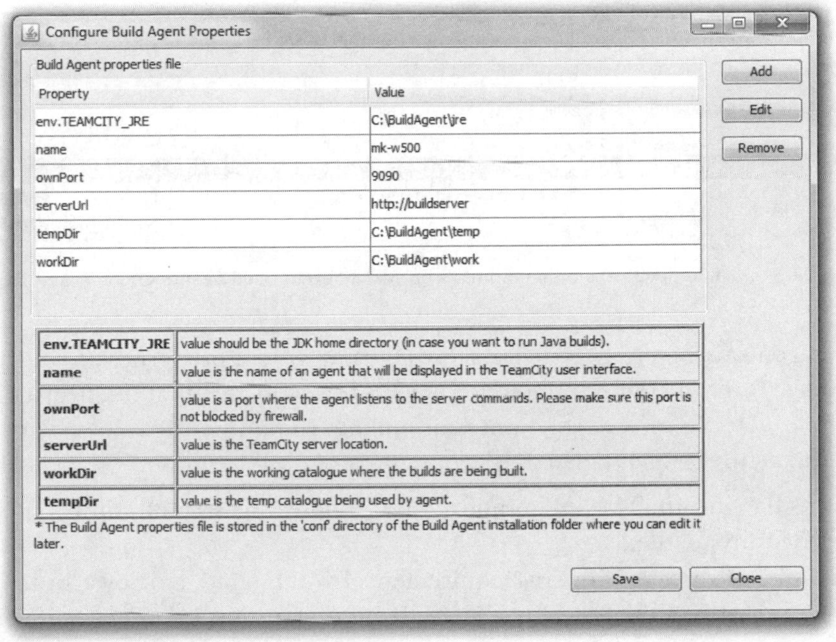

Figure 12.7   Configuring the TeamCity build agent. Pay close attention to the `ownPort` variable (the port needs to be open for communication) and the `serverUrl` variable (it's the TeamCity server location).

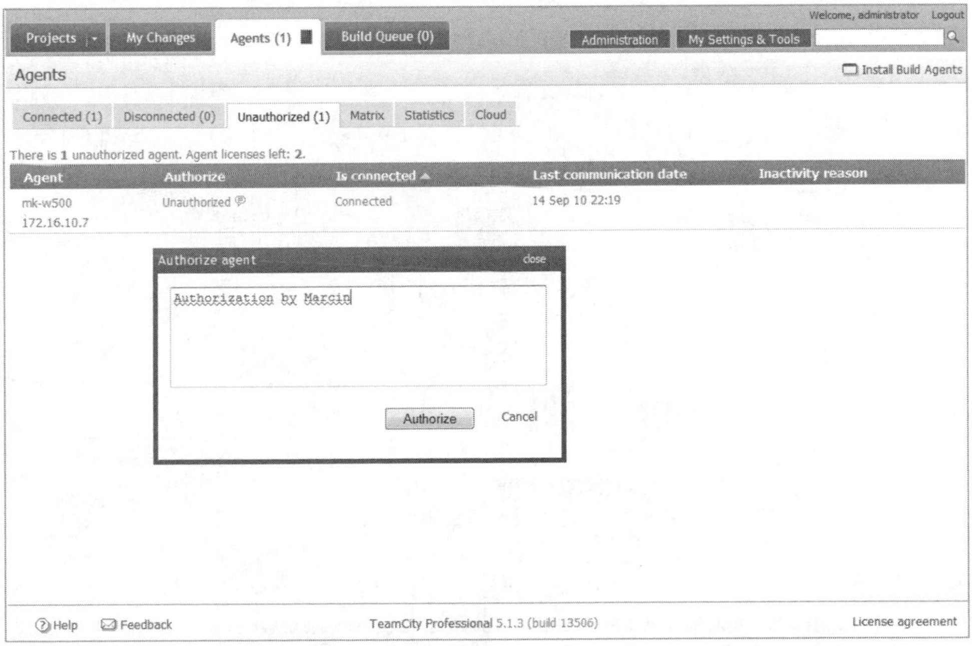

Figure 12.8   Authorizing a new build agent in TeamCity is required to make it work.

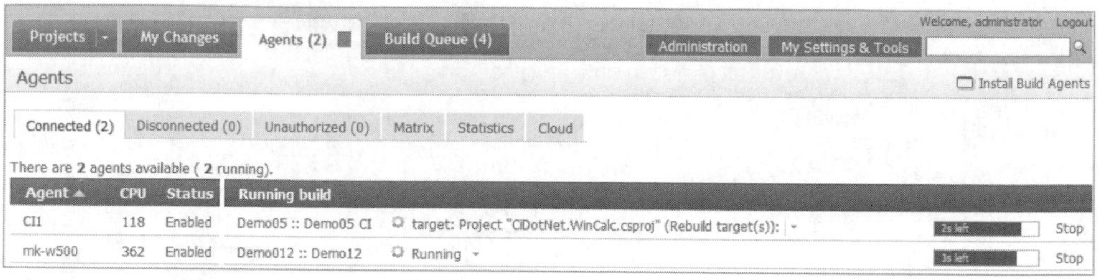

Figure 12.9   Simultaneous execution of builds on two different build agents under TeamCity

Build agents in TeamCity are characterized using system properties and environment variables. You can freely set the requirements for build agents at the project level. For example, you can say that you want your build to run only on Windows machines with .NET Framework 4.0 installed. Let's configure a project to do so:

1   Go to the build configuration, and choose the seventh wizard step: Agent Requirements.

2   Add two system property requirements for the build, as shown in figure 12.10 (you can use the Frequently Used Requirements link on the page if you wish).

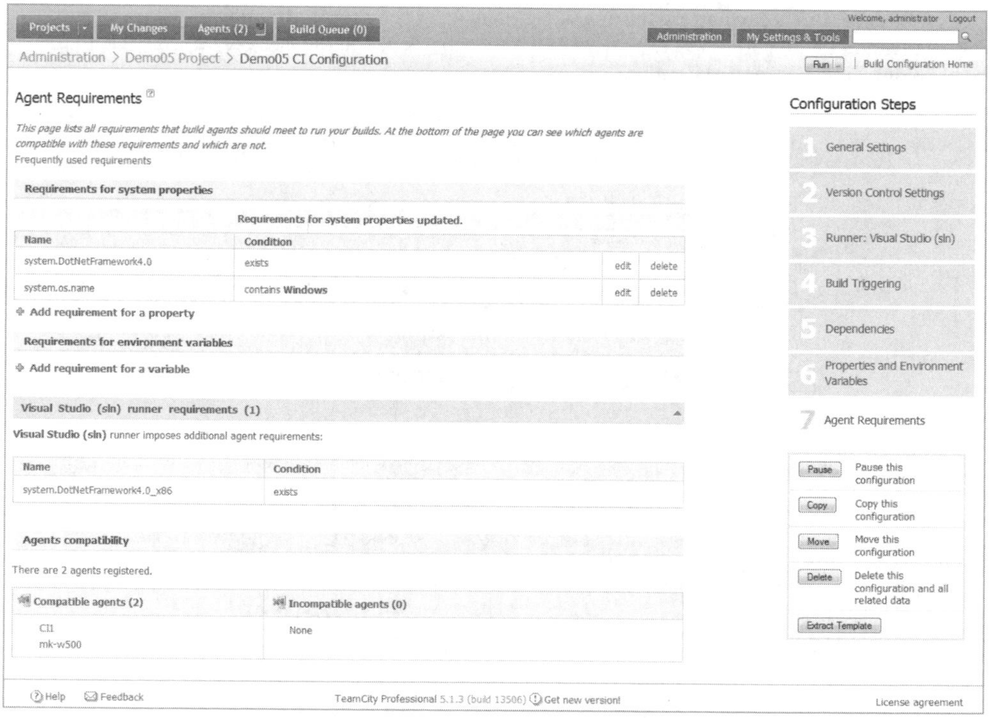

Figure 12.10   Build agent with additional system requirements (Windows and installed .NET Framework 4.0). Both of the connected build agents are compatible.

You can also set the requirements by using environment variables on the build-agent machine. If you wish, you can give your custom variables a condition (like "exists" or "contains") if you like. The condition will be checked before assigning a job to the build agent. If it's fulfilled, the job will be assigned. If not, another build agent will be used.

As you can see, scaling a modern CI server is easy. If you're using CruiseControl. NET, you're in a more difficult situation; you can configure a project trigger to react according to changes on another CCNet server, but you can't design more sophisticated scaling scenarios.

On the other hand, if you're using TFS 2010, you have even more possibilities. You can use build queuing and a grid of build agents to perform simultaneous integrations. You can use TFS Proxy for distributed teams. Let's say your headquarters are in America, and you have one offshore team in Asia. If you let the offshore team connect directly to the TFS server at headquarters, you'll most likely end up with internet traffic as a communication bottleneck. It helps to set the TFS Proxy in the offshore location. The developers connect only to the TFS Proxy server, and it optimizes communication with the main TFS server.

> **NOTE** Some setups use network load balancing with multiple TFS instances to lighten the workload on one TFS application tier. You can find a good paper about scaling TFS 2010 at http://blogs.msdn.com/b/tfsao/archive/2009/11/05/scaling-tfs-2010-beta-2.aspx.

Next, let's change directions and look at softer topics. We'll begin with legal issues related to CI.

12.4 Legal roadblocks

The last thing a developer wants to hear about is a legal roadblock to their application being fully tested and deployed. You may well be in such an environment. Federal, state, or local laws may impose restrictions on moving your application internally in your company.

One such law in the U.S. is the Sarbanes-Oxley Act, commonly called SOX. Passed in 2002, SOX applies to all publically traded companies regardless of size. The bill was created after several major accounting scandals at firms such as Enron, Tyco, and WorldCom. The law creates tough restrictions on corporate accounting procedures and reporting. It requires that documented processes be in place so that similar accounting scandals don't happen again.

But what does a law governing accounting have to do with CI? If you're creating internal applications that do any type of accounting, inventory, financial management, and so on, you may have to comply.

Briefly, to comply with SOX, developers can't touch QA or production systems. QA can't touch production or development systems. Production can't touch QA or development systems. This may make it more difficult for your CI system to function cleanly.

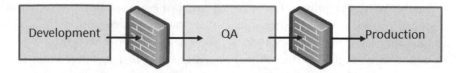

Figure 12.11   Under SOX, there's separation between development, QA, and production. One team can't access the systems of another. It's as if a brick wall exists between the teams.

But here's what you may be able to do. The development CI system compiles the code and runs unit and integration tests. It may run Sandcastle and do static code analysis. It may not run other tests such as acceptance, stress, scalability, load, performance, and so on. It certainly can't push an application directly into production. If the build succeeds, it can push the compiled assemblies or even an install set onto a shared server. Think of it as a demilitarized zone (DMZ) (see figure 12.11) where no work takes place. It's a drop point for the QA files. Source code never goes here.

The QA people have their own CI system that picks up the dropped files and starts running automated tests. Bugs are documented and entered into a bug-tracking system that development has access to.

If a build is deemed ready for release, the QA team pushes the install set out to another DMZ between them and production. The production team then picks up the bits and installs them, and users begin working with the new version.

We must stress that we aren't lawyers and aren't giving legal advice. You should consult with an attorney to determine if any laws pertain to your environment and, if they do, what specifically you need to do to comply with them.

To wrap things up, we now move on to a topic that seems out of place in a book on CI: a CI maturity model.

12.5   *Maturity model for CI*

Different models that show the maturity of a process have grown out of the Capability Maturity Model[2] (CMM). It's a methodology for businesses to help improve their processes. In software, CMM is most often associated with application lifetime management (ALM) in shops that use waterfall project-management methodologies. That said, it seems as though a maturity model has no place in CI, a practice that came out of the Agile movement, which is the complete opposite of waterfall.

But if we look at a maturity model as a way to improve processes, we start to see areas that can be improved. The Enterprise CI Maturity Model[3] (ECIMM) was developed by Eric Minick and Jeffrey Fredrick at Urban Code,[4] a leading company in build

---

[2] Capability Maturity Model is a service mark of Carnegie Mellon University.

[3] You can download the complete Enterprise CI Maturity Model white paper at www.anthillpro.com/html/ resources/default.html.

[4] To learn more about Urban Code and its Anthill Pro CI products, visit www.anthillpro.com.

and release solutions. It was the result of a discussion at the Continuous Integration and Testing Conference (CITCON).

ECIMM breaks a CI process into four distinct areas: building, deploying, testing, and reporting. In each area, five different compliance levels—introductory, novice, intermediate, advanced, and insane—are provided, for ranking a level of compliance. We'll look at these in a moment. Additionally, the industry norm and a best practice target level for each area are identified. You can use ECIMM to rate where your company is compared to others and set a target for where your company should be in relation to best practices. But to do this, you need to understand ECIMM, starting with building.

12.5.1 Building

As we discuss ECIMM, you'll see that many companies are in the introductory stage for most areas. Building (see figure 12.12) is no exception.

Building refers to using a source code repository, and the way your CI process performs the actual build. Look carefully at the introductory level, where most companies are. If you're performing manual builds that check out the latest changes, you're probably at this level.

Compare that to the best practice. Are your builds continuous, meaning that they run with every check-in? Do you use a single machine, or are your builds clustered? (Remember that earlier in this chapter we talked about parallel builds.) What will it

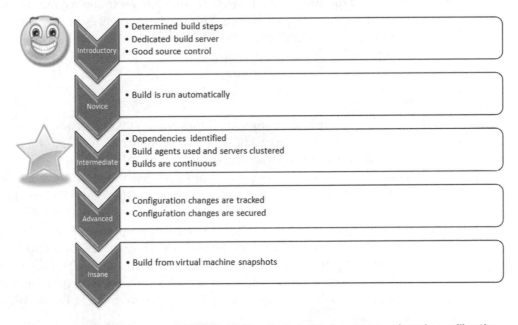

Figure 12.12 The building area of ECIMM specifies levels for storing source code and compiling the application. The industry norm (smiley face) and target levels (star) are specified in the Urban Code ECIMM document. The graphics in this section are adapted from that document.

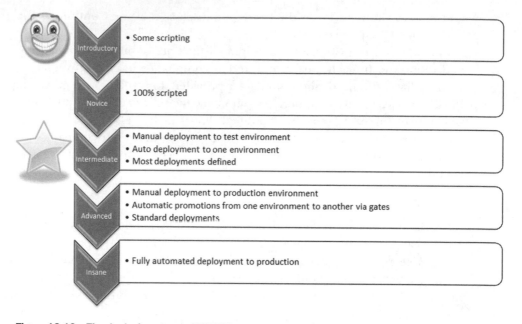

Figure 12.13   The deploying stage of ECIMM maps out levels to help you make your deployment easier and more complete.

take to get you to the intermediate level? If you've been following our advice, you should be well on your way to complying with the best practices of the intermediate level. You should have a dedicated build machine executing build scripts automatically and using a source control repository.

Now it's time to move on to deploying.

12.5.2 *Deploying*

How do you get your application from development into QA? What about getting your application to your users in the production environment? That's what the next step, deploying (see figure 12.13) is all about.

Chances are, you have a few scripts in your CI process that push the compiled bits out to your QA department. But what if QA isn't ready for that build? Did you just overwrite the version they had only partially tested?

You may also have multiple environments that you support, such as 32- and 64-bit. Do you have different configurations of the software for each environment?

Why not let QA pull the latest build when they're ready for it? That's the idea behind self-service test deploys. And a single, standardized configuration for each environment is essential. It not only makes it easier to program, it also makes testing significantly easier.

NOTE Automatic deployment to production, although it sounds ideal, falls into the insane level. It's difficult to do properly, and few companies do it because of the level of complexity. One of the biggest issues here has to do with SOX compliance as discussed earlier in this chapter.

We just talked about your QA department getting the latest build, so it's a good time to examine ECIMM testing.

12.5.3 Testing

We've spent several chapters talking about different types of testing. ECIMM addresses testing your application (see figure 12.14).

Many companies have some areas of unit testing. And perhaps other types of testing have some automation attached to them. But are you doing static code analysis with FxCop or StyleCop? How much unit testing do you have in place? How about security scans? Even managed code can have security issues that need to be addressed.

It's interesting that 100% test coverage is placed at the insane level. We agree with this, because 100% test coverage is not only almost impossible to achieve, but also undesirable. Not everything needs to be unit tested, and doing so slows down the build process.

The final step of ECIMM is feedback.

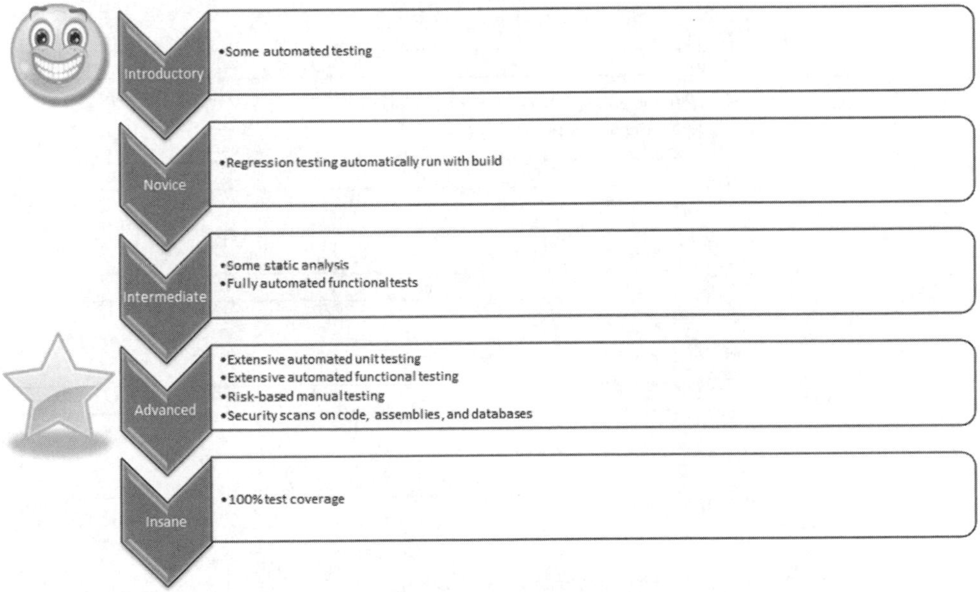

Introductory
- Some automated testing

Novice
- Regression testing automatically run with build

Intermediate
- Some static analysis
- Fully automated functional tests

Advanced
- Extensive automated unit testing
- Extensive automated functional testing
- Risk-based manual testing
- Security scans on code, assemblies, and databases

Insane
- 100% test coverage

Figure 12.14 Application testing levels are an important part of ECIMM.

12.5.4 *Reporting*

Getting good feedback is a key step of any CI process. It's also important to ECIMM (see figure 12.15). After all, without good reporting, you have no way of knowing if your CI process is doing its job or needlessly running through the steps.

Reporting is the only ECIMM stage that has novice as the industry norm. This level is where we find reporting from most CI tools. Think about the reports you get from a build. You see what the latest build result was, how many unit tests passed, and possibly other important information such as other test results, static code analysis, documenting, and so on.

But these standard reports don't give you much in the way of trend analysis. Are bug counts going up or down over time? Is the percentage of code covered by unit tests increasing? Is the speed of the build staying at a manageable level?

Cross-silo analysis is important too. This can involve collecting data across different projects or teams inside your company. One team may be better at creating and running unit tests than another. Perhaps there's something you can learn from this, which you can apply to other teams.

The ECIMM is a valuable tool to use in your business as you expand the use of CI. By using it as a guide for where you should be, you can improve your CI process.

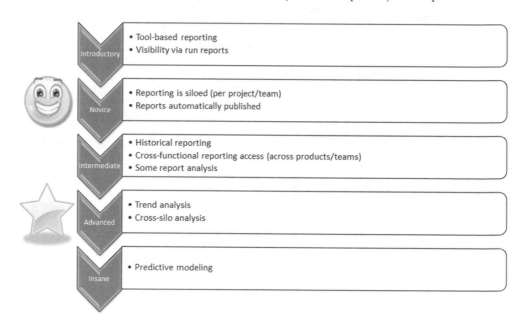

Introductory
- Tool-based reporting
- Visibility via run reports

Novice
- Reporting is siloed (per project/team)
- Reports automatically published

Intermediate
- Historical reporting
- Cross-functional reporting access (across products/teams)
- Some report analysis

Advanced
- Trend analysis
- Cross-silo analysis

Insane
- Predictive modeling

Figure 12.15   Reporting is a key part of the ECIMM.

12.6 Summary

In this chapter, we presented several topics for you to consider as your CI process grows. We discussed areas that cause the build to slow down, including the seven deadly sins of slow builds, and we presented several ideas that you can implement to speed up your CI process.

We then turned to legal issues that can impose roadblocks in moving applications through your company. Specifically, we talked about SOX and one idea for helping you comply with the law.

Finally, we discussed the Enterprise CI Maturity Model, which presents a way for you to determine how your CI process compares with other companies and what you should be targeting as a best practice.

We're at the end of our journey in this book. We've dealt with various aspects of a well-designed CI process. By now, you should know all you need to build your own setup and to maintain and extend it, from creating a solid source control system to automating the build, setting up a CI server, automating various types of testing, performing code analysis, generating documentation, creating setup routines, and incorporating database integration and scaling. You'll profit greatly from this knowledge. We wish you well on your journey with continuous integration in .NET!

index

RELATED MANNING TITLES

The Art of Unit Testing
with Examples in .NET
by Roy Osherove

> ISBN: 978-1-933988-27-6
> 320 pages, $39.99
> May 2009

Brownfield Application Development
in .NET
by Kyle Baley and Donald Belcham

> ISBN: 978-1-933988-71-9
> 416 pages, $49.99
> April 2010

C# in Depth, Second Edition
by Jon Skeet

> ISBN: 978-1-935182-47-4
> 584 pages, $49.99
> November 2010

Dependency Injection in .NET
by Mark Seemann

> ISBN: 978-1-935182-50-4
> 375 pages, $49.99
> August 2011

For ordering information go to www.manning.com